AMERICA'S COUNTERTERRORIST FORCES

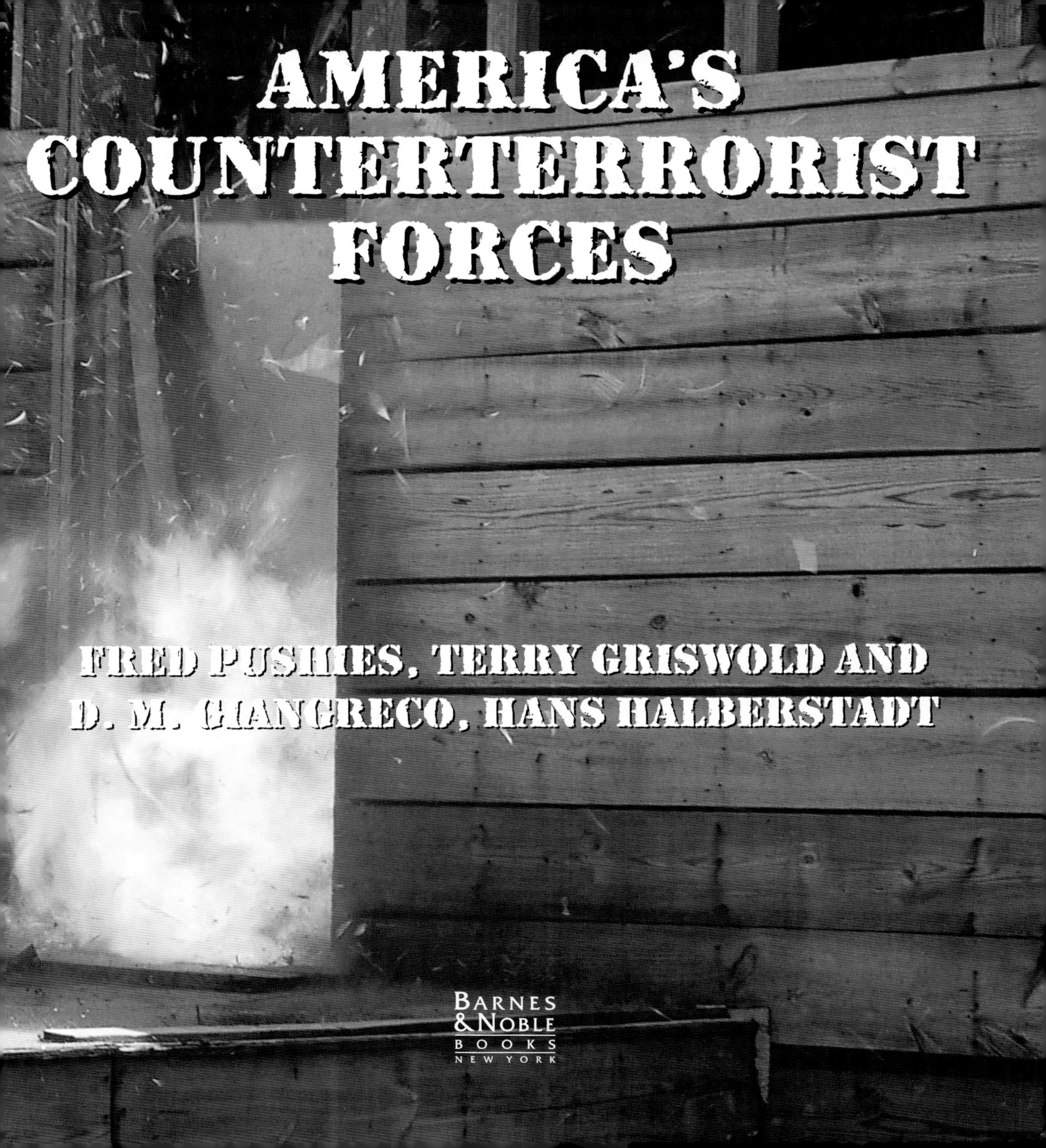

AMERICA'S COUNTERTERRORIST FORCES

FRED PUSHIES, TERRY GRISWOLD AND D. M. GIANGRECO, HANS HALBERSTADT

BARNES
&NOBLE
BOOKS
NEW YORK

First published in 1992, 1993, and 2001
by MBI Publishing Company, LLC
Galtier Plaza, Suite 200, 380 Jackson Street,
St. Paul, MN 55101-3885 USA

This edition published by Barnes & Noble, Inc.,
by arrangement with MBI Publishing Company

2001 Barnes & Noble Books

M 10 9 8 7 6 5 4 3 2 1

ISBN 0-7607-3150-0

U.S. ARMY SPECIAL FORCES © Fred J. Pushies,
2001
DELTA © Terry Griswold & D. M. Giangreco,
1993
U.S. NAVY SEALS © Hans Halberstadt, 1992

Library of Congress Cataloging-in-Publication
Data Available

On the front cover: Insignias of the U.S. Army
Special Forces: the arrowhead patch, worn by
all Special Forces soldiers; the black and silver
crest, emblazoned with the Special Forces
motto, De Oppresso Liber ("To Free the
Oppressed"); and the crossed arrows, worn by
the Special Forces officer. *Fred Pushies*

On the back cover: Special Forces weapons
sergeants are expert in both light arms, such as
the M4A1 carbine (right), and heavy weapons,
such as the AT-4 anti-tank weapon (left). *Fred
Pushies*

On the title page: The Special Forces Advance
Reconnaissance, Target Analysis, and
Exploitation Techniques Course (SFARTAETC)
provides the Special Forces soldiers with the
skills and training required to battle terrorists.
Fred Pushies

Photos on pages 5, 7, 8–9, and 130–131 by
Fred Pushies
Photo on page 256–257 by *Hans Halberstadt*

Printed in China

CONTENTS

DELTA: AMERICA'S ELITE COUNTERTERRORIST FORCE

U.S. NAVY SEALS

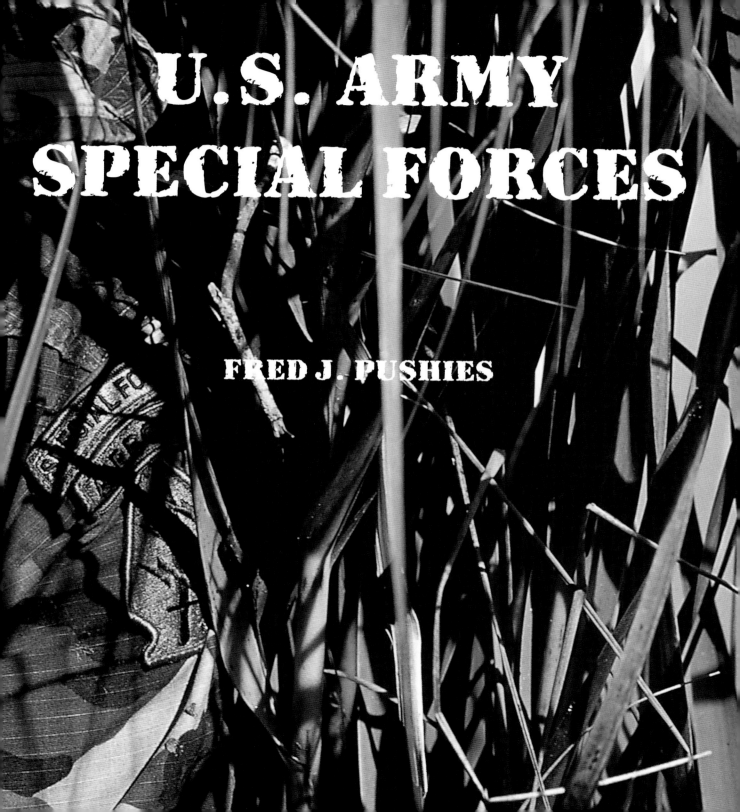

U.S. ARMY SPECIAL FORCES

FRED J. PUSHIES

Foreword

This book pays tribute to a special breed of man, a special breed of Americans, and a special breed of warrior. Special Forces soldiers, commonly referred to as the "Green Berets," are unique— not only due to the types of missions they undertake, the rigorous training they undergo, or the equipment they use, but also because of their character, spirit, and dedication. They are men who step away from conventional methods and conventional thinking to undertake tasks that many experts would deem impossible. They are men who can be ruthless in their quest to accomplish a mission, yet selfless and compassionate, caring for people who are in desperate need of a helping hand. I know this from first-hand experience. I will always be grateful to have had the opportunity to serve alongside, and to be associated with, such courageous and awe-inspiring men.

Although officially only 49 years old, the Green Berets can trace their proud lineage back to the daring and courage of Americans serving in the Revolutionary War. Since the Special Forces inception in 1952, the Green Berets have been at the forefront of nearly every operation involving America's military, from Korea to Vietnam, from Grenada and Panama to Iraq, and from Somalia and Haiti to the Balkans. Often the Green Berets are the United States' only military presence in a number of countries around the world. They stand as both America's vanguard and its good-will ambassadors. The renaissance men of warfare, Special Forces stand ready to undertake any mission, from unconventional warfare, direct action, and rescue missions to peace operations and humanitarian assistance. Our Special Forces provide unique capabilities that are essential to the United States' national security strategy and its ability to provide leadership in an uncertain and troubled world.

Since the creation of the Special Operations Command in 1987, a unified command with headquarters at MacDill Air Force Base in Tampa, Florida, Special Forces has become a vital element of joint and combined military operations. Each regional Commander in Chief (CinC), which includes European Command, Pacific Command, Southern Command, Central Command, and Joint Forces Command, has a Special Operations component manned with Special Forces soldiers. The Green Berets provide forces to conduct operations across the spectrum of conflict as well as the staff expertise to better integrate their unique capabilities and talents into joint and combined operations around the world.

The trend to greater integration is important. The men of the Green Berets and their colleagues in the Special Operations community are recognized not only for their ability to conduct missions for which they are uniquely qualified, but also as a great combat multiplier during conventional military operations.

The future of Special Forces will be tied to its ability to continue to attract and develop quality personnel, as well as maintain its standards of excellence. The United States relies on its technological prowess to stay ahead of potential adversaries—and Special Forces will leverage that technology. But it is the spirit, ingenuity, and professionalism of each individual who wears the Green Beret that maintains the force's vital core, ensuring its long-term efficacy. They are extraordinary men whom we ask to accomplish what others would often consider impossible. As this book underscores, it is the extraordinary caliber of the individual Green Berets that has been the constant source of strength for this incomparable organization. The men who constitute its ranks will continue to be the underlying and undying strength of the Special Forces as it meets the challenges of the new millennium.

De Oppresso Liber!

—*General Henry H. Shelton*
Chairman of the Joint Chiefs of Staff

Acknowledgments

First and foremost, I must acknowledge my thanks to God for His guidance and wisdom in this project. To Michael Haenggi, editor at Motorbooks International; General Henry H. Shelton, Chairman of the Joint Chiefs of Staff; Lt. Colonel Thomas Rheinlander, Carol Darby, Barbara Ashley, SFC Amanda Glenn, Specialist John Creese, U.S. Army Special Operations Command -Public Affairs Office, Ft. Bragg; Major Tom McCollum, Captain Andrew "Dutch" Franz, Major Jonathan B. Withington, Special Forces - PAO, Ft. Bragg; Major Rich Patterson, Special Warfare Center - PAO, Ft. Bragg; Randy Action, President & CEO, U.S. Cavalry; Lt. Colonel Mike Nagata, Major Jack Jensen, Major Patrick Eberhart, Major Douglas Robertson, Command Sergeant Major Melvin Lyles, Staff Sergeant Peter Simchuk, Training Cadre - 1st Special Warfare Training Group; Command Sergeant Major Richard Fitzgerald - Non-Commissioned Officers Academy; Lt. Colonel Clifford C. Cloonan, MC, U.S. Army; Commander Michael Wilkinson, MSC, U.S. Navy; Captain Steve Ellison, MC, U.S. Army Joint Special Operations Medical Training Center; Major Kimm Rowe - Range 37; Mr. Donald Strassburg, Special Forces Arms Facility; Major Thomas Hartzel; CWO4 "Bulldog" Balwanz; Roxanne Merritt - JFKSWC Museum Curator; Mr. Joe Lupyak, CSM (ret.); Mr. David Clarke, CSM (ret.); Cadre 1st SWTG, Colonels "Daniels, Ranger & Mosby" G-Chiefs of Pineland; ODA 914 & ODA 916; Mrs. Catherine Bank; Mr. Noel Corby - Operations - National Training Center, Ft. Irwin; Gordon Sims, President, 1st Special Service Force Association; Colonel Mike Jones - Commander; Major Jeff Kent; Major Craig Johnson; C Company 3rd Battalion: Colonel Jack Zeigler; Major Ken Cobb; Captain Brent Jorgenson; Captain Mike Irvine; ODA-391, ODA-392, & ODA-395, MSgt. Gary Kenitzer, 3rd Special Forces Group (Airborne); CWO2 Michael Roth; MSG Sam Wright; SSG J. DeVerteuil; ODA-774, 7th Special Forces Group (Airborne) A Company 3rd Battalion; ODA-581, Colonel Gary Danley Commander 3rd Battalion, 5th Special Forces Group (Airborne); ODA-052, ODA-055, & ODA-065, Lt. Colonel David Alegre 10th Special Forces Group (Airborne) Company C, 2nd Battalion; Lt. Colonel Daniel Moore G7 Force Integration - USASFC(A); Major Richard Steiner, S-3, 2nd Battalion, 3rd Special Forces Group (Airborne); Captain Drew Bayliss, CWO2 Ken Hodges, SFC David A. Harrington, and ODA-363; SOTIC instructors, NCOIC - MSG Bill Olson, SFC Ron Woolett, SFC George Simmons, SFC Jim Wallace, SFC Dave Garner, Rick Boucher, MSgt. (ret.), Cpl. George Bundy, 2nd Rangers and SSgt. Clifford Richardson, 5th Special Forces Group (Airborne) ODA-546; Captain Brent Epperson - Assistant S-3, Sgt. Mark Williams, Multimedia, NCOIC, 7th Special Forces Group (Airborne); Mr. Emit B. Hutsman, Curator, Ft. Clark Museum - Indian Scouts; Colonel Robert S. Sumner USA (ret.) Alamo Scouts, 6th Army; Robert E. Passanisi, Historian, Merrill's Marauder Association; Mr. Richard Sanne; Mary Scott Smith, Vice President, Barret Firearms Manufacturing, Inc.; Michael J. Winey, Curator, U.S. Army Military History Institute; John W. Goldtrap, Rebe Phillips, General Atomics Aeronautical Systems, Inc.; Kathy Vinson, Defense Visual Information Center; Steve Harrigan, Johnson Controls World Service, Inc. Also Darren Proctor, Robert Bentley Jr., and my family.

Special Thanks to "The Sea Pigs": Captain Brian Ebert, CW2 Tony Bonnell, MSG B.F. Burnham, SFC Mikel Chapman, SSG Jason Clark, SSG Jeremy Jemmett, Sgt. Joe Ferris, SSG Jason Perkins, SSG Doug Peterson, and SFC Greg Green of ODA-173, 1st Special Forces Group (Airborne).

Introduction

Unconventional warfare is nothing new. The Old Testament recounts the story of Gideon, whom God told to do battle with the Midianites approximately 5,500 years ago. The Midianites, an enemy of Israel, had a force so large their numbers were uncountable. Gideon began his campaign with 32,000 men, but twice God told him to reduce the ranks of his troops. Finally, when Gideon's force numbered only 300, God gave him a plan and set the attack in motion.

Gideon divided the 300 men into three companies of 100 each. He armed them each with a trumpet, an empty pitcher and a lamp, which was placed inside the pitcher. During the night the three companies secretly took up preordained positions, surrounding the enemy. Just around midnight, when the Midianites had placed the first watch, Gideon and his men blew their trumpets, broke the pitchers, and raised their lamps. In the ensuing confusion that befell the enemy, the Midianites turned their swords on one another, as Gideon and his band disappeared into the night. This encounter foreshadowed future unconventional methods: employ psychological warfare, stealth, and lightening hit-and-run tactics.

Some 5,000 years later, in 218 BC, a young commander named Hannibal employed yet another facet of unconventional warfare. Hannibal marched his men, roughly 35,000 troops, over the Italian Alps. While such a movement is not unusual, what was unexpected and well out of the ordinary was the fact that Hannibal's invasion force included elephants. To move huge equatorial animals through the frozen expanses of the mountains would be unthinkable today—and it was unthinkable then. Hannibal added more principles for unconventional warfare: Do

the unexpected, tackle the impossible, and succeed at all costs.

Unconventional warfare has been with mankind since the beginning of time. In Greek mythology the Greek warriors feigned retreat and sailed away, leaving behind a large wooden horse. The Trojans believed it was an offering to the goddess Athena, and brought it into the city for luck. Unbeknownst to the jubilant Trojans, the Greeks were hidden inside. As the city slept, the Greeks slipped from the horse, now within the enemy's fortress, opened the city's gates to the returning sailors, and decimated the Trojan forces.

The legendary Trojan Horse was featured on the beret crest when the U.S. Army Special Forces troops carried out postwar activities in 1952 Germany. It was used again in the formation of U.S. Special Operations Command in the 1980s. Currently, the representation of the Trojan Horse embodied in the knight piece can be found on the beret crest of the U.S. Army Special Warfare Center/School. A symbol of unconventional warfare from ancient times, it continues in the heraldry of the modern Special Forces warrior.

From its humble beginnings as a handful of men roaming the Bavarian Alps of post–World War II Germany, the Special Forces has evolved into a critical component of U.S. military operations. Whether performing civic actions and training with the indigenous populace or carrying out clandestine activities in denied territory, these men epitomize the term *warriors*, and bring unconventional warfare to a new level. This is their story—where they have come from, and where they are heading in the new millennium. These are the men of the U.S. Army Special Forces, "The Quiet Professionals."

CHAPTER 1

Special Forces Lineage

The lineage of today's Special Forces soldier begins some two centuries ago in an emerging country called America. It was here during the French and Indian War (1754–1763) that colonists would serve with British forces. In 1756, Major Robert Rogers recruited these Americans into a unit that would number nine companies of men. Although Maj. Rogers did not invent the unconventional warfare techniques, he did

The forerunner of the current Special Forces, Francis Marion, was known as the "Swamp Fox." He and his men brought unconventional warfare tactics to the Revolutionary War, making guerrilla raids against the British. *South Caroliniana Library*

exploit the tactics and establish them into Ranger doctrine. He is credited by some with writing the first Ranger Manual.

The newly founded Ranger companies would learn to assimilate these techniques. Following Rogers' command, they would strike where the enemy least expected them to hit, and they would traverse terrain conventional forces would avoid. The Rangers employed stealth and secrecy in their movements on the enemy. Once in position they would spring the attack and, like a North American rattlesnake, hit fast and hit hard. Major Rogers instituted a plan of action to train his Rangers and personally watched over its execution. He set strict orders for his troops to follow, stressing operational security, readiness, and tactics.

Rogers' tactics contained more than two dozen paragraphs detailing the Rangers' operational techniques. Over the years these techniques have been summarized in what has come to be known as the "Standing Orders—Rogers' Rangers." They are:

1. Don't forget nothing.

2. Have your musket clean as a whistle, hatchet scoured, sixty rounds powder and ball, and be ready to march at a minute's warning.

3. When you're on the march, act the way you would if you was sneaking up on a deer. See the enemy first.

4. Tell the truth about what you see and what you do. There is an army depending on us for correct information. You can lie all you please

when you tell other folks about the Rangers, but don't never lie to a Ranger of office.

5. Don't never take a chance you don't have to.

6. When we're on the march we march single file, far enough apart so one shot can't go through two men.

7. If we strike swamps, or soft ground, we spread out abreast, so it's hard to track us.

8. When we march, we keep moving till dark, so as to give the enemy the least possible chance at us.

9. When we camp, half the party stays awake while the other half sleeps.

10. If we take prisoners, we keep 'em separate till we have had time to examine them, so they can't cook up a story between 'em.

11. Don't ever march home the same way. Take a different route so you won't be ambushed.

12. No matter whether we travel in big parties or little ones, each party has to keep a scout 20 yards ahead, 20 yards on each flank, and 20 yards in the rear so the main body can't be surprised and wiped out.

13. Every night you'll be told where to meet if surrounded by a superior force.

14. Don't sit down to eat without posting sentries.

15. Don't sleep beyond dawn. Dawn's when the French and Indians attack.

16. Don't cross a river by a regular ford.

17. If somebody's trailing you, make a circle, come back onto your own track, and ambush the folks that aim to ambush you.

18. Don't stand up when the enemy's coming against you. Kneel down, lie down, hide behind a tree.

19. Let the enemy come till he's almost close enough to touch, then let him have it and jump out and finish him up with your hatchet.

Rogers' Rangers and these rules lay the groundwork for future generations of Special Operations Forces of the United States.

The tradition of the Rangers continued when the time came for the colonists to fight for their independence during the American Revolution. Active during the Revolutionary War were Dan Morgan's "Corps of Rangers," formed under orders from George Washington, and the Connecticut Rangers, under the leadership of Thomas Knowlton. While Morgan's men were considered expert marksmen, Knowlton's Rangers, a force of hand-picked men, were skilled in reconnaissance techniques.

It was Francis Marion, however, who would bring guerrilla war to the British and establish a firm position in the Special Forces lineage. Born and raised in South Carolina, Francis Marion fought the Cherokee Indians in 1760 as a lieutenant in the militia. During the Cherokee War, Marion learned the fighting techniques of the Indians, how they would initiate a surprise attack and then fade away as quickly as they had begun the assault. After the war Marion retired from service to take up the quiet, peaceful life of a farmer.

The war for independence changed these plans. Due to his past experience fighting the Cherokee, Marion received a commission as captain in the Continental Army and took up arms in the fight for freedom. Eventually, Marion would be promoted to the rank of General.

When Charleston fell to the British, Marion escaped capture and, like the Cherokee Indians he had fought, headed into the South Carolina swamps. Once in the swamp he established his base camp and with 150 men formed what would become known as Marion's Brigade. As the war progressed Marion and his men carried out

The U.S. Scouts, or Indian Scouts, were the first to employ the crossed arrows for their unit insignia in August 1890. Later, in World War II, the 1st Special Service Force would adopt the insignia. The crossed arrows continued their appearance in the SF beret crest and became the ensign of the U.S. Army Special Forces when the Army designated them as a separate branch in 1987. *Ft. Clark Museum*

unconventional warfare tactics against the British. They would ambush British troops, attack their supply lines, and perform hit-and-run raids on the enemy's camps; when done they would fade away into the dark forbidding recesses of the swamps. Try as they might, the British found it futile to attempt to follow these guerrillas into their safe haven of the swamp. A British colonel dubbed Marion the Swamp Fox.

Guerilla and unconventional war tactics reappeared in the U.S. Civil War. Mean's Rangers of the Union Army and Ashby's Rangers of the Confederacy were specialists in scouting, harassing, and raiding. Each did its best to hamper the efforts of the other side. Yet the best-known unconventional warfare troops of this war undeniably were the Confederate Army's Mosby's Rangers. Under the command of Colonel John Singleton Mosby of Virginia, Mosby's Rangers operated behind Union lines, just south of the Potomac. Col. Mosby began with a three-man scout element in

1862. By 1865, Mosby's Rangers had evolved into a force of eight companies of guerrillas.

Col. Mosby was a firm believer in the use of reconnaissance, aggressive action, and surprise attacks. Mosby and his Rangers cut off Union communications and supply lines, wrecked railroads, and raided base camps behind enemy lines. One of their greatest feats was to capture Union General Edwin H. Stoughton by bluffing their way into, and removing him from, his own house. Due to his stealth and uncanny ability to avoid capture, Mosby earned the nickname the Gray Ghost. Mosby's Rangers were well trained and well disciplined, setting a standard for future unconventional warfare forces.

In the years following the Civil War, American "Horse Soldiers" fought in the Great Plains Wars of the Southwest. Aware that hostile forces could not be tracked down by the cavalry alone, the U.S. Army created a new special operations force, known as the Indian Scouts. Drawn primarily from Pawnee, Navajo, and Seminole tribes, they were deployed at length all through the West. The Indian Scouts aided General G. Crook in capturing Geronimo.

With attributes comparable to today's Special Forces soldiers, these Indians Scouts were renowned in such military traits as tracking, field craft, physical courage, and boldness. The language skills, cultural appreciation, and civic action that characterized these forces are quite similar to today's Army Special Forces. The heritage of the Indian Scouts continued in the Crossed Arrows insignia that was adopted by the 1st Special Service Force during World War II.

The history of the U.S. Army Special Forces may be traced to the pre–Revolutionary War time period; however, a more direct lineage and organizational relationship follows from the elite U.S. military forces operating during World War II. Special operations units were active in all theaters of operations, from the jungles of Pacific islands,

Burma, and China, to the expanses of European mountains, woodlands, and towns.

The Second World War added the term Army Rangers to the annals of military history, and to the pages of Special Forces heraldry. Major General Lucian K. Truscott, the U.S. Army liaison to the British General Staff, submitted the idea of an American unit similar to the British Commandos to General George Marshall. The War Department responded with cables to Truscott and Major General Russell P. Hartle, commander of all Army forces in Northern Ireland, authorizing formation of the special unit.

General Truscott liked the term "commandos," but it was a British name and he desired something more American. Looking back on the history of unconventional warfare, Truscott found American troops that met the highest standards of courage, motivation, tenacity, fighting spirit, and ruggedness. The group that inspired him was that commanded by Major Rogers, and a new name was added to the U.S. military— Army Rangers.

General Hartle picked Captain William O. Darby, who had been serving as his aide-de-camp, to recruit, select, and organize the newly formed unit. Darby, a West Point graduate, was intelligent and enthusiastic, demonstrating the capacity to gain the confidence of his superiors and the loyalty of his men. Promoted to Major, Darby took on the task in hand. Major Darby and his handpicked staff officers interviewed volunteers from the 1st Armored Division, the 34th Infantry Division, and other units from the area.

Within a few weeks, the first unit of Army Rangers was selected. On 19 June 1942, in Carrickfergus, Ireland, the 1st U.S. Army Ranger Battalion was activated under the command of Major William O. Darby. This unit would come to be known as Darby's Rangers.

Major Darby and his Rangers would spend three months at the Commando Training Center at Achnacarry, Scotland. Here, under the tutelage of combat-seasoned British Commandos, the American Rangers learned the basics of unconventional warfare. Out of 600 men that began the training with Darby, 500 remained.

Darby's Rangers fought throughout Western Europe, but they achieved their greatest recognition on D-Day, 6 June 1944. The Rangers would scale the cliffs of Pointe du Hoc as part of the Allied invasion of Normandy.

The 1st Special Service Force was officially established at Fort William Henry Harrison, Montana, on 9 July 1942. These unconventional warfare troops comprised both American and Canadian soldiers under the command of Colonel Robert T. Frederick. The 1st SSF was a

Portrait of Brigadier General Robert T. Frederick, commander of the 1st Special Service Force. Known as the "Devil's Brigade," these unconventional warfare troops were constituted of both American and Canadian soldiers. *JFK Special Warfare Museum*

March 1944, at Laganga/Walawbum area, Burma. One of the 5307th's Battalion's I & R (Intelligence & Reconnaissance) Platoons, patrolling the area before the attack at Walawbum. (The 3rd Battalion consisted of two Combat Teams, Orange and Khaki, each with its own I & R Platoon.) Note the men are not carrying their field packs, so they can move about and conceal themselves more easily. *Lt. David Lubin Merrill's Marauders Association*

force of three battalion-size units, with 60 percent of the men coming from the ranks of the American military. Volunteers were sought out from various units; in some cases commanders eagerly "volunteered" some of their troublesome soldiers and sent them out to Montana. Col. Frederick weeded out men who arrived less than highly motivated, from which one could argue he was responsible for instituting the first Special Forces Assessment and Selection (SFAS). As Gordon Sims, president of the 1st Special Service Force Association, relates, "Many people think the American soldiers were roughnecks and yard birds. The truth was, some of these men were more at home in the field than in garrison. What regular Army commanders saw as troublesome actually turned out to be some of the best operators."

Col. Frederick formulated a training schedule for his men that would stress physical conditioning, hand-to-hand combat, weapons training, demolitions, infantry tactics, and mountain work. The soldiers of the 1st SSF were also airborne trained, and schooled in skiing and winter operations. Their specialty was close-quarter combat against numerically superior forces.

The 1st Special Service Force would see combat against the Japanese in the Aleutians and with the Germans in Italy and France. It was in Europe that the 1st SSF got its nickname, the Devil's Brigade. The crossed arrows and distinctive unit insignia of the present-day Special Forces was first authorized to be worn by the 1st SSF by the Secretary of War.

While Darby's Rangers and the Devil's Brigade were conducting their operations in Europe, another group of men was writing its lessons into the journal of unconventional warfare in the Pacific. Here the men of the 5307th Composite Unit (Provisional), under the leadership of Brigadier General Frank Merrill, brought the war to the Japanese in the jungles of Burma.

Organized in 1943, this unit of 3,000 men, all volunteers, was tasked with the mission of long-range infiltration behind Japanese lines. Their objective was to destroy the enemies "jugular"—their communications and supply lines. Furthermore, they were to harass and attack the Japanese at will. This unit would come to be known as Merrill's Marauders.

One of the Marauders' greatest undertakings was the seizure of the Myitkyina Airfield. Merrill and his men infiltrated through the hot, humid, insect- and disease-ridden Burmese jungle. And that was the good news. These unconventional warriors were constantly outnumbered by the enemy, and support was almost nonexistent. Merrill's Marauders' accomplishments are legendary and inspirational, even by today's standards.

Another unconventional raiding force operating in the Pacific was the Alamo Scouts. This unit of highly skilled soldiers was created by Lt. General Walter Krueger, commanding General of the U.S. Sixth Army. Those who volunteered for assignment to this force went through six weeks of arduous training and field exercises encompassing land navigation, hand-to-hand combat, weapons, communications, survival, small boat operations, and advance patrolling techniques. Those who graduated from the training were selected to become Alamo Scouts and formed into small teams, usually one officer and six or seven enlisted men.

These teams would infiltrate the numerous Japanese-held islands throughout the South Pacific, emerging from PT boats and rubber rafts to perform their missions. Their primary mission was originally reconnaissance, but their skills and the demands of war led them to greater challenges. In one of their foremost missions, the Scouts led U.S. Rangers and Filipino guerrillas in an attack on a Japanese prison camp at Cabantuan, freeing all 511 Allied prisoners there. Never numbering more than 70 men, the Alamo Scouts

Team leaders of the Alamo Scouts, left to right: Lt. Bill Nellist, Lt. Tom Roonsaville, Lt. Robert "Red" Sumner, Lt. Jack Dove. Leyte, Philippine Islands, January 1945. In more than 100 missions, the Alamo Scouts never lost a man. *Alamo Scout Association*

conducted more than a hundred missions without the loss of a single soldier.

These unconventional units of World War II were indeed U.S. Army elites. They took the principles founded by Rogers' Rangers and gave them a twentieth-century application, thus establishing a basis for modern special operations forces. Their mission was simple: Hit the enemy, hit them hard with lightning attacks, and disappear into the countryside, whether the mountains and woodlands of Europe, or the jungles of Burma. In addition to units employing lightning raids on the enemy, World War II produced another kind of unconventional warrior—a soldier who could adapt and integrate the types of methods employed by the Swamp Fox and Col. Mosby. This force would combine these principles with new techniques of airborne and guerrilla fighting.

Private First Class Edeleanu prints news bulletin on bulletin board outside Intelligence tent of Kyaukpyu Camp, the day before Office of Strategic Services (OSS), AFU, departure via convoy for Rangoon. Detachment 101, Ramree Island, Burma. *National Archive*

They were know as Shadow Warriors. Their organization would become known as the Office of Strategic Service, or OSS.

Prior to the United States becoming involved in World War II, President Franklin D. Roosevelt realized the need for the collection of intelligence and special operation capabilities. He authorized creation of the Office of the Coordinator of Information (COI), formed under the leadership of William "Wild Bill" Donovan in 1941. The COI flourished, establishing operations sites in England, North Africa, India, Burma, and China.

When the United States entered World War II in December 1941, the COI agency was renamed the Office of Strategic Services. The OSS was instrumental in gathering intelligence and conducting sabotage raids in occupied Europe. It also worked with the French resistance fighting against the Nazis.

In April of 1942, Detachment 101 of the OSS was activated for service in Burma. Under the command of General "Vinegar Joe" Stillwell, this unit conducted operations behind the Japanese line in Burma. Detachment 101 consisted of nearly 11,000 Kachin tribesmen. Starting from scratch, these guerrillas were responsible for killing 10,000 Japanese, while losing only 206 of their own.

On 23 December 1942, the Joint Chiefs of Staff authorized the formation of multi-national Operation Groups (OGs), for which Donovan had been the principal advocate. The OGs were French, Greek, German, Italian, Norwegian, and Yugoslavian. These units included specially selected, trained, and disciplined U.S. Army soldiers who were proficient in conducting operations behind enemy lines. An Operation Group comprised 30 enlisted men and three officers, further split into two 15-man sections. OGs were the forerunners of the Operational Detachments-Alpha (ODAs), or A-teams, of today's Special Forces.

The mission of the OGs was to infiltrate by parachute or sometimes by sea into enemy territory. There they would meet up with existing guerrilla forces and support them in conducting unconventional warfare. Like current ODAs, the OGs were self-sufficient and had the ability to train and coordinate guerrilla operations. Such operations included, but were not limited to, direct sabotage, rescue of downed Allied pilots, and collection of intelligence. Although efforts were made to coordinate their action with the

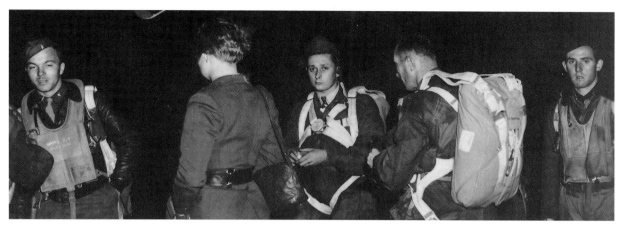

OSS Jedburgh team members prepare to board a B-24 bomber for their parachute drop behind German lines. Operating primarily at night, B-24s of the 801st Bombardment Group, known as the Carpetbaggers, supported missions the same as today's Combat Talons—penetrate enemy airspace and infiltrate special operations teams. *National Archive*

Resistance, the OGs could, and did, conduct raids and operations without any partisan support.

In the early part of 1944, in preparation of the D-Day invasion of France, the OSS began the creation of the first of the Jedburgh Teams, which eventually numbered 96. The name Jedburgh came from the area of Scotland where the Scots carried on a guerrilla war against the British invaders in the twelfth century.

The typical Jedburgh Team consisted of three men—two officers and one enlisted radio operator. These individuals were trained in demolitions, weapons, knife fighting, hand-to-hand combat, infiltration and exfiltration techniques, small units tactics, survival, and a multitude of other unconventional warfare skills to assure them success in their missions behind the German lines.

The mission of the Jedburgh Teams was to infiltrate, via parachute primarily, occupied France, Belgium, and Holland prior to the D-Day invasion. There they would organize guerrillas and conduct unconventional warfare against the Nazis, providing the resistance fighters with supplies and

weapons. Operations began on D-Day to ambush German convoys, disrupt communications, destroy railways, bridges, and roadways and to delay enemy reinforcements from reaching the beachhead at Normandy.

At the conclusion of World War II, President Harry S. Truman deactivated the OSS, yet its legacy lives on today. The intelligence branch of the service is considered the father of the current Central Intelligence Agency (CIA), formed in September 1947. The first directors of the agency were former OSS veterans.

Special Forces thus drew inspiration and tactics from many sources throughout U.S. history and before our nation was formed. With each new conflict, the leaders of unconventional warfare drew on the proven techniques of the past, and added to them with resources and techniques of the time. World War II provided a pressing international stage on which to hone unconventional warfare techniques, and the lessons learned in that conflict have been extended and refined to the present day.

CHAPTER 2

The Birth of the U.S. Army Special Forces

Two OSS operatives, Col. Aaron Bank and Col. Russell Volckmann, remained in service with the U.S. Army. These two officers had been assigned to the Army Psychological Warfare Staff at the end of World War II, commanded by Brigadier General Robert McClure. Gen. McClure had been the director of information in the U.S.-occupied area of West Germany. A strong advocate of psychological warfare, he would take

The original beret crest of the U.S. Army Special Forces—the Trojan Horse centered in a shield with a lightning bolt in the background, resting on a pair of airborne wings. This crest can still be seen in use today at the headquarters of the 10th Special Forces Group (Airborne) at Fort Carson, Colorado, and in Germany.

command of the Office of the Chief of Psychological Warfare (OCPW) on 15 January 1950. The OCPW was divided into three branches, PsyWar, covert deception, and Special Operations.

Working for the OCPW, Cols. Bank and Volckmann developed plans for organizing and training a special operations unit. They worked diligently to convince the Army Chiefs that the post–World War II world held numerous sites of potential conflict that would not be open to conventional warfare, but were prime targets for unconventional warfare tactics and guerrilla fighting. One such area was Eastern Europe, now occupied and dominated by the Soviets. Intelligence indicated that a substantial potential for guerrilla and covert Unconventional Warfare (UW) operations existed in the area.

Special operations units as envisioned by the two colonels, and Banks in particular, would be a force multiplier. Based on the OSS Jedburgh Teams, with striking similarities to today's Special Forces A-Detachments, these small teams could operate behind the enemy's lines and raise havoc and confusion within its ranks. It would be possible for a handful of men to effectively hamper, disrupt, and paralyze a much larger conventional force, e.g., the Soviets.

This was daring and innovative thinking that went against the grain of traditional, conventional concepts. However bold the idea, by 1952 the U.S. Army was at last ready to commence a new era of unconventional warfare.

The new organization would be referred to as "Special Forces," a name derived from the OGs fielded by the OSS in 1944. The Army allocated

2,300 personnel slots for the unit and assigned it to Fort Bragg, North Carolina.

In the spring of 1952, Col. Bank headed to Fort Bragg to choose the location for a Psychological Warfare/Special Forces Center. The area he selected is still the home of Special Forces, located at the corner of Reilly Road and Ardennes. This area was, and remains to this day, Smoke Bomb Hill. Although a remote location at Fort Bragg in 1952, within a decade it would become one of the busiest areas in the U.S. Army.

At this time Col. Bank began bringing together selected officers and NCOs who would serve as the nucleus of the new organization. These men would act as the training cadre to fill in the ranks of the fledgling unit. Col. Bank did

The father of the U.S. Army Special Forces, Colonel Aaron Bank. He was the first Special Forces Commander, commanding the 10th Special Forces Group (Airborne) as it was organized in June 1952 at Smoke Bomb Hill, Ft. Bragg, North Carolina. *JFK Special Warfare Museum*

When first organized in 1952, members of the Special Forces wore the Glider and Parachute airborne patch. Subsequently, it would be replaced with the Arrowhead patch, which is the current shoulder patch of the SF soldiers.

not want any inexperienced soldiers; from the inception of Special Forces, only the best troops were sought, and Banks got them. Among the ranks assembled in the newly formed organization were former OSS officers, airborne troops, Ranger troops, and combat veterans from World War II and Korea.

The individuals who volunteered for service with the newly formed Special Forces were unique, highly motivated men looking for new challenges—the tougher the better! Virtually all the soldiers were fluent in at least two languages, had the minimum rank of sergeant and were trained in infantry and airborne skills. They were all volunteers who were willing to work behind enemy lines. They further agreed to operate in civilian clothes as necessary. This in itself would be dangerous, since soldiers in civilian clothes were no longer protected under the Geneva Convention and most likely would be executed if captured.

But the men who volunteered did not worry about the risks. Mr. Joe Lupyak SF-CSM (ret.) relates that "most of the early SF troops were foreigners." Indeed, many of the early troopers were from Eastern Europe, and had lived through their share of communist tyranny and Nazi rule. They

had fled to America after the end of World War II under the provisions of the Lodge Bill, a law that allowed immigrants from politically persecuted countries to become U.S. citizens by serving in the United States armed forces.

Because of their backgrounds and motivation, the men of the first Special Forces organization were ideally suited for guerrilla operations in Eastern Europe. This was precisely the geographical area Bank had in mind when he designed the

Members of the 10th Special Forces Group (Airborne) take a break in the Bavarian mountainside. A number of the early SF soldiers were not from the United States. They joined under the Lodge Bill, a legislative act designed to allow immigrants from politically persecuted countries to become U.S. citizens by serving in the U.S. armed forces. The soldier on the left is armed with a Czechoslovakian submachine gun. *JFK Special Warfare Museum*

Members of the 10th Special Forces Group (Airborne) during mountain training, seen here wearing the forbidden green berets. In the early years the beret was often worn in the field, but rarely, if ever, worn in garrison. Note the glider and parachute shoulder patch worn by the original SF units. *JFK Special Warfare Museum*

group. Not only were they fluent with the language of the targeted areas, they were also familiar with the local customs, political sentiments, police, and industrial structure, as well as the overall geography.

After months of concentrated preparation, the new unit was ready. On 19 June 1952, the 10th Special Forces Group (Airborne) was activated, under the command of Col. Aaron Bank. On the day of its activation, the 10th SFG (A) had a total complement of ten soldiers—Col. Bank, one warrant officer, and eight enlisted men. This fledgling organization would soon flourish into a formidable force.

Within months of its activation, hundreds of the first volunteers reported to Smoke Bomb Hill as they completed the initial phase of their Special Forces training. As the group grew in size, it was divided into a compilation of three types of detachments or teams: A-teams, B-Teams, and C-Teams.

Students from the Special Warfare Center go through their final exercises in the National Forest area near Ft. Bragg, North Carolina. This exercise, known as Robin Sage, will pit the newly trained SF students against a larger conventional "enemy" force. Uniform of the day is "guerrilla casual" so they can blend in with the locals. *JFK Special Warfare Museum*

The basic operational unit of Special Forces was the A-detachment or A-team. The A-team consisted of twelve men—two officers and ten enlisted men—and was commanded by a captain. The A-team was the core of the new Special Forces. They were the soldiers who would be on the ground deep inside enemy territory. Their job was to make contact with the local resistance leaders and develop the indigenous population into a cohesive guerrilla force. The A-team had two operations and intelligence sergeants, two medical sergeants, two communications sergeants, two weapons sergeants, and two demolition/engineer sergeants. This configuration would allow the A-team to operate in two six-man teams or "split A-teams" if necessary. It was standard operating procedure that

each member of the A-team was crossed-trained in the SF skills. A-team soldiers were highly trained in unconventional warfare and spoke at least one foreign language. To this day the A-team remains the basis of Special Forces operations.

The functions of the B- and C-teams were more organizational. B-teams coordinated the actions of numerous A-teams assigned to specific areas in a designated country. C-teams were at the top of the Special Forces hierarchy. They worked with top leaders of indigenous guerrilla movements, and provided overall guidance to other SF teams in the area.

As soon as the 10th group was large enough, Banks started training his soldiers in the most advanced unconventional warfare techniques. The initial mission of the 10th Special Forces Group was to infiltrate designated areas of enemy territory by land, sea, or air and establish and train indigenous forces to conduct Special Forces operations, with an emphasis on guerrilla warfare. There were also secondary missions, including deep-penetration raids, intelligence-gathering assignments, and counter-insurgency operations. Special Forces operations demanded a commitment to professionalism and excellence unparalleled in the history of America's military, but the men of the 10th Special Forces Group (Airborne) were up to the challenge.

Like today's Special Forces soldier, the men under Col. Banks' newly formed organization were Airborne qualified and many of them had undergone Ranger training as well. Familiar with tough training, volunteers for Special Forces quickly realized this was not a mere review of Ranger tactics. As Banks put the men through their paces, they would learn many more skills, undergo more intense training, practice different mission profiles, and master more complex operations.

The Ranger units of World War II and the Korean War had been created to perform as shock troops and carry out light infantry raids—to hit and run and wait for follow-on forces. Special Forces troops, by contrast, were expected to remain behind enemy lines for months on end, perhaps even years. They would be self-sufficient experts in survival, capable of living off the land. And they would speak the language of the indigenous populace in their area of operation.

The Special Forces soldier would learn all of these skills and many more. Operating as a full Special Forces Group for less than 18 months, the men of the 10th Special Forces demonstrated to the Army that they were masters of these unconventional and very useful skills.

With the political climate heating up in East Germany, half of the 10th Special Forces Group was re-deployed on 11 November 1953 to Bad Tolz, West Germany. These A-teams would be on call to provide support to any resistance movements, if necessary, in Soviet-occupied Europe. The other half of the group would remain at Fort Bragg and was redesignated the 77th Special Forces Group. This split was significant, as it demonstrated that Special Forces had established itself as a vital unit of the U.S. Army.

During the balance of the 1950s, Special Forces would continue to grow, slowly but consistently, into a formidable organization. Special Forces was surveying its interest in the Far East, moving beyond their previous European focus. In April 1956 the 14th Special Forces Detachment (Area) (Airborne) was secretly activated at Fort Bragg; two months later they would deploy to Hawaii, and subsequently to Thailand, Taiwan, and Vietnam.

This detachment of 16 SF soldiers taken from the 77th SFG was tasked with the mission of leading Asian resistance against any communist thrust into Indo-China, Malaya, South Korea, and the surrounding area. Operations in Korea were not new to Special Forces personnel. Near the end of 1952, Special Forces troops had been operating behind enemy lines and had been deployed on classified missions. Special Forces soldiers assisted anti-communist guerrillas who had joined the United Nation Partisan Forces-Korea or UNPFK. These guerrillas were often referred to as "donkeys," from the Korean word for liberty, dong-il. The guerrillas, operating from small islands off the Korean coast, would conduct raids, rescue downed airmen, provide gunnery spotting, and maintain electronic facilities. This would be the first time that U.S. Army Special Forces would operate with guerrilla troops behind enemy lines.

Shortly after the activation of the 14th SFOD, three additional operational detachments, the 12th, 13th, and 16th, were designated for service in Asia and the Pacific. These three SFOD were

President Kennedy speaks with Brigadier General William P. Yarborough at Fort Bragg, 12 October 1961. President Kennedy would later comment that the green beret was "a symbol of excellence, a badge of courage, a mark of distinction in the fight for freedom." *JFK Library*

By 1961 there were three active Special Forces groups securely established in the U.S. Army—the 1st Special Forces Group (Airborne), the 7th Special Forces Group (Airborne) (re-designated from the 77th on 6 June 1960), and the original 10th Special Forces Group (Airborne).

The Cold War produced increased demand for unconventional tactics and soldiers. The Special Forces were in Berlin when the Berlin wall was erected. Special Forces personnel would conduct cross-border operations, some of these missions still classified today. These soldiers were assigned to a unit known simply as detachment "A." When in garrison, they would not wear the SF patches or berets; they would blend in with other conventional troops wearing the Berlin brigade patch. As their Office of Strategic Services (OSS) predecessors, when these soldiers would go out to roam around Germany, they would do so in civilian clothes. The clothes they wore, the shoes on their feet, their rucksacks, and even their underwear were of German origin. There would be nothing to trace them to the United States if they were compromised.

Other missions given to the Special Forces during this time included training Cuban expatriates. Special Forces teams were sent to Guatemala to train soldiers for the possible invasion of Cuba again in October of 1962 during the Cuban Missile Crisis, when the Soviets placed offensive nuclear missiles in Cuba. The U.S. military was put on full alert, including Special Forces teams placed on standby, should the call for their insertion be sent.

If Col. Aaron Bank was the father of the Special Forces, then President John F. Kennedy was to become their godfather. President Kennedy, a military scholar with more than a mere interest in counterinsurgency, recognized the need for a counter-guerrilla force. He referred to this as "another type of war, new in its intensity, ancient in its origins—war by guerrillas, subversives,

eventually combined into the 8231st Army Special Operations Detachment. On 17 June 1957 the 14th and 8231st united to form the 1st Special Forces Group (Airborne) based out of Okinawa and responsible for the Far Eastern area of operation. In the summer of 1959, Special Forces training teams would be inserted covertly into Laos to train soldiers of the Royal Lao Army. These SF teams were designated "White Star" mobile training teams, or MTT. Working under the direction of the Central Intelligence Agency (CIA), the Special Forces MTTs were also used to train Meo tribesmen as a guerrilla force.

insurgents, assassins; war by ambush instead of by combat; by infiltration instead of aggression, seeking victory by eroding and exhausting the enemy instead of engaging him." This, he continued, would require "a whole new kind of strategy, a wholly different kind of force."

During his visit to Ft. Bragg in 1961, President Kennedy found such a force as he reviewed the men of the U.S. Army Special Forces. These dedicated soldiers were what the President was looking for to thwart the spreading threat of communist insurgents around the world. President Kennedy also liked the green beret headgear. These men had a special mission; it was only fitting they have a special symbol to set that mission apart. As the ranks of the Special Forces grew, the green beret became synonymous with Special Forces.

With the support of the President, the Special Forces grew, and additional SF groups were formed. On 21 September 1961, the 5th Special Forces Group (Airborne) was activated, followed by the 8th SFG(A) on 1 April 1963, the 6th SFG(A) on 1 May 1963, and finally the 3rd SFG(A) on 5 December 1963. Members of the Special Forces would also find themselves in Army Reserve and National Guard units with the formation of the 11th and 12th SFG(A)—Reserve and 19th and 20th SFG(A)—National Guard, in 1966.

Nineteen-sixty-three would see the death of the U.S. Army Special Forces' greatest proponent, President John F. Kennedy. He had given them a

On 29 May 1965, the United States Army John F. Kennedy Center for Special Warfare was dedicated. The ceremony was held in front of the first completed building of the Center, John F. Kennedy Hall. John F. Kennedy Hall would be a hub of activity for Special Forces operations during the Vietnam War.

"Bronze Bruce" stands as a memorial to the Special Forces soldier. Depicted as a Sergeant First Class, he is armed with an M16 rifle signifying his readiness to do battle. Yet his other hand is open and outstretched, indicating his willingness to help and provide comfort.

mission, had given them the "green beret," and had set a course for the Special Forces soldier. On 29 May 1965, the date that would have been the president's 48th birthday, the United States Army John F. Kennedy Center for Special Warfare was dedicated. The ceremony was held in front of the first completed building of the Center, John F. Kennedy Hall.

The mission of the Special Warfare Center was to instruct selected U.S. military personnel, civilians, and eligible foreign offices; develop tactics and techniques for the Special Forces soldier in the field—e.g., infiltration methods, target analysis, operations and intelligence, communications, weapons, medical and engineering; prepare training documents in support of instructional programs and special unit training; coordinate with other armed forces and civilian agencies and support training activities of the U.S. Continental Army Command, USCONARC.

Special Warfare was defined at this time as the application of three associated activities as carried out by highly trained soldiers to achieve the nation's objective, whether in cold, limited, or general war. Those three areas were Counterinsurgency Operations, Unconventional Warfare, and Psychological Operations.

Counterinsurgency Operations would include any and all military, political, and economic actions taken to eliminate subversive insurgency. Subversive insurgency, e.g., wars of liberation, had received increased support by the communists as a primary course of action to extend communist control. Counterinsurgency Operations required the integration and coordination of all military and non-military resources to achieve the necessary results.

Unconventional Warfare encompassed guerrilla warfare, evasion and escape, and sabotage against hostile forces. UW operations would be conducted within enemy territory or enemy-controlled areas by establishing, training, and supporting the indigenous personnel in carrying out these missions.

Psychological Operations included PsyWar (psychological warfare) and covered the political, military, economic, and ideological actions necessary to create in enemy, neutral, or friendly forces the emotions, attitudes, or behaviors to support the national objectives.

Throughout the early 1960s soldiers of the Special Forces participated in more than six major exercises and more than 74 smaller FTXs (Field Training Exercises) ranging from Exercise Polar Strike in Alaska to Quick Kick VII conducted in the Caribbean. Soldiers from SF groups would be included in counter-guerrilla and counterinsurgency warfare training with assorted conventional units located in the continental United States.

Many Special Forces soldiers with distinct capabilities as teachers were assigned to Army Special Action Forces (SAF). These units would be tasked with civil affairs, engineer, intelligence, military police, and psychological operations units. Five such units were active: one for Asia, one for Latin America, one for Europe, and two for Africa and the Middle East. SAF instruction in medicine, sanitation, agricultural techniques, local government administrations, communications, and basic commerce was a direct deterrent to the spread of communism.

Simultaneous with these other activities, the Special Forces soldiers and groups constantly prepared for the UW task of infiltrating deep into enemy-controlled territory to contact, organize, train, equip, and advise the local partisans for guerrilla warfare against a common enemy.

During this time Special Forces soldiers were sent all over the globe in MTT. In 1965, for example, 25 MTT were deployed to 14 different countries. These countries included Argentina, Bolivia, Brazil, Ethiopia, Iran, Iraq, Jordan, Mali, Nepal, Nigeria, Pakistan, Peru, the Philippines, and the Republic of the Congo.

The missions of these teams varied by country, but would include aerial delivery methods, communications, engineering/demolition, language interpretation, medical instruction, and other tactical training. Lt. General William P. Yarborough called the Special Forces soldiers "the finest representatives that the United States Army has ever had." These MTT missions assisting friendly foreign countries expanded the role of the SF soldier from unconventional warfare and counterinsurgency to one of today's important SF functions, Foreign Internal Defense.

With the growing success of its teams and their missions, the Special Forces had soldiers who had seen action all over the world. Not all of the missions were benign in nature. While the public's and military's primary attention was directed to the area of Southeast Asia, SF teams were quite active in Latin America. Members of the 8th Special Forces Group (Airborne) operating out of Fort Guick, in the Panama Canal Zone, were involved in operations against communist-backed guerrillas in Latin America. Special Forces soldiers would be involved in the pursuit and capture of Ernesto "Che" Guevara, a known Cuban revolutionary in the mountainous terrain in the country of Bolivia in 1968.

Special Forces was originally created to provide an unconventional warfare force in the event of Soviet aggression in Europe. It would not be the massing of Soviet armor funneling through the Fulda Gap, however, that would give Special Forces the action they were trained to carry out. The small wars of liberation referred to by President Kennedy would be where the Special Forces would come of age. They were the watershed for soldiers of the green beret.

CHAPTER 3

Baptism by Fire: Vietnam

While many people believe America's involvement in Vietnam was initiated by President Kennedy, it was actually President Dwight D. Eisenhower who first committed U.S. troops to southeast Asia. The French debacle at Dien Bien Phu in 1954 left a void in the region, opening it to the spread of communism.

At this time President Eisenhower promised direct aid to the government of South Vietnam. In 1957 the first U.S. Army Special Forces soldiers actually arrived in Vietnam. That summer members of the 1st SFG(A) would train members of the Vietnamese Army at the Commando Training Center located at Nha Trang. This began the official involvement of U.S. Army Special Forces in Vietnam, which would last for 14 years until their withdrawal in February 1971.

During the time period of 1959–1960, South Vietnamese insurgents referred to as Viet Cong (Vietnamese communists) were growing in numbers and in power. The VC, as they came to be called, would move through villages spreading terror, torture, and destruction among the people. Thirty Special Forces soldiers were sent to South Vietnam in May 1960 to set up a training program for the army of Vietnam. It was on 21 September 1961 that the new president, John F. Kennedy, made good his inaugural address, "we shall support any friend, oppose any foe." His deep concern over the communist insurgents in South Vietnam drew the president to the Special Forces and their capability. The 5th Special Forces Group, 1st Special Forces, were made responsible for conduct of all SF missions in Vietnam.

To the average American citizen, places such as Nam Dong, Plei Mei, Kontum, Lang Vei, Dak To, and Bu Brang were unknown locations on a map. To the men of the Special Forces they were home, fortresses where they took a stand for freedom. These names meant camps where SF soldiers labored to build a future for liberty, bunkers where they spilled their blood, and a handful of

Special Forces soldiers were among the first U.S. advisers sent to the Republic of Vietnam. Here members of the 5th Special Forces Group (Airborne) are armed with M1 Garand rifles, carbines, and BARs (Browning Automatic Rifles) and wear an assortment of uniforms, from early issue jungle fatigues to the "duck hunter" camouflage. Note the SF Captain, (kneeling, left) is holding a newly issued AR-15 rifle, the predecessor to the M-16. *U.S. Army Photo*

dirt where some gave the ultimate sacrifice for what they believed in: "De Oppresso Liber." (SF motto: To Free the Oppressed.)

In the early part of U.S. involvement in Vietnam, Special Forces soldiers carried out missions to train a guerrilla force. According to intelligence from the CIA, the SF teams were deployed to the central highlands of South Vietnam to begin training the Montagnards (a French term defined as "mountain people"). The Montagnards numbered more than 500,000 in South Vietnam and came from approximately 20 different tribes. The agency had recognized the Montagnards as a possible ally in the war against the communists.

Special Forces began a program with mountain people that would become known as CIDG, or Civilian Irregular Defense Group. The organization and training of this paramilitary group became the primary mission for Special Forces in Vietnam. From 1961 to 1965 more than eight CIDG camps were built in the isolated countryside of South Vietnam. Each of these outposts was self-contained and manned by a CIDG Strike Force, a complement of South Vietnamese Special Forces and a U.S. Special Forces A-team. The primary role of the A-detachments took a turn from their origins in 1952. Instead of training a guerrilla force to interdict conventional army troops, they were now training indigenous tribesmen to conduct actions against other guerrillas, the Viet Cong.

Over the course of the war more than 250 outposts of A-Camps would be established throughout South Vietnam. Scattered along the Laos and Cambodian boarders, these strategically located outposts of freedom would become a considerable thorn in the side of the Viet Cong and later the North Vietnamese Army.

One such camp was Nam Dong, commanded by SF Captain Roger H. Donlon. Located some 32 miles west of Da Nang, the camp was distinctly in enemy territory. Established 15 miles from the Laotian border, it was placed strategically to inter-

"Green Beret" Staff Sergeant Arthur Fletcher assisted two members of the Vietnamese Special Forces in the repair of a 30-caliber machine gun. *U.S. Army Photo*

dict and harass the VC coming down the Ho Chi Minh from the North. Nam Dong was not like any other A-Camp design the SF soldiers had seen at Ft. Bragg—e.g., Plei Mei was triangular, Dak To circular, Lang Vei a diamond, and so on. This plot of real estate measured approximately 80 yards by 120 yards, looking more like a West Virginia ham than a formidable fortress. Beyond the camp perimeter was another area 350 yards long and 250 yards wide. Here is where the Vietnamese strike force lived, in about a dozen hootches. In addition to the "strikers," there was a contingent of 60 Nungs. (The Nungs were ethnic Chinese mercenaries who fought bravely, and were dedicated to the Special Forces soldiers they fought alongside.) Just beyond the outer fence line there lay a jungle airstrip, courtesy of the U.S. Navy Seabees.

Approximately 5,000 Katu tribesmen live in the area of the Nam Dong Valley. The SF Camp would provide them with medical attention and protection, and hopefully be a source of aggravation for the VC. The team medical specialists, Sgt. Thomas L. Gregg and Sgt. Terrance D. Terrin, would become the "popular" members of the team with the locals, as oftentime happened among the camps.

Nam Dong would be home for the Special Forces soldiers of A-726 (A-team-7th SFG(A)Team #26). What team A-726 did not know was that this civic action mission would turn into a life-or-death battle before they would leave.

At 0226 Monday 6 July 1964, the VC began their attack of Camp Nam Dong. Mortar rounds, grenades, and small arms fire erupted from every direction. The Special Forces soldiers were surrounded. SSG Keith Daniels, shaken out of bed by the first explosion, was now on the camp's radio. He made contact with Da Nang and requested a flare ship and air strike. Hearing explosions coming closer to his position, he knew the communications shed was next. He grabbed his AR-15 and hit the door. Just as he left, the building exploded behind him.

By now the Nungs and South Vietnamese had moved to their fighting positions, and the SF were manning the mortar pits. A typical mortar pit was approximately eight feet around, with sandbags stacked around the edge to provide some protection from small arms fire and flying fragments. Located at the rear of the pit was a cement bunker housing 300 rounds of assorted ammunition for the tube—high explosive (HE) and white phosphorous, either 60mm or 81mm, accordingly.

President Kennedy had referred to the green beret as a "symbol of excellence, a badge of courage, a mark of distinction in the fight for freedom." The men of team A-726 put their training and experience to work that morning. From bunkers, mortar pits, or behind debris piles, the Special Forces soldiers were returning fire

By the spring of 1970, more than 350 U.S. pilots had been captured and held in prison camps in North Vietnam. These pilots and aircrews were exposed to appalling living conditions and subjected to frequent beatings and torture. The majority of American captives in the North were not even allowed contact with other prisoners or the outside world.

In May of 1970, reconnaissance photographs revealed the existence of two prison camps west of Hanoi. At Son Tay, one of the recce photos showed a large letter "K" drawn in the dirt. This was a code for "come get us."

Brigadier General Donald D. Blackburn, who had trained Filipino guerrillas during World War II, recommended that a small hand-picked group of Special Forces volunteers be assembled to mount a rescue operation to liberate these prisoners. For this operation, he choose Lt. Colonel Arthur D. "Bull" Simons to lead the force.

Since the prison compound was located more than 20 miles west of Hanoi, operation planners believed Son Tay was isolated enough to enable a small group to land, rescue the prisoners, and withdraw. A full-scale replica of the prison compound was constructed at Eglin Air Force Base, Florida. Here a select group of Special Forces soldiers trained at night for the mission. The mock compound was dismantled during the day to avoid detection by Soviet satellites. A model of the camp was built that would allow the raiders to view the camp under various light to duplicate moonlight, flares, night vision, and so on. The replica was named "Barbara." To be successful, the troops needed to be prepared, yet time was running out. Evidence, although inconclusive, showed that Son Tay may have been empty.

On 18 November 1970 Col. Simons moved his raiders to Takhli, Thailand, to begin staging for the mission. Only Col. Simons and three others knew what the final mission would be. Five hours before takeoff, 20 November, Col. Simons informed his force of 59 men, "We are going to rescue 70 American prisoners of war, maybe more, from a camp called Son Tay. This is something American prisoners have a right to expect from their fellow soldiers. The target is 23 miles west of Hanoi." As Col. Simons left the room the solders broke into applause.

Approximately 0215, Hanoi time, on 21 November 1970, the raid began. An Air Force C-130 flare ship illuminated the area with flares, and the HH-53 began firing on the guard towers with its twin Gatling guns. The U.S. Navy also provided diversionary fire. The raiders now had less than 30 minutes to land and complete their mission before they would have to face North Vietnamese reinforcements. The only problem was, the helicopter mistakenly set down at another site. Instead of being just outside the prison compound, the support group was some 400 meters away at what was referred to as a 'secondary school' on the maps. This building was a barracks that housed Chinese and Soviet advisers and a large number of NVA troops. The raiders took this force under fire and eliminated them from reinforcing the prison.

After this brief encounter, Col. Simons and the support group re-loaded his HH-53 and moved to the prison compound. Nine minutes into the raid, Col. Simons was outside the prison wall. There, he and the support element augmented the assault and security elements and eliminated approximately 60 guards. However, as they searched from building to building the hard facts begin to sink in, there were no American prisoners. There were no prisoners whatsoever. The Son Tay raid ended after 27 minutes and the raiders were once again airborne. The force had not lost a single man, and al-

The Son Tay Raid Patch

though there were no prisoners to rescue, the planning and execution itself were flawless. To this day the Son Tay raid is often referred to as a "textbook" mission.

"Outpost of Freedom." This aerial photo shows a good overview of an SF camp. Scattered throughout South Vietnam, these fighting camps would serve as bases of operations against the Viet Cong and later the North Vietnamese Army troops. Numerous layouts and plans were tried; this plan, referred to as a star pattern, was one of the later designs. Each tip of the star is a fighting bunker, and as you move in toward the core of the camp you can see additional motor pits or machine gun emplacements. This also is where the "Green Berets" would set up their Tactical Operations Center. *JFK Special Warfare Museum*

toward the rushing horde of VC guerrillas. As the courageous troops fought to defend their camp, the VC kept coming. Two reinforced VC battalions, more than 800 guerrillas, had managed to encircle the camp. They had already penetrated the outer perimeter and were now bearing down on team A-726.

After five hours of intense fighting, the defenders of the camp successfully thwarted the VC attack. Camp Nam Dong had survived, but not without a cost: 55 of the camp's defenders had been killed. Among them, MSgt. Gabriel R. Alamo and Sgt. John Houston, members of A-726, and

an Australian Warrant Officer, Kevin Conway. The body count showed that more than 200 VC had died in the failed attack.

On 5 December 1964, President Lyndon B. Johnson awarded the Medal of Honor to Captain Roger Donlon, who had particularly distinguished himself. The text of the citation explains that "Captain Roger C. Donlon, 7th Special Forces Group (Airborne), 1st Special Forces, distinguished himself on 6 July 1964, while commanding Special Forces Detachment A-726 at Nam Dong, republic of Vietnam. On 6 July, the camp was assaulted in a pre-dawn attack by a reinforced Viet

Cong battalion. During the violent five-hour battle, resulting in numerous causalities on both sides, Captain Donlon directed the overall defense of the camp. He swiftly marshaled his forces and ordered the removal of needed ammunition from a blazing building hit by the initial assault. He then dashed through a hail of small arms and exploding hand grenade fire to a breach of the main gate where he detected and annihilated an enemy three-man demolition team. Exposed to an intense attack and sustaining a severe stomach wound, he succeeded in reaching the 60mm mortar pit. Discovering most of the men in the gun pit were wounded, Captain Donlon disregarding his own injury, risked his own life by remaining in the pit and returning the enemy fire, allowing

Captain Roger H. Donlon returns to the Special Forces camp at Nam Dong, where he was the Officer in Charge when the camp was attacked by the Viet Cong on 6 July 1964 by a force estimated to be of battalion size. He inspects what is left of the mess hall. Captain Donlon was the first soldier to be awarded the Medal of Honor during the Vietnam War. By the end of the conflict, Special Forces soldiers would bring home 17 Medals of Honor, our nation's highest award for gallantry above and beyond the call of duty. *National Archive*

the men to withdraw. While dragging his team sergeant out of the gun pit, an enemy mortar round exploded, hitting Captain Donlon's left shoulder. Suffering from multiple wounds, he carried the 60mm mortar to a new location 30 meters away where he found another three wounded defenders. After administering first aid and encouragement to these men, he left the weapon with them and then raced toward another location, retrieving a 57mm recoilless rifle. With great courage under fire, he returned to the abandoned gun pit, evacuated ammunition for the weapons and crawling and dragging back the urgently needed ammunition, received a third wound on his leg. Despite his critical condition, he crawled 175 meters to an 81mm mortar position and began directing firing operations, which protected the east sector of the camp. Until daylight brought defeat of the enemy forces, Captain Donlon moved from position to position around the beleaguered perimeter, hurling grenades at the enemy and inspiring his men to superhuman effort. Captain Donlon's conspicuous gallantry, extraordinary heroism and intrepidity at the risk

Special Forces with I Field Force Vietnam, Ban Me Thout. Assisted by U.S. Special Forces and indigenous personnel, the people of Buen Tor 1, some 10 miles south of Ban Me Thuot, evacuated their former homes. *U.S. Army Photo*

of his life above and beyond the call are in the highest tradition of the military service, reflecting the utmost credit upon himself, the Special Forces and the United States Army."

At the award ceremony, Captain Donlon said the award belonged to the entire team—to the valiant men of Special Forces Detachment A-726.

This was the first Medal of Honor to be awarded in the Vietnam war, but it would not be the last earned by the Special Forces. Sixteen of the nation's highest award, the MOH, would go to Special Forces soldiers: SFC Eugene Ashley, Jr.*, Detachment A-101, 5th SFG(A)—Lang Vei; Sgt. Gary B. Beikirch, Detachment B-24, 5th SFG(A)—Dak Seang; SSgt. Ray P. Benavidez, Detachment B-56, 5th SFG(A)—Loc Ninh; SFC William M. Bryant*, 5th SFG(A)—Long Khanh Province; Sgt. Brian L. Buker*, Detachment B-55, 5th SFG(A)—Chau Doc Province; SSgt. Jon R. Cavaiani—U.S. Army Vietnam Advisory Group; SSgt. Drew D. Dix—Chau Doc Province; 1st Lt. Loren D. Hagen*—U.S. Army Vietnam Advisory Group; SSgt. Charles E. Hosking, Jr.*, Detachment A-302, 5th SFG(A) Phuoc Long Province; SFC Robert L. Howard, 5th SFG(A); Specialist Fifth Class John J. Kedenburg*, Command and Control Detachment North, 5th SFG(A); SSgt. Franklin D. Miller, 5th SFG(A); 1st Lt. George K. Sissler*, 5th SFG(A); 1st Lt. Charles Q. Williams, 5th SFG(A)—Dong Xoai; Sgt. Gordon D. Yntema*, Detachment A-431, 5th SFG(A)—Cai Cai; SSgt. Fred W. Zabitosky, SOG.

The battle for Nam Dong was not an anomaly. In fact the Special Forces Camps were such a barb in the side of the VC that the communists would sacrifice thousands of their troops to try to dislodge a team or overrun a camp. Occasionally they did succeed, but only after the SF team extracted a heavy toll. If you go to a map of South Vietnam and pick a camp, there will be story for each one—Plei Mei in 1965, a battle so intense it would mark a major turn in U.S. involvement to the ground war in Vietnam; Lang Vei in 1968, where the communists had to employ Soviet-supplied PT-76 tanks in order to overrun the camp; Ben Het, where the NVA laid siege to the isolated post for two months, never taking it over; Dak To, Dak Pek, Dak Seang, Bu Brang, the list goes on. Strange names on a tactical map, hundreds of camps, and a thousand acts of heroism by Special Forces soldiers.

In addition to the tenacity of the SF teams located in these camps demonstrated, they had the versatility to employ various methods of turning the tide in their favor should the proverbial "hit the fan." The U.S. Air Force, Air Commandos flew AC-47 Gunships, "Spooky" and "Puff the Magic Dragon," that were often on call. TAC air, whether A-1E "Spads" or the fast movers, F-4 Phantoms, could be overhead in minutes. There were even times when B-52 bombers would rain down terror to break the assault on a camp in trouble. While all these sources provided outstanding assistance, the Special Forces also had an ace up their sleeves. Organic to the Special Forces, it was a group the camps called in when they were in danger of being overrun: the MIKE Force.

The MIKE Forces were Mobile Strike Forces. Each force consisted of three companies of soldiers, giving them a strength of 600 men. These units comprised elite CIDGs that would act as quick reaction forces to support the SF camps. Because of their loyalty and aggressiveness, Nungs were often well represented in the MIKE Forces. Highly trained in airborne and helicopter operations, the MIKE Forces could be called in to reinforce a camp and turn the tide in favor of the Special Forces soldiers on the ground.

Unlike other assets in theater, the MIKE Force was under direct control of the U.S. Special Forces and commanded by SF soldiers. Under the control of the "C" detachment commander, by 1968 there were five Mobile Strike Force Commands in Vietnam, numbering approximately 2,000 men per command. These forces were highly responsive and

(* *awarded posthumously*)

could be placed into action at a moment's notice. For this reason, members of the MIKE Force seldom had the luxury of sitting around garrison. They would return from an engagement often with only enough time to resupply and load up on the helicopters for the next run. The soldiers of the MIKE Force were the "cavalry" in Huey's, and many a besieged SF camp owes its survival to this group of courageous soldiers, both American and indigenous. By the end of 1966 the 5th Special Forces Group (Airborne) had an operational strength of 2,400 men, with strike forces numbering 33,400 indigenous troops and supported by 2,400 MIKE Force soldiers.

Special Forces soldiers leading indigenous troops were also employed at this time by the Central Intelligence Agency (CIA) to conduct reconnaissance operations. Reconnaissance teams, or RTs, usually consisted of two SF soldiers and four indigenous personnel. These early CIA-sponsored operations were referred to as PROJECT DELTA and filled Military Assistance Command Vietnam (MACV) intelligence requirements across the entire country. The capability of these small teams proved so valuable that subsequent recce missions were formed in the operations known as Projects, GAMMA, SIGMA, and OMEGA.

These small teams were extremely vulnerable to the larger communist forces they were sent to study. Helicopters were regularly called in to extract an RT from a "hot" (enemy engaged) landing zone (LZ). For the times when the helicopters could not land, the RT could be extracted with the use of the McGuire rig, named after Special Forces Sergeant Major Charles McGuire, who invented it. The McGuire rig was a simple rope 100 feet long with a canvas sling attached; it would be lowered to the ground from a hovering helicopter. The team member on the ground could quickly place himself in the sling and hold on, to be snatched from grasp of the enemy as the helicopter pulled him out. Four of these rigs could be fitted on a helicopter at one time.

In addition to providing special reconnaissance, 5th SFG(A) established the MACV Renaissance/Commando School in September 1966, located in Nha Trang, South Vietnam. Known as the "Recondo" School, this three-week course trained the indigenous forces in helicopter insertions and extractions techniques, survival, evasion and escape (E&E), communications, weapons (U.S. and enemy), intelligence gathering methods, and other subjects pertaining to Special Forces operations. Non-airborne soldiers would also receive parachute training. Members of U.S. Long Range Reconnaissance Patrols (LRRPs) and recon troop from Vietnam, Korea, and other allied countries also attended the Recondo School.

Because of the many successes of the CIDG program, in addition to the U.S. buildup of conventional troops in Vietnam during 1965–1966, the Special Forces–led CIDG units shifted to more offensive operations. In late 1966, Colonel Francis "Blackjack" Kelly, then commander of 5th SFG(A), presented the plan for the formation of the Mobile Guerrilla Force (MGF). Col. Kelly envisioned a company-size force that would operate in the same method as Merrill's Marauders operated in Burma during World War II.

The MGF was to be a small, self-contained unit; there would be no artillery support or reinforcements flown in to fill in for casualties. The only support that would be provided would come from a lone Forward Air Control aircraft. Resupply of the MGF would be done not by transport or helicopter but by fighter planes. In order not to compromise the troop's location, A-1E Skyraiders flown by the U.S. Air Commandos would drop napalm canisters, fitted with parachutes, filled with up 400 pounds of food, ammunition, and other supplies. The purpose of the MGF would be to drop in the middle of a known enemy's area of operation and create havoc. Col. Kelly was putting the VC on notice—SF was in town and they were going hunting! Hunting was good. The MGF

A captain from the 6th Special Forces Group (Airborne) goes over a mission plan with his A-team. Planning, rehearsing, and evaluating the mission are all part of the Special Forces operations. Every possible contingency they can think of is discussed and alternate measures developed. Very few things happen that have not been discussed in mission planning. Special Forces are successful because they "sweat the small stuff"! *U.S. Army Photo*

would be engaged in more than 50 battles, called in on countless air strikes against the enemy and involved in assaults on numerous company- and battalion-strength base camps. Mobile Guerrilla Force - Detachment A-303 was also responsible for recovering a highly sensitive "black box" from a U-2 aircraft operating with the SAC, Strategic Reconnaissance Wing, that had crashed.

The MIKE Force and MGF missions were highly successful. These units were large, however, and there was a need for a smaller, more covert unit. In February 1964 the commander of the MACV, General Paul D. Harkins, authorized the creation of

SOG. Officially the name stood for Studies and Observation Group; unofficially, and more exactly, it stood for Special Operations Group. While SOG did engage members of the other services, e.g., Navy SEALs, Air Commandos, and even USMC Force Recon, the majority of personnel came from the 5th Special Forces Group (Airborne).

The purpose of SOG was to conduct covert missions on "the other side of the fence." This meant the insertion of teams into North Vietnam, Laos (codename: Prairie Fire), and Cambodia (codename: Daniel Boone). SOG missions could include guerrilla warfare, direct action, sabotage, psychological operations, E&E nets, and other operations that are still classified. SOG was broken down into three operational areas: Command and Control North (CCN) with forward operating bases (FOB) located in the area of Hue and operating in North Vietnam and Laos; Command and Control Central (CCC), FOB in Kontum, operating in Laos and northeastern Cambodia; and Command and Control South (CCS), FOB located in Ban Me Thout and Quan Loi, operating in Cambodia.

A former SOG member reports that SOG teams would load M-16 cartridges with "pet," a high explosive. "We would wait until we got into a firefight with a [NVA] unit. We would begin our withdrawal and as we left, we'd drop magazines with these doctored rounds. They would be in for quite a surprise when they used them in their captured weapons." The "pet" round would blow up when the enemy tried to fire the weapon. A similar method was used in mortar rounds. A SOG team would infiltrate an enemy base camp and locate its ammunition supply. Instead of rigging it with explosives, the SOG members would plant these "special rounds" in the ammo boxes, and exfiltrate. Again, when the enemy would drop a round into the tube, it would explode. This had a marked psychological effect on the enemy concerning the quality of the ammunition they were receiving.

Although SOG forces regularly overcame overwhelming odds, not every mission dreamed up for them was realistic. One SOG veteran relates that as he was getting ready to go on R&R, he was called into the commander's office. There were rumors floating around that the Soviets had introduced tanks into the south and SOG wanted confirmation of this information. He had been chosen, since he had a background in armor and knew how to drive a tank. His mission was to be inserted "across the fence," locate one such tank, affix a white flag to its antenna and drive it back to friendly lines in the south. His eyes widened at the prospect of such a mission. He was also told that the tank was at a base camp deep inside enemy territory and had a regiment protecting it. This veteran continues, "Even some missions were just too wild for SOG. I said, thanks, then grabbed my bag and headed for R&R." (MACV/SOG would get its verification of the tanks some months later when 11 PT-76 tanks overran Lang Vie Special Forces camp.)

SOG teams took extremely high casualties. Often teams would have to run for their lives moving from one LZ to another hoping the Hueys could get them out in time. It was during the SOG missions that the STABO rig was developed. The name STABO was derived by the three SF soldiers from the Recondo School that developed the device: Major Robert Stevens, Captain John Knabb, and Sergeant First Class Clifford Roberts. For this device the soldier wore a specially designed web harness in place of his normal web gear. When the need for extraction came, the soldier would undo two straps from the back of the harness, secure them around his legs, then attach himself to the STABO yoke via carabiners at each shoulder. This harness differed from the McGuire rig in that it provided a more secure connection and allowed the user to keep his hands free to operate weapons as he flew through the air and out of harm's way.

Another method for extracting special operations personnel from the ground was the Fulton Surface-To-Air Recovery (STAR) system, known as "Skyhook." The STAR device consists of two containers that can be air-dropped to special forces units operating in a covert operation. Upon opening the canisters the soldiers on the ground would find a balloon, two helium inflation bottles, and an insulated flight suit and harness. When inflated, the balloon measured eight feet in diameter by 23 feet in length. Attached to the balloon would be a 500-foot nylon line equipped with marker flags for daylight extractions and strobe lights for nighttime operations. The individual to be extracted puts on the insulated flight suit and harness, hooks himself to the balloon's lines, and then sits facing the oncoming plane as the balloon is released and heads skyward.

A specially equipped MC-130 Combat Talon from the 90th Special Operations Squadron was also part of the Skyhook system. As the aircraft approached the recovery area, the yoke arms or "whiskers" were extended. These arms snagged the line in a locking device. The balloon would break away and the line would be fed into an attached hydraulic power winch in the rear of the

MACV-SOG (Military Assistance Command Vietnam–Studies and Observation Group) ran three AOs, or areas of operations. Command and Control North (CCN) operated in North Vietnam and Laos, Command and Control Central (CCC) operated in Laos and northeastern Cambodia, and Command and Control South (CCS) operated in Cambodia.

aircraft. The individual was then reeled into the ramp door. Along with personnel, the STAR system could also recover up to 500 pounds of equipment or material, if needed.

The soldiers of SOG were tasked with some of the most dangerous missions of the war. Reconnaissance teams became known as Spike Teams. Hatchet Teams, similar to a MIKE Force, would be ready to swoop in on any target the Spike Team exposed. The acronym for their missions said it all: SLAM—Search, Locate, Annihilate Mission. What more can you add? These were the types of missions assigned to SOG. Of the Medals of Honor given to SF soldiers in Vietnam, two went to SOG members.

Whatever the results of the Vietnam War, the men of the U.S. Army Special Forces emerged from the conflict with a permanent place in the history of the U.S. Army. They were highly adaptable in their fighting techniques. Introduced in the unconventional warfare role, they adjusted remarkably well to counter-insurgency, as well as dealing with conventional warfare and civilian irregulars. Whether building and defending an isolated CIDG camp, serving with larger MGFs, or operating on a small SOG team, Special Forces soldiers were highly motivated and determined to accomplish their missions at all costs.

When the Special Forces departed Vietnam, they accounted for 17 Medals of Honor, one Distinguished Service Medal, 60 Distinguished Service Crosses, 814 Silver Stars, 13,234 Bronze Stars, 235 Legions of Merit, 46 Distinguished Flying Crosses, 232 Soldier's Medals, 4,891 Air Medals, 6,908 Army Commendation Medals, and 2,658 Purple Hearts.

Mission after mission these warriors demonstrated their courage and tenacity to tackle the impossible and come out victorious. The men of the U.S. Army Special Forces, known to many as the "Green Berets," did their duty and departed from Southeast Asia with honor.

CHAPTER 4

Special Forces Beyond Vietnam

This modified version of the HUMMV for desert operations during Desert Shield/Storm was dubbed the DUMMV. Currently it's referred to as a Ground Mobility Vehicle (GMV). The ultimate 4x4 vehicle, it allowed SF soldiers to execute their mission at long range, or serve as a Mission Support Site (MSS), from which ODAs operate in their AO. This particular GMV is armed with a Mark 19, 40mm Grenade Machine gun, and is loaded with fuel cans, water, ammunition, and other mission-essential equipment. Attached to the rear of the vehicle is camouflage netting that may be deployed by the team to conceal its MSS.

In the years following the Vietnam war the Special Forces saw a dramatic downsizing. The 1st, 3rd, 6th, and 8th Special Forces Groups were deactivated or consolidated into other groups. Conventional commanders were trying to distance themselves from the war in Southeast Asia and cast their attention anew on the verdant valleys of "cold-war" Europe. Beset by conventional commanders, Special Forces soldiers fought the Army mindset for mere survival. The Special Forces soldier had become an anachronism, and many people considered becoming a member to be a dead-end career path. During the early 1970s, the Army was placing more emphasis on the Rangers, and some of the SF missions were being incorporated into the two newly formed Ranger battalions. In January 1969 the JFK Institute for Special Warfare was renamed the U.S. Army JFK Institute for Military Assistance. (IMA)

In an attempt to maintain their capabilities, Special Forces commanders formulated the SPARTAN program. SPARTAN stood for Special Proficiency at Rugged Training and Nation Building. This program was created to demonstrate the many skills of the Special Forces soldier. It also proved that SF troops were not outdated merely because the United States was no longer engaged in active warfare.

The SPARTAN program sent soldiers from the 5th SFG(A) and 7th SFG(A) to various states throughout the United States, such as Florida, Arizona, and Montana, to work on American Indian reservations. Here the SF soldiers applied their talents on American soil, building roads, schools, medical facilities. They provided medical treatment to the poverty-stricken areas of Hoke and Anson counties in North Carolina. To this day, you can still find SF soldiers working among the American Indian population. Major Tom McCollum, SF-PAO, said, "going to these locations, our soldiers get the feel for real Third World conditions." As honorable as this program was, civic actions were not the primary purpose Special Forces had been intended to serve. Special Forces was created for unconventional warfare, and with the lessons learned in the Vietnam War, Special Forces missions would be broadened beyond Unconventional Warfare (UW) to include direct action in a guerrilla war. They would not have to wait too long for the opportunity to serve this role.

In November 1979 the U.S. Embassy in Teheran, Iran, was captured and its staff taken hostage. While alternate venues were discussed, President Jimmy Carter, after six months, authorized the military option, and Operation Eagle Claw commenced.

What began as an extraordinary attempt by the U.S. Special Operations Forces ended in tragedy in the darkness of an Iranian desert. It was April 1980 when Special Forces Operation Detachment - Delta, better known as "Delta Force," along with supporting Air Force and Marine aircraft and aircrews, met with disaster. Operation Eagle Claw had failed. It resulted in the loss of eight courageous troops and damaged the honor of the United States of America and the credibility of U.S. Special Operations.

Following the disaster at Desert One, a review committee known as the Holloway Commission convened to look into problems within U.S. Special Operations. At the conclusion of its review, the Commission made two major recommendations. First, the Department of Defense should establish a Counterterrorism Joint Task Force (CTJTF) as a field organization of the Joint Chiefs of Staff (JCS) with a permanently assigned staff and forces. The JCS would plan, train for, and conduct

Two members of Company C, 2nd Battalion, 7th SFG(A). Staff Sergeant John Anchex and Sergeant Rodney Allen (left to right) rappel down an icy mountain during Exercise Brim Frost, 1981. Rappelling skills are still used today when necessary to maneuver down a mountain slope, or down the side of a building as in SFAUC. *Defense Visual Information Center Photo*

operations to counter terrorist activities directed against the United States. The CTJTF would employ military forces in the counterterrorism (CT) role. These forces could range in size from small units of highly specialized personnel to larger integrated forces. Second, the JCS should consider the formation of a Special Operations Advisory Panel (SOAP). This panel would consist of high-ranking officers to be drawn from both active service and retired personnel. To be selected a soldier needed a background in special operations or service at a CinC or JCS level with proficient knowledge of special operations or defense policy.

With the election of President Ronald W. Reagan in 1980, the U.S. military would get a much-needed revitalization. The defense policy of the new administration, along with the emergence of anti-Leninist guerrillas in Nicaragua, Angola, Mozambique, and Afghanistan, compelled the United States to take a more dynamic role in combating communism. These situations also heightened the awareness of deficiencies in U.S. Special Operation Forces. A new focus came into being: Low Intensity Conflict, and the Army Special Forces in particular would benefit from this new attention.

On 1 June 1982, the Center for Military Assistance was redesignated the 1st Special Operations Command (Airborne) (SOCOM), and assigned to U.S. Army Forces Command (FORSCOM). FORSCOM was responsible for all activities of Special Operations Forces units. In June 1983 the IMA

During Exercise Team Spirit 1986 a member of the 1st Special Forces Groups (Airborne) assumes a prone firing position to provide security for his team as they secure the perimeter of the Pohang DZ (drop zone). Using his rucksack for cover, he aims his M-16 and watches for any OpFor (Opposition Force) soldiers. *Defense Visual Information Center Photo*

Kuwaiti soldiers from the 2nd Infantry Battalion, 15th Brigade, fire M-16 rifles on the firing line while being supervised by a U.S. Army Special Forces Sergeant First Class. Special Forces troops conducted live fire training with the Kuwaitis and instructed them on the use and care of M-16s and assorted small arms. They were part of the coalition forces who fought in Desert Storm. The working relationship and cultural experience the SF soldiers possess made the members of the SF ODAs (Operational Detachments-Alpha) "the glue that held the coalition together," per General Norman Schwarzkopf. *Defense Visual Information Center Photo*

was again named the U.S. Army John F. Kennedy Special Warfare Center. The qualification course for Special Forces was lengthened and toughened, so only the highest quality soldiers would make it to the SF A-teams. The A-teams were also slightly modified, with the executive officer changed from a lieutenant to a warrant officer. The A-teams remained the backbone of Special Forces. In October 1984 the Army established a separate career management field (CMF 18) for Special Forces soldiers. The warrant officer career

management field (CMF 180) was introduced shortly thereafter on 9 April 1987.

In October 1983 the United States mounted Operation Urgent Fury to rescue American medical students and suppress pro-communist insurgents on the island of Grenada. All the services, consisting fully of volunteer forces, wanted to show what they could do. Within two days of landing on the island on 15 October 1983, the island was secure. U.S. forces were victorious, but

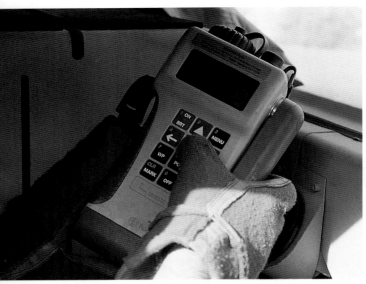

Using the Global Positioning System (GPS) unit, SF teams were able to determine their positions accurately as they performed SR, DA, and other missions across the wasteland of the Iraqi desert during the Gulf War.

it appeared special operations units still needed better coordination.

In 1984 the 1st Special Forces Group (Airborne) was reactivated at Fort Lewis, Washington. On 9 April 1987 the chief of staff of the Army established the Special Forces as a separate office career branch of the service. Special Forces officers would now wear the Crossed Arrow insignia on their uniform collars and Jungle Green was designated as the Special Forces Branch color.

As the Reagan policy unfolded, Special Forces detachments were deployed to numerous countries around the world. Their main mission was Foreign Internal Defense (FID). Other missions included training allied armed forces to defend their countries, humanitarian assistance, medical care, and construction of roads and buildings in various Third World countries. Special Forces played a pivotal role in El Salvador and Honduras, preventing a civil war in Nicaragua from spilling over the borders.

In May 1986, Congressmen William Cohen and Sam Nunn introduced a Senate bill to amend the 1986 Defense Authorizations Bill. The following month, Congressman Dan Daniel introduced a similar bill in the House of Representatives. This bill, signed into law in October 1986, in part directed the formation of a unified command responsible for special operations. In April 1987, the U.S. Special Operations Command (USSOCOM) was established at MacDill AFB, Florida, and Army General James J. Lindsay assumed command.

In June 1988 the SF training program was increased from approximately 21 weeks to a full six months. This increase included a three-week Special Forces Assessment and Selection. SFAS also changed assignment from a PCS (permanent change of station) to TDY (temporary duty); this created a more fluid flow of soldiers who volunteered for Special Forces. This new assessment tested the candidates both psychologically and physically. Consequently, any unsuitable candidate could be removed from the program before ever entering the SF training. Field time was lengthened from 63 to 100 days.

Another milestone for Special Forces came on 1 December 1989, when the U.S. Army Special Operations Command (Airborne) was created under USSOCOM. USASOC, commanded by a three-star general, would be responsible for all Army Special Operations Forces. This would include the Rangers, the 160th Special Operations Aviation Regiment and, of course, the Special Forces.

This new command would have its effectiveness battle-tested when President George Bush ordered the execution of Operation Just Cause in Panama in December 1989. Special Forces would play a proactive part in the invasion, which lasted less than 24 hours.

Members of the 7th SFG(A), Company A, 3rd Battalion under the command of Major Kevin Higgins, secured and held the Pacora River Bridge, a vital crossing point. Special Forces soldiers, along with conventional troops, blocked a Panamanian Defense Forces (PDF) vehicle convoy from bringing reinforcements across the bridge. As they held the convoy, using LAW and AT-4 anti-tank weapons, an AC-130H Spectre gunship orbiting overhead employed precision fire, halting any further PDF movement.

In another part of the country, members of the 7th SFG(A) were tasked with the surgical mission of disabling a television repeater facility at Cero Azul. As Operation Just Cause began on 19 December 1989, two MH-60 helicopters lifted off for their target. Aboard these two aircraft was an 18-man element of Special Forces soldiers, augmented with members of the 1109th Signal Battalion.

Once on site, they fast-roped to the ground and, using explosives, neutralized the target. While the signalmen went to work on the electronics equipment, the SF soldiers swept the building, making sure it was secure, and conducted patrols in the local area. With the mission complete without taking any enemy fire, they extracted by MH-60 Blackhawks.

A year later, U.S. Army Special Forces Command (USASFC), which assumed command of all SF units, was established as a Major Subordinate Command, or MSC. A second MSC, USACAPOC (U.S. Army Civil Affairs and Psychological Operations Command), would be included under USASOC. USACAPOC included all PsyWar and civil affairs units. In June 1990 USASOC also took over command of the JFK Institute and School from TRADOC (Training and Doctrine Command). All of the capabilities and components of the Army Special Operations Forces were now under U.S. Army Special Operations Command (Airborne), or USASOC.

In the beginning of 1991, USASOC and the Special Forces would be called to war again in the vast desert wasteland of Southwest Asia. Operation Desert Shield was launched after Iraq invaded the neighboring country of Kuwait. National Command Authority (NCA) immediately deployed members of the 3rd, 5th, and 10th Special Forces Groups (Airborne), along with Civil Affairs and Psychological Operations units, to the Persian Gulf region. Special Operations Command Central, or SOCCENT, was responsible for the area abutting the Iraqi border, some 60,000 square miles of desert. Unlike their Panamanian mission, when U.S. Special Operations Forces went to war this time, they operated with a new set of parameters: Is this an appropriate SOF mission? Does it support the CinC's campaign plan? Is it operationally feasible? Are the required resources available to execute? Does the expected outcome justify the risk?

The primary mission of the Special Forces soldiers as Operation Desert Shield began was to work with their FID skills in the formation of a defensive posture among the newly formed Coalition Forces. The 5th Special Forces Group's mission of Coalition Assistance came to the forefront at this time. Due to its constant deployment into the theater and working relationship with the local military, the 5th SFG(A) was familiar with the areas, languages, and cultures of these soldiers. They also knew the abilities of these forces and how they operated in this region. This mission also included members of 10th Special Forces Group, who interacted with coalition members from Europe, e.g., British, French, Czech, and so on. Because of the SF soldiers' expertise, they worked with almost every level of Coalition Forces, 109 battalions in total. They were instrumental in establishing working relations with the Saudi, Egyptian, and Syrian military.

Under camouflage netting, the GMVs are well hidden in the MSS. Captain Steve Warman of ODA581 receives a communication over the SatCom radio. While the team leader sends in a situation report, or SitRep, Commo Sergeant Christopher Spence provides security, keeping a watchful eye on the terrain.

During Operation Desert Storm, Special Forces ODAs (Operational Detachments-Alpha) would conduct deep reconnaissance in Saudi Arabia, Iraq, and Kuwait. These recon missions not only provided up-to-the-minute intel on the Iraqi forces, but included analyzing soil conditions to ascertain whether it would support the heavy weight of armored vehicles. In addition to the special reconnaissance (SR) mission, the ODAs would perform direct action (DA) missions, e.g., sabotaging lines of communication, raids, ambushes, and destroying command and control targets. They also assisted in Combat Search

and Rescue (CSAR) missions and supported the Kuwaiti resistance.

As the air war began, SF teams were tasked with behind-the-lines intelligence-gathering missions. One such SR mission was carried out by ODA-525 of the 5th SFG(A), under the command of CWO2 John "Bulldog" Balwanz. Chief Balwanz relates that 5th SFG-Desert Shield basically started with coalition work, beginning with border recon on Saudi and Kuwaiti borders. The group was using DUMMVs—HUMMVs modified for desert operations. They were on the border between Saudi and Kuwait; they were the eyes of the command. ODA-525 was located at the King Fahad airport, along with the 1st Battalion of the 5th SFGF and SOCCENT. This underground command center was known as the "Bat Cave."

Balwanz had his team running training missions—cross country movement, long range movements, including areas in the Northwest portion of Saudi, near the Jordan border. They also began rehearsing such things as building hide sites. There was no SOP for desert hide sites, so in the tradition of good SF soldiers the team scrounged and scavenged material. King Fahad airport was under construction at this time, so procurement was not a problem. Soon the SF troopers had assorted lengths of metal conduit on hand to fabricate their hide site. The basic hide site consisted of a hole, approximately nine feet square and five feet deep dug into the desert. Up from the hole came the center stand, which was an umbrella-like device with arms that stretched over the hole. The whole assembly was then covered with plastic, then burlap, then topped off with sand, making the hide site blend into the terrain. This whole assembly would then be broken down and carried in the soldiers' rucksacks. An average hide site kit could weigh more than 100 pounds.

Finally, the word came down that ODA-525 had its SR mission. Chief Balwanz and his team were moved from King Fahad airport to King Khalid Military City (KKMC), which was the staging area for the 5th Special Forces group. During Isolation, all details of the mission were gone over, and the list of needed equipment was decided upon by the team. When the team inserted into Iraq, each man's rucksack, including the hide site kit, weighed over 175 pounds. Chief Balwanz relates that "Along with the kit, there was 5 gallons of water per man, ammunition, food, shovels, extra batteries, redundant radio systems. We had two SatCom systems, a system to talk with the aircraft, and even a PRC-104 radio for emergencies." In addition to all this equipment, four of the team members carried M-16A2 rifles, two carried M-16s outfitted with M-203 grenade launchers, the last two carried the HK MP5 SD3 suppressed 9mm submachine guns; all members of the team also carried the M-9, 9mm Beretta as a sidearm.

On the morning of 23 February 1991, Chief Balwanz and the men of ODA-525 loaded onto two MH-60 Blackhawks of the 160th Special Operations Aviation Regiment (Airborne)—the "Night Stalkers." This would be the first time in the history of the Army that a warrant officer would lead a team into combat. The team was prepared to stay on the ground for four days. At the end of four days, they would be extracted, or if the ground war had begun by this time, they would link up with the ground force as the corps passed through their position. (They did not know when they loaded the helicopters that the ground war was scheduled to begin the next morning.) Chief Balwanz relates a conversation with Chief Warrant Officer 3 Kenny Collier. CWO3 Collier was a former SF soldier, now a helicopter pilot with the 160th SOAR. He would be piloting one of the MH-60s that would be inserting ODA-525. "Kenny," Chief Balwanz said, "I know you'll get me in . . . [my] concern is you coming back for me." With a smile on his face

Chief Collier assured his friend and fellow warrior, "I tell you, dog . . . you call, we'll haul!"

"Our mission called for us to go about 150 miles into Iraq," says Balwanz. "We wanted to put eyes on a major highway, Highway 7. It ran from Baghdad to Nasiriyah, then cut over to Basara." This put them in the right spot to provide "hard" intel to the corps commander once the ground war began. Were the Iraqis sending in reinforcements, or were they withdrawing their troops? They would locate their hide site in the area of the Euphrates River. Since there would be some vegetation, the SF soldiers opted to wear standard issue woodland BDUs (battle dress uniforms), rather than the desert "chocolate chip" or three-color desert camouflage patterns.

They flew from KKMC to Rahfa, just inside the Iraqi boarder, to refuel the Blawkhawks. Fuel would be a critical factor in inserting the SR team. Mission planners had determined that infil and exfil would be done with only 10 minutes of fuel to spare. This also meant that if ODA-525 hit a hot LZ, they had less than 10 minutes to get the helicopters back out. Timing was also critical because the team needed to be on the ground a certain number of hours to build their hide sites before the sun came up. The plan called for a departure at 2000 hours, refuel at 2200, and getting on site with six hours before first light.

As the two helicopters flew into the Iraqi night, the pilots got word that the mission had been aborted, and they returned toward Rahfa. As they landed in Rahfa, they were told that it was on again. While there is a lot of speculation as to why this happened, no one ever gave clear reason. With the mission back on, the MH-60 needed to refuel. This ate up valuable darkness time and placed the team behind schedule for the insertion.

Fuel tanks now topped off, and the insertion window getting smaller, the MH-60s took off. The pilots were flying on NVGs (night vision goggles) approximately 20 feet above the desert at

During Operation Uphold Democracy, Brigadier General Meade studies maps and aerial photos with a group of Special Forces soldiers. The general is being briefed by the SF members after a grenade attack in Port au Prince, Haiti, that killed five people and wounded another 25. *Defense Visual Information Center Photo*

more than 120 knots. It was hazardous moving so low and fast, and all of a sudden the Blackhawk jerked up. Chief Balwanz, wearing a head set, inquired what had happened. Chief Collier calmly responded, "We just hit a sand dune, probably tore off the rear landing gear."

Well hell, thought Bulldog, if Kenny isn't worried, then I'm not going to worry about it, either.

Shortly thereafter, a flock of ducks flew up from a lake or pond and one got sucked into one of the engines, shutting it down. This still did not deter the pilots of the 160th.

As they got close to their target site, they performed a couple of false insertions. They would intentionally get picked up on enemy radar, then sit down on the ground 10–15 seconds, then move to another site. As they neared their predetermined site, another snag arose. Due to the recall, they had lost global position system (GPS) satellite coverage, so the pilots went to alternate navigational systems that are not as accurate.

As the two Blackhawks touched down, the eight-man SF team—four men from each helicopter—jumped to the ground and assumed a defensive position on the desert surface. They had been told there would be no dogs, but moments after landing the air filled with barking. They removed their PVS7 NVGs and let their eyes acclimate to the night and their surroundings. By now the GPS was back online, and the team found out it was about a mile from its planned insertion spot. The men broke out the map and a compass, hoisted their 175-pound packs, and headed to the spot they had selected for their hide sites.

After moving about 3/4 mile, they stopped to cache the PRC-104, an FM radio capable of Morse code. If everything went south, they could get to the radio and E&E out of the area. Each member of the team had the GPS location of the site; there was also a small palm tree at the position so it would be easy for them to locate.

The team members moved on, finally reaching the canal where they planned to establish their hide sites. When they rehearsed digging hide sites in Saudi, the soil was soft loam, but here the ground was rock hard. There was no way the team would be able to replicate the Saudi-style hide site in the allotted time before daylight. They decided to dig into the side of the canal where the earth was softer. One team set up a hasty hide site in the canal, while the other dropped back a little where the ground was looser. From the highway either site would be invisible.

The team split, digging two separate hide sites 150 meters apart and approximately 300–400 meters from the highways. One group would watch the northbound traffic, the other the southbound. They needed to be close to the road so they could identify "signature items," pieces of equipment that are specific to a particular division or type of unit. As Chief Balwanz explained, "If you could ID the equipment, then you could ID the unit." Close proximity also allowed them to identify whether a tank was a Soviet T-72 or a T-55.

As the sun rose, the men in the hide site heard the sound of children playing. The children came closer to the site and looked inside, seeing team member SSgt. James Weatherford. Startled, the children ran away. Immediately, the team medic, Sgt. Daniel Kostrzebski, and weapons specialist, SFC Robert Degroff, were out the rear of the hide site with their weapons sighted on the fleeing children. They asked Chief Balwanz what they should do. Knowing full well that if the children made it back to their homes, the team would be compromised, he told his men not to shoot. The team gathered in the canal and via the SatCom contacted XVIII Airborne Corps, informing them they had been compromised and requesting immediate exfiltration.

The hide sites being compromised, Chief Balwanz instructed his team sergeants to stay in the canal and once it became dark, they would move to a new location and continue their mission. All was going well, until just after noon. At this time, CWO2 Balwanz was leaning on the parapet of the canal, observing the highway with his binoculars, when another group of children discovered them. A sheepherder also saw them and began heading quickly back to the village. The team again contacted base, requesting an exfil and possibly close air support (CAS). They were told that emergency exfiltration would be mobilized and that CAS was 20 minutes out.

A group of Bedouins came out looking for the team, and shortly afterward, four or five trucks, a Toyota Land Cruiser, and a bus stopped on the highway. An estimated 150 Iraqi soldiers armed with weapons poured from the vehicles and began to move toward the ODA-525's canal site. Sensing an imminent firefight, Chief Balwanz put into effect their emergency destruct plan: All the team's classified crypto gear, radios, and burst equipment were stuffed into one of the rucksacks and rigged with a block of C4 explosive that was then set with a one minute timer. The team piled the rest of their rucksacks on top of it. Carrying only their weapons, load-bearing equipment (LBE), with ammunition and water, and one LST-5 SatCom radio, the SF soldiers ran down the canal. The Iraqis, plus the Bedouins, began maneuvering around the eight-man SF team. As the team tried to put some distance between themselves and the enemy, they heard the C4 explode and the screams of Iraqi soldiers. This meant that the Iraqis were about a minute behind them.

Their pursuers began firing and were trying to outflank them. Chief Balwanz ordered his two M-203 gunners (SFCs Degroff and Hovermale) to start laying down fire. The team was now located in an "elbow' of the canal, with nowhere else to run. Fortunately, the troops closing in on the Americans were not aware they had stumbled on an SF team; perhaps they thought it was just a downed aircrew. Secondly, these were not Republican Guards, they were more militia-type soldiers. They tended to bunch up and walk upright, firing on the SF soldiers. When the 40mm HE rounds went off, these bunches became history. In the first minute of the firefight Chief Balwanz and his men took out almost 40 of the enemy. Another advantage for ODA-525 was that five of its eight men were school-trained snipers. They did not have any sniper rifles, but at 300 to 500 meters, their training made a real difference in the fight. Precise shooting also allowed the team to conserve its ammunition.

Finally, over the LST-5 they could hear the Forward Air Controller calling for the team. Unfortunately, in their haste to destroy the radio gear, the VHF whip antennae for the LST-5 had been left behind. Although the team could hear the aircraft, they could not communicate with them. As a last resort, SFC Degroff pulled his PRC-90 survival radio out and tried to make contact with any coalition aircraft. After a number of attempts, he got a response from an AWACS, which then passed the team's frequency on to the U.S. Air Force F-16s there to provide CAS.

While the Falcon pilots had yet to establish the actual location of the team, their mere presence caused many of the Iraqis to run away from the beleaguered SF team. At last the flight detected the team's position. The first request from the team was to take care of the vehicle and the people on the highway. The F-16s made their run dropping cluster bomb units (CBU). One minute there were vehicles, the next there was nothing but burning scrap metal. Now the attention of the CAS was directed at those enemy soldiers closing in on the team. Flying at 20,000 feet, the F-16 pilots were dropping CBU approximately 200 meters, or "danger close" to the SF soldiers. A total of 16 sorties were flown in support of ODA-525 that day.

As daylight faded, the team fought back down the canal and the fight died down. The helicopters were now inbound. The team returned to the cached PRC-90 radio, which was equipped with a beacon. They turned the unit to beacon mode and after a couple of minutes, two MH-60s descended almost right on top of the team. In less than ten seconds the team was on board. The helicopters lifted into the night sky and headed back to KKMC. Chief Balwanz was awarded the Silver Star, and the balance of the team was awarded the Bronze Star with V-device. The Blackhawk pilots received the Distinguished Flying Cross, and their crew members were awarded Air Medals.

Special Forces ODAs continued to perform similar missions even deeper as Operation Desert Storm began the ground phase of the war. SF teams shadowed the Iraqi Republican Guard, and every move they made was immediately reported to General Schwarzkopf's command center. This gave the CinC the vital, up-to-the minute information he required to mount the offensive that would decimate the Iraqi forces. In one of his briefings, General Schwarzkopf acknowledged that the Special Forces teams "let us know what was going on out there, and they were the eyes out there."

In summation, the ODAs of the U.S. Army Special Forces put their principles of coalition warfare into reality, combining the synergy of three allied corps into a united force that liberated Kuwait. General Schwarzkopf would say of the Special Forces, "They were the glue that held the coalition together."

After the Gulf War, in April 1991, members of the 1st Battalion, 10th Special Forces Groups (Airborne), were deployed to southeast Turkey and northern Iraq to participate in Operation Provide Comfort. Here the SF soldiers were involved in humanitarian operations with more than a half-million Kurdish refugees. As the month wore on, the 2nd and finally the 3rd Battalion would join in the operation, resulting in the deployment of the entire 10th group. The SF teams were instrumental in saving these refugees, as they provided direction, overall ground relief, and security for the operational activities.

As the missions wound down in the Persian Gulf region, Special Forces teams found themselves occupied with training schedules and new missions to carry out, as the latest operations unveiled themselves. Members of the 2nd Battalion, 5th SFG(A), were involved in Operation Restore Hope and Provide Comfort on the continent of Africa. They were placed under the command of the Joint Special Operations Forces, a component command of the Unified Task Force. When the detachment deployed to Somalia, the men established an Advance Operations Base (AOB) and began their initial mission of border surveillance along the Ethiopian boarder. Their mission was to locate and identify members of Somalian factions and bandits using Ethiopia as sanctuary while they carried out raids into Somalia.

In January of 1993, the SF forward operating base, or FOB, deployed to Mogadishu and assumed command and control of Joint Special

The United States leads de-mining operations around the world. Members of the SF are instrumental in teaching host nations' troops the proper methods of safely dealing with the plethora of mines scattered across the battlefields. Here a soldier from the 10th SFG(A) buries an inert land mine, which will be used to teach students the finer points of probing. *Defense Visual Information Center Photo*

Operation – Somalia (JSOFOR). JSOFOR organized and conducted Special Operations in Somalia in support of the UNITAF humanitarian relief efforts.

JSOFOR originated with a small force of one Operational Detachment B, or ODB, five ODA operating out of Belet Uen, and one ODA in Bardera. These forces supported operations under the UNITAF area of responsibility ranging from the Indian Ocean in the South to the Ethiopian boarder in the North. This area was subsequently divided into nine sections referred to as Humanitarian Relief Sectors (HRS); SF would be employed in four of the nine sectors.

The SF ODA units proved themselves a valuable asset to the task force. On one occasion SF soldiers made contact with an Ethiopian boarder post after 10 days of diplomatic efforts had failed. Making this connection with the post created a relationship that would provide valuable intelligence regarding the movement of Somali factions along the border.

While Operation Restore Hope did have some success in Somalia, any benefits these SF soldiers contributed in carrying out their missions faded into the background. Somalia will be remembered by the firefight in October 1993 involving Task Force Ranger, resulting in 18 U.S. soldiers killed and more than 30 wounded; enemy losses were estimated at more than 1,000.

On the other side of the globe, SF soldiers were participating in Operation Uphold Democracy on the island of Haiti. Members of the 3rd SFG(A) were sent to Haiti to establish an FOB, while the bulk of conventional troops of the 10th Mountain Division and later the 25th Infantry secured the city in Port au Prince. SF ODAs would deploy to the FOB and then fan out into the countryside in order to stabilize the remainder of the island.

During Haitian operations, a Special Forces captain and his men were making their way through a village. Three women approached him pleading for their assistance. The women told the SF captain that the local "witch" had placed a curse on their children and they wanted the American officers to help them. The so-called witch in question just sat there glaring at the soldiers. This was definitely something out of the ordinary for these men.

The captain slung his M-4 carbine over his shoulder and pondered the situation. Had the women told him there were rebels in the hills, he could call in helicopters; had he been informed that armored cars were attacking civilians, he had Spectre gunships at hand; but a "witch" was well beyond the scope of normal mission parameters.

As he deliberated over the predicament, the captain stuck his hand in the pocket of his BDU. There he found a small chemical light stick. Secretly he snapped the stick, allowing the chemicals to mix, thus creating a soft glow. Shielding the light from view, he pulled the light stick out of his pocket and held it behind his thumb. With the other hand he removed his combat knife from its sheath. In a deliberate and careful move he cut what appeared to be the tip of his thumb, in reality the top of the chemlight. As the light mixture started to ooze out, the SF captain gently rubbed a small mark on the forehead of each of the children. All eyes, now wide with awe, were on the captain. He told the women this would protect their children from any curses or spells. Then he told the "witch" that she was to leave these mothers and children alone, or he would return. This is exactly what Special Forces soldiers are trained to do, to think "outside the box."

Operational Tempo, or OpTempo, as it is called, remained continually high for members of the Special Forces, as the United States committed more than 20,000 American soldiers to the country of Bosnia. In December 1995, a joint NATO (North Atlantic Treaty Organization) force would deploy to this war-torn country to partake in Operation Joint Endeavor as the military elements of the Dayton Peace Accords. The first of the U.S. units to enter Bosnia-Herzegovina would come from the 10th SFG(A). Further operations in this region would find the SF soldiers of the 3rd & 10th groups involved in Operations Joint Guard and Joint Forge.

Additionally, the 10th SFG(A) would be active in Operation Joint Guardian in Kosovo. As members of the Kosovo Forces (KFOR), SF teams

Staff Sergeant Gary Koenitzer of ODA-126, 1st Special Force Group (Airborne), takes a break with his students in southern Thailand. These Thai troops are being instructed in patrolling, small unit, and unconventional warfare tactics. *Courtesy MSgt. Gary Koenitzer*

employed their unique skills and cultural abilities in this region. During the early stages of American involvement, NATO planes began an air campaign over the skies of Kosovo in spring of 1999. When a U.S. Air Force F-117 Nighthawk was downed, members of the 10th SFG(A) who were on alert for possible CSAR (Combat Search And Rescue) missions were loaded onto waiting helicopters within 10 minutes of getting the information.

Members of the 3rd, 10th SFG(A), and selected SF National Guard units participated in all major operations in the Balkans. Special Forces teams were instrumental in the peacekeeping efforts in this region, and provided SF liaison control elements to the NATO allies and coalition partners. As of this writing, ODAs from the 10th SFG(A) are still active in Bosnia and Kosovo. The 5th SFG(A) has teams active in Kuwait. SF soldiers of the 3rd SFG(A) are conducting missions throughout the continent of Africa as part of the African Crisis Response Initiative (ACRI). ODAs from the 7th SFG(A) are performing FID and Counter-Drug (CD) training for national police and military forces in the jungles of Colombia, and members of the 1st SFG(A) carry out their missions in the Asia-Pacific region. Whether they are part of a larger operation or a single A-Detachment—perhaps the only U.S. military presence in a country—the sun never sets on the U.S. Army Special Forces.

CHAPTER 5

Special Forces Organization and Missions

Today's Special Forces is founded on a rich heritage and warrior lineage. The modern SF soldiers draw their combat skills from the proud tradition of their special warfare predecessors—the "Swamp Fox," the Office of Strategic Service (OSS) Jedburg teams, 1st Special Service Forces, and others. Members of the U.S. Army Special Forces still espouse the ensign held up by President John F. Kennedy. Kennedy gave the men of the Special Forces more than the green beret; he gave them a mission: to uphold democracy at all costs. Over the past five decades this standard has been carried into various conflicts, and the men of the Special Forces have paid the price. At the height of the Vietnam War there were more than a dozen Special Forces Groups, including active, Army Reserve, and National Guard units.

Today, under the command of Brigadier General Frank J. Toney Jr., the U.S. Army Special Forces Command (Airborne), USASFC(A), commands seven major subordinate units (or groups), each commanded by a colonel. The mission statement of the SF Command is "To organize, equip, train, validate and prepare forces for deployment to conduct worldwide special operations, across the range of military operations, in support of regional combatant commanders, American ambassadors and other agencies as directed."

Special Forces units are oriented to specific areas around the world. By concentrating on specific regions, the SF soldiers gain experience in the regional culture and languages of their assigned countries. This also gives them the opportunity to form a bond with the foreign mil-

itary forces and a working relationship with the indigenous population. There are five active SF groups: the 1st SFG(A), 3rd SFG(A), 5th SFG(A), 7th SFG(A), and 10th SFG(A). In addition to these active units, there are two National Guard SF groups, the 19th SFG(A) and 20th SFG(A). In addition to the Special Forces Groups, USASFC(A)

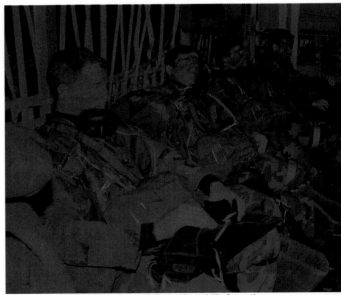

The modern SF soldiers draw their combat skills from the proud tradition of their special warfare predecessors. As with the OSS Jedburgh teams of World War II, airborne insertion is a hallmark trait of the Special Forces soldier. This SF team prepares for an over-the-water insertion via parachute. They wait in the cavernous fuselage of the C-130 for the signal to jump. The red lights allow their eyes to adjust to the darkness.

The SF soldiers may find themselves operating in a variety of environments, from the tropical rain forest of South America to the desert sands of the Middle East; from the jungles of Africa to the snow-covered mountainsides of Europe and the Balkans. Natural surroundings may pose as much danger as any foe. Fortunately, SF soldiers are proficient at dealing with both circumstances.

Beret Flashes of the U.S. Army Special Operations (Left to Right) Top Row: U.S. Army Special Operations Command (Airborne), U.S. Army Special Forces Command (Airborne), U.S. Army John F. Kennedy Special Warfare Center & School (Airborne), and U.S. Army Special Warfare Training Group (Airborne). Middle Row (Active): 1st Special Forces Group (Airborne), 3rd Special Forces Group (Airborne), 5th Special Forces Group (Airborne), 7th Special Forces Group (Airborne), and 10th Special Forces Group (Airborne). Bottom Row (National Guard): 19th Special Forces Group (Airborne) and 20th Special Forces Group (Airborne).

also has two active duty and two reserve chemical recon detachments (not SF personnel) and a 13-man SF detachment, assigned to 1st SFG(A) to support theater war-planning requirements on the Korean peninsula, known as Detachment K or Det-K.

The 1st Special Forces Group (Airborne) has its headquarters in Ft. Lewis, Washington. Their motto is "Warriors First—First in Asia." Under the authority of PACOM (Pacific command) this group has a pre-deployed battalion or ODB stationed on the island of Okinawa. Additionally,

the 1st SFG(A) provides soldiers for Detachment K in Korea. Their area of responsibility (AOR) is the Pacific rim and Asia, which includes all the islands up through India, Manchuria, and China. Also, due to its size, part of Russia also falls under their AOR. The 1st Group maintains a high state of preparedness to carry out special operations in support of USCINCPAC (U.S. Commander In Chief Pacific) in a major theater war.

The 3rd SFG(A) is based at Ft. Bragg, North Carolina, and is assigned to EUCOM (European Command), concentrating mainly on the continent of Africa, excluding the Horn of Africa. Third Group also has one battalion that is on line to support CENTCOM (Central Command), which is

The Special Forces soldier is often the eyes and the ears of a theater commander. Members of the SF teams hold a minimum grade of E-5 sergeant. Each soldier is a mature, physically rugged, morally straight, thoroughly lethal, and highly skilled individual who brings a new level of professionalism to an already elite military unit.

The team leader of the SF ODA (Operational Detachment-Alpha) is a captain. He will spend two years as a detachment commander before he moves on to other assignments within the Special Operations Forces (SOF) community. Occasionally, a team leader will get an additional rotation with the teams; however, this is the exception rather than the rule. Unique in their operations from a conventional infantry commander, the SF captain team leaders take on missions and encounter obstacles that not only require unconventional military measures, but also require unorthodox thinking.

responsible for the Middle East. One of the major missions involving the 3rd SFG(A) is the African Crisis Response Initiative, or ACRI. This is a prime example of an SF collateral mission, that of security assistance. ACRI is a U.S. Department of State-supported program intended to enhance the security and peace in selected countries on the continent of Africa. SF ODAs (Operational Detachments-Alpha) will train soldiers from these countries into highly effective and rapid-deployable peacekeeping units. With this training, the local forces can be used as peacekeeping forces, thus limiting or perhaps even eliminating the need for large U.S. involvement.

Next is 5th SFG(A), located in Ft. Campbell, Kentucky. It is the lead Group under CENTCOM. Their AOR is from the Horn of Africa up through the Central Asia Republics of Kazakhstan, Turkmenistan, and Tajikistan. While it does not have a forward deployed battalion, like the 1st Group, the 5th SFG(A) does regularly rotate an ODA through the Middle East, maintaining a constant presence in Kuwait. The exploits of the 5th Group are legendary. From the jungles of Vietnam to the desert wastelands in Iraq, the men of 5th SFG(A) have set a benchmark in Special Forces operations.

If you travel north on Ft. Bragg's Yadin Road and hang a right at 77th SFG Way, you'll locate the HQ for the 7th SFG(A). Its motto is "Lo Que Sera, Cuando Sera, Donde Sera" (Anything, Anytime, Anyplace). They operate the SOUTHCOM (South Command) AOR in Central and South America and the Caribbean. One company of the 7th SFG(A) is forward based in Puerto Rico, at Roosevelt Roads Naval Air Station, or "Roosey Roads," as it is called. Additionally, members of the 7th have been selected to participate in the Army WarFighter Experiment exercises, to test new SF doctrine, organization, and equipment.

Finally, under EUCOM, is the 10th Special Forces Group (Airborne) based out of Ft. Carson, Colorado. It also has a forward deployed battalion in Panzer Kaserne, Boeblingen, Germany. This AOR for the 10th Group comprises Europe and countries of the former Soviet Union, including Russia (except for the part handled by 1st SFG(A)). The 10th Group holds the honor of being the original SF Group. If that seems confusing, it was meant to be. The Special Forces were created in the early 1950s to prepare a specialized force in the event of a World War III. They were to conduct guerrilla operations behind enemy lines, should the Soviets invade Europe. The U.S. Army only had one Special Forces unit at this time, but it did not want the Soviets to realize this—hence, this Special Forces Group was designated the 10th. The 10th SFG(A) was stationed in Bad Tolz, Germany, during the Cold War, and subsequently relocated to the Stuttgart area in July 1991. While the 10th Group encompasses all of the SF doctrinal missions, its ODAs hone their skills in unconventional warfare (UW), and they remain the premier mountain and winter troops among the U.S. Army Special Forces.

In November 1990, the Reserve SF Groups were deactivated, leaving only the National Guard Groups. The 19th SFG(A), a National Guard outfit with headquarters in Salt Lake City, Utah, has units spread throughout the western United States. The 19th group is a "jack of all trades." It operates in the Pacific, it has the ability to operate one battalion in Central Command, and it performs duties around Europe. The other Guard

If the SF team is the eyes and the ears of the CinC, then the eyes and ears of the SF ODA are the Operations and Intelligence Sergeants. These senior non-commissioned officers (NCOs) "run" the teams. They are the quintessential SF soldier. They thrive on ambiguity and uncertainty, thinking the unconventional and daring the uncommon. They see obstacles as something to be overcome, surroundings as environments to be adapted to, and tasks as opportunities for improvisation. A team sergeant will immerse himself in the art, science, and history of war.

outfit is the 20th SFG(A) with headquarters in Birmingham, Alabama, and units throughout the eastern United States. The 20th operates mostly in the Caribbean and Central and South America.

When you look around the world, you do not see large armored or infantry divisions in all places, yet Special Forces has a constant presence. So valuable are the SF groups that the CinC of EUCOM recently requested two additional SF Groups for his AOR.

The purpose of the SF Group is to establish, support, and operate a Special Forces Operational

The SF Weapons sergeants are responsible for the employment of weapons using conventional and UW tactics and techniques. They will serve as the detachment armorer. Here can be seen both light arms, M4A1 carbine, and heavier weapons, the AT-4 anti-tank weapon. The weapons sergeant will be an expert on both U.S. and foreign weapons systems and the best way to employ them.

Base, SFOB, and Forward Operational Base, FOB, to provide special operation command and control units to conventional headquarters. The SF Group is responsible for training and preparing the SF ODA for deployment, and directing, supporting, and sustaining those ODA once deployed. Under each of these Groups, you'll find a Headquarters/Headquarters Company (HHC), a Support unit, and three SF Battalions.

The HHC plans, coordinates, and directs SF operations, either separately or as part of a larger force. This includes training and preparing SF teams for deployment, providing command and staff personnel to operate an SFOB, and providing advice, coordination, and staff assistance on the employment of SF assets to a joint Special Operations Command (SOC), Joint Special Operations Task Force (JSOTF), or other major headquarters. The Support Company will provide military intelligence, signal support, and general aviation support. Each of these Battalions in turn comprises a Headquarters and three SF Companies.

The SF Battalion operates like the Group on a smaller scale. It conducts and supports any special operation in any operational environment, whether in peace, conflict, or war. The SF Company, also referred to as SFODB (Special Forces Operational Detachment-B or B-Team), consists of five ODAs or A-teams. SFODB has the capability to plan and carry out SF missions; train and prepare ODA for deployment; infiltrate and exfiltrate by air, land, or sea; conduct operations in remote areas and hostile environments for extended periods; and organize, equip, and train indigenous troops up to a regimental size. When you total all the personnel, you end up with approximately 1,200 people per SF Group, or 10,000 worldwide.

Each SF battalion will have one HALO (High Altitude Low Opening) team, schooled in Military Free Fall, MFF; one SCUBA (Self-Contained Underwater Breathing Apparatus) team, trained as Combat Swimmers; and one CT or Counterterrorist team. The balance of the teams are referred to as ruck teams, and they use the "low impact" method of insertion—by foot.

The A-team

The ODA remains the essence of the U.S. Army Special Forces. Here is where the "rucksack meets the ground," where missions are carried out. No matter how you got to that point, HALO, SCUBA, Ground Mobility Vehicle (GMV), Zodiac, or Helicopter, here is where the planning is put into action. The ODA is specifically designed

Without a doubt the **green beret** headgear sets the U.S. Army Special Forces soldier apart from other troopers. It has become part of American folk history like the coonskin hat and cowboy hat. The hat was first sported by the members of the 10th SFG(A) in the Bavarian mountain ranges. The men would order the berets from a woolen company in Canada at their own expense, usually $7 to $8, in 1955. According to Mr. Joe Lupyak SF-CSM-ret., "The berets were only worn in the field, during exercises. [The Army] would not allow the wearing of the berets in garrison."

The green beret was originally designated in 1953 by Special Forces Major Herbert Brucker, a veteran of the OSS. Later that year, 1st Lt. Roger Pezelle adopted the beret as the unofficial headgear for his A-team, Operational Detachment FA32. Soon it spread throughout all of the Special Forces troops—much to the dismay of the U.S. Army and conventional commanders.

In 1961, President John F. Kennedy planned to visit Fort Bragg. He sent word to Brigadier General William P. Yarborough, the commander of the Special Warfare Center, that all Special Forces soldiers were to wear the green berets for this visit. President Kennedy felt that since they had a special mission, Special Forces should have something to set them apart from the rest of the conventional troops. Coincidentally, even before the presidential request came, the Department of the Army had reversed its objections to the headgear and sent a message to the center authorizing the green beret as part of the Special Forces uniform.

When President Kennedy arrived at Fort Bragg on 12 October 1961, Brigadier General William P. Yarborough wore his green beret to greet the commander-in-chief. The president said, "Those are nice. How do you like the green beret?" Yarborough responded, "They're fine, sir. We've wanted them a long time."

President Kennedy sent a message to General Yarborough, stating, "My congratulations to you personally for your part in the presentation today . . . The challenge of this old but new form of operations is a real one and I know that you and the members of your command will carry on for us and the free world in a manner which is both worthy and inspiring. I am sure that the green beret will be a mark of distinction in the trying times ahead."

On 11 April 1962, in a White House memorandum for the United States Army, President Kennedy showed his continued support for the Special Forces, calling the green beret, "a symbol of excellence, a badge of courage, a mark of distinction in the fight for freedom."

Over the years, the custom of the green beret changed in Special Forces. When the first Special Forces wore the berets, they would only wear them in the field and never in garrison. Today, 50 years later, the green berets are worn only in garrison and rarely, if ever, are they worn in the field or on operations. There are a few exceptions to this rule. When meeting foreign military for the first time, the SF captain or sergeant may wear his green beret to receive instant credibility. Also, an NCOIC, or Non-Commissioned Officer In Charge, who is training local troops might wear the beret for immediate recognition by the indigenous troops.

Talk to some SF soldiers and they will tell you it is just a headgear, while others will explain that the green beret is the quickest way of identifying a member of the U.S. Army Special Forces, when starting to discuss Special Operation Forces. Either way, when an SF soldier places that green beret on his head, he walks a little straighter, and stands a little taller.

The **arrowhead** patch is worn by members of the Special Forces around the world. Drawing from the heritage of American Indians, the arrowhead depicts the field craft, stealth, and tactics of these tenacious warriors. The upturned dagger is symbolic of the nature of Special Forces unconventional warfare missions. The three lightning bolts represent the three methods of infiltration—land, sea, and air. Lightning is also characteristic of intense speed and strength. The color gold exemplifies fortitude and inspiration, and the teal blue background represents the Special Forces' encompassing of all branch assignments.

The distinctive **Special Forces crest** is black and silver, emblazoned with the Special Forces motto: De Oppresso Liber. This Latin phrase translates into To Free the Oppressed. A fighting knife is upturned and placed over two crossed arrows. The arrow symbolizes the Special Forces' role in unconventional warfare, and the knife reflects the attributes of a Special Forces soldier, straight and true. Both arrow and knife were silent weapons employed by the American Indians, thus providing a further link to the warrior spirit of this great nation.

In April of 1987 a new and separate branch of the Army was created for Special Forces officers. Prior to this time, officers assigned to Special Forces would wear the symbol for their branch of service on their collars, e.g. infantry, engineers, etc. With the creation of a separate branch, the crossed arrows were designated for the Special Forces officers. The Special Forces officer branch inherited this insignia from the Indian scouts, several of whom were awarded Medals of Honor for their actions with U.S. forces. The **crossed arrows** were also used by the 1st Special Service Force in World War II. During the 1960s, it was not uncommon to see SF officers sporting the crossed arrows on their uniform collars.

In July of 1983 the **Special Forces Tab** was authorized to be worn by SF qualified personnel. Upon completion of SF training the soldier is authorized to wear the tab on the left shoulder. This tab is worn above the Airborne tab and SF arrowhead. If an individual is also Ranger qualified, he may wear the Ranger tab as well. It would be located between the SF tab and the Airborne tab.

SF Insignias

Special Forces engineer sergeants are just as skilled in building bridges as demolishing them. As part of their mission, they may do "nation building" with a hammer and saw as well as C4 and Det-cord. The ODA engineer sergeants perform and instruct in all aspects of combat engineering, light construction, and demolitions techniques. Here an SF engineer sergeant prepares a charge of military dynamite for a training mission. It should be noted that dynamite is not the first explosive of choice; however, SF are taught to use what they have, and in a Third World setting or UW role, this may be the only explosive material available.

to organize, train, advise, direct, and support indigenous military or paramilitary forces in UW and FID operations. The units are capable of training a force up to a battalion in size. Unlike a conventional unit, which will deploy with its full chain of command, staff officers, and support and logistics units, SF does not. The 82nd

does not send an infantry squad out on a mission and say, "By the way, sergeant, it's all yours." On the other hand, that is exactly how an SF ODA deploys; often the SF team is the only U.S. military presence in a country.

The Special Forces ODA is commanded by a captain (18A00). He may also command or advise

Call him "Doc" or "18-Delta," the SF medical sergeant is one of the most capable medical specialists in the U.S. military. He is trained in first aid, trauma care, dentistry, and veterinary skills. He functions as an independent medical care practitioner in a remote environment, and takes care of the A-team's medical needs as well as those of any indigenous personnel. Although he is a medical specialist, the SF 18D is also a combatant. He not only knows how to perform a tracheotomy, he can perform a CAS strike or take out an enemy sentry with the same precision. When the other members of the team head out on a patrol with their LBE and loads, he will also be carrying a medical pack or trauma bag filled with assorted medical supplies.

up to a battalion-size group of indigenous combat troops. He is proficient in those tasks that support the detachment's mission-essential task list, or METL, with knowledge of a broad spectrum of common and special operations tasks. Not only must the SF captain know the skills that will make him mission-capable during independent special operations, he must also be able to operate in

concert with conventional forces in large-scale operations. As the team leader, he is accountable for everything that happens on that team, right or wrong. He is tasked with mission planning—working with the team specialist to establish the best possible strategy for mission success. As Captain Steve Warman, of ODA-581, 5th SFG(A) sums it up, the team leader "is responsible for the men and their equipment, and makes sure that everything happens the way it is supposed to happen."

When you look at the difference between an SF captain and the captain of a conventional unit,

The two Communications "Commo" Sergeants of the ODA advise the detachment commander on communications matters. They install, operate, and maintain FM, AM, HF, VHF, and SHF radio communications in voice, CW, and burst radio nets. Here SFC Greg Green of the 1st Special Forces Group (Airborne) performs a communications check. He is using an AN/PSC-5 Multi-band, Multi-mission communications terminal, with SatCom antennae.

A Special Forces sergeant takes aim with his M4A1/M203. He will be ready to provide cover fire for his team members as they move stealthily through the wooded marsh.

you see the vast chasm in their operational capabilities. A typical infantry, airborne, or armor captain will operate usually within 10 kilometers of his command and control. He'll have full logistical support and medical facilities nearby, and his operations will be in concert with other larger units. His need for E&E skills is limited, and he will normally fight within range of artillery support. Conversely, the SF captain will operate in isolated areas, often over 100 kilometers from his headquarters. Logistical support will be little, if any, and often he'll live off the land; availability for MedEvac is limited and will depend on the team medical specialist. ODAs will operate independently of other units. The need for survival and E&E skills

is high, and the SF captain will rarely operate within the range of friendly fire support.

The executive officer of the ODA is the detachment technician, a warrant officer (WO) (180A0). He serves as second in command, ensuring that the detachment commander's decisions are implemented. His tasks also include administrative and logistical aspects of area studies, briefbacks and operational plans (OPLANs), and operational orders (OPORDs). He will assist in the recruitment of indigenous troops and the subsequent training of these combat forces up to and including a battalion size. In the event the mission requires the ODA to run a "split team op," the WO would command one of these teams.

What makes SF soldiers special? An SF sergeant summed it up best when he said, "You look at his shoulder, that tells you his Quals [Qualifications, e.g. Airborne, Ranger, Special Forces tabs]. You look at his chest, that tells you his schools [e.g. Air Assault, Airborne, EIB (Expert Infantry Badge),etc.]. You look in his eyes, that tells you what kind of a man he is."

The next man on the team is the operations sergeant (18Z50), the "team sergeant." He is the senior NCO on the detachment. A master sergeant, he advises the ODA commander on all training and operational matters. His job also entails providing the team with tactical and technical guidance and support. He will prepare the operations and training portion of the area studies, briefbacks and OPLANs, and OPORDs. In the absence of the WO, the "team sergeant" will fill in this position.

Directing the ODA's intelligence training, collections, analysis and dissemination is the assistant operations and intelligence sergeant (18F40), a sergeant first class (SFC). As the name implies, he assists the operations sergeant in preparing area studies, briefbacks, and so on. He is also responsible for field interrogation of enemy prisoners. He briefs and debriefs SF and indigenous patrols, and will fill in for the ops sgt. when necessary.

The operations and intelligence sergeant comes from the ranks of Special Forces. He will have been on an ODA for some time and will have attended the Advanced Non-Commissioned Officers Course at the NCO Academy, USAJFK-SWC/S at Ft. Bragg.

Next on the team are the two weapons sergeants (18B40) and (18B30), an SFC and staff sergeant (SSG) respectively. They are responsible for the employment of weapons using conventional and UW tactics and techniques. They will train the indigenous troops as well as other team members in the use of small arms (e.g., pistols, rifles, assault weapons), crew-served weapons (e.g., machine guns, mortars), anti-aircraft (e.g., stingers) and anti-tank weapons (e.g., LAW, AT-4). They may assist the operations sergeant, and they can organize, train, advise, and command up to a company-size indigenous force.

Two engineer sergeants (18C40) SFC and (18C30) SSG supervise, lead, plan, perform, and instruct all aspects of combat engineering and light construction. They are knowledgeable in demolitions and improvised munitions. They will plan and perform sabotage operations. As the weapons sergeants, they can organize, train, advise, and command an indigenous force up to a company size.

Two medical sergeants (18D40) SFC and (18D30) SG provide emergency, routine, and long-term medical treatment for the ODA and associated allied or indigenous forces. They will train, advise, and direct detachment members and indigs in emergency medicine and preventive medical care. In the event of a prolonged mission, they will establish a medical facility and are also trained in veterinary care. They are considered physician substitutes and can provide emergency, routine, and long-term medical care for the ODA, allied forces, and host nation personnel. One other unique capability of the SF medical sergeant is that he is fully schooled in the SF skills and is a combatant. As are the other team members, he is capable of training and commanding up to a company-size force.

Finally, the last two members of the ODA are the communications sergeants (18E40) SFC and (18E30) SSG. These two soldiers advise the detachment commander on communications matters. They install, operate, and maintain FM, AM, HF, VHF, and SHF radio communications in voice, CW, and burst radio nets. They prepare the communications portion of briefbacks, OPLANs, and OPORDs. They will train members of the ODA and indigenous personnel in the use and maintenance of the communication equipment. They can advise, train, and command indigenous forces up to a company in size.

According to Major Tom McCullom, SF-PAO, "A SF soldier is a highly skilled, extremely capable soldier, there is very little he as an individual cannot figure out how to do; but as a team, the team is unstoppable, because each SF soldier builds off the others' strengths. The commo sergeant may know everything to know about commo, but may be weak in demolitions; meanwhile the team has an engineering sergeant that knows everything there is to know about demolitions. And he can help out the commo sergeant. . . . A good team does not just do their job and go home at the end of the day, they socialize together, they know each other. Special Forces are a type A personality times three! SF soldiers have a lot of initiative, [and] the ability to think on their own. They've got to be mature enough that when they are on their own they will be making the right decisions."

While conducting an SR mission, the SF soldier may use a ghillie suit to camouflage his position. He will report his observations using the SALUTE method—Size, Activity, Location, Unit, Time, and Equipment. Special Forces also include their proximity to the target. High command will determine what ordnance to use against the target and whether the SF team's position is considered Danger Close.

Members of the 5th Special Forces Groups (Airborne) practice their lethal trade. Here the Ground Mobility Vehicle (GMV) has pulled off the road into a partial defilade position. While the team sergeant mans the Mark 19, 40mm Grenade Machine Gun, other members of the ODA provide 360 degrees of cover fire, if necessary.

Special Forces Missions

Originally created to train and maintain a guerrilla force against communist aggression in Europe, their primary mission in 1952 was that of unconventional warfare. Over the years the geopolitical world has changed and so has the mission of the Special Forces soldier and ODA. Today, the Special Forces comprises five core missions, and while UW is one of them, they are prepared to conduct and execute any of them. These core missions are the following:

Special Reconnaissance (SR), is defined as the reconnaissance and surveillance activity conducted by Special Operations Forces (SOF). Performed by SF teams, this covers the area of HUMINT (HUMan INTelligence), placing U.S. "eyes on target" in hostile, denied, or politically sensitive territory. An SF team could be tasked to conduct these missions. This means putting warm bodies on the ground in a specific location to accomplish what no satellite can do. An ODA performing an SR mission will be infiltrated into enemy area to report back to their commanders necessary information needed to carry out ongoing attacks. Special Forces teams may be utilized to acquire or verify, by visual observation or other methods available, information concerning the capabilities, intentions, and activities of an enemy force. SR may also include the placement of remote sensor equipment in enemy territory. Special Reconnaissance includes recording meteorological, hydrographic, and geographic characteristics of the objective area. Additionally, SR comprises target acquisition, bomb damage assessment, and post-strike reconnaissance. Reconnaissance provides the CinC with intelligence needed to conduct operations.

SR provides intelligence that is *strategic*—data that is required by national decision makers in formulating national or foreign defense policies, *operational*—details and reports used by theater level commanders to plan and conduct their campaigns, and *tactical*—information that commanders need for fighting battles.

Direct Action (DA), involves small-scale offensive actions, normally of a short-term duration conducted by SF teams. Such actions include seizure, destroying, capture of enemy personnel—any action that would inflict damage on enemy personnel or material. Direct action missions may also include the recovery of sensitive items or isolated personnel—e.g., POWs. SF units are highly trained and may employ raids, ambushes, and

Qatar soldiers listen to a class given by SFC Tim Keck of the 5th Special Forces Group (Airborne), on the proper procedures for clearing enemy forces from buildings. *DOD Photo*

A SF captain from ODA 052, 10th Special Forces Group (Airborne) pauses to check his map. Wearing snow camouflage, he blends in well with his surroundings. While some units still have the three-color snow camo, he is wearing the newly issued "All White" camo.

other small unit tactics in the pursuit of these mission goals. They may employ mines and other demolitions or conduct attacks by employing fire support from air, ground, or sea assets. Direct action may employ stand-off weapons, such as a sniper team or an SF team with a SOFLAM (Special Operation Force Laser Acquisition Marker) who lase a target for terminal guidance ordnance—e.g., precision-guided "smart bombs."

Foreign Internal Defense (FID) is a primary means of providing U.S. military SOF's expertise to other governments in support of their internal defense and developmental efforts. FID is one of the SF's primary peacetime tasks. By providing such training, SOF may eliminate the need to deploy conventional forces in a particular region of the world. Yet by employing SF ODAs in this mission, teams stay prepared for their role as combat advisers in the event of war. FID missions have included basic static line parachute training, MFF, and jumpmaster training; light infantry tactics, encompassing counterinsurgency operations, advance patrolling, urban combat, and advance marksmanship/sniper training; water operations, including riverine ops, small boat ops, and scout swimming; and engineering and communications training. Medical and veterinary training are also incorporated in the SF FID missions.

Unconventional Warfare (UW), the origin of SF, encompasses guerrilla warfare, the use of irregular forces—normally indigenous personnel operating in enemy-held territory—and other direct offensive, low visibility, covert, or clandestine operations. Incorporated in the UW mission are the indirect activities of subversion, sabotage, intelligence gathering, and evasion and escape nets. Armed rebellion against an established force or occupying power is often within the scope of UW. In wartime, Special Forces may be tasked with directly supporting any resistance or guerrilla force. This is commonly accomplished by infiltrating operational detachments or A-teams into denied or sensitive areas for the purpose of training, equipping and advising, or directing indigenous forces.

Counterterrorism (CT) consists of the offensive actions taken to prevent, deter, and respond to terrorism; this includes intelligence gathering and threat analysis. SF troops are ideal for engaging in antiterrorism and counterterrorism missions. Such assets could be on station in the rapidly changing environment of a CT operation,

Although one of the five core missions of Special Forces, CT, or Counterterrorism, is not talked about openly by USASOC. They do not want to give the terrorist any edge. This member of a CT team is "armed for bear"; he carries the M4A1 carbine with dual magazine, vertical grip and sight, a Berretta M9 pistol, flash-bang grenades, and numerous ammo magazines at the ready. He wears special head and eye protection.

greatly enhancing flexibility in meeting the critical demands of the situation. The CT mission could include training of host nation counterterrorist forces, conducting hostage rescues, recovering sensitive material from terrorists, or performing DA on the terrorist infrastructure to reduce the effects of international or state-sponsored terrorist activities.

Collateral Missions

Due to the nature of SF soldiers, who can adapt, overcome, and improvise according to ever-changing missions and environments, they are frequently called upon to perform Collateral Activities, in addition to the five core missions.

These activities include **Humanitarian Assistance**, as in Operation Provide Comfort (the highly trained medical specialists in SF are often called for such missions); **Security Assistance**, training and advisory roles; Personnel Recovery, from **Combat Search and Rescue** (CSAR) to **Non-Combatant Operations** (NEOs), such as Operation Assure Lift in Sierra Leone, where members of 3rd SFG(A) extracted Ambassador Ann Wright from her embassy in 1997; **Counter-Drug (CD)** efforts, supporting counter drug operations inside the United States in cooperation with JTF-6 and in various locations OCONUS (OutsideCONtinental US); and **Counter Mine**, conducting several demining initiatives worldwide. The United States is the world leader in removing mines, and the SOF and SF lead this initiative. Finally, there is the area of **Special Activities**, which is classified.

Selection and Training

In addition to the active and National Guard SF groups, two additional groups come under the command of USASOC. They are the U.S. Army John F. Kennedy Special Warfare Center and School (Airborne) and U.S. Army Special Warfare Training Group (Airborne). These two groups are tasked with the training of the Special Forces soldiers. Their mission is to assess, select, train, and qualify Special Forces soldiers in preparation

Land navigation is an essential skill for SF soldiers. While they are well versed in the use of high tech gear, like the Global Positioning System (GPS), they are just as comfortable with a map and compass. The SF soldier will use whatever means are available, even if that means navigating from the stars.

for assignment to an Operational Detachment-Alpha, or ODA.

The JFK Special Warfare Center and School is responsible for special operations training, leader development, doctrine, and personnel advocacy. The center and school's training group conduct the full spectrum of training in special operations. The 1st Battalion administers Special Forces Assessment and Selection (SFAS) and the SF Qualification Course, or Q-Course. The 2nd Battalion is responsible for advanced SF skills, military free fall (MFF); combat diving (SCUBA); the SERE (Survival, Escape, Resistance, and Evasion) course; Special Operations Target Interdiction course; Special Forces Advanced Reconnaissance, Target Analysis & Exploitation Techniques course, and Advanced Special Operations Techniques. The 3rd Battalion teaches civil affairs, psychological operations, Special Forces warrant officers, language training, and regional area studies.

What makes an SF soldier special? What makes him stand head and shoulders above any other soldier in the world? He is in a class by himself. He is a mature, highly skilled, outstandingly trained individual, and without a doubt the finest unconventional warfare expert in the world, bar none. He is a teacher, a fighter, and oftentimes a diplomat. And a warrior of uncommon physical and mental caliber, ready to serve at a moment's notice anywhere his mission may take him. An SF sergeant summed it up best when he said, "You look at his shoulder, that tells you his QUALs [Qualifications, e.g. Airborne, Ranger, Special Forces tabs]. You look at his chest, that tells you his schools [e.g., MFF, SCUBA,

The subdued patch of the John F. Kennedy Special Warfare Center and School. This instructor is also Ranger and SF qualified.

"Airborne, All The Way!" All members of the U.S. Army Special Forces are Airborne qualified. This training takes place at the U.S. Army Airborne School, Ft. Benning, Georgia. Upon successful completion, a soldier is awarded the "Silver Wings" and is no longer considered a Low Energy Ground soldier, or "LEG."

Pathfinder, and so on]. You look in his eyes, that tells you what kind of a man he is."

One of the unique characteristics making the Special Forces "special" is the fact that soldiers who make it into this branch of the Army are triple volunteers. First, an individual must volunteer for service with the U.S. Army. Second, they volunteer for Airborne training. Then, after serving in their Military Occupational Specialty (MOS), they volunteer for Special Forces. When the time comes for the SFAS, the soldier has a couple years under his belt. This ensures that SF

soldiers are well grounded in conventional Army tactics before undergoing Special Forces training.

During the 1970s and early 1980s, an individual could enlist directly into the SF field. He would go through Basic Combat Training, Advanced Individual Training, Airborne School and then go on for Special Forces training. Today, the SF "direct" enlistment option is no longer available. Special Forces is a "nonaccession" branch of the Army, which means SF does not accept entry-level personnel. Any male soldier may volunteer for SFAS. At this point he

Where the journey into SF begins—the Special Forces Assessment and Selection phase at Camp MacKall. The purpose of SFAS is to identify soldiers who have the potential for Special Forces training.

The SF weapons sergeants are trained on more than 80 weapons—U.S. and foreign, friend and foe, old and new. You never know what weapons the host nation will be using, so you train up on everything you can get your hands on. Brass flies into the air as two members of ODA-173, "The Sea Pigs," send some .45 caliber rounds down range using the M3 submachine gun, also known as the "Grease Gun." A World War II–era weapon, it is still in use today.

may not be Airborne qualified. If he makes it through SFAS, he will have to go through Airborne training before entering the Qualification Course.

To join Special Forces the soldier must be a proven performer, having risen to the rank of captain or sergeant. Warrant officers come out of the SF senior NCO ranks. Here is the training progression, beginning with Airborne, SFAS, and then the Q-Course.

Airborne

The separation of the SF trooper from his fellow soldiers begins in the hot Georgia sun. Airborne training for the prospective Special Forces trooper is conducted at the U.S. Army Airborne School at Ft. Benning, Georgia. For the next three weeks he will be at the mercy of the Army's "Black Hats," the Airborne instructors of the 1st Battalion (Airborne), 507th Parachute Infantry Regiment, who will convert a "leg" into an "Airborne" trooper. He will learn what it takes to hurl oneself out of an airplane for the purpose of infiltrating into his mission drop zone (DZ). And he will run.

He will also learn a new mantra, which he will repeat over and over during the three weeks at Ft. Benning. He will shout out, "Motivated! Motivated!! Motivated!!! Airborne!" and he will run. He will repeat the mantra, "Fired up! Fired up!! Fired up!!! Airborne!" and when his body is aching and cannot move another inch, he will run some more. These veteran Airborne qualified instructors wearing the "Black Hats" ensure these potential Green Berets are indeed motivated and fired up! This is far more than an evolution. This is Airborne!

Basic airborne training is broken into segments of a week each: Ground, Tower, and Jump Week.

SF Engineers receive extensive training in building and construction. Often, nation building is accomplished with a hammer and saw rather than an M4A1 and Claymore. There are times, of course, when what has gone up must now come down. It has been said that most problems can be solved with the proper amount of high explosives. Here an SF engineer sergeant is preparing a timing fuse for an explosive charge.

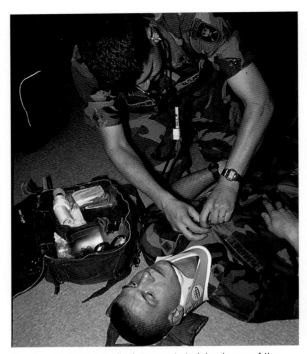

The Special Forces medical sergeants training is one of the most exhaustive training programs in the SF/SOF arena. Very often the SF medic will be the only source of medical care to which the team or indigenous personnel have access. He is trained and capable of serving as a physician substitute in the austere environments where the Operational Detachment-Alpha (ODA) operate.

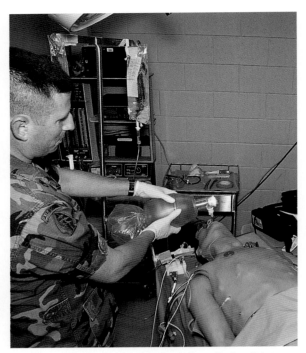

Special Forces 18D students practice their medical proficiency on the Human Patient Simulator. This highly sophisticated simulator, in use at the JSOMTC, is capable of producing normal and abnormal physiological responses to myriad anesthetic, medical, and surgical events. Lungs fill with and empty of air, eyes can become fixed and dilated, and so on. The benefit of the simulator is that these conditions are repeatable, thus removing a variable in the restoration or demise of the patient. By using the patient simulator, there is no risk to live patients during this phase of training.

During Ground Week, our trainee will start an intensive program of instruction designed to prepare the trooper to complete his parachute jump. He will learn how to execute a flawless parachute landing fall (PLF) to land safely in the landing zone (LZ). The PLF uses five points of contact designed to absorb the shock of landing and distribute it across the balls of the feet, calves, thighs, buttocks, and the push-up muscles of the back. He will learn the proper way to exit an aircraft using mockups of a C-130 and a C-141. He will climb up a 34-foot tower, where he will be connected to the lateral drift apparatus and upon command will assume door position and jump. Proper body position will be evaluated, and he'll do it over and over until the "Black Hats" are happy; and he will run.

Next comes Tower Week. Now that our trainee has learned how to exit, position, and land, he will have this second week to refine those skills. Using a training device known as the swing landing tower (SLT), where he is hooked up to a parachute harness, he jumps from a 12-foot-high elevated platform. The apparatus provides downward motion and oscillation to simulate an actual parachute jump. To make things more challenging for the student, the instructors have control of the SLT and can determine if they want to land him hard or soft. As one student rushes toward the ground, hands clinging to his harness, the instructor yells at him, "Hazard left!" and leans into the rope controlling the drop. He watches as the airborne trainee hits the ground, and he had better land in a manner to avoid the imaginary obstacle, or the "airborne sergeant" will have a few choice words for him and a number of pushups, too. During week two the student gets to ride the "tower." The tower is designed to give the student practice in controlling his parachute during the descent from 250 feet, and in executing a PLF upon landing. He will learn how to handle parachute malfunctions, and he will run.

Finally, week three, Jump Week. The potential SF trooper will perform five parachute jumps. First, an individual jump with a T-10B parachute. Next a mass exit with equipment and T-10B chute; then another individual exit with MC1-1B parachute and tactical assembly. His fourth jump will be a mass exit at night with a T-10B and tactical equipment. And finally the fifth jump is either an individual jump with an MV1-1B, or a mass jump with a T-10B parachute.

The United States Army's "Guide for Airborne Students" states, "Airborne training is a rite of passage for the warrior." Upon graduation he will be awarded the coveted Silver Wings and is now qualified as an airborne trooper.

Special Forces Assessment and Selection (SFAS)

What is SFAS? The purpose of SFAS is to identify soldiers who have the potential for Special Forces training. The career management

Adapt, Overcome, and Improvise is the hallmark of an SF soldier. The SF Commo Sergeant is instructed in numerous communications devices, from the basic Morse code to high-tech satellite communications. Here is an improvised radio antenna. It has been built with branches, 550 cord, spoons from a Meal Ready to Eat (MRE) and commo wire. It may seem crude, but it works. Want to be more creative? One ODA has practiced using a kite get an antenna aloft; now that is thinking outside the box!

field (CMF) 18 includes positions concerned with the employment of highly specialized elements to accomplish specifically directed missions in times of peace and war. Many of these missions are conducted at times when employment of conventional military forces is not feasible or is not considered in the best interests of the United States. Training for and participation in these missions is strenuous, somewhat hazardous, and often sensitive in nature. For these reasons it is a prerequisite that every prospective Special Forces soldier successfully complete the 24-day SFAS program. SFAS is conducted by the 1st Battalion, 1st SWTG(A) at Rowe Training Facility, Camp MacKall, approximately an hour's drive from Ft. Bragg.

The SFAS program assesses and selects soldiers for attendance at the Special Forces Qualification Course (SFQC). This program allows SF an opportunity to assess each soldier's capabilities by testing his physical, emotional, and mental stamina. SFAS also allows each soldier the opportunity to make a meaningful and educated decision about SF and his career plan. Any male soldier may volunteer for SFAS. A normal progression will see a number of RANGERs volunteer; however, a large portion comes from soldiers with varying MOSs.

Applicants volunteering for SFAS must meet the following criteria: male soldier in rank of E-4 to E-7; U.S. citizen with a high school diploma or GED (General Education Development certificate); airborne qualified, or a volunteer for airborne training (candidates not airborne qualified will be scheduled for airborne training at the completion of SFAS); able to swim 50 meters wearing boots and battle dress uniform (BDU); meeting Special Forces fitness standards; eligible for a "Secret" security clearance; and not a prior Airborne or SF voluntary terminee.

All candidates participate in a variety of activities designed to place them under various forms of physical and mental stress. The training assesses potential and qualities through behavioral observation, and analysis of performance measures and recorded data. All tasks are performed with limited information and no performance feedback. What this means is no praise, no encouragement, no harassment; tasks are assigned and rated, period. SFAS assesses a candidate's potential for being independent, yet a team player and a leader. Instructors look for the soldiers to demonstrate the following individual attributes: motivation, accountability, maturity, stability, teamwork, intelligence, physical fitness and trustworthiness. Leadership traits include communications, influence, judgment, decisiveness, and responsibility.

The SFAS program has two phases. Phase one assesses physical fitness, motivations, and the ability to cope with stress. Activities during this phase include psychological tests, physical fitness and swim tests, runs, obstacle course, basic First Aid, land navigation, ruckmarches, and military orienteering exercises. An evaluation board meets after the first phase to determine which of the candidates will be allowed to continue the program. The second phase assesses leadership and teamwork skills. SFAS not only serves to select the proper soldier for Special Forces training, it screens out those individuals who are lacking the qualities and potential to complete training. Only those soldiers who have demonstrated the potential to complete Special Forces training successfully are allowed to continue. At the end of the 24 days, another board meets to select those soldiers who may attend the SFQC. Fewer than 50 percent of the soldiers that start SFAS are selected for Special Forces training.

After a soldier is selected through SFAS, he will return to his unit and wait for his slot in the SFQC. This process may take several months before the soldier will actually begin SF training. Those soldiers selected for MOS 18B (weapons) and MOS 18C (engineer) report directly to Ft. Bragg to begin their training. Soldiers selected for MOS 18E (communications) will first complete a course in Advance International Morse Code (AIMC) before attending the SFQC.

SFQC and SFDOQC
(Special Forces Detachment
Officer Qualification Course)

Each branch of service that produces special operations personnel has its own unique training. This specialized training not only emphasizes physical prowess and military skills, but also serves to bring about teamwork, unit cohesiveness, and esprit de corps. For the U.S. Air Force's Special Tactics Teams, it is accomplished with Indoctrination and the Pipeline; for the U.S. Navy SEALs it is achieved with BUD/S and "Hell Week." For the Special Forces soldier it is the "Q-Course."

The SFQC/SFDOQC teaches and develops the skills necessary for effective use of the SF soldier. Duties in CMF 18 primarily involve participation in Special Operations interrelated fields of unconventional warfare. These include foreign internal defense and direct action missions as part of a small operations team or ODA. Duties at other levels involve command, control, and support functions. Frequently, duties require regional orientation, including foreign language training and in-country experience. SF emphasizes not only unconventional tactics, but also knowledge of nations in waterborne, desert, jungle, mountain, or Arctic operations.

The CMF 18 is subdivided into five accession MOS: detachment commander -18A; SF weapons sergeant - 18B; SF engineer sergeant - 18C; SF medical sergeant - 18D; and SF communications sergeant - 18E. Each SF volunteer receives extensive training in a specialty, which prepares him for his future assignment in an SF unit. SF units are designed to operate either unilaterally or in support of and combined with native military

and paramilitary forces. Levels of employment for Special Operations Forces include advising and assisting host governments, involvement in continental United States–based training, and direct participation in combat operations.

After successful completion of SFAS, officers who have not already attended their Advance Course will attend either the Infantry or Armor Officer Advance Course. For the enlisted soldier, the SFQC is currently divided into three phases. Phase I is Individual Skills, Phase II is MOS Qualification, and Phase III is Collective Training. The enlisted applicant's SFQC training will be scheduled upon successful completion of SFAS.

Phase I—Individual Skills

During this time, soldiers in process are trained on common skills for CMF 18, skill level three. Training is 40 days long and is taught at the Camp Rowe Training Facility. The training covered during this phase includes land navigation (cross-country) and small unit tactics. This phase culminates with a special operations overview.

Phase II—MOS (Military Operation Specialty) Qualification

For the enlisted soldier, the decision on which of the four specialties he will receive training in will be made based upon his background, aptitude, and desire, and the needs of Special Forces. Training for this phase is 65 days and culminates with a mission planning cycle. During this phase, soldiers are trained in their different specialties:

18A - SF detachment commander. Training includes teaching the officer student the planning and leadership skills he will need to direct and employ other members of his detachment. He will be trained in escape and recovery; infiltration (Infil) and extraction (Exfil) techniques; SF weapons, engineering, medical and communications skills; Military Decision Making Process, MDMP; terrain analysis; Direct Action; Special

Reconnaissance; Foreign Internal Defense; and Unconventional Warfare. Training is conducted at Fort Bragg, North Carolina, and is 24 weeks long. The culmination of this training is an FTX called the Troy Trek, held in the Pisgah National Forest or at Ft. A.P. Hill.

18B - SF weapons sergeant. Training includes learning the characteristics and capabilities of more than 89 types of U.S. and foreign light weapons—e.g., handguns, submachine guns, rifles, machine guns, mortars, anti-tank weapons, and man-portable air defense weapons. The trainee will learn range planning, tactics, indirect fire operations, weapons emplacement, and integrated combined arms fire control planning. He will learn how to teach marksmanship and the employment of weapons to others. Training is conducted at Fort Bragg, North Carolina, for 24 weeks.

18C - SF engineer sergeant. Training includes planning and constructing buildings, bridges, and field fortifications, as well as the use of demolitions for their destruction. The trainee learns how to read blueprints, as well as developing carpentry, electrician, and plumbing skills. Training also includes target analysis and demolitions techniques, including electric and non-electric firing systems. He will be taught the latest demolitions techniques and how to improvise with substitutes for ammunition and explosives. Training also includes land mine warfare and de-mining techniques. The program is conducted at Fort Bragg, North Carolina, for 24 weeks.

18D - SF medical sergeant. This course also includes U.S. Navy SEAL corpsmen, U.S. Army Ranger medics, and U.S. Air Force pararescuemen. The medical training is divided into two portions. First, trainees go through the Special Operations Combat Medic course (SOMC). Upon successful completion of this program, they move on to the more advanced Special Forces Medical Sergeants course.

At the SOMC, which lasts 24 weeks, the soldiers undergo a curriculum of concentrated medical training specifically designed for special operations medical personnel. They receive emergency medical technician-basic (EMT-B) and paramedic (EMT-P) training and certification. They also get certified by the American Heart Association in basic life support and advanced cardiac life support. SOMC training teaches students how to manage trauma patients prior to evacuation and provide them with medical treatment. This includes minor field surgery, pharmacology, combat trauma management, advanced airway treatment, and military evacuation procedures. Students will actually be assigned to hands-on patient care both in emergency and hospital settings as part of their training. This is conducted during a four-week assignment in one of the country's largest metropolitan areas, New York City.

The second major phase of this program is the Special Forces Medical Sergeants Course Training. This course provides skills in trauma management, infectious disease, cardiac care, life support, basic dentistry, basic Veterinary skills, X-ray, anesthesia, surgical procedures, team medical care, and indigenous population care. Training is conducted at the Joint Special Operations Medical Training Center located at Fort Bragg, North Carolina. Training takes approximately 57 weeks.

18E - SF communications sergeant. The purpose of this course is to train and qualify the SF soldier in the basic skills and knowledge required to perform duties as the SF communications sergeant on a Special Forces ODA. Training includes AIMC—encompassing instruction in radio telegraph procedures, military block printing, and exercises in transmitting and receiving Morse code; cryptographic systems; burst outstation systems; and common radios found throughout the Army. Students become familiar with antenna theory and radio wave propagation

continued on page 86

Just east of John F. Kennedy Hall, Fort Bragg, North Carolina, behind a tall fence topped with barbed wire, is the U.S. Army Joint Special Operations Medical Training Center (JSOMTC). Here, the 18-Deltas, or Special Forces Medics, learn their trade. This facility is responsible for the training of all enlisted medical personnel within the United States Special Operations Command. Over a decade in development, the JSOMTC is the result of an effort to create a single medical training facility for all Special Operations Forces (SOF) enlisted medical personnel. The JSOMTC was created for the centralized training of Special Forces medics, the Special Forces Medical Sergeants Course (SFMSC), and a new training program for all non-SF SOF medics, called the Special Operations Combat Medic Course (SOCM). With all SOF enlisted medical personnel now training at a single site, and with all becoming certified EMT-Paramedics, the level of medical training and of medical interoperability within SOF has been significantly enhanced.

According to LTC. Clifford Cloonan of JSOMTC, this Department of Defense (DOD) training center was established to consolidate and standardize medical training among all DOD SOF, while continuing a mission to provide first-class medical training to U.S. Army Special Forces (SF) medics (18D). Beginning in 1986, in an effort to consolidate enlisted medical training for all DOD SOF, the headquarters of the United States Special Operations Command (USSOCOM) and the U.S. Army Medical Department Center and School, began preliminary discussions on the feasibility of integrating Special Operations medical training in a single facility at Fort Bragg, North Carolina. The training of Special Forces medics had formerly been divided between programs at Fort Sam Houston and Fort Bragg and there existed no specialized advanced medical training for non-SF special operations medics, e.g. Rangers, SEALS, and USAF Para-rescue. In 1996 the JSOMTC was open for business.

The expected benefits were improved training for non-SF SOF medical personnel (who were formerly trained only to the conventional force standard), reduced training costs, and standardization of all SOF medical training leading to enhanced interoperability. Early in the process of designing the joint SOF medic training program to be taught at this new facility, it was decided that training and certification as a paramedic to National Registry EMT-Paramedic standards would be an integral and requisite part of the course.

This new training center uses the latest training techniques and technological advances to impart medical skills and knowledge to SOF medical personnel. The JSOMTC is designed to support the training of multiple classes simultaneously. Located on 9.6 acres of land, the 74,000-square-foot main building houses the offices, classrooms, and ancillary facilities necessary to support training. There are 17 large and small classrooms available for small group sessions and lecture, the largest of these capable of seating 200 students. Additionally, there are more than two acres of enclosed woodlands on the grounds of the JSOMTC to support training in simulated field environments.

A barracks facility constructed near the JSOMTC houses 140 single and unaccompanied students and an identical barracks is currently under construction immediately adjacent to the existing barracks. Upon completion of the second barracks all single and unaccompanied students will reside within immediate proximity to the JSOMTC.

A host of other facilities dedicated to instruction for the SF & SOF medical specialist are located within the JSOMTC. Ten operative procedure rooms modeled after modern hospital operating rooms are equipped for instruction in surgical techniques. Two 800-square-foot laboratory classrooms are available for student instruction and can accommodate up to 48 students each. These laboratories would be the envy of contemporary university facilities, each having a five-headed microscope with mounted digital camera. A modern anatomy and physiology teaching laboratory is well equipped for instruction. A dedicated x-ray suite is available for teaching radiological techniques with field x-ray equipment. These specialized areas are supported by a large medical logistics division complete with instrument sterilization equipment and supply storage areas. Between five and eight cadaver specimens are available for each class through arrangement with a local university. In addition to the "specimens," JSOMTC has a state-of-the-art patient simulator. This sophisticated computer patient can be programmed with an assortment of maladies that the student must identify and treat properly. It simulates all the correct body responses—eyes dilate, chest rises and falls, it can be intubated, IVs can be administered to it, or it can be charged "back to life."

Funding obtained from USSOCOM in 1998 allowed for the creation, within the JSOMTC, of an SOF-focused medical library and a student computer lab. The JSOMTC currently has holdings of more than 700 titles covering a wide range of topics of relevance to SOF medicine. In addition to books, the library subscribes to a variety of medical journals of SOF relevance, and has videotapes that can be viewed in the library. The 1,300-square-foot library allows for approximately 40 patrons to sit and study. Students can facilitate their learning on interactive CDs and via the Internet at 44 state-of-the-art computer work stations located in the library and in a separate computer lab. Access to MEDLINE and other full-text databases allows patrons to read the latest journals in the field and search for relevant articles of interest.

Special Forces medical specialists often have to deal with animals of the region. For this purpose there is also a 9,000-square-foot veterinary facility that supports veterinary and medical skills training. Complete with automated feeding equipment and air exchange mechanisms, this facility incorporates the newest animal care provisions and emulates the finest facilities of this type in the country. The latest in computer, electronic, and fiber optic technology has been incorporated into the design of the JSOMTC.

Instruction at the JSOMTC is provided by a skilled and experienced group of permanently assigned officers and enlisted personnel from all branches of the military. Dean of the JSOMTC is a colonel army physician with a special operations background. The Navy and the Air Force each provide an assistant dean with medical, educational, and special operations training and experience. Day-to-day operation of the facility is the responsibility of the Special Operations Medical Training Battalion, which is commanded by a lieutenant colonel Special Forces branch officer. Included in the staff are officers selected for their professional expertise and special operations experience from the Medical, Dental, Veterinary, Nursing, and Physician Assistant branches. Enlisted instructors are assigned from SOF in the Army, Navy, and Air Force. Enlisted technicians specializing in pharmacy, radiology, laboratory diagnostics, surgery, animal care, and logistics and personnel management provide additional support. A group of civilian employees with backgrounds in education, personnel management, information management, and pre-hospital emergency medical care complete the staff of the JSOMTC.

U.S. Army Special Forces students attend the 46-week Special Forces Medical Sergeants (SFMS) course, which is Phase II of a three-phase, 58-week-long Special Forces Qualification Course conducted at Ft. Bragg. Students in this course must successfully complete the 24-week SOCM curriculum before continuing on for an additional 22 weeks of specialized training in medical, surgical, dental, veterinary, and preventive medicine subjects. Upon completion of this course, students are qualified to function as independent health care providers. USN personnel qualified for this advanced training attend a similar course of instruction at the JSOMTC, known as the Advanced Special Operations Combat Medic course (ADSOCM), which is also 22 weeks in length. Upon completion of this course, the Navy awards these students the title of Independent Duty Corpsman (IDC).

Joint Special Operations Medical Training Center, Ft. Bragg, North Carolina.

In addition to the four weeks of clinical training provided during the SOCM portion of their training, U.S. Army SFMS and USN ADSOCM students receive another four weeks of clinical experience (called Special Operations Clinical Training, or SOCT) at selected military health care facilities throughout the eastern and central United States. During this rotation, the students will perform ride-alongs with city EMS units and serve in the emergency rooms of various metropolitan hospitals.

The JSOMTC participates in the continuing medical education or medical sustenance training of SOF medical personnel in numerous ways. Qualified Special Forces Medical sergeants receive two weeks of medical instruction at the JSOMTC as part of their Advanced Non-Commissioned Officers Course. Advanced Cardiac Life Support Instructor certification is available to qualified personnel through JSOMTC-taught instruction. Qualified SOF medical personnel may also attend Advanced Trauma Life Support courses that are conducted periodically by the Defense Medical Readiness Training Institute using JSOMTC facilities. In addition, a number of initiatives are being pursued that will provide JSOMTC instruction via distance learning to SOF medical personnel worldwide. In the near future, SOF personnel will be able to continue their medical education or receive support in the field by logging on to a JSOMTC World Wide Web home page via the Internet.

Currently, the JSOMTC is tasked with the execution of two complete courses of instruction, the SFMS, and the SOCM. Also provided is instruction for two modular courses, the USAF EMT-I course for Air Force Pararescue (PJs) not assigned to a special operations unit, and the USN ADSOCM for senior SEAL corpsmen. In addition, portions of two other Special Warfare Center and School Courses, the 18D Special Forces Medic Advanced Non-Commissioned Officer Course and the Special Forces officer orientation course, are also taught at the JSOMTC.

and learn how to teach these skills to others. They will be taught how to install, operate, and maintain FM, AM, HF, VHF, UHF, and SHF communications in voice, continuous wave, and burst radio nets, and learn SF communication operations procedures and techniques. Training culminates with an around-the-world communications field training exercise called Maxgain. Training is conducted at Ft. Bragg, North Carolina, and Camp Gruber, Oklahoma, and lasts 32 weeks.

Phase III - Collective Training

The third and final phase of the SFQC is a 38-day training period conducted at Camp MacKall. Soldiers are instructed in Special Operations, Direct Action, Isolation, Mission Planning, Air Operations (LZ/DZ, MPU, Resupply), and Unconventional Warfare (UW) training. In collective training all the instruction, hard work, and preparation come together. This field training exercise combines and strengthens both the specialty training and common skills. Soldiers from each of the SF skills areas and a detachment commander will put their training to the test. Approximately 160–170 students form 10–12 "A-teams," or ODAs. These ODAs will vary in size ranging from as few as eight to as many as 15 students.

The ODAs will be deployed as separate teams throughout the Uwaharrie National Forest for a UW exercise. Each of the ODAs will have a Training Group cadre member who will be their evaluator for their "final exam." This exercise comes complete with some 120 opposing force (Op Force) soldiers, a guerrilla force (Gs) numbering around 200, and a civilian auxiliary. The students will have to work with the guerrilla force just as they would in a real-world situation. While the SF and Gs are learning to deal with each other, they are being hunted and often attacked by OpForce troopers. This exercise will last for two weeks and is known as Robin Sage.

Robin Sage

The Robin Sage exercise takes place in the fictional country of Pineland on the continent of Atlantica, located in the Atlantic Ocean between America and Europe. Surrounding Pineland are OpForLand, DozerLand, and NeutraState. Pineland is of strategic importance to the United States. For this reason, members of the 9th Special Forces Group (Airborne), also a fictitious unit, have been tasked to provide military assistance. The guerrilla forces have been fighting for some time. The ODA-914 of 9th Group will be sent in to establish a link with these forces and train them in UW techniques.

Depending on their mission profiles, the student ODAs will be inserted by helicopter, parachute, boat, or truck. Regardless of how the team infils, it will ultimately be humping a ruck through some of the roughest terrain in the state of North Carolina, that is, Pineland.

After a day or two, depending on the scenario and how good the team is, the men will make contact with the guerrilla force. If they thought humping an 80–100 pound rucksack for a day or so was rough, it's nothing compared to the task ahead, meeting the guerrilla chief.

The G chief is played by an experienced SF soldier, usually a senior NCO, or perhaps a retired SF soldier brought in to test the mettle of these students who seek to join their ranks. These people know their business and will not spare the fledgling team, or their detachment commander. Whereas the Navy Seals' BUD/S "Hell Week" involves a week of sleep deprivation and 90 percent physical effort, Robin Sage is a thinking man's game.

The ODAs will meet and have to deal with a number of different scenarios and the G's. During their initial meeting, the guerrillas and their leaders are instructed to give the A-team a hard time, to be aloof, stand-offish, perhaps even a little hostile or threatening. One guerrilla comments to

Phase III—Robin Sage. Here is where all the training comes together. The SF students are matched up into functional A–teams, or ODAs, and sent into Pineland. Here they will put to use the skills set they have learned, and discover whether they have what it takes to wear the green beret.

the student, "We have been fighting for years. How much combat do you have? None? How can you tell me how to fight?" One of the G chiefs does not like officers, so he will only deal with the senior NCO of the team. This throws a definite curve to the team and can be unsettling to a detachment commander with too big an ego. When another team meets the G's, the chief's right-hand man is not happy with the situation and tries to convince the ODA to overthrow the chief. These are the types of mind games the G chief and the Gs will force upon the team—and some of these G's take this role-playing very seriously. This sense of realism adds to the intensity of the exercise, and an ODA only has to spend a few days in the base camp before beginning to believe that he really is in Pineland.

Time is a factor, however, since Robin Sage lasts only two weeks. Unless the team really

The team leader of ODA914 converses with the resident guerrilla chief. The G Chief is played by an SF sergeant with many years of experience under his belt. He will ensure that the young captain and his team receive the "Pineland" experience.

Five-Star accommodations, à la SF. While running the Phase III-Robin Sage exercise, this is about as good as it gets—a poncho on the ground and one hanging overhead. "Hey, where is the concierge? My MRE is cold!"

messes up, the Gs will eventually warm to them. Now the team will place into action what they have learned. The weapons specialist will teach the guerrillas how to establish a defensive perimeter around the base camp, the medics will teach hygiene and first aid. The engineers will teach the Gs how to build, and how to take down a target with a very large boom, while the commo specialist provides instruction on radio equipment and procedures. The trainees teach the guerillas small unit tactics, raids, and ambushes. By teaching and doing, the students will learn the hallmarks of a successful raid: Surprise, Speed, and Violence of Action.

Slowly the Gs will evolve from a ragtag bunch of individuals into an organized fighting force. Missions will be planned and executed, all under the watchful eye of the Training Group evaluator. This evaluator is a cadre member of the 1st Special Warfare Training Groups (Airborne). After one such mission, an assault on an OpForce position, the evaluator will sit down with the student and go over his performance. Did you perform the proper Warning Order? It's 98 degrees out here, why didn't you instruct your squad to carry more water? Did you do a recon of the target? Why didn't you wear any face camo? Did you have an alternate plan if you got compromised?

Q-Course student goes over a mission plan with one of the Gs. The hallmarks of a successful raid are surprise, speed, and violence of action on the target. The prospective SF soldier will explain these traits to this guerrilla prior to an assault.

On and on the questions go, and the evaluator will mark the progress or lack of progress of a student. All of these evaluations will go into a leadership assessment that will be used to determine whether the student has what it takes to be a member of the Special Forces.

Trainees must also respect and employ the skills of others on the "island." The OpForce includes soldiers from active military units who have been tasked to assault or engage the team from time to time. The Gs usually possess a modest form of infantry skills, as well as those of clerks, cooks, truck drivers, and so on. The third group who makes up the population of Pineland

During the two weeks of Robin Sage, the SF students get numerous opportunities to apply their skills and exercise their talents. Here a medical sergeant student administers an IV to one of the Gs suffering from heat exhaustion.

Engineer Sergeant student Joe Ferris prepares timing fuses for a future mission. Note that in training, as in combat, his M4A1 carbine is close by, should the need arise. Even in the relative safety of the G Camp, the SF students may come under attack from the OpForce troops at any time.

are the Auxiliary. These are civilian players who for the most part remain anonymous. They offer their homes or barns as "safe houses" for the ODA and Gs; they may provide transportation for a mission, or perhaps bring in some good old home cooking for the freedom fighters of Pineland. Along with the G's supporters, there are those who support the OpForce—e.g., the local sheriff may see the unfamiliar face of an ODA member surveying a target, and lock him up. These local people of the Auxiliary have been assisting in the Robin Sage exercise since the 1960s; indeed, they add a sense of realism to missions.

The exercise ends with a final mission: The ODA has trained the Gs, and they now take on an OpForce target. At this point, Robin Sage is over. The teams will return to Camp MacKall, clean their weapons, gear, and themselves, and await the results of the exercise.

As the evaluations come in, the students are notified whether they have passed or failed the Q-Course. Depending on the recommendation of the evaluators and cadre, a student who does not pass may be recycled for another chance, or he may be dropped. Those who are dropped are sent back to their units.

According the mission brief of the 1st SWTG(A), the soldier who passes will, "Thrive on ambiguity and uncertainty. Think the unconventional and dare the uncommon. Overcome obstacles and persevere when others fail. Adapt to his surroundings and anticipate changes. [He is] physically rugged, morally straight and thoroughly lethal. Triumphs through genius as well as force of arms. [And] immerses himself in the art, science and history of war." Those soldiers who have made it through the course will become members of the U.S. Army Special Forces. They will attend a regimental dinner where they will receive the Special Forces tab, and the coveted green beret. The following day will be the official graduation ceremony from the Q-Course.

Throughout the two weeks of the Robin Sage exercise, the student ODAs will be evaluated on every nuance of their training. Here a Pineland evaluator writes up an "eval" of one of the students following a raid on an OpFor installation.

Every SF Soldier goes through language training. Here members of the 7th Special Forces Group (Airborne) are studying Spanish. Their instructor, who may be from Mexico or South America, is a native speaker. SF soldiers may also learn via computer self-paced training, and from members of the ODA.

The training does not stop here. One of the qualifications of the Special Forces since its inception was that the soldier be conversant in a foreign language. Our newly "tabbed" soldier will now attend language training. Depending on which SF group the soldier will be assigned to, he will be trained in Spanish, French, Portuguese, German, Czech, Polish, Russian, Persian-Farsi, Tagalog, Thai, Vietnamese, Korean, or Modern Standard Arabic.

This training ranges from 17 to 23 weeks, depending on the language. The training stresses basic communications skills with an emphasis on military terminology. Language skills are taught by an instructor indigenous to that country—e.g., the Thai instructor is from Thailand, and the Russian teacher is from Russia, and so on. This assists the SF troops not only in the language, but also with dialects, as well as customs of the country. Each of the Special Forces Groups will also have a language lab for follow-up training.

The next step for the new Green Beret is going to SERE (Survival, Escape, Resistance, and Evasion) School. An SF soldier, or ODA, may be deployed to any location in the world. It may be in the middle of the desert or the side of a mountain; it may range from the extreme heat of the jungle or the frigid cold of subarctic

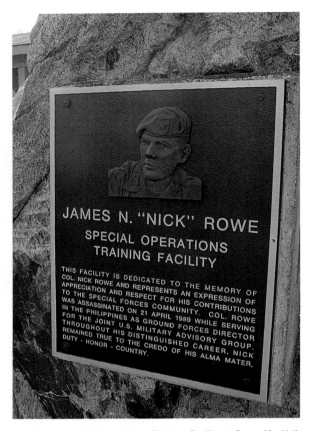

On 8 February 1990, the Rowe Training Facility at Camp MacKall was dedicated in honor of Colonel James N. "Nick" Rowe. Colonel Rowe had survived as a prisoner of war in Vietnam for a period of five years, until he managed to escape from his captors. Colonel Rowe was killed in the Philippines during his tour as senior adviser to that country.

lines; and it is not outside the realm of possibility that he will be captured. The SERE School was developed for these reasons and is mandatory training for all SF soldiers. The school is located at the Colonel Nick Rowe Training Facility, at Camp MacKall. Here, members of Company A, 1st SWTG(A), will impart their survival skills to the students.

The key word for the course is S-U-R-V-I-V-A-L. The students will learn that each of these letters represents a technique. By learning all eight of the skills, they will afford themselves a greater chance of staying alive and returning to base. The eight skills are as follows: S: Size up the situation (the surroundings, your physical condition, equipment); U: Undue haste makes waste; R: Remember where you are; V: Vanquish fear and panic; I: Improvise; V: Value living; A: Act like the natives; and L: Live by your wits (or for the new students, L: Learn basic skills). Put them all together and they spell SURVIVAL, the difference between life and death.

The objective of the course is "to provide students with an understanding of what to expect if captured; explain the Code of Conduct and provide a clear understanding of what is expected of them should they become a prisoner of war (POW); prepare the student to survive in unique and adverse conditions, and to evade the enemy; teach resistance to exploitation by the enemy if captured, and to escape captivity and return home with honor." The SERE course lasts 19 days, ending in an evasion exercise that will expose the SF soldier to increased levels of physical and mental pressure, testing their endurance as well as their resolve. During this course, students will also receive instruction in hand-to-hand combat and sentry take-down techniques. Upon successful completion of the course, the students go through a critique and graduation. At this point the SF soldier will head off to his appropriate group as a new member of an ODA.

regions. Most of the time the team will be working together, and will draw on each other's strengths. There may be times, however, when an SF member could find himself alone, with little or no personal equipment. Due to the very nature of the Special Forces missions, it is very likely he will find himself behind enemy

Warrant Officer Technical Certification Course

The 1st SWTG(A) also teaches the Special Operation Warrant Officer Technical Certification course. The training provides for growth within the SF organization, as it draws from senior Special Forces NCOs. The experienced sergeants, who will have already taken the Army's basic warrant officer program, will receive additional training in special operation command structure, missions, mission preparations, doctrine, SERE, UW classes, isolation, and briefbacks. The training duration is 19 weeks, and culminates with a field training exercise (FTX), Mystic Watchman. Those soldiers graduating from this program are commissioned as warrant officers and go on to serve as the executive officer on an SF ODA.

Advanced Special Forces Skills

Training for the Special Forces soldier never ends. While he continues to hone the skills learned during the Q-course, he will also receive additional training in a variety of techniques to assist him in executing his mission with the greatest probability of success.

Military Free Fall (MFF)

Further airborne infiltration training is available to SF soldiers through the U.S. Army Military Freefall Parachutist School at Ft. Bragg, North Carolina. The mission of the school is to train personnel in the science of HALO (High Altitude Low Opening) military free-fall parachuting, using the Ram-Air Parachute System (RAPS). MFF parachuting enables the theater commander to infiltrate an SF team into an area that would prohibit the use of static-line parachute operations. Special operations missions require rapid and covert infiltration into operational areas.

During week one of this course, the future SF troopers will go through the normal in-processing

High Altitude Low Opening (HALO) and High Altitude High Opening (HAHO) techniques are taught to those SF members who are assigned to a HALO team. Here a member of the 7th Special Forces Group (Airborne) floats down to earth on the Ram-Air Parachute System (RAPS). This jumper is prepared to drop his rucksack, which is suspended by webbing straps. Note the M4A1 carbine tucked along his left side.

and be issued their equipment. At this time they will be assigned to a HALO instructor who will remain with them throughout the four-week training cycle. It is also during week one that they will be matched up with a "jump buddy." Their "buddy" will be approximately the same weight and height, so they will fall at the same rate.

In ground school they will learn about the ram air parachutes, substantially different from the usual T-10B or MCI-1B that they jumped with at Basic Airborne School. The MC-5 ram air parachutes are rectangular shaped as opposed to circular, and are extremely maneuverable. Course students learn about equipment, rigging, and repacking the parachutes. They also learn special jump commands, as well as use of the oxygen systems employed in high altitude jumping.

In case of trouble, the course also teaches emergency procedures involving parachute malfunctions, cutaways, entanglements, and how to recover. These exercises are run over and over until they become second nature to the jumpers. Falling at a rate of over 180 feet per second, you do not have the luxury of thinking about the problem—you must react.

During week one, the candidate spends time in the Military Free Fall Simulator Facility. Completed at Ft. Bragg in 1992 at a cost of $5 million, this 11,000-square-foot facility contains an enclosed vertical wind tunnel, 32 student classrooms, an operator control room, and communications and equipment rooms. "This facility is a marked improvement," says Carol Darby of the Special Warfare School. "Prior to having the facility, the students had to practice [body stabilization] by lying on table tops."

The simulator is approximately 18 feet high and 14 feet in diameter, and it can support two jumpers with equipment up to 375 pounds each. The simulator's fan generates winds up to 132 miles per hour. Suspended in a column of air, the students will learn and practice body-stabilization techniques. The wind tunnel will simulate the effects of free-falling at a speed of approximately 200 feet per second.

After they complete ground week, the students will travel to Yuma Proving Grounds, Arizona. Weeks two through five will find our candidates jumping, jumping, and jumping again, beginning at 10,000 feet with no equipment, and working up to 25,000 feet with full equipment load and oxygen system. The course provides in-the-air instruction, where the student will concentrate on stability, aerial maneuvers and parachute-deployment procedures. Each student will receive a minimum of 16 free fall jumps, which include two day and two night jumps with oxygen and full field equipment.

SCUBA Training

U.S. Army Combat Divers School is in Key West, Florida. At this location, our man will learn to use SCUBA gear to stealthily infiltrate his target area. This training is essential to the SF teams, since they may be asked to infiltrate into denied territory via underwater methods. Unlike U.S. Navy SEALs operations, for the most part Special Forces missions do not take place in the water. The water is merely a means of infiltration and/or transportation to their deployment or objective.

Training will include waterborne operations both day and night. Students will be taught ocean subsurface navigation, deep diving techniques, marine hazards, how to read tides, waves, and currents. They will also be instructed in the proper procedures of submarine lock-in and lock-out, the method of entering and exiting a submerged sub. Training in both open-circuit and closed-circuit equipment will be taught. This is no recreation diving, as depths in training go down to 120 feet under diverse operating conditions.

This training phase will last four weeks. Week one begins with PT, and further physical conditioning to get the trainee prepared for the balance of the class. Week two will find the trooper in the water receiving training to build up his confidence and strengthen his swimming. In week three, students will dive, dive, and then dive some more.

In the final week each student will perform an underwater compass swim. It is not sufficient

Some SF soldiers are trained on SCUBA (Self-contained underwater breathing apparatus) techniques. When necessary for an over-the-horizon insertion, the SF may use LAR-V rebreathers or open circuit systems. This combat swimmer has come ashore to perform a beach recon prior to bringing the balance of the team onto the shore.

to just know how to SCUBA dive; he must be able to execute his mission via underwater ingress. Equipped with a compass board, SCUBA tank, weapon, and rucksack, he will carry out an infiltration to a point on the beach. Final week brings more night dives, a Field Training Exercise, and graduation.

Special Operation Target Interdiction Course (SOTIC)

The SOTIC, as explained by Major Kimm Rowe, commander Company D, 2nd Battalion 1st SWTG(A), "trains SF personnel in the technical skills and operational procedures necessary to deliver precision rifle fire from concealed positions to selected targets in support of special operations forces missions." This is also known as sniper training. SOTIC students all volunteer for this training. They must have a rating of expert with their weapon, pass a number of psychological evaluations, and have Secret clearance. SOTIC is a Level 1 category course for Special Forces and Rangers. This means those who graduate from the course are qualified to instruct U.S. troops, train soldiers from foreign nations, and shoot at close proximity to U.S. troops and noncombatants. What that means in simple terms is that a SOTIC sniper can drop an enemy if he is standing right next to you.

The class has a ratio of one SOTIC instructor for every four students, and the students learn the ins and outs of the M24 Sniper Weapon System (SWS), a bolt-action, single-shot rifle chambered in 7.52mm x 51mm; the Leuopold Mark IV M3A 10 power rifle scope; XM144 15x-45x spotting scope; and M19/22 binoculars. They will familiarize themselves with the Soviet SVD 7.62mm x 39mm, the Barrett M82A1, 50 caliber, the Stoner SR25, 7.62mm x 51mm and various other U.S. and foreign sniper weapons. They will also receive training in the use of night vision devices, and in the technique and creation of the ghillie suit.

The ghillie suit is a camouflage suit that is used to break up the outline of the sniper. There are a number of options and it often boils down simply to personal preference. The two most common versions, however, are the one-piece, made from a flight suit, and the two-piece BDU version with separate shirt and trousers. The student sews netting onto the clothing, attaches various lengths

SF soldiers may also attend the Special Operations Target Interdiction Course (SOTIC) at Ft. Bragg, North Carolina. SOTIC, better known as sniper training, is the best the U.S. military has to offer. SOTIC is a Level 1 category course for Special Forces and Rangers. Level 1 means, in simple terms, that an SOTIC sniper can drop an enemy if he is standing right next to you.

of burlap to the netting, and then strip by strip shreds the burlap until the outline of the uniform has vanished. A "boonie hat" is often given the same treatment to break up the silhouette of the sniper's head, and then is used for concealment once in position. Vegetation is often added to the burlap for further camouflage. The instructors at the SOTIC favor a mix of 30 percent burlap strips and 70 percent vegetation, which is stuffed into the netting and held in place by rubber bands. One of the SOTIC instructors explains, "By using the local vegetation, the sniper will blend into his surroundings." Students also learn to adjust the foliage in the suit as they move from one position to the next to remain invisible.

During one of the stalking phases, the student-sniper must get to within 200 meters of the spotters. These spotters are SOTIC instructors with ranger finders and binoculars who scan the woodline for the students as they stealthily approach. When the student has reached his position and is confident he has not been sighted, he will fire a blank round. The instructor will call in one of the "walkers" who are out in the brush. They are there to tag the student out if he is spotted. SOTIC instructor, SFC George Simmons, radios to the walker, "Move three feet to your left . . . sniper there." The walker, who knows where the snipers are but does not tell the spotters, responds that he is not within three feet of the sniper who has just fired. Sergeant Simmons then holds up a white card with a number on it. Radio contact is again established with the walker, "Have the student ID the card." The walker responds that the student correctly identifies the number "7." Having moved into position without being sighted, the student is allowed to take a second shot. This time the instructors are looking for telltale signs of a sniper—things like the muzzle blast of the weapon, or the movement of the foliage as the shot is taken. If it's a nada, zip, zero, this student has done well and gets a passing score for the stalk.

During this six-week course, 24 students will be taught the skills of advanced rifle marksmanship, sniper marksmanship, field shooting, field craft, judging distance, observation techniques, camouflage, stalking, counter stalking, and airborne insertion. In the final exercise, the students jump in, move over land, and take a final shot. In a third of the scenarios, they must make a first round hit, or else they don't graduate. Those who do graduate will return to their ODA where they will take up their position as one of two snipers on the team.

Special Operation Training (SOT)

The SOT course was formed back in the late 1970s. SOT trains SOF solders in the tactics, techniques, and procedures required to conduct direct action and unilateral special operations that are of limited scope and duration. SOT also develops the precision marksmanship needed in the MOUT (Military Operations in Urban Terrain) environment. According to Major Rowe, "The real intent for SOT is to train somewhat organic teams together, thus strengthening team cohesion."

Training emphasis is on advanced marksmanship, ballistic and mechanical breaching, limited explosive breaching, building climbing and rappelling, and Close Quarters Battle (CQB)

in various building environments, culminating in a 24-hour FTX.

SFARTAETC

This is the third course carried out by the instructors of Company D, 2nd battalion, 1st SWTG(A).

This rather long abbreviation stands for Special Forces Advance Reconnaissance, Target Analysis, and Exploitation Techniques Course. Although the course is highly classified, the unclassified description states that "SFARTAETC provides the basic entry level training in the tactics, techniques, and procedures needed by personnel being assigned to a theater CinCs in extremis force (CIF).

Special Forces Advance Reconnaissance, Target Analysis, and Exploitation Techniques Course (SFARTAETC). SFARTAETC provides the basic entry-level training in the tactics, techniques, and procedures needed by personnel being assigned to a theater. These skills include precision marksmanship, integrated CQB, and interpretability with other specifically designated forces.

These skills include: precision marksmanship, integrated CQB, and interpretability with other specifically designated forces."

This eight-week course is a counterterrorism (CT) type of CQB usually involving a hostage, POW, or similar situation. Training will also encompass engaging linear targets. Training emphasizes advanced marksmanship, close proximity shooting; ballistic mechanical and explosive breaching techniques for doors, windows, and walls; building-climbing and -rappelling procedures; fast rope techniques; CQB in multi-team and multi-breach points along with multi-story and multi-building environments; and interoperability techniques. Weapons training includes the M4A1 carbine with Aimpoint and tactical light systems, M9 pistol with tactical light, HK MP5, Remington 870 breaching shotgun, ballistic protection, breaching devices, night vision devices, M155 & MK141 flash bangs, fast rope, and climbing equipment.

SFAUC

Special Forces Advanced Urban Combat (SFAUC) was developed by the U.S. Army Special Forces Command in response to the ever-increasing number of urban operations confronting the SF soldier. The driving force behind the program is Major General William Boykin, who had been in charge of the SF Command until March of 2000, when he assumed command of the Special Warfare Center and School.

The general is very familiar with the cost of urban combat on special operations forces, as he was the commander of 1st Special Operations Detachment - Delta in October 1993. It was during this time that Task Force Ranger, the 160th SOAR(A), and Delta Force were engaged in a firefight for their lives in the streets of Mogadishu, Somalia.

General Boykin initiated the SFAUC program in May 1999 with a plan to have every SF soldier

trained in the three-week session. Each of the SF groups are responsible to disseminate these techniques and procedures to their ODAs. Major Richard Steiner, Operations Officer, 2nd Battalion, 3rd Special Forces Group (Airborne) explains, "The intent of Special Forces Advanced Urban Combat is to improve Special Forces soldiers' already formidable skills in CQB, especially as it concerns direct action missions, raids and ambushes—and especially as they apply to conducting direct action missions in an urban environment." The world is urbanizing, the population is becoming more and more dense, and SF must be able to operate in that environment. According to Major Steiner, "National Command Authority assumes when they commit Special Operations Forces in general and Special Forces in particular they're getting soldiers that can apply lethal force with a high degree of precision. SFAUC is not necessarily for hostage rescue, rather to pick an enemy out and engage that enemy without a number of unwanted casualties or unwanted collateral damage. SFAUC may be applied in the force protection arena. Where zero U.S. casualties in peacetime or in combat is the goal, then SF must be dominant in CQB tactics. This would include during a DA or even in a SR mission, anywhere in the world. He will have the capability of doing that in a dominating way while still maintaining the precision of U.S. SOF."

SFAUC is operations in urban terrain, involving engaging only hostile or theater enemy forces, sophisticated shooting techniques, identifying the target and engaging, breaching and entering buildings. The SF soldier is trained for every contingency, from bamboo huts to reinforced steel doors—get in and leave the building standing. This is contrary to the Russians' approach: One only has to look at Chechnya to see how they define urban combat—lots of rubble, not very precise.

SFAUC is taught in three phases. Phase I is Combat Marksmanship, advanced shooting skills

As the world urbanizes and the population becomes more dense, the SF soldiers must be able to operate in that environment. SFAUC—Special Forces Advanced Urban Combat—is operations in urban terrain. The skills taught involve engaging only hostile or theater enemy forces, sophisticated shooting techniques, identifying the target and engaging, breaching, and entering buildings. The U.S. Army Special Forces continually hone these skills to ensure they remain the premier special operations fighting force.

with the M4A1 carbine and the M-9 pistol. Targets are engaged from 0 to 50 meters—single targets, multiple targets, from the prone, kneeling, and standing positions. Targets are engaged head-on and laterally and in depth. During this time the soldier will undergo stress firing, 2-1/2 minutes to ID and engage 20–25 targets in various scenarios. He will also face pop-up targets, reactive, and non-reactive targets, from 3–25 meters. He will fire and reload using his primary weapon (M4A1) and secondary weapon (M-9).

Phase II covers Breaching/CQB. Mechanical breaching involves the use of sledge hammers, battering rams, crowbars, and glass and bolt cutters.

Ballistic breaching is using a shotgun with a variety of ammunition, such as #9 bird shot and "shock locks" and other specialty ammo to defeat a door, primarily the locking mechanism. Explosive breaching covers a diverse selection of explosives and techniques—flex linear charge, det-cord, C-4. A favorite is the silhouette charge—a cardboard silhouette with one to three wraps of det-cord around the perimeter, with a charge to the center does a good job of cutting through a door. Replace the det-cord with the proper amount of C-4 and the silhouette will now blow out a substantial passageway through a cinder block wall. Assorted initiators are also taught for instant detonation.

Phase III is CQB. During this phase the SF will be trained in and practice single-man, two-man, and four-man entry into a room, engaging targets, and collapsing on their sector. They will learn how to "stack," which is lining up for dynamic entry into a room or building. The SF soldiers will conduct a breach, enter the building, clear the room, secure the structure; if on a DA mission, they will recover personnel or equipment, or destroy the target, and clear the structure.

While each mission will vary, the standard deployment for SF CQB is the four-man entry team. From the time the team members initiate the breach, enter the room, collapse and secure their sector, finally clearing the room, it will take an average of four seconds.

The SF primary weapon for SFAUC training is the M-4 carbine. Choice of scopes range from standard iron sight, ACOG 4x scope, Aimpoint with red dot, or ACOG Reflex sight—the latter two are used with both eyes open. Additionally the M-4 carbine may be fitted with a white light that has a pressure on/off switch. It may be used for securing an individual, or searching a room once secure. The SFAUC troops may choose a more stealthy approach and go in with weapons suppressed. Major Steiner says, "Since the 5.56mm round is supersonic, you will hear the bang. What the suppressor does for you is buy you some time while the bad guys are trying to figure out, 'what was that?' 'Where did it come from?' By the time they figure out what is going on, you should be in dominance of the situation." Suppressors will also keep the muzzle blast to a minimum, assisting the entry team in situation awareness.

Weapons are not the only edge the SFAUC Green Beret has in his kit. Currently the SF ODAs are looking at a new headgear for CQB, a combination Kevlar and communications helmet. In the meantime, they will continue to train with the current Kevlars. During the three-week session, with an average of 36 students, the SFAUC course will expend more than 75,000 rounds of 5.56mm ball, 75,000 rounds of 9mm ball, 15,000 rounds of simmunitions (simulated munitions, using a plastic bullet), and hundreds of 12 gauge assorted loads.

There is a reason for the amount of ammunition used. Some would call it "muscle-memory," in which the body automatically brings the weapon up to the ready. Others called it automatic response. Whatever term you choose, SFAUC trains the SF soldier in the fundamentals of sight alignment and trigger control. Once you can reflexively apply those two skills, you will get hits, whether you are standing on the corner, sitting in a HUMMV, or jogging down the street. The SF soldier is taught to neutralize the hostile until he is no longer a threat.

SFAUC is about engaging hostiles in a DA or SR mission. This is not intended to replace the training for hostage rescue. The techniques and procedures taught in this course will aid the SF soldier as he takes down a radar installation or command post, recovers equipment, or deals with guards. SF takes weapons skills so seriously that there are four "shooting houses" on Ft. Bragg alone. Major Tom McCollum, SF Command, relates, "These guys are just about artists at their profession. The training is repetitive, and you build on those skills. Then you begin to use your imagination, to think outside of the box: What if . . . ? Suppose we do this . . . ? Then you build in the contingencies for the what-ifs."

All of the training, and the acclimation of that training, is the reason the SF soldiers are in constant demand around the globe. Their advanced training is what makes them the Quiet Professionals within the U.S. military, and provides the expertise that makes the Special Forces soldiers the most lethal warriors on earth.

7 *Equipment and Techniques*

S pecial Forces soldiers are schooled in unconventional techniques and procedures that will prove beneficial to their missions. The communications sergeant is capable of rigging up a radio antenna with some branches, 550 cord and Meal Ready to Eat (MRE) spoons. The engineer sergeant, with items from under the kitchen sink, can construct an explosive devise to take out a target, while the weapons sergeant is able to assemble an assortment of lethal weapons, from slingshots to shotguns. SF soldiers are trained to be effective with whatever is at hand. But in real-world situations, where they are almost always vastly outnumbered, these men are equipped with the best weapons and technology available to fulfill their missions.

Weapons

Special Forces soldiers are familiar with and expert in numerous types of weapons systems, U.S. and foreign, new and old, allied and enemy. They must know how to operate a World War II German MG34 machine gun being used in a Third World country, or the latest Mark 19, 40mm Grenade Machine Gun, in use with Coalition Forces. They are masters of small arms, such as revolvers, semi-automatic pistols, rifles, and submachine guns. Use of crew-served weapons, like the 60mm and 81mm mortar, and recoilless rifles is a common task for the SF troopers. Where is the best place to position a .30 caliber or .50 caliber machine gun? The SF will instruct in the placement, fire lanes, and interlocking fields of fire to maximize these lethal instruments. Engaging an enemy tank or bunker? The Operational

Detachment-Alpha (ODA) will survey which system will best do the job—e.g., the AT-4, Carl Gustov, or M-72 LAW. Whether engaging personnel, tanks, helicopters, buildings, or aircraft, the Special Forces soldiers are the best trained fighters in the world to accomplish this mission.

To cover all of the weapons systems in use by the Special Forces Groups would require volumes.

The M9 9mm Berretta pistol was adopted by the Department of Defense to standardize the 9mm round for U.S. and NATO forces. The M9 is the standard issue pistol for all U.S. military troops including the Special Forces. While it is an acceptable weapon, there are many within the special operations community who still favor the .45 caliber round.

Consequently, we will address those weapons organic to the ODA, the primary firearms intrinsic to the team.

SOPMOD M4A1

All Special Forces soldiers are currently issued the Special Operations Peculiar Modification (SOPMOD) M4A1 Carbine. The M4A1 from Colt Arms of Connecticut is a smaller, compact version of the full-sized M16A2 rifle. This weapon was designed specifically for the U.S. Special Operations Forces. The M4A1 is designed for speed of action and light weight. The barrel has been redesigned to a shortened 14.5 inches, which reduces the weight while maintaining the gun's effectiveness for quick-handling field operations. The retractable butt stock has intermediate stops allowing versatility in Close Quarters Battle (CQB) without compromising shooting capabilities.

The M4A1 has a rifling twist of 1 in 7 inches, making it compatible with the full range of 5.56mm ammunitions. Its sighting system contains dual apertures, one for 0–200 meters and a smaller opening for targets at 500–600 meters. Selective fire controls for the M4A1 have eliminated the three-round burst, replacing it with safe semi-automatic and full automatic fire.

The SOPMOD Accessory Kit allows the SF soldier to modify the weapon per mission parameters. Using the Rail Interface System (RIS), numerous components may be secured to the weapon. The kit includes a 4x32mm Trijicon Day Optical Scope, allowing the soldiers to judge range and deliver more accurate fire out to 300 meters; Trijicon Reflex sight, designed for close-in engagement; and Infrared Target Pointer/ Illuminator/Aiming Laser AN/PEQ-2 (for use with night vision devices), which places a red aiming dot on the target—very useful in building and CQB. Additionally, the kit includes Visible Light, a high-intensity flashlight mounted on the rail system; backup iron sight (since the carrying handle of the M4A1 can be removed, this backup sight can be employed in the absence of the handle); and a forward hand grip, which helps in stabilization of the weapon and keeps the user's hands away from the hand guards and barrel, which tend to heat up in combat. Finally, the kit includes a sound suppressor, which significantly reduces the noise and muzzle blast.

The primary weapon for the Special Forces soldier is the Colt M4A1 Carbine. This shortened version of the M16A2 rifle features a collapsible stock, a flat top upper receiver with an accessory rail, and a detachable handle and aperture sight assembly. The M4A1 fire selector has three settings: safe, full automatic, or single shot. The M4A1 shown here has been modified with the Special Operations Peculiar Modification (SOPMOD) accessory kit. A special Rail Interface System (RIS) allows the attachment of numerous aiming devices and accessories depending on the mission. This M4A1 has been modified with a Trijicon ACOG (Advanced Combat Optical Gun-sight) 4x32 scope; on the hand-grip is a AN/PEQ-2 Infrared Target Pointer/Illuminator/Aiming Device. The PEQ-2 emits a laser beam for precise aiming of the weapon. It may also be used for lasing targets for the delivery of smart bombs. Finally, attached to the barrel is a Quick Attach/Detach Sound Suppressor. With the suppressor attached the muzzle, blast, flash, and sound are significantly reduced.

The M203 grenade launcher is a lightweight, single-shot breech loaded 40mm weapon specifically designed for placement beneath the barrel of the M4A1 Carbine. With a quick-release mechanism, the addition of the M203 to M4A1 carbine creates the versatility of a weapon system capable of firing both 5.56mm ammunition as well as an expansive range of 40mm high explosive and special purpose munitions.

Colt M203

The M203 grenade launcher is a lightweight (three-pound), single-shot, breech-loaded 40mm weapon specifically designed for placement beneath the barrel of the M16A1 and M16A2 rifles and M4A1/M16A2 carbines. Attached with a quick-release mechanism, the M203 creates the versatility of a weapon system capable of firing both 5.56mm ammunition as well as an expansive range of 40mm high explosive and special purpose munitions.

The most commonly utilized M203 ammunition is the M406 antipersonnel round. This grenade has a deadly radius of five meters. Another option is the M433 multi-purpose grenade, which in addition to the fragmentation effects is capable of penetrating steel armor plate up to two inches thick. Other types of ordnance available are buckshot, tear gas, and various signal rounds.

The receiver of the M203 is manufactured of high-strength forged aluminum alloy. This provides extreme ruggedness, while keeping weight to a minimum. A complete self-cocking firing mechanism, including striker, trigger, and positive safety lever, is included in the receiver. This will allow the M203 to be operated as an independent weapon, even though attached to the M16A1 or M16A2 rifle or M4A1/M16A2 carbine. The barrel is also made of high-strength aluminum alloy, which has been shortened from 12 to 9 inches, allowing improved balance and handling. It slides forward in the receiver to accept a round of ammunition, then slides backward to automatically lock in the closed position, ready to fire.

Special Operations Forces depend on rapid deployment, mobility, and increased firepower. Where the emphasis of a small unit, such as the SF, is placed on "get in and get out" fast, the M203 lends added firepower to the already-proven and outstanding family of M16 weapons.

M9 Beretta

Since 1985, the M9 has seen service as the standard issue side arm for U.S. troops, both conventional and special, in Operation Urgent Fury in Grenada, Operation Desert Shield/Storm in Kuwait, Operation Restore Hope in Somalia, and with IFOR in Bosnia and KFOR in Kosovo. Along with the standardization of the 9mm round, the M9 brought the armed forces a larger-capacity magazine. The M9 holds 15 rounds, compared to the Colt 1911's seven or eight rounds. Although the 9mm ammunition was lighter and smaller, it was viewed as ade-

The M240B replaces the M-60 machine gun in the ODAs (Operational Detachment-Alpha). The highly reliable 7.62mm machine gun delivers more energy to the target than the smaller caliber M249 Squad Assault Weapon (SAW) in use with the Rangers and other Army troops.

quate for line troops. This trade-off also allowed the troops to engage more rounds in a fire fight before having to reload. The original M9 was viewed with some apprehension among operators in the Special Operations community because +P ammunition reportedly caused stress fractures of the weapon's slides. Beretta addressed this problem and today's M9 has an average life of 72,250 rounds.

The slide is open for nearly the entire length of the barrel. This facilitates the ejection of spent shells and virtually eliminates stoppages. The open slide configuration also provide a means for the pistol to be loaded manually. As with all weapons in use with Special Operation Forces, the operators are always trying to get that extra "edge." One of the most likely features to be added to the M9 was a sound suppressor. For such a device the military turned to Knight Arma-

ment Company. The smooth cylindrical suppresser is manufactured of anodized aluminum with a steel attachment system. Weighing a scant 6 ounces, it can be replaced or removed in three seconds. Carrying over the Vietnam-era name, the suppressor was dubbed the "Hush-Puppy."

M-240 Medium Machine Gun

After extensive operational testing, the U.S. Army selected the M240B medium machine gun as a replacement for the M60 family of machine guns. Manufactured by Fabrique Nationale, the 24.2 pound M240B medium machine gun is a gas-operated, air-cooled, linked-belt-fed weapon that fires the 7.62 x 51 mm round. The weapon fires from an open bolt position with a maximum effective range of 1,100 meters. The rate of fire is adjustable from 750 to 1400 rounds per minute through an adjustable gas regulator. It features a folding bipod that attaches to the receiver, a quick-change barrel assembly, a feed cover and bolt assembly enabling closure of the cover regardless of bolt position, a plastic butt stock and an integral optical sight rail. While it possesses many of the same characteristics as the older M60, the durability of the M240 system results in superior reliability and maintainability.

M249 Squad Automatic Weapon (SAW)

Fielded in the mid-1980s, the M249 SAW is an individually portable, air-cooled, belt-fed, gas-operated light machine gun. A unique feature of the SAW is the number of alternate ammunition feeds. The standard ammunition load is 200 rounds of 5.56mm ammunitions in disintegrating belts. These rounds are fed from a 200-round plastic ammunition box through the side of the weapon. The normal link ammunition for the SAW is four rounds of M855 ball ammunitions followed by one round of M85 tracer. Additionally, it can use standard 20- and 30-round M16 magazines, which

M249 SAW is an individually portable, air-cooled, belt-fed, gas-operated light machine gun. The standard load is 200 rounds of 5.56mm ammunitions in disintegrating belts. These rounds are fed from a 200-round plastic ammunition box through the side of the weapon. Additionally, the SAW can utilize standard 20- and 30-round M4A1/M16 magazines, which are inserted in a magazine well in the bottom of the SAW. Using the same 5.56mm ammunition as the M4A1, it allows the ODA to carry common ammunition loads. The M249 is capable of engaging targets out to 800 meters.

The weapon of choice for the Special Forces sniper is the M24 SWS, or Sniper Weapon System. Based on a Remington 700 action, it is equipped with a Leupold Mark IV 10 power fixed scope referred to as the "Ma-3 Alpha." The M24 SWS is a bolt-action rifle capable of engaging a target at well over 500 meters.

are inserted in a magazine well in the bottom of the SAW. Since the SAW uses the same 5.56mm ammunition as the M4A1, it allows the ODA to carry common ammunition loads. The M249 is capable of engaging targets out to 800 meters.

M24 Sniper Weapon System (SWS)

The current issue sniper rifle for the Special Forces is the M24 SWS, two per ODA. The M24 is based on the Remington 700 series long action. This action accommodates chambering for either the 7.62x51mm or .300 Winchester Magnum round. The rifle is a bolt-action six-shot repeating rifle (one round in the chamber and five additional rounds in the magazine). It is issued with the Leupold Mark IV 10 power M3A scope, commonly referred to as the "Ma-3-Alpha." The sniper

may also make use of the weapon's iron sights. Attached to the scope is the M24/EMA ARD (Anti-Reflection Device). Less than three inches long, this honeycomb of tubes cuts down the glare of the scope. The M24 SWS does come with a Harris bipod; however, most of the time the bipod remains in the deployment case. The rifle weighs 12.1 pounds without the scope and has an overall length of 43 inches, with a free-floating barrel of 24 inches. The stock is composite Kevlar, graphite, and fiberglass with an aluminum-bedding block. The stock has an adjustable butt plate to accommodate the length of pull.

Heavy Sniper Rifle

When the mission calls for a Hard Target Interdiction (HTI) at very long range, e.g., over 1,000 meters, the SF will turn to the big guns. HTI would be taking out such targets as an airplane, helicopter, or vehicle. Currently, the SF has the M82A1 in their inventories. It is a one-man portable, semi-automatic rifle with a magazine

When hard targets must be engaged over 1,000 meters away, the SF will turn to the Barrett M82A1 semi-automatic .50 caliber rifle. Here a member of the 5th Special Forces Group (Airborne) is inundated with the desert sand as he sends rounds down range. The M82A1 currently in the SF armory will soon be augmented with the M107 bolt-action, magazine-feed .50 caliber rifle.

Mark 19, 40mm Grenade Machine Gun is a self-powered, air-cooled, belt-fed, blow-back operated weapon. The MK19 is designed to deliver accurate, intense, and decisive firepower against enemy personnel and lightly armored vehicles.

holding up to 10 rounds of .50 caliber Browning machine gun (BMG) ammunition. These are group weapons and are drawn out per mission requirements. Now that the SF soldiers are in the new millennium, USASOC will add a new .50 caliber weapon to their Table of Organization and Equipment (T.O.& E). Each ODA will now be issued one Barrett M107 .50 caliber rifle. The M107 weighs 23 pounds, with a length of 45 inches. It can be reduced in size by further takedown of the weapon, allowing for more covert transport. Using a bullpup design, it is a bolt-action system with a removable five-round magazine, and is chambered for all NATO .50 caliber BMG cartridges. Other features include a quick-detachable bipod with spiked feet, iron sights, and an M1913 (Picatinny) optical rail to accommodate various sighting and aiming devices. The addition of the M107 to the T.O.&E. will give the Special Forces more punch, readily accessible to the A-teams.

Vehicles

GMV (Ground Mobility Vehicle)

The GMV has its origins in Desert Storm. During the Gulf War, the Special Forces modified HUMMVs for extended desert missions, dubbing them DUMMV (pronounced "Dum-Vee)." The modifications included a heavier suspension, more powerful engine, and an open bed and back for storage of water and fuel and other mission-essential item. The GMV has a cupola on top, similar to that used for mounting a tow system. It is used for mounting various weapons systems, e.g., M2, .50 caliber

The Ground Mobility Vehicle, or GMV, had its origins in Desert Storm. During the Gulf War, the Special Forces modified HUMMVs for extended desert missions, dubbing them DUMMVs, pronounced "Dum-Vee." The modifications included a heavier suspension, more powerful engine, and an open bed and back for storage of water and fuel and other mission-essential items. The GMV has a cupola on top, similar to that used for mounting a TOW missile system. It is used for mounting various weapons systems, e.g., the M2 .50 caliber machine gun and the Mark 19, 40mm Grenade Machine Gun.

The F470 Zodiac Inflatable Boat is the mainstay of water-borne operations with Special Forces. Extremely versatile, it can be launched from submarines and other boats. It can be air dropped via parachute or other deployment methods from an assortment of fixed- and rotary-wing aircraft. When using the outboard motor, the Zodiac is fast and quiet.

machine gun and the Mark 19, 40mm grenade machine gun.

Used by the SF Mounted Teams, the basic make-up is four GMV per team, with a crew of three men per vehicle. The GMV greatly enhances the capability of the mounted ODAs, extending their mission endurance and flexibility.

According the Colonel Gary Jones, Commander 3rd SFG(a), Mounted Team soldiers attend special schools, such as the Rod Hall

Advanced Military Off-Road driver training in the desert of Nevada. Here they are taught how to drive the GMV safely and effectively in on-road and off-road environments. The Special Forces soldiers learn techniques such as brake modulation, which allows them to work the ups and downs of the harsh environment and navigate over rocky, uneven terrain. The soldiers also learn how to maintain the vehicle and make necessary repairs in the field.

Zodiac Rafts

The F470 Zodiac Inflatable Boat is the mainstay of water-borne operations with Special Forces. Extremely versatile, it can be launched from submarines and other boats. It can be air dropped via parachute or other deployable methods from an assortment of fixed- and rotary-wing aircraft. When using the outboard

Wearing PVS7 Night Vision Goggles and carrying M4A1s, two members of the 3rd Special Forces Group (Airborne) infiltrate under the cover of darkness. The Klepper Arius 2 Military Canoe, more commonly referred to as a sea kayak, features speed and stealth. The canoe gives the lowest signature of all the surface vessels in use by U.S. Special Operations Forces.

motor, the Zodiac is fast and quiet. Each fuel bladder will allow the craft approximately one hour of operation with an average load of six men and equipment. The low profile and the fabric provide little or no radar signature to be detected by hostile forces. An interesting cache method that can be deployed in a team insertion is to totally submerge the Zodiac, caching the boat, outboard, and other equipment. Upon mission completion, the team will return to position, locate the boat and, using special compressed air tanks, reinflate it, power up the outboard, and exfil the area.

Klepper Arius 2 Military Canoe

The Klepper is more commonly referred to as a sea kayak. It possesses many of the Zodiac's advantages, except for air droppability and motor operations. The sea kayak features speed and stealth. Using the paddles, a crew of two can travel extended distances in a relatively short time. The canoe gives the lowest signature of all the surface vessels in use by U.S. Special Operations Forces. The two SF soldiers sit just below sea level with only their upper torsos elevated above the clandestine craft. Their Load Bearing Equipment and mission-essential equipment are placed in storage positions within the craft.

Snow Terrain Vehicle

For operations in snow-covered mountains, the Special Forces teams employ a snow terrain vehicle, "mil-speak" for snowmobiles. Currently in the inventory of the 10th SFG(A) are Polaris Model 600, wide track, 500cc machines. Each man on the ODA will have his own snowmobile, allowing the team to run split-team operations and provide backup transportation of team members should one of the snowmobiles break down or become disabled in combat. The SF soldiers load up the snowmobiles with kit gear, snowshoes, snow shovel, tent, and food. The M4A1 weapons are placed in an M1950 rifle case mounted on the side of the unit. Additionally, each member will carry a minimum of three five-gallon cans of fuel. One of the techniques employed by the 18Ds is placing IV bags in an

The Army calls it a Snow Terrain Vehicle, more commonly known as a snowmobile. This Polaris Model 600 is currently in use with the 10th SFG(A). Each man on the ODA has his own snowmobile, which he will load up with his kit gear, snowshoes, snow shovel, tent, and food. The M4A1 weapons are placed in an M1950 rifle case mounted on the side of the unit.

ammo can under the cowling next to the engine. In the event one must be used, it is not only not frozen, but warm so as not to lower the patient's body temperature when administered. Team members have also found this procedure useful for warming their Meals Ready to Eat (MREs). In addition to the snowmobiles, the teams also employ sleds called "Pulks" to carry their rucksacks and other mission-essential equipment.

Global Positioning System (GPS)

While all Special Forces soldiers are trained in land navigation using the standard issue Lensetic Compass, sometimes the A-team must have pinpoint accuracy, as when conducting an SR mission through the desert, or across the frozen tundra, in enemy territory, in the middle of the night. They will need to know the position of an enemy division, a radar station, or perhaps a SCUD when reporting in to headquarters. For such instances they will use a device known as a Global Positioning System or GPS.

The GPS is a collection of satellites that orbit the earth twice a day. During this orbiting they transmit precise time, latitude, longitude, and altitude information. Using a GPS receiver, special operations forces can ascertain their exact location anywhere on the earth. It is the same technology used by certain civilian automobile navigation services.

GPS was developed by the U.S. Department of Defense (DOD) in the early 1970s to provide a continuous, worldwide positioning and navigational system for U.S. military forces around the globe. The complete constellation, as it is called, consists of 24 satellites orbiting approximately 12,000 miles above the earth. These 22 active and two reserve or backup satellites provide data 24 hours a day for 2D and 3D positioning anywhere on the planet. Each satellite constantly broadcasts precise time and location data. Troops using a GPS receiver receive these signals.

Members of the 5th Special Forces Group (Airborne) call in the position of their Mission Support Site. Using the Rockwell "Plugger" GPS unit, they can convey their exact position to higher headquarters.

By measuring the time interval between the transmission and the receiving of the satellite signal, the GPS receiver calculates the distance between the users and each satellite. Using the distance measurements of at least three satellites in an algorithm computation, the GPS receiver provides the precise location. A special encryption signal is used in the military's Precise Positioning Service. A second signal called Standard Positioning Service is available for civilian and commercial use.

The Special Forces ODAs are issued the Rockwell "Plugger" or PSN-11. The precise name for the unit is PLGR+96 (Precise Lightweight GPS Receiver). The PLGR96 is the most advanced version of the U.S. DOD hand-held GPS unit. It serves the increasingly demanding requirements of the SF soldiers, as well as all the U.S. Special Operations Forces.

Secure (Y-code) Differential GPS allows the user to accept differential correction without zeroing the unit. Differential accuracy can be less than one meter. Other features of the "Plugger" include Wide Area GPS Enhancement for autonomous positioning accuracy to 4 meters CEP, jammer direction finding, targeting interface with laser range-finder, remote display terminal capability, and advanced user interface features.

Weighing in at a mere 2.7 pounds (with batteries installed) the GPS unit is easily stowed in the cavernous rucksack carried by the ODAs. In addition to hand-held operation, the PLGR+96 unit can be installed in various vehicles and airborne platforms.

For missions requiring underwater infiltration, there is the MUGR, Miniature Underwater Global Positioning System Receiver. This small device weighs 1.2 pounds and provides the team with position and navigational information needed for infil/exfil, fire support, Special Reconnaissance, and target location. Once the unit acquires the satellite fix, the waterproof MUGR can be taken to a depth of 33 feet. Alternately, the unit may work underwater employing the optional floating antenna.

SOFLAM

Special Operations Forces - Laser Acquisition Marker (SOFLAM). Special Forces soldiers would use this equipment in a direct action mission for the direction of terminal guided ordnance. This technique is referred to as "lasing the target." When it absolutely, positively has to be destroyed, you put an SF team on the ground and a fast mover with a smart bomb in the air; results—one smoking bomb crater. This newly issued laser marking

Communications is the lifeline of the SF team. Here a member of the 10th Special Forces Group (Airborne) uses the AN/PSC-5 (V) "Shadowfire" by Raytheon.

device is lighter and more compact than the current laser marker in service with the U.S. military. It can be used in daylight, or with the attached night vision optics it can be employed at night.

Radios

Communications is the lifeline of the SF team. For long-range communications, the Special Forces use the AN/PSC-5 (V) "Shadowfire" by Raytheon, issued two per ODA. The PSC-5 is a multi-band, multi-mission communication terminal with capability for UHF/VHF (Ultra High Frequency/Very High Frequency) Manpack LOS

Another useful communication device is the PRC-137. This ultra-lightweight HF radio is unique to Special Operations Forces. Using a small keyboard, the SF soldier will type in the message to be sent; it is then down-loaded into the radio. He then may continue on his mission. When the base station comes online, an automatic link will be established with the PRC-137 and the message will be up-loaded.

(Line-Of-Sight) and satellite communications (SATCOM). For satellite use, the set provides both TDMA (Time Division Multiple Access) and DAMA (Demand Assigned Multiple Access). This device supports the DOD requirement for a lightweight, secure, network-capable, multi-band, multi-mission, anti-jam, voice/imagery/data communication capability in a single package. The Shadowfire weighs 11.7 pounds without the battery, 8 pounds heavier with it.

For tactical intra-team communications, Multi-band Inter/Intra Team radios provide the SF teams with the ability to communicate on user-selected frequencies from 30 to 512 MHz using a single hand-held unit. The radios have power up to 5 watts in VHF/FM, VHF/AM, UHF/AM, UHF/FM(LOS) for ground-to-ground and air-to-ground connectivity. Weighing only 31 ounces, the radios come in two versions, immersible to six feet and 66 feet. The units have embedded COMSEC (Communications Security) for full digital voice and data operations. The MI/IT radio will replace the current AN/PRC-126, AN/PRC-68, Saber I/II/III, and MX-300 Series.

Rappelling

This old mountaineering technique has served SF troops since the first Special Forces soldiers operated in the mountains of Bavaria, near Bad Tolz, Germany. Whether working in a mountainous terrain, or in an urban environment, rappelling is a valuable skill. Often, traversing a steep hill carrying an 80- to 100-pound rucksack, it is the best way down the contour.

SF teams will train in this procedure with full combat gear, as well as rappelling with a casualty. Attaching to a regular military assault line through carabiners, or a specially designed rappelling device (known as a "Figure 8"), the team will negotiate down the side of a mountain like a mountain goat, or the side of a building as rapidly as Spiderman.

This member of the 7th Special Forces Group (Airborne) is suited up for a High Altitude Low Opening (HALO) parachute jump. HALO is one of the means by which SF teams can be inserted into denied or hostile territory. The jumpers are capable of exiting an aircraft at 25,000 feet using oxygen. They will then free fall to a designated altitude where they will open their RAPS and then form up together. This jumper has his rucksack strapped in front and his M4A1 attached to his left side, ready to go.

FRIES

The Fast Rope Insertion/Extraction System is the way to insert your assault force on the ground in seconds. This system begins with small woven ropes made of wool, which are then braided into a larger rope. The rope is rolled into a deployment bag and the end secured to a helicopter. Depending on the model of chopper, it can be just outside on the hoist mechanism of the side door or attached to a bracket off the back ramp. Once over the insertion point the rope is deployed and even as it is hitting the ground the ODA members are jumping onto the woolen line and sliding down, as easily as a fireman goes down a pole. Once the team is safely on the ground the flight engineer or gunner, depending on the type of helicopter, will pull the safety pin and the rope will fall to the ground. Such a system is extremely useful in the rapid deployment of Special Forces personnel. An entire ODA can be inserted within 12–15 seconds. FRIES is the most accepted way of getting a force onto the ground expeditiously. Unlike rappelling, once the trooper hits the ground, he is "free" of the rope and can begin his mission.

The second part of FRIES is the extraction method. Although both insertion and extraction systems were originally referred to as SPIES, or Special Procedure, Insertion & Extraction System, the Army has combined both methods into one term. While fast-roping gets you down quickly, there are times when you have to extract just as fast. The problem is, there is no Landing Zone for the Blackhawk of the 160th SOAR to land, and the "bad guys" are closing in on your position. This technique is similar to the McGuire and STABO rigs developed during the Vietnam War. Both used multiple ropes, which often resulted in the troops colliding with one another; the latter at least let the user fire his weapon while on the ride up. The techniques that served the Special Forces troops of the 1960s have been refined to the new FRIES method.

Fast Rope Insertion/Extraction System or FRIES is the fastest method of inserting Special Forces soldiers. An entire ODA can be inserted within 12–15 seconds. Once over the insertion point the rope is deployed and even as it is hitting the ground the ODA members are jumping onto the woolen line and sliding down, as easily as a fireman goes down a pole. Extremely useful in the rapid deployment of Special Forces personnel, FRIES is the most accepted way of getting a force onto the ground expeditiously. Unlike rappelling, once the trooper hits the ground, he is free of the rope and can begin his mission.

The second part of FRIES is the extraction method. Originally referred to as SPIES, or Special Procedure, Insertion & Extraction System, the system was changed by the Army to combine both methods. While fast-roping gets you down quickly, there are times when you have to extract just as fast. A single rope is lowered from the hovering helicopter. Wearing a special harness, the SF member or team attaches to the rope via snap links. Once the men are secure to the line, the helicopter will whisk the team out of harm's way. *Defense Visual Information Center Photo*

To extract with FRIES, a single rope is lowered from the hovering helicopter. Attached to this rope are rings, woven and secured into the rope at approximately five-foot intervals. There can be as many as eight rings on the rope. The SF soldiers, wearing special harnesses similar to a parachute harness, attach themselves to the rope via the rings. This is accomplished by clipping in a snap link that at the top of the harness. Once all team members are secured, a signal is given and the soldiers are extracted out of harm's way. This method allows the team members to maintain covering fire from their weapons as they extract. Once the SF soldiers have been whisked out of enemy range, and an LZ can be located, the helicopter pilot will bring the troops to ground again.

At this time they will disconnect from the rope and board the chopper to leave the area.

Rubber Duck

A "rubber duck" is the term SOF troops use to describe a mission involving deployment of a Zodiac raft. In a Soft Duck, a fully inflated Zodiac raft is deployed from the rear cargo ramp of a "NightStalker" MH-47 Chinook, or an AFSOC MH-53 Pave Low. The raft is slid out the back of the helicopter and the ODA follows right behind. Once in the water, the team jumps in, fires up the outboard engine, and heads out on its mission. An alternate to this is the Hard Duck, which involves a craft with a metal bottom delivered in the same manner as the Soft Duck. The Zodiac may also be

Members of the 3rd Special Forces Group (Airborne) perform a Rubber Duck operation from an MH-47E. Immediately after the Zodiac raft has cleared the ramp, the SF team will follow it out. Swimming to the raft, they will then load in and continue their insertion to their target area.

deployed via parachute, as would be the case when delivered via AFSOC assets such as a Combat Talon or Combat Shadow. Moments after the loadmaster releases the package, the SF troops will shuffle to the end of the ramp and parachute in after it. An additional method is the Double Duck, where two Zodiacs, fully inflated, are stacked and deployed via parachute together, again via the Hercules aircraft.

Delta Queen

While the Rubber Duck is used for inserting a SF team, the Delta Queen is a method for retrieval and extraction of the team. Upon mission completion the team will return to the Zodiac, and go "feet wet" into the water, whether an ocean, a lake, or river. The team will meet up with an MH-47E Chinook of the 160th Special Operation Air Regiment (Airborne). The pilot will bring his aircraft to a hover, then bring the heli-copter down, closer and closer to the water's surface. He will continue his descent until the rotary-wing craft actually rests on the water.

With the rear cargo ramp lowered, the MH-47E will begin to take on water. Wave after wave begins to cascade over the ramp and soon the flight engineers are standing in water over the tops of their boots. As the Zodiac begins to line up with the rear of the chopper, the crew member holds a red-filtered light to signal the team. The exfiltrating team guns the engine, ducks their heads, and aims for the ramp and the now-flooded fuselage. With a splash and a thud, the team is aboard and already the ramp begins to raise slightly. The pilot raises the behemoth aircraft from the surface, creating what looks like a small version of Niagara Falls as the water pours from the rear of the helicopter. The extraction complete, the NightStalkers and the Special Forces team or return to base.

"Mission complete. Request Exfil." Called a Delta Queen, the Night Stalker pilot of this MH-47E Chinook will set the large helicopter down so the aircraft is literally taking on water. Guided by members of the flight crew signaling with a flashlight, the SF ODA will then pilot the Zodiac up the ramp and into the fuselage. Once secure, the pilot will lift off and return to base.

CHAPTER 8

Special Forces in the 21st Century

When the Special Forces was formed in 1952, the biggest threat to world peace and democracy was from the Soviet Union. The A-teams of the 1950s practiced for Unconventional Warfare (UW) against the Russian "Bear" and made preparations to conduct guerrilla activities in World War III. With the collapse of the Soviet Union, there is a new perspective on warfare. The predication of World War III with masses of Soviet T-80 tanks rolling

Around the world, around the clock. Members of the U.S. Army Special Forces stand poised to defend freedom on a moment's notice. From the frigid Arctic winds to the humid, insect- and snake-infested jungles, the men of the Green Beret carry on in the tradition of their predecessors to defend liberty at all costs.

As the U.S. Army Special Operations Command advances further into the 21st century, the dynamic world of today will find the Special Forces soldier in the position of warrior, diplomat, and commando. Once shunned by conventional troops and commanders, the Special Forces today are in constant demand by U.S. ambassadors and theater CinCs.

across Europe has been replaced with discussions of Operations Other Than War (OOTW) and Small Scale Contingencies.

As the years have gone by the Special Forces have adapted to the geopolitical nature of warfare.

Whether preparing for all-out war or OOTW due to the regional instability around the world, they stand poised, mission capable to deploy, on a moment's notice, a threat-adaptive force. During the Cold War the U.S. deterrent to a nuclear holocaust was the Strategic Triad: Inter-Continental Ballistic Missiles in silos, Strategic Air Command bombers flying around the globe, and submarines on patrol. The Special Forces of the 21st Century comprise a new "Triad" for democracy: the Operational Detachment-Alphas (ODAs), the regional orientation of the teams, and the latest specialized equipment.

The Special Forces soldier of the 1950s and 1960s has evolved from a guerrilla/counter-guerrilla fighter to the consummate paragon of special operations. In today's dynamic world the Special Forces soldier is warrior, diplomat, and commando. Once shunned by conventional troops and commanders, the Special Forces today are in constant demand by U.S. Ambassadors and theater CinCs. The ODAs of this century possess strategic agility, ubiquitous presence, state-of-the-art equipment, and the latest intelligence for information dominance.

Strategic agility is the Special Forces' capability to meet the contingency needs of the regionally engaged CinC and Special Operations Command with forces based Outside of Continental United States (OCONUS) and forward-based forces.

Ubiquitous presence is evident in the forward deployed teams, e.g., Europe, Korea, and the Caribbean. In addition to these teams, there are regionally assigned SF Groups to support various engagement plans of the theater CinCs. This regional deployment creates a cultural exchange, establishes credibility, and builds trust and relationships between the SF soldiers and host nation forces. These Foreign Internal Defense (FID) missions can have long-term benefits. A sergeant that a SF team trains in patrolling today may be a

Special Forces ODAs are heavily engaged throughout the world. They are a highly relevant force of choice when circumstances require the use of small specialized teams. Capable of easy transition from peacetime to conflict, the SF teams are known as the "Quiet Professionals." These low-key forces are earning trust, building relationships, and establishing credibility around the world.

future colonel. That captain with whom they share a Meal Ready to Eat may someday be the leader of the country. By teaching these countries how to defend themselves, it may mean the United States does not have deploy multiple divisions of troops to an area. Establishing a warrior bond with these host nation soldiers may very likely create a strong ally for the United States in the future.

In addition to mastering the established conventional skills and military occupational specialties, SF soldiers are taught many special skills to develop the unique proficiencies that give them a wide variety of capabilities. They stand ready to execute their missions in any environment by any means of infiltration, air, land, or sea. This sergeant from the 7th Special Forces Groups (Airborne) in HALO equipment is ready to jump in to perform an FID, UW, SR, DA, or any other mission he is tasked.

The M2 Selectable Lightweight Attack Munition, or SLAM. Weighing a mere 2.2 pounds and small enough to fit in a BDU pocket, it is a low-volume, multipurpose munition. The M2 is self-contained, can be easily emplaced, and is compatible with other munitions for anti-material, anti-vehicular, and anti-personnel uses. It has four detonation modes, passive IR, magnetic influence, time delay, and command detonation.

Part of the Special Operation Forces Demolition Kit. This kit provides the SF soldier the capability to custom build, attach, and waterproof demolitions charges for specific target and operational scenarios. Seen here is the Explosive Form Penetration device or EFP. The device is packed with C4, thus creating a shaped explosive charge. For stability and deployment, it is placed upon a tripod. The EFP has a picatinny rail on the top; this allows an aiming device, such as an Aimpoint, in this case, to be attached. Once the target has been sighted in, the optical sight is removed and the EFP is set for detonation. This explosive device will penetrate concrete walls or rolled hardened armor.

I am an American Special Forces soldier. A professional! I will do all that my nation requires of me.

I am a volunteer, knowing well the hazards of my profession.

I serve with the memory of those who have gone before me: Rogers' Rangers, Francis Marion, Mosby's Rangers, the First Special Service Forces and Ranger Battalions of World War II, the Airborne Ranger Companies of Korea. I pledge to uphold the honor and integrity of all I am—in all I do.

I am a professional soldier. I will teach and fight wherever my nation requires. I will strive always to excel in every art and artifice of war.

I know that I will be called upon to perform tasks in isolation, far from familiar faces and voices, with the help and guidance of my God.

I will keep my mind and body clean, alert, and strong, for this is my debt to those with whom I serve. I will not bring shame upon myself or the forces.

I will maintain myself, my arms, and my equipment in an immaculate state as befits a Special Forces soldier.

I will never surrender though I be the last. If I am taken, I pray that I may have the strength to spit upon my enemy.

My goal is to succeed in any mission—and live to succeed again.

I am a member of my nation's chosen soldiery. God grant that I may not be found wanting, that I will not fail this sacred trust.

GREEN BERET

SYMBOL OF EXCELLENCE···BADGE OF COURAGE··· MARK OF DISTINCTION IN THE FIGHT FOR FREEDOM····PRESIDENT JOHN F. KENNEDY

The Green Beret is more than a headgear issued to graduates of the Q-Course. Today, as when it was adopted, it stands for liberty, freedom, and professionalism. The SF soldier who dons a beret colored forest green is a diplomat, a soldier, and a warrior. Ask a collection of SF soldiers, and they will tell you, "the beret is hot in the summer, and cold in the winter; but don't even think of taking it away. It's like the flag."

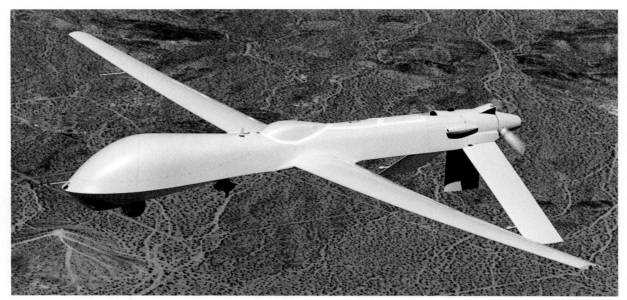

The RQ-1A Predator is a medium-altitude, long-endurance Unmanned Aerial Vehicle or UAV. This aerial craft is considered a joint forces air component, and is deployed for reconnaissance, surveillance, and target acquisition in support of the Joint Force Commander. More than a mere aircraft, the Predator is a system, equipped with color camera in the nose, a day variable aperture television camera, a variable aperture infrared camera (for low light/night). It is also equipped with a synthetic aperture radar for looking through smoke, clouds, and haze. The Predator UAV system can provide real-time imaging that will assist in the often unique missions tasked to Special Forces ODAs. *Photograph provided by General Atomics Aeronautical Systems, Inc.*

Good intelligence can mean the difference between success or failure, life or death, on the battlefield. Information Dominance is a focus of new technology to keep the Special Forces at the leading edge. Referred to as "Ground Truth," officially it is called "IT-21" for Information Technology for the 21st Century. It is designed to enhance Command and Control, Communication, Computers and Intelligence (C4I), and to ensure connectivity with joint, combined, and coalition forces, while maintaining situational awareness.

Today's SF team will deploy with the latest state-of-the-art equipment, yet it is constantly looking at ways to improve its edge in combat. For this purpose, U.S. Army Special Operations

Command (USASOC) has Lieutenant Colonel Daniel Moore, the G-7, Force Integration. The job of the G-7 is strategic planning, force structure, and equipment for the next decade to ensure the ODAs are appropriately equipped to meet future contingencies. From thermal underwater to body armor, from remote reconnaissance camera systems to complex combat simulations, if it will enhance the ODA, you'll find a file covering it on the G-7s PC.

New explosive devices are finding their way into the rucksacks of current SF ODAs—items like the M2 SLAM, or Selectable Lightweight Attack Munitions. The SLAM weighs a mere 2.2 pounds and is small enough to fit in the pocket of a battle dress uniform (BDU). The explosively formed penetrating warhead can pierce targets of 40mm rolled homogeneous armor out to 25 feet. It has four operating modes: Bottom attack (magnetic influence fuse)—as a vehicle passes over the M2, it will sense the magnetic signature and will detonate upward; Side attack (passive IR)—detonation occurs when sensing a passing vehicle's infrared signature; Time demolition of a target in four settings—15, 30, 45, and 60 minutes; and finally, Operator-initiated command detonation, using the standard Army blasting caps with the new time delay firing device (TDFD).

Another useful explosive device is the M150 Penetration Augmented Munition (PAM). The PAM is a lightweight man portable demolition device developed for special operations forces. It is compact at 33 inches, weighs 35 pounds, and can be emplaced by a single SF soldier. The primary use of the munition is against reinforced concrete bridge supports, piers, walls, and abutments. The munition can easily be carried in the rucksack or affixed to the soldier's Load Bearing Equipment without restricting his ability to walk, climb, rappel, or fast rope. It can be ignited by any standard military detonation device.

The PAM is hung against the target. The warhead consists of a forward charge, which cuts any rebar; a hole-drilling charge, which forms a hole in the target; and a follow-through charge, which is propelled to the bottom of the hole where it detonates. The explosion fractures the structure and results in a loss of at least 75 percent of the load-bearing capacity. The PAM's efficiency at destabilizing a structure allows two SF soldiers with two PAM units (70 pounds) to set up the devices and be ready to exfil in two minutes.

In the realm of information dominance, the G-7 shop is looking at the use of Unmanned Aerial Vehicles, or UAVs, to provide up-to-the-minute

Currently under consideration for possible addition to the SOPMOD kit is the Lightweight Shotgun System or LSS. Similar to the M-203, 40mm Grenade launcher, the LSS would be mounted under the barrel of the M4A1 Carbine. The LSS is a 12-gauge weapon that would most likely be carried by the point man, giving him an extra punch. It would also prove useful in the Special Forces Advanced Urban Combat role and Close Quarters Battle operations. *USASOC*

With the demise of the Soviet Union, the world is seeing numerous wannabe dictators and terrorist threats to U.S. and allied interests alike. The U.S. Army Special Forces are prepared for such contingency operations. By training its soldiers in the Special Forces Advance Reconnaissance, Target Analysis, and Exploitation Techniques Course, USASOC is mission capable of handling any threat. Pictured here is a terrorist's worst nightmare, a SFARTAETC trained stack ready to perform a dynamic entry.

aerial reconnaissance of the battlefield. A prime example of such a craft is the RQ-1A Predator UAV, manufactured by General Atomics Aeronautical Systems Inc. The Predator is a medium-altitude, long-endurance UAV. It is a Joint Forces Air Component Commander–owned theater asset for reconnaissance, surveillance, and target acquisition in support of the Joint Force command. The Predator UAV is equipped with a color nose camera, a day variable aperture TV camera, a variable aperture infrared camera for low light/night, and a synthetic aperture radar, for looking through smoke, clouds, or haze. The camera produces full-motion video and SAR still-frame radar images. The three sensors are carried on the same air frame but cannot be operated simultaneously. With a speed of 80 miles per hour and a range of 400 nautical miles, the Predator can loiter up to 25,000 feet for a period of 24 hours. With a gross weight of 2,250 pounds, this is definitely a support aircraft. However, USASOC is looking at the feasibility of small UAVs that could be carried into enemy territory in a rucksack. The small hand-held versions of the UAV could provide the team with immediate imaging of their AO.

Along with the UAV and numerous satellites with Multi-speed Transient Imaging (MTI), Multi-Hyper Spectral Imaging (HSI), and Synthetic Aperture Radar (SAR), NASA's shuttle missions have been used to map the world to within a meter. When you combine all of this input and run it through a simulator, you have an extremely accurate view of your target area. Throw in some blueprints and 3-D modeling software and you now have a full mission profile from insertion to exfil, all inside the computer. Teams can use such a simulation to actually plan their missions: What is the best route in? There, from the Northwest. Where is the best vantage point for the sniper? There, just beyond that outcropping of rocks. The team can even enter the building and recon, all from the safety of the simulator in the Isolation Facility. It is called "Virtual Recon." The unclassified look was amazing—one can only imagine what the classified version looks like.

Communications devices will also get a revamping as the technology improves. Eventually, we'll see the iridium phone and radio technology becoming so prevalent that instead of an ODA carrying a large PSC-5 and MBIIT radios, each SF soldier will have his own personal communication device small enough to fit into the pocket of the rucksack, or in an M16 magazine pouch. The device will have all the current features, including SATCOM communications with the Mission Support Site, CinC, group, or even National Command Authority, if necessary, all on a secure uplink.

One last item from the G-7 shop is fused imaging. This technology will combine thermal imaging with image intensifiers, day/night vision, integrated HUD (Heads Up Display) with a laser target reticle of the weapon, and a Global Positioning System microchip, all in one set of glasses. All of this technology is here today; it is just a matter of time before it is incorporated into a working unit.

Without a doubt USSOCOM and USASOC provide the best weapons and equipment for the men of the Special Forces Groups. Their efforts are paramount in providing the SF soldier with what is necessary not only for mission success, but also personnel survival. However, it is still the man on the ground that makes the difference—the sergeant who hoists a 150-pound rucksack on his back; the SFC who serves as the only U.S. military presence in a foreign country; the ODA that HALOs out of an MC-130 and lives in the bush for weeks, months, or longer. You only have to spend a short amount of time with the men who wear that woolen headgear and have that tab on their shoulder to understand that the Green Berets are warriors par excellence. Whether equipped with the SOPMOD M4A1, a SLAM and a UAV overhead, or a K-Bar, a block of C4, and a map, the SF soldier will execute his mission.

A command brief from the 7th SFG(A) lists the following SOF Truths: Humans are more important than hardware. Quality is better than quantity. Special Operations Forces cannot be mass produced. And, competent Special Operations Forces cannot be created after emergencies occur. With the experience gained over the years through sweat and blood, continuing in the heritage of those who have gone before, the Special Forces soldiers are trained, prepared, and equipped to operate in any environment, anywhere on the globe, anytime they are needed.

The Special Forces are a lethal, intelligent, decisive, and high-risk force for combat. Whenever needed, they will be ready to answer the call. The green beret remains "the symbol of excellence, a badge of courage" for the "Quiet Professionals" of the U.S. Army Special Forces.

Steeped in the heritage of the last five decades . . . armed with the lessons of those who gave the ultimate sacrifice . . . trained to master the art and science of unconventional warfare . . . ever vigilant to their creed and the motto, "De Opresso Liber," To Free The Oppressed: The men of the U.S. Army Special Forces remain the tip of the spear.

Glossary of Terms

AT: Antiterrorism. Defensive measures used to reduce the vulnerability of individuals and property to terrorism.

C4I: Command, Control, Communications, Computers, and Intelligence.

CinC: Commander in Chief.

Civil Affairs: The activities of a commander that establish, maintain, influence, or exploit relations between military forces and civil authorities, both governmental and nongovernmental, and the civilian population in a friendly, neutral, or hostile area of operations in order to facilitate military operations and consolidate operational objectives. Civil Affairs may include performance by military forces of activities and functions normally the responsibility of the local government. These activities may occur prior to, during, or subsequent to military action. They may also occur, if directed, in the absence of other military operations.

Clandestine Operation: Activities sponsored or conducted by governmental departments or agencies in such a way as to ensure secrecy or concealment. (It differs from covert operations in that emphasis is placed on concealment of the operation rather than on concealment of identity of sponsor.) In Special Operations, an activity may be both covert and clandestine and may focus equally on operational considerations and intelligence-related activities.

Close Air Support (CAS): Air action against hostile targets that are in close proximity to friendly forces. Each action requires detailed integration with the fire and movement of those forces.

Collateral special operations activities: Collateral activities in which Special Operations forces, by virtue of their inherent capabilities, may be selectively tasked to participate. The activities may include security assistance, humanitarian assistance, antiterrorism and other security activities, counter-drug operations, personnel recovery, and special activities.

Counterproliferation: Activities taken to counter the spread of dangerous military capabilities, allied technologies and/or know-how, especially weapons of mass destruction and ballistic missile delivery systems.

Counterterrorism: Offensive measures taken to prevent, deter, and respond to terrorism.

Covert Operations: Operations that are planned and executed so as to conceal the identity of, or permit plausible denial by, the sponsor.

Crisis: An incident or situation involving a threat to the United States, its territories, citizens, military forces and possessions or vital interests that develops rapidly and creates a condition of such diplomatic, economic, political, or military importance that commitment of U.S. military forces and resources is contemplated to achieve national objectives.

Direct action mission: In special operations, a specific act involving operations of an overt, covert, clandestine, or low-visibility nature conducted primarily by a sponsoring power's special operations forces in hostile or denied areas.

Ducks - Types of Zodiac deployments.
  Double: Twin Zodiacs
  Hard: Zodiac with hard metal bottom
  Soft: Zodiac raft

Exfiltration (Exfil): The removal of personnel or units from areas under enemy control.

First Line Belt: Specially designed webbing with shock cord inside, used when traveling on aircraft. One end has a standard carabiner, and the other end a quick-release carabiner.

Foreign Internal Defense (FID): Participation by civilian and military agencies of a government in any action programs taken by another government to free and protect its society from subversion, lawlessness, and insurgency.

Guerrilla Warfare: Military and paramilitary operations conducted in enemy-held or hostile territory by irregular, predominantly indigenous forces.

Host Nation: A nation that receives the forces and/or supplies of allied nations and/or NATO organizations to be located on, operate in, or transit through its territory.

Humanitarian assistance: Assistance provided by Department of Defense forces, as directed by appropriate authority, in the aftermath of natural or manmade disasters to help reduce conditions that present a serious threat to life and property. Assistance provided by U.S. forces is limited in scope and duration and is designed to supplement efforts of civilian authorities that have primary responsibility for providing such assistance.

Infiltration (Infil): The movement through or into an area or territory occupied by either friendly or enemy troops or organizations. The movement is made either by small groups or by individuals at extended or irregular intervals. When used in connection with the enemy, it implies that contact is avoided.

Insurgency: An organized movement aimed at the overthrow of a constituted government through the use of subversion and armed conflict.

Internal defense: The full range of measures taken by a government to free and protect its society from subversion, lawlessness, and insurgency.

Inter-operability: The ability of systems, units, or forces to provide services to and to accept services from other systems, units, or forces and use the services so exchanged to enable them to operate effectively together.

Low-intensity conflict: Political-military confrontation between contending states or groups below conventional war and above routine, peaceful competition among states. It frequently involves protracted struggles of competing principles and ideologies. Low-intensity conflict ranges from subversion to the use of armed force. It is waged by a combination of means employing political, economic, informational, and military instruments. Low-intensity conflicts are often localized, generally in the Third World, but contain regional and global security implications.

Maquis: Active guerrilla groups, World War II.

Military Civic Action: The use of indigenous military forces on projects useful to the local population at all levels in such fields as education, training, public works, agriculture, transportation, communications, health, sanitation and others contributing to economic and social development.

Mission: A statement of an entity's reason for being and what it wishes to accomplish as an organization.

Nation Assistance: Civil and/or military assistance rendered to a nation's territory during peacetime, crises, or emergencies, or war, based on agreements mutually concluded between nations. Nation Assistance programs include, but are not limited to, security assistance, FID, other DOD Title 10 programs, and activities performed on a reimbursable basis by federal agencies or international organizations.

NCA: National Command Authority. The President and the Secretary of Defense together, or their duly deputized alternates or successors. The term signifies constitutional authority to direct the Armed Forces in their execution of military action.

Objectives: Specific actions to be achieved in a specified time period. Accomplishment will indicate progress toward achieving the goals.

Operator: See "Shooter."

Psychological operations: Planned operations to convey selected information and indicators to foreign audiences to influence their emotions, motives, and objective reasoning, and ultimately the behavior of foreign government, organizations, groups, and individuals. The purpose of psychological operations is to induce or reinforce foreign attitudes and behavior favorable to the originator's objectives.

Ranger Assist Cord: 550 parachute line, used to attach anything and everything to an operator.

Shooter: Special Operations Forces trooper, e.g., U.S. Army Special Forces, U.S. Navy SEAL, U.S. Army Ranger, SAS (British or Australian), etc.

Special Reconnaissance: Reconnaissance and surveillance actions conducted by special operations forces to obtain or verify, by visual observation or other collection methods, information concerning the capabilities, intentions, and activities of an actual or potential enemy or to secure data concerning the meteorological, hydrographic, or geographic characteristics of a particular area. It includes target acquisition, area assessment, and post-strike reconnaissance.

Strategy: Methods, approaches, or specific moves taken to implement and attain an objective.

Unconventional Warfare (UW): A broad spectrum of military and paramilitary operations conducted in enemy-held, enemy-controlled, or politically sensitive territory. Unconventional warfare includes, but is not limited to, the interrelated fields of guerrilla warfare, evasion and escape, subversion, sabotage, and other operations of a low visibility, covert, or clandestine nature. These interrelated aspects of UW may be prosecuted singularly or collectively by predominantly indigenous personnel, usually supported and directed in varying degrees by (an) external source(s) during all conditions of war or peace.

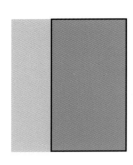

Abbreviations

ARSOC	Army Special Operations Command
AT-4	Anti-Tank Weapon
CAS	Close Air Support
CIA	Central Intelligence Agency
COIN	Counterinsurgency
COMINT	Communications Intelligence
CSAR	Combat Search And Rescue
CT	Counterterrorism
CQB	Close Quarters Battle
DA	Direct Action
DAM/T	Direct Action Mission/Team
DIA	Defense Intelligence Agency
DOD	Department of Defense
DZ	Drop Zone
E&E	Evasion and Escape
ELINT	Electronic Intelligence
FID	Foreign Internal Defense
FOB	Forward Operation Base
FOI	Forward Operating Location
FRIES	Fast Rope Insertion/Extraction System
GPS	Global Positioning System
HAHO	High Altitude High Opening
HALO	High Altitude Low Opening
HE	High Explosive
HUD	Heads Up Display
HUMINT	Human Intelligence
INTREP	Intelligence Report
JCS	Joint Chiefs of Staff
JSOC	Joint Special Operations Command
JSOF	Joint Special Operations Forces
JSOTF	Joint Special Operations Task Force
JUWTF	Joint Unconventional Warfare Task Force
LBE	Load Bearing Equipment
LZ	Landing Zone
MFP	Major Force Program
MGF	Mobile Guerrilla Force
MPU	Message Pickup
MRE	Meal Ready to Eat
MTT	Mobile Training Team
NOD	Night Optical Device
NVG	Night Vision Goggles
OPCON/M	Operational Control/Command
OPSEC	Operational Security
PSYWAR	Psychological Warfare
SEAL	Sea Air Land (U.S. Navy Special Operations Forces)
SAR	Search and Rescue
SAS	Special Air Service
SBS	Special Boat Squadron
SF	Special Forces (U.S. Army)
SFAUC	Special Forces Advanced Urban Combat
SFARTAETC	Special Forces Advanced Reconnaissance, Target Analysis & Exploitation Techniques Course
SFOB	Special Forces Operating Base
SOCOM	Special Operations Command
SOF	Special Operations Forces
SOFLAM	Special Operations Forces Laser Acquisition Marker
SR	Special Reconnaissance
SWS	Sniper Weapon System
USASOC	U.S. Army Special Operations Command
USASFC	U.S. Army Special Forces Command
UW	Unconventional Warfare
WM	Weapons of Mass Destruction

DELTA
AMERICA'S ELITE COUNTERTERRORIST FORCE

TERRY GRISWOLD AND D.M. GIANGRECO

Preface

**This is another type of war, new in its intensity, ancient in its origins—
war by guerrillas, subversives, insurgents, assassins . . . seeking victory
by eroding and exhausting the enemy instead of engaging him.**

President John F. Kennedy, 1962

The success of Fidel Castro's Cuban revolution in 1959 and rising tide of insurgencies around the globe made it clear to newly elected President of the United States John F. Kennedy that the focus of communist expansionism had shifted to the Third World. Kennedy firmly believed that the communist's ominous Cuban foothold in the Western Hemisphere could be countered by a program aimed at stimulating peaceful evolution instead of violent revolution. His response to the communists' challenge was the Alliance for Progress.

The Alliance for Progress was a serious effort to promote stability in Latin America through political reform, as well as economic and social development, and it served as a model for similar US commitments in other less–developed regions. Embryonic communist insurgencies threatened this evolutionary process, and Kennedy moved quickly to blunt their threat by devising and implementing a doctrine of counterrevolutionary warfare. More than thirty years later, the descendants of his elite, unconventional warriors continue to assist dozens of potential or fledgling democracies while specifically tasked, direct–action arms of the Army, Navy, and Air Force stand ready to fight an insidious by–product of Third World instability and the recent Cold War: terrorism.

In the years following the Iran hostage crisis and disaster at *Desert I*, a great deal has been written on the 1st Special Forces Operational Detachment–DELTA. Most of the focus has been on the origins of the failed rescue attempt, the major players, technical problems, and in some cases, the strategic and tactical leadership of the units involved. However, the guts and backbone of DELTA and similar units is the individual trooper. For the most part, he is typical of those in the special operations community.

But there is more to the soldiers who make up DELTA. Each man is a self–starter who not only displays personal initiative but can work well when part of a team. They are mature individuals, confident in themselves and their unit, who are unquestioned experts in their craft. These qualities are more than just factors in what makes a good DELTA trooper, they are the essence of DELTA. And while most of the unit's officers stay around long enough to learn the art of counterterrorist (CT) operations, it is still the old hands, the highly professional noncommissioned and warrant officers, that keep DELTA on the straight and narrow. This story examines CT training and operations from their viewpoint: the elite special operations team members who must wade into the dirty business of counterterrorism to protect US lives and interests.

In a free—and financially strapped—society, there is immense pressure on units costing the taxpayer millions of dollars to produce and show results. Because of the clandestine nature of DELTA's mission, however, the full story of this extraordinary and sophisticated unit cannot be told no matter how important its unique capabilities are to the ongoing war against international terrorism. This relative anonymity makes DELTA an easy target for congressional budget cutters searching for a "quick fix" and the unit may well find itself as an expensive toy up for funding cuts in the austere future. Such actions would be disasterous.

The information in this book is based upon the research and experience of the authors and does not represent the positions or policies of any official, agency, or department of the United States government, British government, or any other government. The information was derived from unclassified publications and sources and is intended to neither confirm or deny, officially or unofficially, the views of those governments.

Uncredited photos in this book were taken by US armed forces personnel and are in the public domain. The names of current DELTA troopers are classified and, unless otherwise noted, all names given for soldiers below the rank of colonel are pseudonyms.

Chapter 1

Out of the Desert

The takeoff had to go right the first time. There would be no second chance. As the last item on the pre–flight list was checked off, the pilot revved up the EC-130E's Allison turboprops to gain maximum power. Releasing the already–straining brakes and pushing the throttles to the firewall, the pilot nursed his aircraft slowly forward out of the jumbled mass of wheel ruts furrowed deeply into the Iranian desert. The straining engines created a mini sandstorm that all but obliterated the ghastly funeral pyre they were leaving behind. Resembling some prehistoric bird of prey, the dark Hercules sluggishly lifted away from the makeshift desert runway and the disaster that Operation *Eagle Claw* had become.

This aircraft was one of the last special operations birds leaving Iran after the aborted rescue attempt to free American hostages in Teheran. The Ayatol-

---

RH-53D Sea Stallions from the USS *Nimitz* practicing low–level formation flying before the attempted rescue of American hostages in Iran.

---

lah Khomeini's Revolutionary Guards had held their fifty–three prisoners in the captured US Embassy compound for nearly six months and the half–dozen Hercules had been slated to play a key role in rescuing them. Now, as five heavily loaded aircraft flew into the early morning darkness, an EC-130E tanker and RH-53D Sea Stallion helicopter lay blazing in the desert. Through the swirling sand, passengers with portholes could clearly see what each had never believed possible: failure. Despite well–laid plans, the team's efforts had ended in an inferno of exploding ammunition and twisted, burning aircraft.

What happened at the refuel site code–named *Desert I* has been argued about and even embellished in a Hollywood adventure film, but the basic facts remain the same. The six special operations aircraft that penetrated Iran on the night of April 24–25, 1980 were configured either as tankers to re-fuel the Sea Stallion helicopters or as transports to bring in the assault teams and their ground support. After reaching the site, the mission was scrubbed

and the force had to prepare for exfiltration.

The decision to abort was made after three of the eight Sea Stallions either failed to reach *Desert I* or could not proceed because of mechanical difficulties. Not enough helicopters were available to carry out the mission, so there was nothing for the rotary and fixed–wing aircraft to do but return to their separate starting points. In preparation for the exfiltration, one of the RH-53Ds had to be repositioned. During that maneuver, the helicopter's main rotor smashed into the cockpit of a parked EC-130; both aircraft erupted into flame, and the explosions turned the stark desert night into a ghastly beacon. During the hasty evacuation of the site, the remaining Sea Stallions were left behind.

On board the EC-130E were members of America's newly formed counterterrorist unit known simply as DELTA. The unit had been activated in November 1977 but was untested or, as military professionals would say, "unblooded," and this was to be their first operational mission. But while the troopers anticipated that their baptism of fire would soon come in Teheran, they instead found themselves trapped in a terrifying inferno fed by thousands of gallons of aircraft fuel. As one of the survivors would later report, the DELTA Blue Team troopers and air crew from the stricken EC-130 struggled to "unass the muther" as best they could, bearing their injured with them.

Caught in the tanker's burning, smoke–filled cargo bay, Master Sergeant Leonard M. Harris was quickly overcome by smoke as he attempted to rescue an Air Force crewman. Luckily for both men, they were pulled from the burning plane by other members of DELTA.

Harris and the other survivors were loaded into various aircraft for the trip out. Now, as the last Hercules flew in a rough trail formation through the inky darkness toward the Indian Ocean and safety, Harris began to regain consciousness. Watery eyes fixed on a light on the cabin roof and then wandered down to scan the confusion around him in the crowded cargo bay. DELTA troopers, dressed in Levis, boots, and black field jackets, were interspersed with air crews, combat control team members, and other support personnel. Some sat in stunned silence, still wearing their woolen naval watch caps, while others were stripping off layers of body armor, web gear, and sweat–stained clothing. Checking his own physical condition, Harris was surprised that, despite his brush with death, the only damage that he was able to perceive, other than a raw throat from smoke inhalation, was a good singeing of his field jacket and a relatively minor burn across the back of his left hand.

Looking down at his recently black–dyed field jacket, he absently picked at the melted tape that covered the only insignia on the assault teams' tactical uniforms: a small American flag sewn on the right jacket sleeve. The troopers were to have displayed the flags after entering the Embassy grounds so that the hostages would readily follow them out during the exfiltration. After all, in their uniforms, the rescue team looked more like muggers in a New York subway than members of an elite counterterrorist unit.

Peering across the red–lighted cargo compartment, Harris realized that he and the rest of the passengers were sitting, lying, or in some other way trying to get comfortable while riding on the bouncing fuel bladder covering the length of the plane. While team medical personnel provided aid, others appeared to be sorting out what had happened to them. Regaining a sense of stability, Harris was

---

(**Top**) RH-53D Sea Stallions on the aft hangar bay of the USS *Nimitz* before launch and (**left**) a burned–out hulk at *Desert I*. Note the .50cal machine guns mounted in the cabin doors at the extreme left and right of the top photo. *Wide World Photos*.

helped into a sitting position by another trooper. He noticed that his palms were wet with sweat, and not really knowing if it was from fear or just shock, he wiped them on his faded Levis. Leaning his head back against the cold metal skin of the Hercules, he muttered, "Good ol' Herky Bird." The vibration and steady hum of its engines made him think of his airborne instructors at Fort Benning, Georgia. "Damn if they weren't right," he thought. "The 130 *is* a living creature."

In the absence of the fear and pain that fatigue brings, he began to reflect on the events that brought him to this godforsaken situation. "How in the hell did I get in this mess?"

The Reception Committee

As the last of the special operations aircraft lifted off from the chaos of *Desert I*, another intense drama was taking place in the Iranian capital. From a clandestine communications site well outside Teheran, Dick Meadows, a highly decorated and skilled former Green Beret, received word of *Desert I's* disaster. His vulnerable advance party of Special Forces soldiers had infiltrated the city only a few days earlier under various cover stories designed to hide all traces of their true identity and mission. Now, however, events beyond their control had forced them to immediately execute their own escape and evasion plans.

Nearly six months before *Eagle Claw*, on November 4, 1979, "subject matter experts" from all relevant military and civilian agencies were drawn to-

Revolutionary Guard checkpoints in Teheran surreptitiously photographed by Army personnel. They are armed with a variety of 7.62mm Heckler & Koch G3 rifles manufactured in Iran under a license obtained from the West German firm. (**Top**) A Revolutionary Guard is carrying several weapons to comrades up the street while, (**left**) the mountains ringing Teheran are clearly visible.

gether to form an ad hoc joint task force (JTF) charged with both the planning and execution of the hostage rescue. Like so often in the military, the "old boy" network was initially used to fill the JTF. This approach brought in many talented people whose broad range of expertise at first quickened the planning phase of the operation. Unfortunately, though, interservice and interdepartmental bickering soon created coordination problems. Despite later denials, virtually everyone either wanted a piece of the action or seemed intent on distancing themselves from the operation. The resulting problems—demonstrated by the initial lack of cooperation from the Central Intelligence Agency (CIA) and State Department officials—tended to frustrate rather than facilitate planning by the JTF's staff officers under the stewardship of Major General James B. Vought, a highly respected paratrooper who had much experience working with Rangers.

Ideally, CIA operatives would have already been in the "area of interest" providing current intelligence and would have been responsible for obtaining critical items such as "safe houses" and locally procured trucks in Teheran. However, at this time in its history, the agency was undergoing a number of reorganizations prompted by highly publicized criticism of its role in major incidents going back as far as the Bay of Pigs invasion of Cuba. Sensational reports of alleged assassination attempts on foreign leaders, Vietnam's numerous "black" or covert operations (including the unjustly maligned *Phoenix* program), and the increasing number of former CIA employees who turned into authors of "tell–all" books added to the growing public perception of a bumbling group of spies running amuck.

After Jimmy Carter assumed the presidency in 1977, he installed a fellow Annapolis graduate, Admiral Stansfield Turner, to oversee the restructuring of the CIA and the institution of his administration's "Georgia approach" to governmental man-

142

agement. Under Turner, hundreds of experienced personnel were laid off (referred to in the government's bureaucratic language as a reduction in force or RIF). The agency soon became heavily dependent on mechanical and technical means as the primary method of intelligence gathering instead of using them in conjunction with, or as a complement to, human intelligence collection, or HUMINT. By the time the Embassy in Teheran was seized, Middle Eastern operations were in a major decline; in fact, the last full–time operative in Iran had already slipped into the warm embrace of retirement.

Despite the CIA's reinfiltration of one of its agents into Teheran, DELTA's thirst for intelligence on a broad range of matters was not satisfied. The "black boxes" were clearly failing to produce the information required to carry out this delicate operation, and the *Eagle Claw* planners in DELTA began to look within the special operations community for HUMINT collection means to make up the shortfall. The search led them to Dick Meadows.

(**Top**) A mass demonstration at "Freedom Square" on Eisenhower Avenue about a half–dozen miles west of the US Embassy. In the unlikely event that Iranian mobs would react quickly enough to threaten the rescue mission, an orbiting AC-130H Specter gunship would perform "crowd control" around the embassy and prevent the armored vehicles based at an army ordnance depot to the north and the police headquarters near the Ministry of Foreign Affairs to the south from intervening. If the Specter found itself hard–pressed to keep the threats at bay, a second gunship covering Mehrabad International Airport to the west, would destroy Iranian F-4 Phantom jets, capable of chasing down the rescue aircraft, and assist at the embassy. (**Left**) A Revolutionary Guard bunker in central Teheran. The broad avenues which criss–crossed the capital, such as Roosevelt, which ran between the embassy and the soccer stadium and north to the army depot, were fed by an intricate—but well–mapped—maze of narrow streets fully or partially blocked by these randomly placed defensive positions.

This was not the first time that Meadows had participated in an effort to free US prisoners. Ten years before, he had been in charge of the compound assault team during Operation *Ivory Coast* (more commonly known as the Son Tay Raid), an airborne assault on a prisoner of war camp only twenty miles from Hanoi in North Vietnam.* Other exploits in Southeast Asia included the capture of North Vietnamese artillery pieces in Laos and the recapture of a major CIA outpost in that same country. He was an expert in what are referred to as "low–visibility insertions" and "takedowns."

Meadows had become a civilian advisor to DELTA after retiring from the Army, and his extensive background in clandestine cross–border operations, as well as his completion of the British Special Air Service (SAS) selection course, carried a great deal of weight in choosing him to enter Teheran ahead of the rescue force. Above all, the JTF planners knew he could be trusted to do his best to accomplish the mission––and, besides, he knew DELTA inside and out. This knowledge, however, could prove to be a rather negative aspect of his qualifications if he were caught.

Meadows' orders were to infiltrate the chaos of Teheran, establish a safe house, locally procure covered trucks to transport the rescue force, and guide the rescuers from the landing zone to their assault positions near the Embassy. In military terms, he was the reception committee and, on paper at least, this part of the operation was one of the less–complicated portions of the entire plan. One critical concern of Meadows was his cover and its associated background information and the story

---

*The over four dozen US prisoners were held at the camp but were moved shortly before the raid and remained in captivity until after the 1973 signing of the Paris Peace Accords. One side benefit of the operation, however, was an accidental attack on a nearby compound that apparently killed as many as 200 East Block or Soviet specialists involved in upgrading North Vietnam's air defenses.

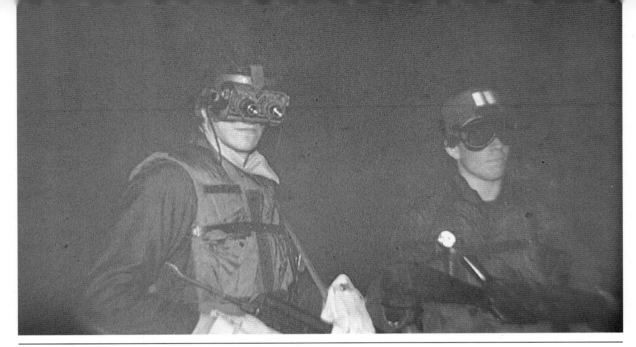

A force of a dozen US Army Rangers and DELTA members made up two teams to secure the road running through the *Desert I* refuel sight. (**Above**) Troopers armed with a Colt M16 assault rifle and Walther MP-L submachine gun peer intently through the night. The relatively heavy PVS-5 night vision goggles, used during the operation, could only be worn for about thirty minutes at a time before a pilot or trooper would have to hand it off to a designated partner to wear. Within minutes after they rode their Yamaha motorcycles out of the belly of the first MC-130 to land, the team captured a bus with forty–four Iranian civilians, blew up a gasoline tanker truck with a light antitank weapon, and ran off another truck.

Although *Eagle Claw* planners were later criticized for establishing the refuel site in a moderately traveled area, mission parameters left them little choice, and DELTA planned to fly any Iranians taken into custody back to Misirah Island on the returning MC-130s. The Iranians would then be flown back to Iranian territory and released at Manzariyeh Air Base the following night. There were never any plans to hold any detained Iranians in exchange for the US hostages (such a move would have had disastrous political repercussions), and if the mission were aborted after they had been flown from *Desert I*, the Iranians would be speedily turned over to the International Red Cross for repatriation.

fabricated to explain what brought a Westerner to this hostile land. CIA liaison officers supplied him with an Irish background, including all the necessary documentation and accessories, while the JTF provided additional backups and an enhanced language capability in the form of three sergeants recruited in Germany, two from a covert Special Forces unit and one from the Air Force.

Unlike Meadows, these men already had covers and were conducting their daily lives under that blanket of anonymity. All were foreign–born nationals who had joined America's armed forces and were now US citizens. One of the men was a native of Germany and was intimately acquainted with the murky world of working with and supporting intelligence requirements levied on the Army by other agencies such as the CIA. Another of the operatives was born in the British Isles and was easily cloaked with the mantle of a Scottish background. The third (who had undergone no previous Special Forces training) was a native of the Middle East and was fluent in Farsi, the primary language of Iran. These men would provide Meadows with the additional skills required of the advance party.

When it was discovered, rather late in the planning, that three high–ranking hostages were being held in the Ministry of Foreign Affairs building six miles from the Embassy, an additional thirteen soldiers were recruited from a clandestine unit in Germany. Not enough time was available to change the basic plan as well as shift existing personnel to other targets, so it fell upon these men to fill the operational void created by the last–minute intelligence. Special Forces detachments like theirs had been preparing to fight potential Soviet invaders in the extensively built–up areas of western Germany since the late 1950s and were composed of experts in urban warfare.

Eagle Claw's mission profile called for the advance team to rendezvous with the DELTA rescue force staging out of a little–used airfield near Qena, 300 miles south of Cairo in central Egypt. Upon receipt of the execution message, the 132 men of the rescue force and additional support personnel flew on two C-141s from Egypt to an air base operated by British and Omani personnel on the large Arabian Sea island of Misirah. At the same time, the helicopter element located on the aircraft carrier USS *Nimitz* "patrolling" nearby in the Gulf of Oman prepared to launch its RH-53D helicopters to an isolated spot, code–named *Desert I*, in Iran's Dasht–e Karir (Salt Desert). While all this was taking place, a contingent of four AC-130E and H Specter gunships were readied for their launch the following night. They would fly directly from Qena to Teheran where they would support the rescue. The Specters would be refueled by KC-135 tankers as they passed over Saudi Arabia.

The next phase of the operation called for DELTA's surgical assault force, along with its security and support element, to take off from Misirah in EC- and MC-130Es of the 8th Special Operations Squadron.

Their destination, *Desert I,* had already been surveyed by an Air Force Combat Control Team member who placed remotely operated infrared beacons along the "hasty" landing strip. After the force successfully rendezvoused at *Desert I* near Garmsar, 265 nautical miles southeast of Teheran, the assault element was to load onto the helicopters and fly on to *Desert II* in the rugged, mountainous region just southeast of the capital. Once there, the choppers would be hidden nearby, at a site codenamed *Figbar,* while the assault force linked up with the reception committee before dawn.

The assault force would settle in for the day while the DELTA commander, Colonel Charlie A. Beckwith would infiltrate Teheran along with a select group of twelve troopers who would receive the trucks gathered by Meadows' team near the city at a secure warehouse called the "Mushroom." It was their job to drive the small convoy out of the city on the second night of the operation and collect the rest of the rescue force from the hide site. After transferring to the six large, tarpaulin–covered Mercedes trucks and a Volkswagen van, 106 DELTA and Special Forces troopers would journey to the capital where final preparations for the impending rescue would be made. The plan called for the rescue force to depart from *Desert II* at 2030 hours and be in their designated assault positions by 2300 hours. Meadows would take Colonel Beckwith on a personal reconnaissance of the target before the attack at approximately the same time that the AC-130s were lifting off in Egypt.

The main assault group's three teams (code–named *Red, White,* and *Blue*) and Foreign Ministry assault group would use the principles of surprise, shock, and coordinated movement to take out the Ayatollah's Revolutionary Guards. As soon as the short, violent rescue operation erupted at the walled Embassy compound, the hidden RH-53D helicop-

(Top) An M151 roars over a a sand dune in Egypt. The soldiers given the mission of guarding the dirt road running through *Desert I* were not picked until after the main body of Rangers, slated to seize Manzariyeh Air Base, had arrived at Qena, Egypt. Intensive training was immediately begun for both the road–watch and airfield–seizure teams. (Above) Before operations could begin, Air Force ground personnel had to be flown into both Qena and the British–Omani air base on Misirah Island to set up communications and logistics for the thirty–four special operations tankers, transports, and gunships involved in *Eagle Claw*.

ters would emerge from their camouflaged position near *Desert II*. One would head for the large park surrounding the Foreign Ministry, while the rest would fly to sites at the rear of the Embassy compound and the Amjedeih soccer stadium across the street, where both hostages and rescuers would be picked up. If the compound site couldn't be cleared of obstructions in time, all extractions would be conducted from the stadium.

Throughout the ground phase of the operation, one AC-130 gunship would orbit over the target area providing fire support, and another would cover the two Iranian F-4 Phantom jets on strip alert at Teheran's nearby Mehrabad International Airport. Two additional Specters would orbit close by in reserve. All parties concerned were fully confident that the massive firepower the Specters could bring to bear on the surrounding area would be more than enough to suppress any Revolutionary Guards attempting to reinforce their Embassy security force and prevent the infamous Iranian mobs from interfering with the rescue. As one of the gunship pilots was later to explain, the Specters' awesome firepower was the "best crowd–control measure" available.

While the AC-130s dominated the area, the helicopters would leave the chaos of Teheran for nearby Manzariyeh Air Base only thirty–five minutes away. Manzariyeh was to have already been secured by a seventy–five–man Ranger contingent and support personnel flying directly from Qena on four MC-130s. This elite light infantry unit was composed of experts in airfield seizure. Using M151s (commonly, if erroneously, referred to as jeeps) and commercial off-road motorcycles, they were capable of gobbling up the sprawling but lightly defended facility in a matter of minutes.

Throughout the exfiltration, F-14A Tomcat fighters and KA-6D Intruder tankers from the USS *Nimitz* would orbit over Persian Gulf waters—on call to knock down any hostile aircraft coming after the vulnerable transports, and gunships leaving Manzariyeh. If all went well, the entire force—Rangers, Special Forces, Meadows' team, support personnel, DELTA, and their newly rescued char-

Sea Stallions receiving preflight preparations on the deck of the USS *Nimitz*. The RH-53Ds had been freshly painted to mimic the look of Iranian helicopters and also carried green, white, and red Iranian identification roundels that could be added to further confuse prying eyes.

ges—would be quickly loaded aboard a pair of C-141s, which had made a quick dash from Dhahran, Saudi Arabia, and exfiltrate to Qena before the Iranians could take any effective countermeasures. There was no way to fly the helicopters out of Iran, and they were to be destroyed before the last Rangers left the airfield.

The catastrophe at *Desert I* changed all that. After Meadows received word over a clandestine radio to abort the mission, he notified the team, which dispersed from the safe house, and all made their individual ways to the passenger terminal at Teheran's Mehrabad International Airport. Security within the terminal was visibly increased. Unshaven and clad in an irregular mix of civilian and military clothing, the pride of Iran's Revolutionary Guard nervously paced back and forth near entrances, fingering their newly acquired Heckler & Koch G3 rifles. The menacing looks—as well as a healthy respect for the weapons' stopping power—caused Meadows to give each of the guards a grudging deference. Swallowing hard, Meadows entered the terminal entrance and walked directly to the Swiss Air ticket counter. Very deliberately, and somewhat slowly, he reached into the inner pocket of his corduroy jacket for the cash necessary to open the

first of many doors to the waiting jet and freedom.

While being processed, he noticed that his "Scottish" comrade was in another part of the terminal area, being heavily questioned by a combination of Revolutionary Guards, customs officials, and men in soldiers' uniforms. Meadows later learned that the large amounts of US currency that had initially brought this unwanted attention to the Scotsman stayed in Iran with that "interested" group of officials. The newfound hatred of the "Great Satan" obviously did not extend into financial matters, and well-placed bribes of American greenbacks continued to do the trick.

Reaching down to retrieve his carryall, Meadows realized that despite the fact that word had been received about an "invasion" to the south, the security efforts within the airport remained disjointed and uncoordinated. Walking at a casual but determined gait toward the Swiss Air jet, he wondered what things were like at the Embassy.

Chapter 2
A New Game in Town

Kill one and terrorize a thousand.

Sun Tzu, 500 BC

Festering Arab resentment of America's direct and substantial support of Israel grew steadily after the United States became the Jewish state's chief sponsor in the wake of the 1967 Six Day War. By 1973, when massive American arms shipments played a critical role in blocking an Egyptian–Syrian victory in the Yom Kippur War, the United States was firmly planted on a collision course with the rising tide of pan–Arab nationalism. From now on, Americans would no longer be incidental victims of terrorist attacks. They would be the targets.

During the Six Day War, the sweeping successes of the Israeli military machine made it clear to the Arab world that change could not be guaranteed by conventional forces alone. One of the key audiences watching from the sidelines with a great deal of interest were the millions of Palestinians living in forced exile not only in the Middle Eastern countries, but also in Europe. Across the Atlantic, the United States was focused on the problems of the war in Vietnam, internal strife centered on the civil

rights movement, and there was growing unrest on college campuses. Against this background, the United States hoped that every effort would be made to solve the numerous long–standing issues in the Middle East peacefully. Failing that, preventing disagreements from boiling up into open warfare was the least that could be strived for. But as world affairs would have it, the Palestinian issue exploded to the surface, amid smoke and gunfire, in the Hashemite kingdom of Jordan.

When shoved into a corner by Soviet–sponsored, Syrian–armed Palestinian forces intent on using his country as a staging area for raids on Israel, King Hussein ibn–Talal used his army to drive the Palestinians into Syria and reasserted his authority. The king and his Hashemite followers had never enjoyed an easy relationship with the various *fedayeen* groups making up Yasir Arafat's Palestine Liberation Organization (PLO), and its military arm, the *Fatah*, which was openly encroaching on the country's control of the Jordan River Valley. One faction, George Habbash's Popular Front for the Liberation of Palestine (PFLP)—the largest and most anti–Hashemite of the *fedayeen*—had worked feverishly to undermine Hussein's throne

---

One of the terrorists holding Israeli athletes at the Munich Olympics relays demands to German negotiators in front of millions of television viewers.

Television crews and reporters line the balcony of the Beirut International Airport terminal during the nine–day hijacking of a TWA jet, June 22, 1985. The media was—and continues to be—one of international terror-ism's most important weapons. *Wide World Photos*

long before the bloody confrontation.

The intense fighting for the capital of Amman and across northern Jordan in September 1970 caused a great deal of worry in the Western world, and supplies were sent in from a number of countries. Military forces were also alerted to move in and provide help, but the Jordanian Army succeed-ed without them. This stunning defeat of the *Fatah*–led Palestinians, however, laid the ground-work for the emergence of full–fledged terrorist or-ganizations such as Black September, a radical group that operated as an arm of the "moderate" PLO until it split off on its own. The name itself commemorates the *fedayeen's* expulsion from Jor-

dan, and they took their revenge on the man who directed King Hussein's forces, Premier Wafsi Tal, by assassinating him the following year in Cairo.

While terrorists have never hesitated at murder-ing any Arab leader who was not in strict agree-ment with the dogma of their particular group, it is generally not considered socially acceptable to blame other "brother" Arabs for their numerous defeats to Israel. The fledgling terrorists saw the Western world as the cause of virtually all Arab problems—whether perceived or real—and several factors combined to make Western Europe an ex-cellent target for their activities. Initially, these countries made particularly juicy targets because of their close proximity to the Middle East and the fact that their open societies allowed the terrorists. a remarkable degree of freedom to carry out their activities.

These new terrorists were also a particularly media–savvy bunch who fully understood the rami-

The grand finale of the Palestine Liberation Organization's September 1970 hijacking of three civilian airliners. Their 300 passengers were held for a week and, after their release, the aircraft were blown up at an abandoned airfield near Amman, Jordan.

fications of the still–evolving revolution in global telecommunications. Recent advances in television technology allowed the terrorist networks to increase their range beyond the printed word of newspapers, and much of the world's population now lived with their acts as a daily fact of life. Ratings–conscious news agencies and the viewers themselves had enabled the television camera to become one of the terrorists' chief weapons.

The use or threat of violence against individuals to affect a much larger, related group is not a new phenomenon; what is call "terrorism" today is a tactic of warfare that has been employed throughout history. Bombing, hijacking, assassination, and kidnapping are simply facets of this type of warfare magnified a thousand–fold by the electronic media. In the early 1970s, the world was introduced to such new television stars as Black September* and the Baader–Meinhoff Gang. Their activities were caught on television in 1970 when several commer-

cial airliners were hijacked and taken with their 300 passengers and crew to Dawson Field, a desert airfield 40 miles from Amman that had formerly been used by Britain's Royal Air Force. After a week, the hostages were removed from the aircraft which were then blown up in full view of the world. But the event having the deepest and most far–reaching impact was the drama which unfolded at the 1972 Olympic Games in Munich, West Germany.

*One of the many organization names used by Sabri Khalil al–Banna (alias Abu Nidal) in an effort to sow confusion in the West as well as make the "armed struggle" against Israel appear larger than it is. In addition to Black September, other names used by the Abu Nidal Organization include: Fatah Revolutionary Council, Black June Organization, the Arab Revolutionary Brigades and Revolutionary Organization of Socialist Muslims.

Viewers were stunned by image after image of the wanton murder of innocents flashing across the screen, and governments in the West soon felt their power to control events slipping from their hands. Terrorist actions—or even the threat of such actions—were increasingly shaping policy decisions on major questions.

One ramification of these terrorist attacks not observed by the public was the new requirements

As an instructer looks on, a member of SAS takes position and returns fire against mock terrorists during a training exercise. He is positioned behind the engine block, which can provide adequate protection against most conventional pistol and rifle ammunition.

placed on international law enforcement and military forces. After the failure to negotiate or rescue successfully for the release of the Israeli athletes, West Germany's security needs were scrutinized from every possible angle with Teutonic efficiency. The findings were many, but the realists who would have to face the next round of fighting concluded that virtually every Western nation was now in the battle with this ancient form of warfare. The emergence of a new combatant—the counterterrorist—marked Western Europe's response.

Each country dealt with the new problem based on its own perception of how various political, economic, social, and, in some cases, religious factors af-

fected security considerations. The Germans established a special unit within its border police—later presented to the world as GSG-9, short for *Grenzschutzgruppe 9*—and the French formed the *Groupe d'Intervention de la Grendarmerie National* (GIGN). The British turned to their old standby, the SAS, while the Americans took the approach of wait and see, or more typically, "This will not happen to us." Yet, as the world continued to spin through the early 1970s, it was painfully obvious that the terrorists were moving a step or two ahead of the various national security forces and could attack whenever or wherever it was to their advantage. The organizations established to blunt terrorist attacks would, however, soon prove that they were forces to be reckoned with.

In October 1977 at Mogadishu Airport in Somalia, the German GSG-9 took revenge for their country's embarrassment at Munich by accomplishing a difficult aircraft "takedown" in response to a hijacking. Unknown to the terrorists, the Germans had learned much from the tragedy of Munich, and, with the help of two SAS commandos who blew open the aircraft's doors, a thirty-man GSG-9 force stormed the plane during the early morning hours. Later, in May 1980, the SAS gained international fame by conducting one of the most daring and highly publicized hostage rescues, when Pagoda Troop of B Squadron, 22nd SAS Regiment, launched their spectacular assault on the Iranian Embassy in Princess Gate, London, as television cameras broadcast the action around the world.

Preceding these events was the most famous rescue operation of the period: the raid on Entebbe Airport in Uganda, conducted by the Israeli special forces. Launched from bases within their own borders, more than 2,500 miles to the north, the commandos of Unit 269 flew directly into the site where 103 hostages were held. In the early morning darkness of July 4, 1976, Operation *Thunderbolt* was

Great Britain's 22nd SAS and US Special Forces have enjoyed a long, close relationship which began in earnest during the late 1950s. (**Above**) Lieutenant General Sir Charles Richardson, Britain's Director General of Military Training, inspects an SAS unit during an exercise with 5th and 7th Special Forces Groups at Camp Troy, North Carolina, September 28, 1962. General Richardson's visit turned out to be a pivotal event for the SAS. While the conservative British military establishment had grudgingly conceded the regiment's value in certain situations, the unit was generally thought of as little more than a "private army" of ill–disciplined mavericks that skimmed some of Britain's best soldiers from the top of traditional regiments. A tour with the SAS could kill a young officer's career.

At Camp Troy and Fort Bragg, Richardson witnessed SAS troopers studying advanced demolition and field medicine techniques plus engaging in specialized training in foreign languages, as well as a worldwide assortment of weapons. He left North Carolina greatly impressed with what he saw, and the almost immediate improvement in the attitude of the British military establishment toward the SAS was credited to the general's glowing report.

The same month that General Richardson visited SAS elements training in the United States, the US Special Forces soldier who would later found DELTA, Charlie Beckwith, was leading a troop from A Squadron, SAS, in a combined exercise with the French "paras" of the *1st Bataillon de Parachutistes de Choc* in Corsica. Beckwith had been attached to the regiment as part of an ongoing exchange program and, in 1963, would ship out to Malaya with the SAS to take part in deep–jungle penetration missions against guerrillas along the Thai border. The tour nearly cost him his life but, upon his return to Fort Bragg, he pushed hard (very hard) to have SAS training and organizational techniques adopted by Special Forces.

Israeli commandos, circa 1960, are representative of the high degree of individuality commonly found in elite special operations units. Informally dressed in a variety of military jackets, coats, scarves, and sweaters, they are a diverse lot with members who might easily pass themselves off as Britons, Arabs, Frenchmen, or Americans. Indeed, they may have once been Britons, Arabs, Frenchmen or Americans before emigrating to Israel. Such elite troopers from Unit 269 were responsible for the successful hostage rescue at Entebbe. Note the use of personal weapons of different types and calibers attuned to the taste of the individual soldier. The soldier in the center is armed with the standard Soviet assault rifle of the day, the 7.62mm Kalashnikov AK-47, while the others carry 9mm Uzi submachine guns, which were based on earlier Czechoslovakian weapons but designed and produced in Israel.

carried out with clockwork precision. Keeping it simple, the rescue force landed in four C-130s (why jump your men in when they can be landed in a nice neat package?). The lead Hercules casually taxied to within 200 yards of the terminal building holding the hostages, and a black Mercedes sedan—the standard mode of transportation of all Ugandan officers from company commander on up—rolled serenely down the ramp. The sedan cruised up to the brightly lit building, followed by a pair of nondescript Land Rovers, and suddenly disgorged nine Unit 269 commandos.

Within minutes, the Israeli strike force had secured the terminal area and airfield perimeter, removing a potential problem by blowing up the Ugandan MIG fighter aircraft and then loaded up the rescued hostages. The rescue force commander, Colonel Jonathan Netanyahu, was killed, as well as the entire terrorist gang and an undetermined number of Ugandan soldiers protecting the hostage takers. All but one of the hostages, an elderly woman who had been taken to a hospital and was later murdered, were quickly freed and flown to Nairobi, Kenya, where casualties were transferred to a waiting jet airliner equipped for medical emergencies. The GSG-9 chief, Colonel Ulrich Wegener, had also accompanied the Israelis, probably because two West German terrorists were involved in the hijacking.

Americans Become Targets

The United States entered the CT arena as a very unwilling participant. The primary reasons were America's deeply engrained tradition of keeping military and police powers well separated and the resultant conservative approach of the US military leadership when dealing with what they felt was inherently a police problem. Neither the political nor military hierarchies originally supported the view, held by many in the lower echelons, of the increasing danger to the United States and its interests by media-savvy terrorists.

US intelligence agencies gained their first direct lessons from the *nouveau* terrorists during the September 1970 uprising in Jordan. It was feared that *Fatah* insurgents would seize the US Embassy in Amman, and US paratroopers were alerted to, if necessary, seize the International Airport, allow an armored force to land, race into Amman and retake the Embassy.

As with Operation *Eagle Claw* some ten years later, the Jordanian rescue plan was complicated, unwieldy, and fraught with unnecessary risks. For example, the 509th Airborne Infantry, which was selected to seize the airport, would have had to fly to Jordan via an extremely lengthy, circuitous route from their staging area in West Germany. Instead of taking the normal route over continental Europe to reach the eastern Mediterranean, their operational plan called for a flight out into the North Sea and Atlantic Ocean around Spain to the Gibraltar slot, and then travel the length of the Mediterranean. The force would have to take this roundabout route because the "allies" of NATO would not grant overflight rights—a situation unpleasantly similar to what F-111 pilots would find sixteen years later during a retaliatory raid on Libya for sponsoring a terrorist bombing.

American planners were faced with a number of similar situations over the next two years, and missions were not approved for execution. Either White House or State Department jitters prevented the launching of airborne or Special Forces units to counter terrorist assaults. Terrorist networks in the Middle East, however, could easily strike soft targets and continued to target Israeli citizens. Americans stationed in Germany, as well as West Germans, found themselves the targets of former antiwar students now turned terrorists. In May 1972, the Baader–Meinhoff Gang, also known as the Red Army Faction, finally forced the issue on the United States by conducting six separate bombings.

Their targets were such sacred areas as the officers' club in Frankfurt and the headquarters building of US Army, Europe, located in the sleepy university town of Heidelberg. The news media provided some coverage of these strikes but, understandably, only a fraction of the blow–by–blow reporting which characterized the debacle of that year's Olympic Games.

While the taking of American hostages was not yet a problem, perceptive military leaders realized that the United States needed to be ready and able to respond to terrorism, and units within the Army's Special Forces community were tasked to conduct rescues using what is commonly referred to as the "hasty option response." In lay terms, this means that if the hostage takers begin to harm their prisoners, the team attempts a rescue as quickly and efficiently as possible. The lives of the hostages are of utmost concern, but the hasty response does not allow for the meticulous planning, coordination, and rehearsals that are required to carry out the surgical strikes so often associated with the highly skilled CT units. The hasty response is the operation that all counterterrorists hope they never have to conduct. It is the option that makes a commander wake up at night in a cold sweat.

Due to command relationship conflicts and the numerous constraints on personnel and funds, which prevent in–depth training, the hasty option mission is still found in a number of Army Special Forces groups around the world. This approach, however, leaves little for the in–depth training required to perfect even the most fundamental aspects of aircraft or room entry techniques.

Soon after Munich, a number of American military and civilian advisors recommended that a suitable force be established to fight terrorism. But it was not until the increased threat was brought home to President Jimmy Carter and the feasibility of creating a unit like those who struck at Entebbe

The aftermath of a Red Army Faction car bomb explosion at Rhein–Main Air Base outside Frankfurt, West Germany, August 8, 1985. Over twenty people were injured and the blast killed one US airman and the wife of another. The explosives were packed into a car with forged US license plates and driven to the parking lot outside the headquarters of the 435th Tactical Air Wing. It is believed that the terrorist who drove the vehicle gained access to the base by using the identification card of a US serviceman murdered the previous night.

and Mogadishu that the United States acknowledged the need to establish its own full–time, state–of–the–art counterterrorist response unit. The success of Operation *Thunderbolt* further confirmed the idea that many US planners had been fostering. The United States needed to have a small, surgical force capable of carrying out such operations. It was their contention that, despite the claims of the airborne community, Ranger companies and battalions were neither trained nor equipped for hostage rescues.

From the smoke of military infighting and political intrigue, 1st Special Forces Operational Detachment–DELTA was formed in 1977. Its name is derived from standard Special Forces terminology. Six ALPHA detachments (A teams), commanded by captains, make up a company–sized BRAVO detachment (B team), commanded by a major. A CHARLIE detachment (C team) is a battalion–sized organization commanded by a lieutenant colonel. Since the 1st Special Forces Operational Detachment was commanded by a full colonel and structured along completely separate lines, following the squadron–troop structure of Britain's famed SAS, it became a DELTA detachment. Using the concept of the troop and the squadron as the building block or base, it initially trained to conduct counterterrorist operations. Recent activities in Iraq and Kuwait, however, reveal that DELTA's one–dimensional media image of a super–secret counterterrorist team falls well short of reality. The 1st Special Forces Operational Detachment is a multifaceted unit much like its counterpart, the SAS.

DELTA and *Blue Light*

Both DELTA's sponsors and opponents within the military held firm—and diametrically opposed—ideas on who should respond to the terrorist challenge. The majority of DELTA's sponsors were typical of America's military leadership. They were extremely conservative officers who were slow to respond to the terrorist threat, but once convinced that it was very real indeed, they were bulldogs in their support of the unit. And, like its sponsors, those who had worked hard to undermine or sidetrack DELTA (primarily because they didn't understand the nature of the threat) eventually gave it their full support when ordered.

At the top was Army Chief of Staff General Bernard Rogers. This astute Kansan and Rhodes scholar watched as the armies of Great Britain and West Germany rapidly took on what most American policymakers refer to as "police powers" normally kept out of the military's hands. After the Carter White House made it clear that they wanted a unit with specialized capabilities, Rogers gave his blessing for DELTA's formation. He told the relevant senior planners that he wanted the unit operational—and wanted it now!

The individual most instrumental in DELTA's birthing process was Lieutenant General Edward C. "Shy" Meyer. As the Deputy Chief of Staff for Operations, he was one of the most influential senior officers on the Army staff. It was from his office, that plans and policy for how the US Army would operate were issued. General Meyer took a direct, personal interest in DELTA. From the time that the need for a counterterrorist force was identified through its birth and Operation *Eagle Claw*, Meyer was always present in some form, providing guidance and support. The rest of the Army may have called him "Shy," but to DELTA he was "Moses" because he always seemed to be able to part the waters for them.

Next in the line of supporters came General William DePuy, commander of the Training and Doctrine Command. General DePuy was *the* expert in training; even though he was as conventional a soldier as any, he clearly recognized that a force was needed "like the SAS," as he was often quoted as saying during major policy meetings. He had to be won over before General Rogers and others could be addressed, but that proved to be easy after his inquiries about similar organizations in Europe demonstrated that an effective CT unit could be formed within the US Army. He would provide the training support.

The remainder of the cast were found at Fort Bragg, North Carolina. Fort Bragg has often been referred to as "home of the airborne" because of the vast numbers of parachute and related units based there. Bragg was also the home turf of the members of the US Army's Special Forces. The individuals making up these organizations possess unique skills, and it was from this elite body that DELTA's supporters and opponents would come.

The architect of DELTA was the commandant of the Special Forces School: a gruff veteran of the guerilla wars in Southeast Asia named Colonel Charlie Beckwith. Not only did "Chargin' Charlie" have a wealth of experience in the realm of unconventional operations, but he also knew who the power brokers were and how to use them. For example, in 1975, when General "Iron Mike" Healy was reassigned from his command at the John F. Kennedy Special Warfare Center at Fort Bragg, his replacement was Major General Robert "Barbed Wire Bob" Kingston. Kingston's association with Beckwith could be traced back to the days when Beckwith was an exchange officer with the SAS and Kingston was with the British Parachute Regiment. The two had also just served together at the Joint Casualty Resolution Center in Nakhon Phanom, Thailand, in 1973–1974. Kingston would work closely with General Meyer to establish an SAS–type unit.

It was during Colonel Beckwith's tour as commandant that the special operations community watched Europe's response to the outrages of various extremist groups. Located in an area known as "Smoke Bomb Hill," members of the Special Forces refined their traditional skills and added the hasty response to their repertoire. Special Forces, however, were responsible for carrying out a wide range of missions and could not dedicate much of their training efforts toward hostage situations.

Other soldiers who lent their guidance and support during this critical period were the commander of the 10th Special Forces Group, Colonel Othan "Shali" Shalikashville; General Frederick J. "Fritz" Kroesen, of Forces Command, who controlled all units stationed in the United States; and the XVIII Airborne Corps's chief of staff, Brigadier General James Lindsay. At one point during DELTA's shaky beginning, Shalikashville lined up all his senior commissioned and noncommissioned officers and told them flatly, "The job that Colonel Beckwith has to do is more important than the job we have to do. I would encourage anyone who has the desire to try out for this unit." As for Lindsay, when General Kingston's successor refused Beckwith's request to move DELTA into Bragg's underutilized post stockade, he saw to it that the unit would get it, reasoning, "Here we've got a nice stockade facility where we're keeping eleven bad guys. . . . Why don't we take the eleven and put them downtown in the Fayetteville jail? Your use of the stockade is better than the use it's being put to now. Colonel, you've got it!" Beckwith was obviously pleased that his problem had been solved so quickly but believed that the general would never see another promotion because he was just too practical. Ten years later, however, Lindsay would wear a total of eight stars on his shoulders and become the commander of the newly created Special Operations Command responsible for providing combat–ready special operations forces for rapid deployment to other unified commands around the world.

Still, support of the special operations community was not very strong at this point. Meticulously trained Special Forces units had conducted numerous missions during the Vietnam War, but now there was not a need for such specialists—or so the conventional leadership thought. And the conventional leadership controlled the Army and downsizing in forces that was taking place. Providentially, control of Special Forces fell to the commander of the JFK Special Warfare Center, and since General Kingston, his boss, was in control, Beckwith had the degree of freedom required to bring DELTA on line.

Charlie A. Beckwith of DELTA, circa 1979.

Complaints by the Rangers that DELTA would deepen their current manpower problems (partially true) and that the unit duplicated some of their functions (untrue) were brushed aside early on. Beckwith's only real opposition came from the commander of the 5th Special Forces Group at Bragg, Colonel Robert "Black Gloves" Montell, who believed that the shoot–from–the–hip hasty response was perfectly adequate. Montell was one of the Army's most professional and experienced officers. Always impeccably dressed, he wore what was commonly referred to as the "Bad Tolz" uniform. With pistol belt stripped and worn over olive drab jungle fatigues, spit–shined jungle boots, and an ever–present pair of black gloves topped off by the coveted green beret, he provided even the most hard–eyed professional with a source of pride in those days after Vietnam.

About the time that the DELTA program seemed to be a sure thing, Kingston was transferred to Korea, and Major General Jack "Bobo" Mackmull assumed command. No doubt Mackmull had received his marching orders from Washington to keep the program on track, but as a West Pointer and aviator, he was not very familiar with the missions and capabilities of this strange little unit under his command and, unfortunately, made little effort to learn. Once DELTA was approved for activation, Mackmull was told to come up with a backfill unit until DELTA was certified for operations some two years in the future. Montell's 5th Special Forces Group received the nod.

To meet this requirement, Montell selected forty Special Forces troopers from within the community and trained them in hasty response techniques. This unit was code–named *Blue Light*. Operating under the principle that a bird in the hand is worth two in the bush, Mackmull threw his weight *Blue Light's* way regarding both funding and personnel. Despite reassurances from insiders, it appears that Beckwith feared that Montell's stalwart professionals would derail DELTA before it had a chance to prove its concept. If Beckwith lost his support in Washington, he would lose his unit. And DELTA was truly his.

As with most endeavors, it is not necessarily who is the best qualified, but who has the most support. Initially, that is what kept DELTA and its concept of a full–time, low–visibility CT organization alive. When General Rogers discovered that expected resources were being routed away from DELTA, he, as they say, "went ballistic." From that point on, through the support from the chief of staff on down the line, DELTA was allowed to gain the necessary breathing room to grow from nothing to a full–fledged force.

After 1st Special Forces Operational Detachment–DELTA was activated in October 1977, Beckwith had to select and train his new unit. DELTA troopers would have to be able to blend perfectly into the civilian world, when required, and possess unique skills that included everything from the relevant military arts to climbing the sides of buildings and hot–wiring cars. As luck would have it, DELTA had just completed their certification exercises. The date was November 4, 1979.

Weapons and Equipment

Pistols

In the special operations community, an oft–repeated comment on the controversy over which round is better, the .45cal ACP (automatic Colt pistol) or the 9mm parabellum, goes like this: "Opinions are like assholes, everyone has one." Stopping power, mass versus velocity, number of rounds versus weight—the argument seems neverending but, over time, weapons firing the 9mm (.38cal) round have become respected additions to DELTA's arsenal.

Modern conventional warfare generally calls for relatively light–weight, high–velocity rounds such as the Colt M16's .223cal/5.56mm or NATO's standard .308cal/7.62mm, that are effective out to ranges of several hundred yards. For the takedown of a hostage holding site, however, 100 feet is considered an extreme range. What the counterterrorist needs is a heavy slug that will knock a man down with as few shots as possible, and rounds smaller than .45cal have often proven themselves to be inadequate against a determined enemy. As early as the beginning of this century, Moro warriors battling US soldiers in the Philippines were not stopped by government issue .38cal pistols and, most recently, in the GSG-9 operation against aircraft hijackers at Mogadishu, Somalia, the German commander was forced to empty his snub–nosed .38cal into a psyched–up terrorist who continued fight even as six bullets ripped into his body. For this reason, many operatives prefer to have a bigger weapon.

A big (*very* big) round like that from the Smith & Wesson .44cal Magnum will drop a hijacker in his tracks but, unfortunately, the high–powered bullet is likely to go through its intended target as well as several seats and passengers before it stops. Moreover, the .44 Magnum's substantial kick when firing can delay reacquisition of the same or other targets—possibly with disastrous results. The .45 ACP round fired by the Colt or Springfield Armory M1911A1 and other automatic pistols has a great advantage over its famous friend during takedowns. An old joke among shooters is that the .45's bullet travels so slowly that, for an instant, you can actually see it speeding towards the target. With such a low muzzle velocity—at roughly 830 feet per second, it's almost half that of the .44 Magnum—hostage safety is greatly increased since there is more likelihood that the captors' bodies will stop the bullets.

But while this would seem to make the .45 the obvious weapon of choice for takedowns, many shooters have gravitated to the 9mm Beretta Model

---

(**A**) The basic Colt 5.56mm M16A2 assault rifle, (**B**) Colt 9mm submachine gun, and (**C**) Colt 5.56mm Model 733 Commando assault rifle. (**D**) The Mossberg 12–gauge Cruiser 500 shotgun; (**E**) the Remington 7.62mm M40A1 sniping rifle mounting a ten–power US Marine Corps telescope instead of the Redfield twelve–power telescope commonly used by DELTA; and (**F**) the Springfield Armory 7.65mm M21 sniping system based on the M14 rifle. (**G**) The Beretta 9mm Model 92F pistol, called the M9 by the US Army and (**H**) the Colt .45cal M1911A1 automatic pistol. (**I**) The General Motors Guide Lamp Division .45cal M3 submachine gun often described as "a pleasant gun to shoot"; (**J**) the Walther 9mm MP-K submachine gun, which served as a useful bridge between the M3 and (**K**) the Heckler & Koch 9mm MP5 submachine gun. (**L**) The Heckler & Koch 9mm MP5 SD3 submachine gun with integral silencer.

When DELTA was formed, its armorers developed special lighting equipment that could be attached to weapons for night operations. Today, such devices can be obtained off-the-shelf from manufacturers or are integral to the weapons. (**Top**) A Hensoldt aiming point projector fitted to a Heckler & Koch MP5 A2 submachine gun and (**bottom, lower left**) a laser pointer built into the forearm of a Mossberg 12-gauge shotgun. Also note the Stabo rings attached to the soldier's tactical vest and the flash/bang grenade (an SAS invention) ready for use in his left hand.

92 pistol. The high velocity of its 9mm parabellum slug is easily brought below 1,000 feet per second by reducing the round's charge, and, depending on which variant of the Model 92 is carried into a fight, the counterterrorist can count on making almost twice as many shots before reloading than he would if he carried a conventional .45cal automatic.

The automatic pistol made by Colt and the higher-quality product manufactured by the Springfield Armory, normally fire from eight- and seven-bullet magazines respectively, and can each carry an additional round in the chamber, while the Model 92 and its variants have thirteen- and fifteen-round magazines. The tradeoff is that while 9mm bullets are indeed smaller, their size is *adequate* and the Model 92 has more of them. Moreover, the ammunition a DELTA trooper carries on his body and in his weapon is all that he can count on having available

to him during a takedown. If everything goes as planned, there will be very little shooting. If the operation "goes sour," its just DELTA and the terrorists in a high–intensity shootout of unknown duration. A situation can easily develop where the first side to run out of bullets loses and, with a weight nearly half that of a .45cal bullet, 9mm rounds can be carried in great quantity without encumbering a trooper.

Submachine Guns

The same holds true, of course, for submachine guns. Although pistols are preferred in most hostage situations, submachine guns become a necessity when large target areas or many terrorists (four and up) are involved. DELTA initially settled on the domestically produced .45cal M3A1 "grease gun," a World War II vintage weapon that went out of production in the early 1950s and was generally shunned by the US Army. Interestingly enough, though, the very features that made it unpopular with most soldiers, enabled it be an extraordinarily effective tool for room–clearing: a low muzzle velocity which allowed its heavy slugs to slam into— not through—a terrorist and a rate of fire slow enough to enable single shots to be squeezed off

The Heckler & Koch MP5 SD3 fires 9mm ammo and, with its collapsing stock and integral silencer, it is an outstanding weapon for the closein fight. The sound supressor is a two–stage external silencer. The first stage of the system will absorb gasses while the second absorbs the muzzel blast and flame. The bolt noise is absorbed by buffers made of rubber. If you use subsonic ammo, the report cannot be heard more than fifteen to twenty feet away.

without disturbing the shooter's aim.

Acquiring adequate replacement parts for the weapon was an armorer's nightmare, however, and the old friend soon made way for a variety of submachine guns. Selection of weapons is a personal choice that often revolves around such factors as weight, reliability, how often must you clean it between firings, amount of ammo per magazine, and accuracy after it has been beat up in a parachute jump. The Heckler & Koch MP5 and the less expensive, easily concealable Walther MP-K are both German arms that fire 9mm rounds, as does the Colt submachine gun that has many parts common to the M16 rifle. The compact Colt Model 733 Commando assault rifle also benefits from this commonality and can be used on missions requiring its higher velocity 5.56mm round.

Trooper in southeastern Iraq armed with a Colt Model 727 carbine. Note the troopers sterile uniform (no identification or other markings) and longish hair. A three–power telescopic site is mounted on the carbine.

Shotguns

Shotguns are also useful in a variety of situations but are most commonly associated with forced entry techniques. Heavy rifled slugs can be depended on to supply the pure smashing power needed to quickly and efficiently blow the hinges off most doors. Sabot rounds, on the other hand, allow deeper penetration of the target and are best employed

against vehicle or aircraft engines and door–locking mechanisms. After initial entry has been gained at a hostage holding site, shotguns can be used to force additional doors or, if necessary, against the hostage takers.

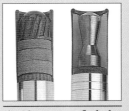

A 12–gauge rifled slug (**left**) and 12–gauge sabot slug (**right**).

Ammunition

Terrorists cannot be reasoned with and will attempt to kill their captives if a rescue is attempted, so when choosing ammunition, CT specialists want a man stopper that will knock a terrorist down and keep him down. While the heavy .45cal remains an ideal round for hostage situations, the lethality of smaller slugs, like the 9mm, can be greatly enhanced by using "soft–point" bullets with hollow or flat tips. The unusual point causes the soft, lead slug to expand into a broad, mushroom–shaped projectile upon entering the body, often doubling in diameter and increasing its shock effect dramatically. In a war where the armed forces of one nation are openly pitted against those of another, the rules of land warfare prohibit the use of such ammunition. DELTA troopers participating in a hostage rescue, however, are not subject to the restrictions of the Geneva Convention. Like their police counterparts, they can legally use hollow–point ammunition (or exploding rounds that shatter on impact) to subdue captors and save the lives of the hostages.

(**Left** to **right**) Flat–point, hollow–point and conventional bullets.

The actual weapons and ammunition used on a mission are determined by the nature of the target.

A takedown of an oil platform, for example, is a very different affair from that of an airliner cabin crowded with hostages sitting upright. Only the team members assaulting areas likely to contain the platform's captive crew need to worry about carrying weapons with limited velocity.

Advances in technology have also complicated matters for DELTA and other CT specialists by adding dangerous factors to the equation such as handguns and bombs with almost no metal parts. Initially, only law enforcement agencies and the military had access to the lightweight body armor made from Kevlar fabric (which, incidentally, does *not* set off metal detectors). Over the passage of time, however, this type of highly effective armor has greatly proliferated and, if not already in terrorist hands, can be easily obtained by third parties or simply stolen. When worn in thin, easily concealable layers, Kevlar will stop the low–velocity slugs normally required for passenger safety. Technology and tactics have provided solutions to these and other problems but the decades–old argument over the most appropriate weapons to use is something that will die harder than any flesh–and–blood fanatic.

Sniper Rifles

Nearly all DELTA weapons—whether old or new—have been "accurized" to some degree by the unit's own gunsmiths. Loose–fitting parts typically found even in quality mass–produced weapons are replaced by custom–built pieces with closer tolerances, specialized trigger mechanisms, and better sights. For example, before it was superseded by the heavy–barrelled 40XB sniper rifle (which was specially manufactured for DELTA by Remington Arms), modifications were made to the trusty old M14A1 to upgrade its already formidable performance as a sniper rifle.

Modifications typically included polishing and hand fitting of the gas cylinder and piston to im-

prove operation and reduce carbon buildup. Barrels were always carefully selected to ensure correct specification tolerances and are bedded into the forearms with a fiberglass compounds. Trigger housing groups were carefully fitted and polished to provide a crisp hammer release and suppressors fitted to eliminate sound and flash which could give the sniper's position away. Receivers could also be individually fitted to stocks using a fiberglass compound. The US Army now purchases an off–the–shelf versions of this weapon from the Springfield Armory called the M21 sniping rifle. DELTA troopers often use this weapon during training and it also receives considerable reworking such as having plastic spacers added to customize the length of the stock. The M40A1 and M24 sniping systems,

Flash/bang grenades with no–snag caps in an Eagle Industries hip pouch. Center pockets hold thirty–round clips for 9mm Heckeler & Koch submachine guns.

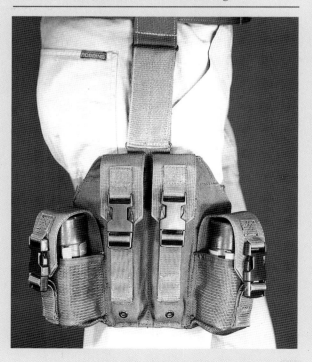

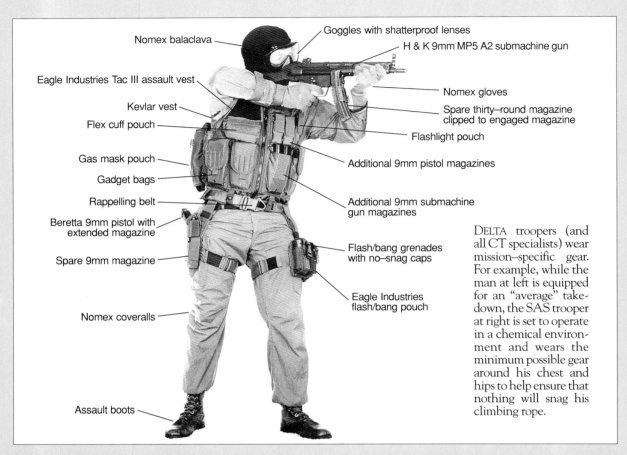

Nomex balaclava

Eagle Industries Tac III assault vest

Kevlar vest

Flex cuff pouch

Gas mask pouch

Gadget bags

Rappelling belt

Beretta 9mm pistol with extended magazine

Spare 9mm magazine

Nomex coveralls

Assault boots

Goggles with shatterproof lenses

H & K 9mm MP5 A2 submachine gun

Nomex gloves

Spare thirty–round magazine clipped to engaged magazine

Flashlight pouch

Additional 9mm pistol magazines

Additional 9mm submachine gun magazines

Flash/bang grenades with no–snag caps

Eagle Industries flash/bang pouch

DELTA troopers (and all CT specialists) wear mission–specific gear. For example, while the man at left is equipped for an "average" take-down, the SAS trooper at right is set to operate in a chemical environment and wears the minimum possible gear around his chest and hips to help ensure that nothing will snag his climbing rope.

standardized versions of the 40XB, are also being acquired by the Army and Marine Corps.

Grenades

The famous "pineapple," more properly known as the Mk II fragmentation hand grenade, is what most people think of when this type of weapon is mentioned, but the long–obsolete pineapple was pulled from front–line service with the US Army over a decade before DELTA was formed. A cylindrical canister, about the size of a shaving cream can, is used for concussion grenades, chemical grenades (such as tear gas), and the flash/bang grenade (a description of the grenade's employment is on page

57). This design allows the grenade's user to gently role it a predictable direction and distance into a room, unlike the Mk II and its similarly shaped or round descendants which are designed for throwing and, if rolled, could wobble almost anywhere— including back up against the very wall that a troop-er is using for shelter! Before the recent fielding of the flat–sided M560 series fragmentation grenades, if a mission profile called for use of an antipersonnel grenade with a predictable roll, an M57 or M61 would have to be soldered into an appropriately sized tin can to achieve the desired effect. Once the pin was pulled and the safety lever fell away, a nearly perfect roll could be achieved every time.

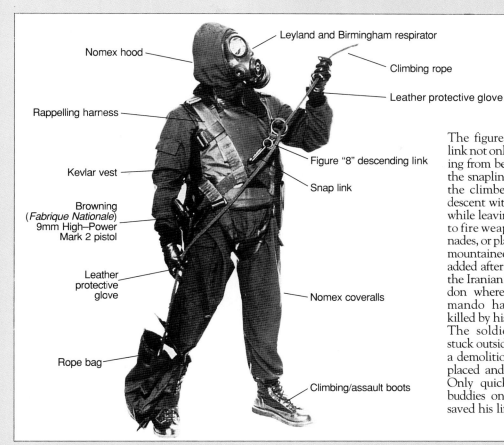

Nomex hood

Leyland and Birmingham respirator

Climbing rope

Leather protective glove

Rappelling harness

Figure "8" descending link

Snap link

Kevlar vest

Browning
(*Fabrique Nationale*)
9mm High–Power
Mark 2 pistol

Leather
protective
glove

Nomex coveralls

Rope bag

Climbing/assault boots

The figure "8" descending link not only prevents clothing from being dragged into the snaplink but also allows the climber to control his descent with only one hand while leaving the other free to fire weapons, throw grenades, or place charges. This mountaineering device was added after the operation at the Iranian Embassy in London where an SAS commando had almost been killed by his own explosives. The soldier had become stuck outside a window after a demolition had been emplaced and its fuse ignited. Only quick action by his buddies on the roof above saved his life.

Clothing

From the early days of hasty option operations, counterterrorist equipment has steadily evolved. Lightweight, highly rigid specialized clothing and equipment has now become a standard for CT teams. Several European units such as the SAS and Germany's GSG-9 found out through practical experiences at the Iranian Embassy in London and at the Mogadishu airport that general issue equipment is great for conventional forces but suffers from dangerous shortfalls when used during specialized operations. Much of the evolution in equipment has focused on the tactical assault vest and modular pouches attached to the upper torso and hips.

They incorporate such items as extra ammo, radio, and first aid pouches along with rappelling rings. Counterterrorist operations are very personal affairs. Despite the fact that the soldiers belong to teams, each man puts a great deal of faith in his individual gear. The equipment *must* be capable of accommodating number of modifications to handle, for example either flash/bang or gas grenades; MP5 magazines or Colt 733 Commando magazines. The problem was solved by creating a basic vest capable of handling interchangeable sets of pouches and holders for the problems specific to a given mission.

Chapter 3

The Making of a DELTA Trooper

In the 82d Airborne, I was better than any guy in my company. Over here I gotta hustle just to keep up.

a DELTA trooper

Joining a counterterrorist unit is very similar to breaking into the big leagues of pro sports. There are a few differences, however. Major league ball clubs have quite a few rookies on the squad, whereas the CT arena requires that units be composed exclusively of veterans with basic special operations skills already refined to a razor edge. And an error in the major leagues won't cost you your life or the lives of your team members.

CT units are composed of senior noncommissioned officers (NCOs) and several rather well–qualified officers. Continuous assignments in such units have not always been career enhancing, and despite the Army's recent elevation of Special Forces to full branch status, few officers stay around for more than one or two tours with the Special Forces groups. Those who do are usually *extremely* dedicated to their units, its troops, and the basic

US and German counterterrorists conducting a joint exercise involving rappelling, door–busting, and room–clearing techniques.

idea that the worldwide terrorist threat and its network of supporters should be met head–on and eliminated. They usually hold the respect of their fellow team members, who are not as concerned with an officer's rank as they are with his ability to shoot straight and back up his team.

Counterterrorism is only one of the missions assigned by law to the special operations community. The men who are charged with carrying out these low–visibility operations are chosen from a wide range of backgrounds and spheres of our society. Each is selected based on his talents and the unit's need to fill particular slots within its ranks. The question, "How does the whole process start?" begins with this fundamental requirement to fill open positions.

Selection and Training

Special operations units, and especially the close–knit counterterrorist outfits, recruit in several different ways. Special attention is given to the "old' boy network." As with any other business or

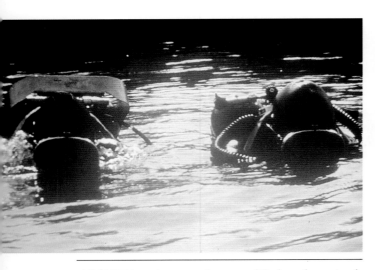

All DELTA trainees are jump qualified, and previously acquired skills, such as scuba diving are further refined during training. Troopers are assigned to specialized teams containing soldiers with the same skills. Many teams and elements are multidisciplined.

occupation, word of mouth and vouching for someone are key ingredients in the selection process. A second method is to simply advertise the need for people. DELTA recruitment teams make the rounds of training centers, troop posts, and such facilities as the Command and General Staff College or NCO advance schools. These recruitment drives preceed DELTA's fall and spring selection and assessment courses. Recruitment letters are also routinely mailed from Army personnel centers and, more recently, as the unit has edged out of the black into a rather dark grey, volunteers have been openly solicited in Army journals.

DELTA's rigid entrance requirements are clearly spelled out for career officers and NCOs who may be enticed to leave behind the warm comforts of their current postings for a new adventure. The pitch is always straightforward and unambiguous:

"ASSIGNMENT OPPORTUNITIES are available in the 1st Special Forces Operational Detachment—DELTA. DELTA is the Army's special operations unit that has been organized to conduct missions that combine rapid response with the surgical application of a wide variety of unique skills and the flexibility to maintain the lowest possible profile of US involvement. . . . DELTA gives commissioned and noncommissioned officers unique opportunities for professional development. . . ."

A fourth and less–known method is for soldiers to be individually sought out by recruiters, based on a screening of their official records. This method may also be used with word–of–mouth recommendations. Recruiters are usually looking for specific assets, such as language skills, key past assignments, military qualifications, or schools attended. From the compiled list of likely candidates, individuals are contacted and asked to volunteer.

Drawn from the Active Army, Army Reserve, and Army National Guard, all DELTA members must pass a background security investigation, be at least twenty–two years old, male, and a US citizen. Each soldier's records are screened for psychological abnormalities or recurring discipline problems, and those accepting the challenge receive very thorough physical and eye examinations. Commonly referred to as the Scuba/HALO physical, it is akin to the in–depth exams pilots receive.

After getting the thumbs up from the doctors, or "chancre mechanics," the prospective counterterrorist is subjected to a battery of tests to determine if he is psychologically sound. The last thing a unit in the midst of a mission needs is to find itself saddled with a would–be Rambo or a real–life psycho. The cost of not conducting extensive psychological tests was graphically displayed as early as the Munich incident in 1972. At one point, the terrorists moved into the sights of the German sharpshooters who then froze. The results were quite unsatisfactory from the Israelis' standpoint.

Approximately 100 prospective counterterrorists receive intensive physical testing every session and high scores are an absolute requirement. In DELTA's formative stage, its selection process closely followed the British SAS model. This was due to the fact that many of the individuals who had a hand in setting up the unit were the products of SAS–Special Forces exchange programs and the close working relations these units have always had. This aspect of the month–long selection process has not changed.

The candidate's ordeal begins with six grueling events which must be completed within a designated period and earning a minimum of sixty points each. The candidates are, of course, expected to do better than the minimum. Periodically, small modifications are made to the test; examples of what is expected of the volunteers include: forty–yard inverted crawl in twenty–five seconds; thirty–seven situps in one minute; thirty–three pushups in one minute; run, dodge and jump course in twenty–four seconds; two–mile run in sixteen minutes, thirty seconds; and 100–meter swim while fully clothed and wearing boots.

Following the test, the candidate has the opportunity to show how well he can accomplish a speed march. The route covers eighteen miles, and the

Soldiers using the Stabo technique to land on a Fort Bragg rooftop. Hanging free from the helo during their approach, the men land simultaneously instead of one at a time. The target area is framed with a two–by–four barrier in case any of the soldiers loses his footing.

individuals must traverse it as rapidly as possible. Since this is one of the psychological problems to overcome, the passing times are never published. However, most of those who have passed it seem to agree that ten–minute miles are almost too slow!

Those who have made it this far into the selection process now receive a real treat. Just like in the SAS course, the candidates now are asked to really show what they are made of and are taken to one of several sites for a combination speed march, compass course, and survival exercise. Tests were originally conducted near Troy, North Carolina, in the Uwharrie National Forest, but are now done on the even more rugged terrain of Camp Dawson, West Virginia; recently, a test site has been added in the secured areas of Nellis Air Force Base, Nevada.

The Freedom to Fail or Succeed

If you were one of the few candidates to reach the forty–mile land navigation exercise, you'd find that the basic scenario goes like this: With all the ceremony of going off to a maximum–security prison, you and the other candidates are trucked out to the test site, where each is dropped at separate starting points. As dawn begins to break, you are given a set of instructions that amount to little more than a compass heading and a point on the map marking the final destination perhaps a half–dozen miles away. You are to pick out your route, keeping in mind that the object is to get there as quickly as possible.

Off you go. As soon as you leave the gentleman who gave you the instructions, your thoughts run the gamut of, "What the hell am I doing here?" to "I hope I can pull this off." Even though you made some rough calculations at the starting point, you drop off to the side of the trail to double check the situation and ensure your initial calculations are correct. (Besides, you didn't want to look indeci-

sive in front of the guy at the drop–off point.) Squinting more closely at the map, you find that the contour lines are so close together that they look like some gigantic drunk worm. In other words, it is all up and down, with a few nice cold creeks in between. Off again, you settle into the comfortable trot the old hands taught you back at Bragg's Smoke Bomb Hill or Fort Benning. As usual, it starts to rain a little, but for the average Airborne, Ranger, or Special Forces type, rain is not a stranger. Checking your compass to keep oriented, you now settle into the routine. In most cases, the trial would be more enjoyable if you didn't remember that this was much more than just an exercise. You are here to show someone that you can hack whatever it takes to be part of that group called DELTA.

As you navigate along the trail, the shoulder straps of your fifty–five–pound rucksack begin to make themselves known to you—especially as the ruck gets wetter. Sweat trickles down your armpits, gets in your eyes, and seems to find refuge in your already chaffed crotch. After about the first hour and a half, the experience factors of Ranger School and the Special Forces qualification course, along with the numerous Special Forces Group exercises, take over. So it's time to stop, take stock of the situation, and drink some water. Pausing along the trail, you look around the dense hardwoods that make up much of the terrain along the mountains. Sensing something in the underbrush near your left jungle boot, you slowly retreat a few steps as "Jake no shoulders" decides to rattle a friendly greeting. Your mind comprehends the danger, but in some ways you really do not want to think about what could have happened, especially if he got upset as you were sitting down to check your feet.

Moving down the trail, you find a better place to get out of the drizzle and change your socks and apply some Vaseline to your sensitive areas. You get your bearings one more time and are off. Whether you are running the selection course in the mountains of Appalachia, with its forests and numerous streams, or driving on in the Sierra Nevada wastelands, the expected results are the same. Just like General Forest, get there "firstest with the mostest." In your case, get there fastest— period.

You've been at this all day, the sun dipped below the wooded hills uncounted hours ago, and at each rendezvous, you hope that it will be the one site where you will be told to throw your ruck into the truck and get aboard. But for some bizarre reason, the only words you hear at each brief stop are the location of your next rendezvous. After about a dozen hours of this, many volunteers begin to rest too long or slow down so much that they are unable to make the twenty–hour time limit. Even good soldiers begin to look for excuses to quit, and many inevitably find them. But not you. Cold, wet,

An exhausted instructor from the John F. Kennedy Special Warfare Center training group, after negotiating a demanding confidence course like DELTA's. He is indicative of the highly motivated, professional soldiers in the US special operations community.

and numb with exhaustion, you move off again, continuing in search of whatever you are out here for until well after midnight, when you are unceremoniously informed that the exercise is over. The survivors rarely remember exactly where they've been and, as with the speed march, even know how far they went or how long it took.

By now, the steady attrition of volunteers has weeded the field down to perhaps a dozen or so survivors. Many of those returning to their home units have been cut because they were unable to meet the tough physical and navigational challenges, while others were sidetracked for other legitimate reasons, such as knee, ankle, or back injuries. Some, however, drop out because they simply were not mentally prepared to follow the course through to the end without the accustomed "you can do it!" prodding that had been an integral part of all previous training. The NCOs overseeing the selection course steadfastly refuse to provide this encouragement. In any event, DELTA makes a great effort to ensure that those not selected know that they are

A trainee negotiates stairsteps to a room mock–up during entry technique training at the SOT. The object is to engage the pop–up silhouette targets from uncomfortable angles while in motion.

not failures. Each candidate receives a certificate of training and is simply told he was not selected.

Looking back at the physical side of the selection process, a key aspect becomes crystal clear: It is structured to put the maximum psychological pressure on those being tested. The individual is provided the freedom to succeed or fail on his own. A candidate not only must know his physical, mental, and emotional makeup, but must be able to use it to his advantage. In the CT arena, there are many occasions where individual actions are required, and in those life–and–death situations, you get only one chance to succeed. As Sun Tzu pointed out

so long ago, you have to know yourself as well as your enemy. If you are not ready to run in seemingly aimless directions for hours through the dark, wet, torturous terrain of overgrown, forested mountains, the cross–country land navigation exercise is not for you. If you are not ready to know what real fear is, to meet it head on and beat it, DELTA is not for you.

The trip back to Fort Bragg takes on an unreal atmosphere after what has occurred. Every selection course will have a variable number of thoroughly exhausted candidates who will go on to face the final and, according to some, hardest part of the selection process: the interview. A board of DELTA veterans grills the survivors and determines who goes on for training.

"So you're infiltrating an unfriendly area prior to taking down a terrorist hideout. Say you come across two little girls. You can't leave them. Do you take them along, tie them up, or do you kill them?"

"Tell us a little about Machiavelli."

"What were the arguments for and against our acquiring the Virgin Islands during World War I?"

"Was President Truman right or wrong to fire MacArthur?"

By this point in the four–hour grilling, some volunteers have taken on the look of frightened animals. The questions are asked seriously, and the DELTA veterans expect serious answers.

"Well, Sergeant, you've given a fine performance so far. Now tell us what you tend to blow it on."

"Why should we take you? What can you offer DELTA?"

"You're a good soldier!? So what!? Sergeant, we're up to our ears in good soldiers. Tell us about your unique skills, what you're really good at that's not military related."

In this tension–charged atmosphere, there are few right or wrong answers. The board is looking at the individual as a whole: his values and how he is able to handle himself in this situation.

The objective of the selection course is to find individuals who can both work with the team and yet operate independently without orders. In the end, only about ten percent or fewer of the initial candidates actually make it into DELTA; and a rumor circulating through the special operations community contends that one group moving throughout the selection process lost virtually every man before the assessment was finished. While such an occurrence could certainly wreak havoc with the manning levels of a small, highly specialized organization, such problems can be ironed out if they are not persistent. Moreover, the nature of DELTA necessitates that its emphasis must remain focused on the quality, not quantity, of personnel entering the unit.

The SOT

As the new DELTA trainee drives along Gruber Road past MacKeller's Lodge, he thinks back to the recent events of the selection course. Now the staff sergeant is at Fort Bragg, reporting in for some of the finest—and toughest—training in the world. To his right, he sees a high cyclone fence and dirt road used by the security force who patrols it. Beyond the fence and nestled within the rough horseshoe formed by Gruber, Lambert, and Manchester Roads is the secure training facility constructed for the training of America's elite CT units and the home of DELTA. Called the Special Operations Training Facility (SOT), the multimillion–dollar complex became a reality through the increased support from congress and the president for the war on terrorism in the early 1980s.

Almost as if the world has opened up its secrets, the SOT unfolds in the form of large two– and three–story buildings and training areas for heliborne insertions. The staff sergeant is immediately struck by how easy it is for virtually anyone to get a look at this surprisingly well–publicized facility. With counterterrorism such a security–conscious business, this visual access seems odd, but he writes it off as the price DELTA must pay for being on an "open post" like Fort Bragg and chuckles to himself when he remembers what started the whole process that led him to Gruber Road today: a public announcement in his branch journal, *Infantry*, that "assignment opportunities" were available in DELTA.

The newcomer passes the SOT's entrance and continues to drive north toward Manchester Road. He is rewarded with a clear view of numerous open–aired and enclosed ranges he'll be seeing a lot of over the next two years. A thrill rushes through him. This is going to be the ultimate adventure! Coming back to the reality of the moment, he makes an unauthorized U turn and pulls up to the brick guardhouse at the gate. His identification is scrutinized

A trainee practices pistol shooting at multiple targets at one of the SOT facility's numerous ranges. Note the semi–crouch stance and two–handed pistol grip.

against the incoming roster for the day, and he is directed to park and await his escort. The games, as they said in ancient Rome, are about to begin.

So far, everything the trainee has seen speaks well of the command emphasis placed on the Army's counterterrorist mission, from the White House down through the major subordinate headquarters, the Joint Special Operations Command (JSOC). In military terminology, it is a "high–speed" operation. As DELTA's newest recruit waits for his escort, he is startled to see an MH-6, bristling with darkened human figures instead of gun pods, zoom overhead. Along each side is a trio of soldiers buckled into special side platforms for rapid egress. Unseen by the trainee, the six commandos slip wearily from their "Little Bird" just a moment later at a helicopter pad near Lambert Road.

This specially modified Hughes chopper belongs to another important part of the team, the 160th Special Operations Aviation Regiment (Airborne), or SOAR. This unit is a result of the many problems experienced during *Desert I* and objectively outlined in its after–action review. Commonly referred to as the Holloway Report, it pointed out that a major area to restructure, if future missions were to stand a chance, was helicopter operations, and the covert aviation unit was duly formed at Fort Campbell, Kentucky. Originally named Task Force 160, it soon became the major US Army aviation support element for DELTA.

The commandos clearing the aircraft have darkened faces and wear a patrol, or "Ranger," cap. Clad in sturdy, olive drab jungle fatigues plus a wide assortment of specially made vests and other web gear, they also carry rappelling gloves, snaplinks and nonstandard Heckler & Koch MP5 submachine guns. As the SOAR 160 bird rises back into the sky, its stubby, rounded frame gives it the appear-

American counterterrorist team practicing pistol shooting from several different positions. Ranges such as this one provide enclosed areas to practice room–clearing methods out of sight of prying eyes.

ance of an overweight bumblebee or lethargic beetle attempting to gain flight.

Most CT operations require lightning fast entrances into the target area, along with shock effect and disorientation of the hostage takers. Carrying out such complicated maneuvers requires a great deal of training, teamwork, and the building of mutual respect for each member's abilities. That is what the new recruits are to learn during DELTA's five–month operators course at the SOT.

The facility's mission is to teach new methods and refine old skills in the art of counterterrorism. Many writers and observers have referred to the skills of eliminating a terrorist situation as antiterrorism. This, however, is incorrect. Antiterrorism is a term that refers to skills and techniques used by people or organizations which will help *prevent* them from becoming the victim of a terrorist attack. There are schools and courses where basic antiterrorist methods and tactics are taught, but the SOT addresses the final options of dealing with a terrorist incident that has *already occurred*. This is where DELTA comes into play: the counterterrorist arena.

Whenever the complex subject of counterterrorism is raised for discussion or debate, the argument that a specialized unit for CT operations is too expensive in terms of manpower and money usually comes to the fore. Regardless of whether this view is correct, it is undeniable that the political impact of a successful terrorist attack is often immense; the economic costs alone can run into the tens of millions of dollars, and priceless, innocent lives are put at risk or even lost. That is why dedicated units tasked to conduct CT operations are a must. How such units are configured is the decision of each country that fields them. Yet, one piece of the equation remains firm: Counterterrorist skills are highly perishable and must be kept at razor's edge if the team hopes to succeed. Appropriate training and constant studying of the enemy's methods, personnel, and organizational structure are an absolute necessity. The required skills and support apparatus are manpower– and resource–consuming, but countries employing counterterrorist units must be prepared to accept the costs. In the long run, it is a low–budget affair when compared to the economic and human costs of a successful terrorist strike.

A CT operation is composed of several distinct phases. First, the unit must get to the area of operations— possibly many hundreds or even thousands of miles away— by reliable, secure transportation. Simultaneously, immense amounts of intelligence must be collected, analyzed, and disseminated by a number of supporting agencies. A critical issue at this phase is who is in charge. The Army's Special Operations Command (SOCOM) supports the DELTA's training and related operational requirements but, in time of crisis, JSOC bypasses the SOCOM link and directs the unit and the nation's other CT assets. Once deployed, the State Department is the key desision–making element for foreign operations, while the Justice Department deals with problems within the United States. This clean, simple chain of command allows a "stovepipe" of direction and support to the unit and cuts out a number of middlemen who would unintentionally hinder the execution of a mission.

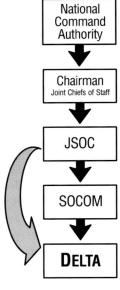

After arriving at the site of the "incident," the next phase deals with preparation. In its simplest form, this means that target surveillance is begun; outer and inner security rings are checked; command, control and liaison functions are established; and incoming intelligence is analyzed. After all the players are satisfied (or the situation forces the issue), the next phase is the assault, or "takedown," of the objective. Closely on its heels is the swift withdrawal of the force back to their homebase.

With this as background, where does the new trooper fit in? He is likely to fill a number of roles or positions, and his titles may be many. As he progresses within the organization, he will use his past skills and experiences to benefit the team he is assigned to. For example, he may be a sniper because he went to sniper school while assigned to a Ranger battalion. If his demolitions background is good, he may find himself dealing with some very exotic toys designed to blow off the smallest locks or take down the entire wall of a room with minimal disturbance to the occupants of the next room. As a "door kicker" or "shooter," his skills will be fine–tuned in the art of lockpicking, room entry, and target identification. Common phrases often associated with the skills or strengths of these unique professionals include the "double tap," "happiness is a head shot," and "reach out and touch someone."

The SOT provides troopers with various methods of entry, seizure, and exit of terrorist situations. They learn to rappel into second– and third–story windows to get at the terrorists and their victims, as well as how to most effectively kick open a door, use specially manufactured stun grenades to disorient the terrorists and then closely follow the blast into the room. Each member of a four–man team must know not only where he is going, but also precisely where his teammates will be and in which direction their fields of fire are directed.

In this closely orchestrated ballet of death known as close–quarters battle, the troopers learn to pick their targets quickly and then instantly place a minimum of two shots in an eye socket–sized kill zone from as far as fifty feet away. This technique is known as the double tap. Moving quickly through the area, the team learns to secure everyone (regardless of who they are) with plastic flex cuffs and leave the sorting out and medical treatment to the follow–on police forces. These strong, yet pliable, restraining bands not only are easy to use, but a large number can be carried by one man.

It is this type of assault that most people associate with counterterrorist forces. During a takedown, terrorists and hostages alike see only dark apparitions, akin to *Star Wars'* Darth Vader, entering behind the stun or flash/bang grenades. From the top down, every trooper is clad in a modern array of sophisticated armor. Heads are protected by a dark gray or black Kevlar helmet identical to current military issue. Under his "Fritz" helmet is fitted a flame–resistant Nomex balaclava. An earphone and/or microphone provides him instant tactical communication with the rest of the unit. The principle is that everyone involved in the decision–making process and execution must be provided with real–time information in order to control the unfolding operation.

Depending on the situation, a trooper is wearing eye protection in the form of either shatterproof goggles or a protective chemical mask which also provides a degree of eye safety. His upper torso is encased by a Kevlar vest, for gunshot and blast fragmentation protection, over a dark Nomex coverall or a tactical battledress. Over this, a variety of general equipment is worn, along with items that will support his specific tasks. Some troopers will have ammunition and myriad survival aids, such as powerful miniature flashlights and radio receivers. Others will have a variety of grenades, different types of ammo and first–aid equipment or knives. When medical assistance is not likely to be immedi-

ately available, CT teams carry a medical pouch containing assorted dressings, IV tubing, saline solutions, and tourniquets.

As with everything else, individual weapons are dictated by the situation. Of course, everyone has a particular favorite, but training on all available CT weapons is a must. Most room entries begin with the lead man using a submachine gun or a semiautomatic pistol. To expedite door–kicking procedures, shotguns firing a sabot or lead slug will be used to blow off the barrier's hinges. Many team members will insist that a submachine gun or shotgun, which can be carried in one hand, is the ideal weapon, and some even mount laser pointers or mini flashlights on their weapons for operations in buildings or dimly lit areas. Plenty of ammo is always strategically placed around his uniform.

Regardless of how much equipment the team member has, each man is aware that one lucky shot or a well–placed booby trap can ruin the best–laid plans. From the soles of his Gore–Tex assault boots to the crown of his Kevlar helmet, a team member's equipment is constantly reviewed and updated. A takedown is an affair that one must come properly dressed for.

Training generally falls into two categories. First the FNG (f——ing new guy) will go through individual skills training designed to break old habits that come from the conventional side of the Army, such as not shooting outside of the prescribed safety limits, and much emphasis is placed on individual action and initiative. New habits, like the double tap, are instilled in the FNG. These come from lessons learned through both successful missions and failures. In the case of the double tap, a pumped–up terrorist in the midst of a takedown cannot be reasoned with or talked into surrendering.

Once this basic training is completed, the FNG enters the team training phase where he is taught how to handle himself in any close–quarters battle,

(**Above**) A CT operative demonstrates how to use a shotgun during a window entry. (**Above right**) A close–up of a "best–case" anchoring system, with abundant safety features. In the heat of a fast–paced takedown, such fine points often have to be bypassed. (**Right and below right**) An assault team conducting a forced entry and room–clearing demonstration of a "hotel conference room." Lock picking is conducted with a charge of C4 plastic explosives. Also note the 360–degree protection and the Walther 9mm P5 pistol and MP-K submachine gun, protective masks, and ballistic (bulletproof) helmets. Expertise with personal weapons while wearing a variety of different equipment combinations is a requirement. (**Below**) If you can't go through the door or a window, go through the wall! Like high tech termites, two US operatives prepare to follow the blast into the next room.

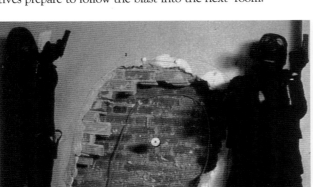

or CQB, whether it is conducted in a building, train, or aircraft. For example, the trooper will be given his first taste of an aircraft takedown at a large mockup of a generic civilian passenger liner at the SOT before training on a great variety of actual aircraft happily supplied by the major carriers at various sites around the country.

Additional CT training is also conducted to teach numerous infiltration methods for moving into isolated target areas. These include parachuting into the area using high–altitude, low–opening (HALO) or high–altitude, high–opening (HAHO), underwater rescue operations using Scuba techniques and miniature submersible vehicles for long–distance travel, and rappelling and fast–roping from helicopters. Teams may also have to learn techniques for driving various types of all–terrain vehicles. Lock-picking is also taught.

Upon completion, the FNG is assigned to a team, and maintenance of his new skills is begun within his troop. Regular cross–training will now occur with related foreign and domestic CT units, such as Britain's SAS or our own Navy SEAL (Sea–Air–Land) teams. Some DELTA troopers will also find themselves temporarily assigned "personal protection duty," providing security to key US personnel, such as ambassadors in Central America and the Middle East.

The Killing House

Take a break you heroes."

The team sergeant chuckles to himself every time he uses that line. If everything is going as it should, his jibe would either cause a rush of sarcastic curses and catcalls or receive a deep–throated moan from the assembled trainees. This time, the muted response indicates that the humid North Carolina weather is having an impact on the strength of the team. More importantly, it was a good indicator of the amount and type of training that should be con-

ducted for the remainder of the day. Based on his observations, the team sergeant decides to deviate from the published training schedule and walk through a room–clearing exercise without the required live ammunition. Training accidents are acceptable in this business but are not sought after.

Fifty meters to the west of this training area, a second and much more experienced team is also working its way through the day's training. Having just finished with their own room–clearing exercise, the men are given one of the most beloved commands in the lexicon of military language: "Take a break."

The break is planned for thirty minutes, but to the team members, it should be longer. Sprawled in various positions underneath the pines, each trooper brushes pine cones out of the way and tries to find a comfortable position while attempting to keep equipment from becoming too dirty with grit and sand. Small rivets of sweat trickle down grimy faces as nomex gloves are removed and calloused hands reach up to brush the sweat away from bloodshot eyes. Each team member wears an assault suit of black Nomex, and some of the team had already removed their black Kevlar helmets and flashproof balaclavas. Goggles, used to provide protection from flying debris, lay in the crown of the helmet, along with sweat–soaked gloves and face masks. Sensitive individual communications earpieces and microphones are inspected to ensure they were switched off.

Each trooper wears body armor, designed to protect throat and chest areas, and "armored shorts" to protect vulnerable groin areas. Some troopers have also added knee and elbow pads under their assault suits, while shin protectors are pulled on by some of the veterans who have grown tired of the bruises and cut shins received in the furniture–cluttered "killing house." Individuals are equipped with either a special–purpose Mossberg automatic shotgun

"Walk–throughs" of room–clearing operations are run with troopers wearing progressively more equipment so the men will gain a clear idea of how different protective sets restrict vision and movement. They must attain extreme levels of proficiency while wearing all combinations of gear. (**Above**) Troopers in coveralls prepare to enter a SOT "killing house" and (**opposite**) perform their ballet of death. Note the mannequin terrorists and hostage in closet.

or a 9mm Heckler & Koch MP5 submachine gun. Most of the free world's CT forces swear by this weapon, and some even argue that it is the best export the Germans have had since *Fräuleins*, Mercedes and beer. In addition to the MP5s, the sniper teams on this exercise are equipped with M24 sniper rifles. Though there are more advanced systems, the accurized Remington 700 bolt–action rifle with five–round fluted, detachable magazine is still the favored standby. Its stainless–steel barrel, and hefty .300 Winchester Magnum round provide this team with the power required to "reach out and touch someone." All members of the sweeper team carry 9mm Beretta Model 92F pistols: the standard sidearm of the US Army.

While some troopers "smoke and joke," others inhale nourishing liquids from canteens and jugs. Like the fondness each man has for his individual weapons, team members also have a distinct enjoyment of anything liquid. Gatorade, bottled spring water, juices, or just plain H_2O is found in the individual backpacks. Unlike what Hollywood would have one believe, hard–drinking troopers are not the norm. The shakes are not conducive to good teamwork. And to the experienced eye, the soldiers are an organized and tightly knit group of professionals, men who can easily operate as either individuals or a team, making decisions that could have far–reaching impacts at world levels.

"Saddle up, you assholes."

Staff Sergeant Dawkins hated it when the sergeant major tried out his hard, John Wayne voice, and comments sarcastically, "I really wonder if John Wayne ever called anyone an asshole." A number of other uncomplimentary thoughts are voiced as the troopers slowly rise to their feet and adjust their equipment. Gathering around the team leader, Sergeant Major Greg Tusconey, the men fall in to form a loose formation facing their boss.

Looking up from his notebook, Sergeant Major Tusconey begins with an in–depth critique of the morning's past exercise. He cites their strengths as well as their weaknesses. When finished, he faces his soldiers and says in a matter–of–fact tone, "OK, girls, let's get our shit together and try it again." The resounding reply to the implication that there is a collective lack of masculinity within the unit is indicative of a team who can give as much as it can take.

Sauntering back to their briefing area, the team members arrange themselves on wooden benches placed in front of a graphic representation of the

rooms within the killing house. A key factor in these exercises, as well as an actual assault, is the need for critical, accurate, and up–to–date information about the physical layout of the passenger aircraft or building, as well as the locations of the hostages and their terrorist keepers. Stepping up in front of the diagram, the sergeant major begins to describe the mission for the team in clear, concise, and pointed terms:

"At 1730 hours last night, terrorists assaulted the US Embassy, and took sixteen State Department employees as hostages. Two US Marines were killed during the initial assault. We are to prepare for a deliberate takedown of the building on order from higher." Stopping to scan the team for questions, he continues. "Outer security has been established by the local police, and inner security has been established by the hasty response team from the 10th Special Forces Group until after we arrive and take over responsibility for the mission. Recon of the building has been conducted, along with a debrief of our people and the locals who have solid, current intel."

Tusconey proceeds to outline the rehearsal schedules and timetables, who is responsible for what, and how he envisions the takedown will be accomplished. After the thorough briefing is completed, individual troopers are quizzed and then individual and team rehearsals are begun. As the last rays of the fading sun are engulfed by the approach of a cool, wet front, the last preparations are wound up. For this exercise, the chopper support for the takedown will come from "the Task Force" as the 160th SOAR is usually referred to.

The team is divided into sniper and assault elements, which coordinate the operation's precise timing, and move out. The two sniper teams each consist of a spotter and a shooter. They are linked together with the assault team, sweeper team, and command center by radio. Each sniper team moves along individual routes previously reconned and takes positions offering vantage points overlooking the target area. The assault element, meanwhile, is moving toward their pickup zone, or PZ, to rendezvous with an inbound chopper. The word circulates that the order has been received. The mission is on.

Because the operation will take place at night, infrared reflective tape is added to each member's equipment. Strips are applied around the chest, wrists, ankles and helmet. Using AN/PVS-7 night vision goggles (NVGs), all assault members will be easily seen in the heat of night combat. The sun has long ago set, and a steady drizzle falls through the tall pines as the team divides evenly and prepares to board the chopper. Right on schedule, the air is disturbed by the pounding of rotor blades beating the heavy night mist. Like a giant dragonfly, the MH-60 Black Hawk glides into the PZ, where the team immediately loads through the side doors. The pilot's eyes are unaided but his copilot wears aviator's AN/AVS-6 NVGs. Immediately, the team leader places the spare set of headphones over his ears and communicates with the pilot.

"Evening," says the pilot in a slow, Southern drawl.

"How's it going?" replies the sergeant major.

Formalities exhausted, Tusconey quickly briefs the aircrew on how the team will carry out the infil as the aircraft nears the target. Due to the lousy weather, the landing zone, or LZ, will be the building's sloping rooftop, and the team will drop onto a very small area at its peak, where a flat space had been located during photo recon analysis. Normally, the team would rappel or fast–rope in, but the wet weather and reduced visibility give them an added advantage and they'll be able to get closer to the target. With clockwork precision, the Black Hawk angles into the rooftop LZ and flares out level and steady. Looking through his NVGs, Tusconey sees that everyone is ready and in a low, distinct voice says, "Stand by, stand by." Prompted by his warning, the sniper teams report in: "Sniper One, ready. Target sighted." "Sniper Two ready. No target." At his hand signal, the lead team members prepare to exit. Taking a deep breath, he gives the command, "Go!"

The soldiers leap onto the mist–shrouded roof and fan out across its tricky incline in a predetermined (and well–rehearsed) pattern. Almost as quickly as the bird arrived at the LZ, it disappears into the gloom. Two team members attach green nylon climbing ropes to anchor points, drop them over the sides of the building along predetermined entry sites, and kneel in anticipation after attaching their snaplinks. Six other men move to a rooftop door and, after determining that it is locked, move into a tight file along the outside wall. The door hinges will have to be shot off.

The Number One man, armed with a Mossberg 12–gauge shotgun, prepares to blast the offending hinges off the wooden door. Despite the fact that every soldier is in communication with the rest of the team, discipline is absolute and the only sound breaking the silence is the constant hiss over each man's earpiece.

It has been ten seconds since the team landed. At the command, "Go!" the hinges disintegrate in a shower of sparks and splinters as the shotgun's solid lead slug crashes into each hinge, starting with the top and working down. Yanking the door to the side, the Number Two trooper rapidly steps into the doorway, where he immediately places his back to the dimly lit stairwell wall. Sweeping the staircase with his NVG, he breathlessly alerts follow–on troopers to the situation he is observing. Number Three now bursts through the doorway and in calculated steps moves down the stairs and secures the top floor stairwell. Peering down the hallway, he speaks in clear, crisp, and rapid tones into his micro-

phone: "Number Three, hallway clear." Trooper Number Four is immediately at his side, having followed his partner down the stairs. As Number Three moves to the right, Number Four moves left and blends into the darkened hallway. Both troopers' H&Ks move in measured arcs: ceiling to floor, left to right. Whenever a trooper's eyes move under their NVG, the stubby barrel of his MP5 follows, ready to spit out a lethal three–round burst along that same visual arc.

The second assault element of four men moves along the right side of the hallway toward a door on the right. The lead man (Number Three) senses motion in the room. Reaching down along his left thigh, he extracts a pop can–sized flash/bang grenade from his leg pouch. Bringing it up to his right hand, which still clutches an MP5, he slides the grenade's pullring over his right hand's gloved thumb. While holding the safety spoon, he pulls the ring. Gently rolling the grenade into the room, he flattens himself against the wall as he warns his teammates. "Grenade" reverberates through the soldier's earphones and, almost immediately, "Go!" is commanded before the nonlethal grenade has expended its package.

Number Five slides into the left side of the doorway as the room erupts in multiple flashes and explosions designed to disrupt, disorient and illuminate. As he moves through the door, Number Six follows and slides into the black, smoke–filled room along the doorway's right wall. He is followed by Numbers Seven and Eight who had entered the floor through windows on the other side of the building. Number Seven backs Number Five by taking on any targets from his twelve– through three–o'clock (the right hand wall). Number Five already has acquired a target through his NVG in his twelve– through nine–o'clock area along the left wall.

A masked terrorist is wildly trying to bring his Polish–made AK-47 assault rifle to bear on a young

(**Above**) A team wearing ballistic helmets takes up position along the wall, to avoid being silhouetted against an open door, as their shooter takes aim at a European-style door latch with a pump shotgun. (**Opposite**) After entry, the team fans out along the walls before picking targets.

woman strapped to a chair near the center of the office. Number Five squeezes a three-round burst into the throat of the terrorist, who goes down in a spasmatic heap.

As Number Seven checks the terrorist for other weapons and vital signs, Number 5 maintains a steady aim on the lifeless corpse. Flipping the terrorist over on his stomach, Number Seven expertly pins his wrists together with flex cuffs. After a quick check of the room, Numbers Six and Eight now check the bound female for booby traps. More than one rescue has ended in disaster when the rescuers failed to check for explosives secreted somewhere on a hostage. A grenade or stick of dynamite can turn a rescue into a sticky affair. After the check is completed, the team exits the room. Eight seconds have passed. As the leader leaves, he announces "Number Two, one terrorist down, one hostage secured, main room, top floor" to the command post and the other team members. Now it is up to the sweepers and backup police forces to take charge of the room.

This ballet of death will continue until the "embassy" is cleared of terrorists and all the hostages are accounted for. After the team exits the building, they move to an assembly area and are whisked away for an in–depth debriefing. If this had been a real takedown, actual terrorists and hostages would be considerably more unpredictable than the mannequins and pop–up targets the team had to deal with. Local police and medical personnel, as well as the sweepers, would have also been moving simultaneously through the building to deal with the carnage left behind and make a complete record of what happened. It may have to be used later as evidence.

This is a typical exercise.

During such exercises, the trooper is trained not to fall into the Rambo approach to CT operations: Never fire from the hip and always extend your folding stock. Fire at close range and don't waste ammo. You learn how to move: dropping to a crouch, firing, dropping and firing again, and moving to the next position. You learn to move quickly through doorways and get in position and maintain proper trigger control.

Chapter 4
Decade of Frustration

> General [Bernard] Rogers told me of a note from the President. It had surfaced in the tank earlier in the day [October 18, 1977] and asked, "Do we have the same capability as the West Germans?" Much discussion ensued before it was decided that we did not. One of the generals present had said, "Well I'm not going over to the White House and tell him we don't."
>
> *Colonel Charlie A. Beckwith, US Army (Retired)*

Throughout the 1980s, DELTA was beset by a number of events that might have caused lesser organizations to collapse. The troopers trained hard but were seldom deployed. They watched helplessly as Americans were whisked from streets and university offices in Beirut and seized in large groups in hijacked airliners and ships. Worse yet, the men found themselves gearing up for rescue operations that were cancelled time and again for a variety of reasons. During this same period, the unit also found themselves on the receiving end of a disturbing amount of unwanted publicity. In addition to a highly publicized financial scandal involving DELTA members, the easy visual access to the Special Operations Training Facility (SOT) may have been a factor in the media's knowledge of deployments during several hostage crises.

A US flag burns on the Rhein–Main Air Base perimeter fence during a period of mass left–wing demonstrations and terrorist strikes against American targets in Germany.

Although it's shocking to think that a unit on the cutting edge of America's war on terrorism was—and still is—in appearance at least, so vulnerable, it was only the tip of the weak links plaguing counterterrorism. In addition to the expected security problems associated with CT operations, numerous interdepartmental squabbles and convoluted command and control issues abounded. An excellent example concerned justification for CT operations within the continental United States. The Justice Department's Federal Bureau of Investigation is responsible for tackling terrorist incidents at home, yet DELTA had to provide badly needed assistance during both the 1986 Statue of Liberty centennial in New York City and the 1984 Olympics in Los Angeles in spite of numerous jurisdictional and legal problems.

When CT operations are planned for overseas, numerous diplomatic issues become critical elements in the military/political equation, and the State Department steps to the forefront. Probably

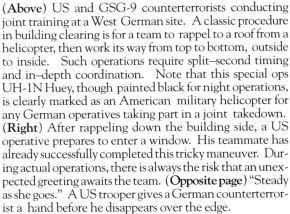

(**Above**) US and GSG-9 counterterrorists conducting joint training at a West German site. A classic procedure in building clearing is for a team to rappel to a roof from a helicopter, then work its way from top to bottom, outside to inside. Such operations require split–second timing and in–depth coordination. Note that this special ops UH-1N Huey, though painted black for night operations, is clearly marked as an American military helicopter for any German operatives taking part in a joint takedown. (**Right**) After rappeling down the building side, a US operative prepares to enter a window. His teammate has already successfully completed this tricky maneuver. During actual operations, there is always the risk that an unexpected greeting awaits the team. (**Opposite page**) "Steady as she goes." A US trooper gives a German counterterrorist a hand before he disappears over the edge.

the most basic question that must be asked before contemplating operations on foreign turf is: What sovereign nation wants to relinquish command and control to United States military forces conducting such highly visible operations on their soil? It has to be remembered that no matter how discreetly DELTA may conduct itself in the run–up to an operation, every hostage rescue is undeniably a high–visibility operation *after* its well–publicized conclusion. The implication for the nation hosting DELTA is, of course, that it does not have the re-

sources to take care of its own internal problems. The domestic, as well as international, political ramifications for a government can be enormous. Add to this mess the fact that the Joint Special Operations Command, the direct link between DELTA and the president (known as the National Command Authority) and the Joint Chiefs of Staff (JCS), can receive marching orders from both. The JCS is better qualified to oversee any operations involving DELTA, but common sense remained a missing ingredient in this war, as can be seen by the less–than–desirable results in Grenada.

Aftermath

The fallout from the inferno of *Desert I* was complicated and far reaching. Not only did President Jimmy Carter lose his bid for re–election, but Egypt's supportive president, Anwar Sadat (who was already on a number of hit lists for his part in the Camp David Accords), was now a principal target of Iranian–sponsored fanatics for allowing the "Great Satan" to launch Operation *Eagle Claw* from his country. He would soon die at the hands of Muslim fundamentalists.

JCS planners continued their work, and soon a new mission to rescue the hostages in Iran, code–named *Honey Badger,* was put together under the direction of the renowned and much–respected General Richard Secord. Armed with the proper special operations support—and the hard–learned lessons gleaned from *Eagle Claw*— he assembled a powerful force of special operations aviators, Special Forces and DELTA troopers, intelligence collectors, and agents who were prepared to go it again. But it was not meant to be. Some two minutes after Ronald Reagan was sworn in as President of the United States, the hostages were released.

To help dampen the firestorm of criticism that erupted after *Desert I*, a six–officer review group was appointed by the chairman of the JCS, General David C. Jones. It was chaired by Admiral James L. Holloway, and the balance of its membership consisted of generals from the Army, Air Force, and Marines who had experience in either special or clandestine operations.

These investigators came to the conclusion that *Eagle Claw* was plagued by untested operational methods, poor communications procedures, and a dangerously informal command structure lacking unity of command. Training for the mission, moreover, had been conducted by its various compo-

nents at different sites without a full dress rehearsal using all the assigned elements—something that would have highlighted the most glaring operational and equipment shortfalls. The commission recommended that "a permanent field agency" of the JCS be established with "assigned staff personnel and certain assigned forces" and that a "murder board" of military experts be formed to independently examine mission plans before execution.

As for Colonel Beckwith, he was asked by General Meyer to formalize an earlier proposal for a permanently operating joint task force that would fall directly under the JCS and combine dedicated Army, Navy, and Air Force elements during its training and planning. Beckwith and others had long voiced the opinion that this type of organization was needed, and Major General John Singlaub put it best when he stated *Eagle Claw* didn't work because "we tried to bring disparate units from all over the Armed Forces—from all over the world— and then put them into an ad hoc arrangement to

A key ingredient in CT operations is covert intelligence collection. Here, an intel specialist supports a DELTA training mission by conducting surveillance operations from a concealed site.

do a very complicated plan."

Beckwith's proposal to establish a Joint Special Operations Command (JSOC) was approved by Meyer in May 1980, and he was soon transferred from DELTA to the newly formed, independent organization he helped create. He badly missed the excitement of leading a combat team, though, and remarked that his staff billet "ain't as good a job [as DELTA]." He retired to the Lone Star State in 1981 and opened a security service. Harkening back to his days with Britain's Special Air Service, he gave his company the name SAS of Texas.

The establishment of the JSOC was one of many honest attempts to put teeth in America's counterterrorist effort in the wake of *Desert I*. As expected, the new government programs became battlegrounds for interdepartmental squabbles. The major catalyst for this fighting was, of course, money since counterterrorism was now in vogue and took funding away from other programs.

DELTA's friends in high places went to even higher places, and the post–Beckwith organization thrived during this period. The unit's strength before *Eagle Claw* of just over 100 men, making up two small A and B squadrons plus support, grew to a relatively stable force of 300 during the early 1980s— enough for three full–sized squadrons— with its selection and training as brutally efficient as ever. The unit also benefited greatly from production of *Task, Conditions and Standards for DELTA*, or, as it is more commonly known, "the Black Book." This document was produced only because General Meyer essentially grabbed Beckwith by the shoulders, pushed him down into a chair, and forced him to compose it.

Meyer, now the Army's chief of staff, was anxious that DELTA not reinvent the wheel with each new commander and wanted to ensure that it would retain its SAS–type structure, one that is unique within the US Army. Four troops of approximately sixteen men make up a squadron, with each troop able to reconfigure itself into eight–, six–, four–, three–, or two–soldier teams or elements. This degree of flexibility is one of the key ingredients in DELTA's ability to handle virtually any terrorist scenario.

DELTA also moved its headquarters from the old post stockade to the new, state–of–the–art SOT, appropriately nicknamed "Wally World" after a lavish theme park in the *National Lampoon's Vacation* movie. But, in a sense, it wasn't just DELTA that came up a big winner from the increased awareness of the terrorist threat. The whole military benefitted because it was identified as the obvious candidate to receive the now readily available funds. And the funds did flow: to Air Force special operations, Navy SEALs, Army aviation, Rangers, and Special Forces, as well as a large supporting cast in the various services, such as the Army's Intelligence Support Activity (ISA).

The State Department, however, was soon to emerge as the biggest winner. Being in the best position to judge the political ramifications of US actions on a host nation's territory, it received the responsibility for overseeing all overseas counter-terrorist operations. But despite the fact that the United States now had its CT apparatus well–organized and in place, the future proved to be not so rosy as the optimists hoped.

Operation *Urgent Fury*

After Ronald Reagan assumed the presidency in 1981, he "let it be known to friend and foe alike" that he had learned from the hard lessons of his predecessors. Surrounded by capable and, in some cases, hawkish advisors, President Reagan was determined that, like the sheriffs of the Old West, he would clean up the world and make it safe for women and children. All he needed was a place to start and the force to sweep up the mess. He didn't have long to wait. At the southern end of the Antilles chain lies the beautiful Caribbean island of Grenada. A former ward of the British Empire, this idyllic eight– by fifteen–mile island was to be the testing ground for the new president and the changes that had been made in the special operations community since *Desert I*.

On October 19, 1983, Grenada's Marxist prime minister, Maurice Bishop, and several cabinet members were lined up along the walls of old Fort Rupert and executed by former associates who formed an even more radical "Revolutionary Military Counsel." Bishop had aligned himself with the Soviets and their Cuban surrogates, who had, among other things, constructed a large military communications facility, a 10,000–foot runway capable of handling long–range transports, and extensive airfield support facilities, ostensibly to support its meager tourist industry. While a single air base would not allow a hostile force to control the entrance into the southern Caribbean during a war, it would provide an excellent stopover for aircraft bringing in material and personnel support for "peoples' revolutions" in Central and South America.

MH-6 Little Birds of the 160th SOAR operating in the Persian Gulf. Among other operations they took part in was the September 1987 capture of an Iranian mine–laying vessel that threatened oil tanker traffic.

With the execution of the genuinely popular leader, widespread protests broke out on the island, and when the military opened fire on the demonstrators, the die was cast. The threat to the region caused an uproar among the neighboring Caribbean nations, and the Reagan administration believed that a radical, Marxist government (that thought nothing of shooting its own citizens) would, sooner or later, get around to using the roughly 600 American students at the island's medical school as pawns in a dangerous game to keep the US military from closing down the airfield. The young students were a hostage situation waiting to happen, so the United States moved quickly to launch Operation *Urgent Fury*.

Leading the assaults were several of the US military's elite as well as (until then) classified units. UH-60 Black Hawks of Task Force (TF) 160 flew directly from the United States to a nearby island launch site, with the help of additional internal fuel tanks, while MH-6s were brought in by Air Force cargo planes. During the early morning hours of

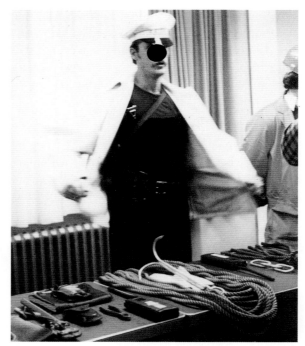

Counterterrorist specialists must be able to use any ruse or disguise to get close to hostage holding sites, such as an aircraft or buildings. Here, US Army CT operatives display equipment and various disguises during a briefing for General Bernard Rogers, Supreme Allied Commander, Europe, in the early 1980s. (**Left**) One of the typical "European businessmen" holsters his 9mm Beretta pistol and (**right**) a "street cleaner," standing beside a "municipal worker," shows off his protective vest and ammunition belt. Note the equipment on display.

October 25, the expert aviators of TF 160 ferried their ground counterparts, DELTA, to targets near the airfield at Point Salines, where they were to carry out a direct action mission ahead of two Ranger battalions parachuting in at dawn. Their target was the airfield control facilities which, it turned out, were heavily ringed by misplaced, but marginally effective, automatic weapons. A second mission entailed the takedown of Richmond Hill Prison, where one Black Hawk was lost to Soviet–made

ZSU-23-2 (twin 23mm) antiaircraft guns. In both cases, men and aircraft were lost (some figures are still classified). The lack of timely, on–the–spot, intelligence had again raised its ugly head.

Several members of the elite Navy SEAL Team 6 have privately related that they had an especially rough time as DELTA and the TF 160 units were running into their own problems in the south. One deadly incident occurred when four of their members parachuted into rough seas to conduct a linkup with a surface vessel that was to take them in close for a water infiltration. The drowning of these four men did not stop the mission, but it did tragically demonstrate that even the best of the best are sometimes incapable of overcoming the odds.

A major concern during *Urgent Fury* was the safety of the British government's representative. Tasked to keep the gentleman from falling into the hands of the Grenadan "Peoples' Revolutionary

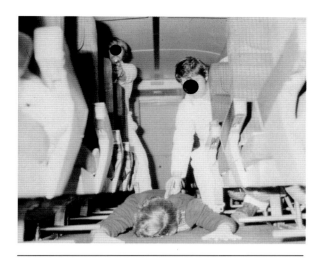

(**Above**) Unlike situations depicted in movies, actual aircraft takedowns must be accomplished quickly, violently, and with surgical precision. Here, a suspected hijacker in a mock airliner cabin is controlled the best way: with a pistol to the head. (**Right**) "Tickets please!" A terrorist's view of a US operative taken during a train–clearing exercise in Europe.

Armed Forces," twenty–two other members of SEAL Team 6 flew in by chopper, fast–roped onto the rooftop and grounds of the governor's residence, and took control. A stunned Grenadan defense unit located nearby summoned help from two Soviet supplied BTR-60 armored personnel carriers mounting multiple machine guns. The sudden appearance of substantial hostile elements forced the planned evacuation of Government House to be hastily cancelled. They were, as one SEAL member later described, "in a world 'a shit" and had to fight in place. With neither antiarmor weapons nor good communications, the team held out as best they could until a Specter gunship came to their rescue and eliminated the problem. But even with the help of the AC-130's massive firepower, up to half of the rescue party is reported to have been wounded by the time Marines reached them on the second day of *Urgent Fury*.

Months later, a veteran SEAL discussing the operation sighed after draining his beer and said, "Thank God it was just the Grenadans." When pressed, he continued, "Every time some nonqualified son of a bitch plans or directs our operations, we get our asses handed to us on a silver platter. It just ain't right." Right or wrong, the end result from the problems of *Urgent Fury* was that closer control over the planning of special operations would, at least for a while, be handled by people who "had been there," which means thoroughly qualified in special operations planning.

An interesting wrinkle on special operations on Grenada came from the media's coverage of *Urgent Fury*. Although the Army had refused to either confirm or deny the use of special operations forces for nearly eight years, ABC News was able to extract a concession that one TF 160 captain was killed and eleven DELTA troopers injured after

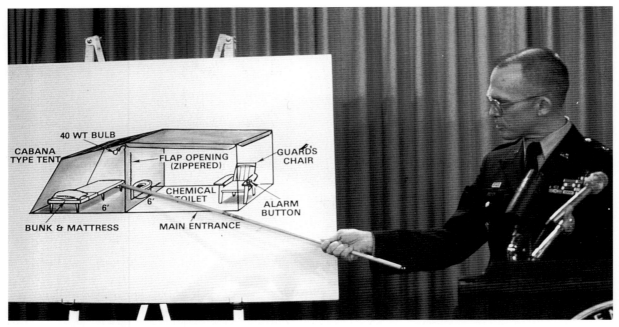

broadcasting footage of the downing of his Black Hawk— an event previously unaccounted for in the Pentagon recap of the operation. An American resident of Grenada had shot the film; other footage showed MH-6s, aircraft for which no procurement information had been publicly released. They were identified by ABC News as Hughes 500 helicopters, its civilian designation.

After the operation, increasingly bitter complaints over the "veil of secrecy" surrounding special operations were heard from some quarters of the media. Also being made was the highly dubious claim that only the American public was being denied access to information since the Soviets supposedly already knew all about such activities. While this is a subject that will certainly never be concluded to everyone's satisfaction, it is an undeniable fact that even relatively low losses can have a severe impact on the capabilities of a small unit. And if the small unit performs a mission of vital strategic importance, that loss may be magnified a hundred-

fold. Not only do Western intelligence agencies monitor terrorist networks, but the terrorists themselves monitor CT organizations, with the assistance of various friendly governments that track Western units and capabilities largely through press reports and, occasionally, espionage. It is not in the best interests of the United States to reveal losses in key covert units within days—or even months— after they were suffered. In this case, freedom of information must take a back seat to security

Trouble in the Mediterranean

Almost immediately on the heels of *Urgent Fury*, members of Italy's own homespun terrorist organization, the Red Brigade, abducted an American one-star general named James L. Dozier from his apartment on December 17, 1982. Authorities were later to learn that Dozier was not the intended victim, but, instead, a Navy admiral had been the group's actual target. Regardless of who was snatched, the impact all over Europe was the same: NATO military

facilities soon became prison camps for the Allies. Virtually every senior officer seemed to see himself or his family as a prime target for the terrorists.

Against this background of confusion, the experts from various special operations units converged on Italy. Much to their credit, the Italians told everyone to kindly go home since this was their turf. But while all door kickers were sent packing, they did keep some special operators who could assist with such exotic needs as radio and telephone intercept.

When the alarm was sounded, one of the units offered was the European Command's own hasty response detachment. Its commander found himself on the first plane into the area. He was also on the first plane out. The Italians recognized incompetence when they saw it, and had enough problems of their own without having to wet–nurse a rookie counterterrorist in addition to the US State Department. With the help of the US signal intercept folks, the Italians found and rescued the kidnapped general, and American CT "experts" learned one

General Dozier's kidnappers erected a tent inside a safehouse room to hold their prisoner. (**Opposite**) Dozier displays a diagram of the tent and nearest guard position after Italian counterterrorists forcibly freed him from the Red Brigade. (**Above**) Lebanese rescue workers and US Marines gather outside the flattened Marine barracks in the aftermath of a terrorist truck bombing. The suicide driver had driven directly past Marine guards, who had been ordered not to carry loaded weapons. There were lessons to be learned: Listen to the warnings of counterterrorist specialists, plus shoot first and worry about CNN later.

more lesson in dealing with the real world.

In 1982, Iran had sent roughly 2,000 of their fanatical Revolutionary Guards to the Lebanese free–for–all civil war as "volunteers." While a good number of them would go to paradise after falling in regular combat against Christian militiamen (and leftist Shiites and Druz militiamen and renegade Palestinians and US Marine snipers, as well as Israeli, Lebanese, and Syrian soldiers), a select few were destined to meet Allah in a less conventional man-

The television image of a TWA pilot being prevented from talking with reporters by an armed hijacker at Beirut airport in June 1985.

ner. These "martyrs" drove explosives–laden trucks into barracks, embassies, or other high–priority targets. On the night of April 18, 1983, forty French paratroopers and 241 US Marines were killed by a pair of these truck bombers after failing to heed the lessons of a similar attack earlier that year on a US Embassy building.

Another incident in late October of that year concerned members of the 10th Special Forces Group who were billeted in a downtown hotel while training and advising the Lebanese Army. The group's commander, Colonel Richard Potter, was warned by associates with connections to the Shiite fundamentalists that the group's quarters were targeted for yet another suicide bombing. Potter, DELTA's former deputy commander and a veteran of *Desert I*, was not about to let such warnings go unheeded and immediately moved his force to a Lebanese Army base north of the city. In this case, the training of one man, along with past friendships nurtured over years of frustration, spared the wives of the 10th Special Forces a visit from a chaplain and the ever present survivor assistance officer.

On December 4, 1984, DELTA was sent to assault a Kuwaiti airliner hijacked on its way to Pakistan. Two American passengers were killed during the incident, and the aircraft was forced to fly to Iran, where both the terrorists and hostages were released before the unit could intervene. Six months later, on June 14, the unit was sent back to the region in preparation for an assault on TWA Flight 847, but the affair ended before they could be employed; one off–duty Navy serviceman on board was singled out and murdered. DELTA failed to come to grips

Throughout the 1970s and 1980s, terrorists in Germany were like fish swimming in a great sea of militant leftist/ Marxist/ecologist/misfit/nationalist extremists and sympathizers. (**Right**) A masked demonstrator protesting outside the US air base at Rhein–Main and (**below**), an arms cache believed to have been hidden by Germany's Red Army Faction. Terrorist groups rely heavily on hidden caches of arms and other supplies.

with terrorists again in October, during the *Achille Lauro* affair, and the resulting fiasco at Sigonella Naval Air Station, Sicily, pointed out that the Italians were not about to change their position on whether they or the Americans have jurisdiction on Italian turf. Members of SEAL Team 6 attempted to take the hijackers into custody and were re-

minded that they were not the ones in charge.

The Palestinian extremists who commandeered the Italian vessel had been persuaded to leave it at Alexandria, Egypt, in return for safe conduct to friendly Tunisia, where the PLO maintained its headquarters. They boarded a commercial passenger jet and left Egypt immediately ahead of DELTA's arrival but was quickly intercepted by US F-14 Tomcat fighters, which diverted it to the US–Italian air base. Once the airliner was forced to land, it was quickly surrounded by the SEALs, who were, in turn, surrounded by Italian *carabonari*, who also blocked their C-141 with security vehicles. Since both groups were attempting to carry out their orders and

(**Above**) The unmarked limousine of General Frederick Krossen, commander of US Army forces in Europe, after a failed assassination attempt by Germany's Red Army Faction in September 1981. Only a month before, the general had finally heeded the advice of West German counterterrorists and obtained the special armored Mercedes that deflected the blast of the Soviet–made rocket–propelled grenade away from the car's interior. In the car was the general, his wife, an aid, and a German driver/bodyguard. (**Right**) A West German wanted poster for known terrorists. As various fugitives were apprehended or killed, they were crossed off the poster by the US CT team that mounted it on their headquarters' wall.

apprehend the hijackers, a tense situation developed between the senior US officer present and Italian officers. The situation quickly degenerated and the *carabonari* loaded and locked their trusty Berettas and drew down on the equally well–armed SEALs. It was an Italian standoff until the diplomats intervened and determined that it was in ev-

eryone's best interest to let the Italians take charge.

Yet another incident occurred the following month, when a commercial airliner was hijacked to Malta by Palestinian extremists. This time, DELTA was on hand but not used. In fact, they were initially not even allowed to land. Since the hijacked aircraft was Egyptian, that country's commandos, trained by US special operations personnel, were allowed to conduct the takedown. It turned sour, and fifty–seven hostages lost their lives.

Troubles at Home

From 1970 through the mid–1980s, more than 1,000 Americans had been killed, taken hostage, or otherwise injured by foreign terrorists. Virtually all of these incidents had occurred overseas, but CT planners believed that America's luck might not hold out much longer: The upcoming 1984 Summer Olympics to be held in Los Angeles was an awfully tempting target. As part of the $1 billion effort to provide security from possible attacks, DELTA deployed to a nearby naval facility and stood ready to counter any terrorist situation. Along with DELTA was a massive CT force incorporating city and state SWAT (special weapons and tactics) teams and the Federal Bureau of Investigation's Hasty Response Team, commonly referred to as HURT. All were given varying degrees of responsiblity to counter threats, depending on their level of expertise and available manpower.

One interesting sidenote to DELTA's deployment at the Olympics was their use of a mobile command post disguised as a Budweiser beer truck for surreptiously transporting a response team to the site of an incident. While mention of such a vehicle almost invariably brings snickers to the mouths of listeners accustomed to seeing similar tricks on scores of television cop shows and films as diverse as *Good Neighbor Sam* and *Stripes*, the fact remains that a vehicle camouflaged in this unconventional manner looks like it "belongs" and can move virtually unnoticed if that is what is required. Thankfully, the truck was not needed, but it had to be a comforting sight to those in the know.

Unlike the funds spent on producing the Budweiser truck, not all monies funneled through Army covert accounts were spent wisely or even legitimately. Army auditors discovered a number of irregularities in a covert account between 1981 and 1983. A disturbing amount of double–dipping had taken place and such items as a hot–air balloon and Rolls–Royce sedan had been purchased supposedly to support clandestine operations.

In a climate that one DELTA member described as "sheer hysteria," standard cost–accounting techniques were applied to ongoing covert operations and training. The result was dozens of reprimands and perhaps a score or more transfers resulting from nonjudicial punishments in lieu of court–martials. Some soldiers, however, were not so lucky. Nor did they deserve to be. In one case, an ISA lieutenant colonel, who supported DELTA set up a firm named Business Security International as a conduit for covert funds and misappropriated more than $50,000 in just six months. In a series of discreet courts martial and a civil criminal trial running through 1986, at least two officers were "assigned to the long course" and are still serving prison terms at Leavenworth Penitentiary.

For most DELTA troopers, though, life remained at its grueling, hurry–up–and–wait pace. Troopers continued their meticulous training and provided advice and support to CT units around the world as they did during the Los Angeles Olympics, when a team was quickly dispatched to Willemstad, Curacao, in the Dutch Antilles, to assist in the takedown of a hijacked Venezuelan DC-9. Both fanatics were killed and seventy–nine passengers were freed. Meanwhile, in Lebanon, kidnappings continued unabated and two of the hostages were murdered, CIA station chief William Buckley in 1985 and Marine Colonel William Higgins in 1989. Frequent changes in hostage holding sites and lack of solid US intelligence sources within the terrorists' camp prevented rescues from being undertaken, and at least one major operation involving DELTA and the SEALs was scrubbed. The professionals at DELTA were, in effect, all dressed up with no place to go. Sometimes, though, this was distinctly good news— as was the case when New York City's vulnerable Statue of Liberty centennial celebration passed without a hitch in July 1986.

On other occasions, events took care of themselves— as in San Salvador and Manila. On November 21, 1989, DELTA was dispatched to the Salvadoran capital of San Salvador to rescue Green

West Berlin police sifting through the rubble of the La Belle discotheque, a bar popular with American servicemen, where a soldier and Turkish woman were killed by a bomb. Intelligence analysts soon discovered that the explosives were planted by Libyan agents based out of their embassy in communist East Berlin.

Beret trainers trapped in the Sheraton Hotel during a guerrilla offensive. The trainers escaped unharmed, however, before the detachment could be put into action. Almost two weeks later, DELTA received another alert for a possible rescue attempt, this time in the Philippines. American citizens were again trapped, this time by an Army coup d'état, but emerged unscathed when the revolt fizzled.

Berlin presented a more interesting—and long-lasting—problem for US, as well as British and French, CT units stationed in the city's Western sectors. Along the seven crossing points through the Wall between East and West, Communist East German border guards, called *Vopos*, checked passports to prevent East Germans from passing into the West, while the British, French, and American guards allowed people to pass unimpeded both ways since they didn't, for political reasons, view East Berlin as a "foreign" territory. A situation was thus created where potential terrorists, finding some access restrictions from Western nations, could simply cross into the city from East Berlin, where the Syrians, Lybians, Iranians, and even the PLO, maintained diplomatic missions. A US hasty response team was always on a high state of alert and an active exchange program was conducted with DELTA. They operated in close conjunction with Berlin's other Western security organizations, but could not prevent terrorist attacks like the April 5, 1986, bombing of the La Belle discotheque, a club fre-

quented by many American servicemen, in which two people were killed and 230 others were injured. The twilight world of terrorism and counterterrorism, espionage and counterespionage, did not end until the East German communist system finally collapsed of its own weight, bringing the Berlin Wall down with it.

Throughout it all, the frustrations and false starts, DELTA troopers maintained their high degree of professionalism and managed to keep their sometimes–irreverent sense of humor. All knew that the beeper clipped to their belts could sound its annoying electronic bleep at any time to signal a recall and they'd casually drop whatever they were doing with an offhand, "Looks like it's time to head on back to the Ranch,"* and disappear out the door for who knows how long.

*The affection of some shaggy–haired troopers for Levis, chewing tobacco, and cowboy boots led their original headquarters at Fort Bragg's old stockade to be called "the Ranch," and even after the unit moved to its new digs at Wally World, the name persisted.

(**Top**) The US Army's hasty response team in Berlin and several DELTA troopers pose for a group photo during a break in a training exercise. (**Above**) During antiterrorist training in West Berlin, an American serviceman is "snatched" by a group of mock terrorists.

Operation *Just Cause*

A public affairs release from Operation *Just Cause* stated simply that all units from the "special operations command participated" in the operation. DELTA's most publicized mission was the rescue of an American businessman and Rotary Club member held in Panama's notorious Modelo Prison. Kurt Muse was a resident of Panama and, in concert with fellow Panamanian Rotarians (dubbed the "Rotarians from Hell" by *Soldier of Fortune* magazine), had been causing Panama's strongman, Manuel Noriega, trouble by operating a clandestine radio station, filling the air waves with propaganda and, in some instances, reporting misleading or confusing instructions to the Panamanian Defense Forces (PDF) on military radio frequencies. Muse was eventually turned in by the wife of a former co-conspirator and was jailed at Modelo, located a stone's throw from Noriega's command post/headquarters turned fortress called the *Comandancia*.

In the early morning hours of December 19, 1989, Muse was rescued by members of DELTA in a classic CT operation. Transported to the rooftop of the prison by an MH-6, the assault team, backed up by a man on the inside who disabled the facility's emergency generator, cleared the upper floors from the top down and fought their way to the cell holding area where Muse was imprisoned. White beams of light from the troopers' weapon–mounted pointers pierced the smoke–filled cell, after its door was blown, and Muse was whisked to the roof up a darkened stairwell as Specter gunships pummeled the *Comandancia* across the street.

Armed with MP5s of various configurations, the troopers took out the armed guards with lethal shock and firepower and used just enough explosives to open the door without harming Muse. The waiting MH-6 was piloted by a lone soldier from the 160th SOAR. Two troopers fought their way to Muse's cell, two more provided security on the stairwell, and four more were on the roof, exchanging fire with prison guards in the barracks beyond a small courtyard. The operation, so far, had unfolded with the clockwork precision of a Wally World exercise. As the security and rescue teams loaded into the helo and along its outside–mounted seats, the heavily laden Little Bird lifted into the night sky.

What Muse saw was as close to a living hell as Wagnerian opera. AC-130s were tearing great chunks out of the *Comandancia's* defenses, while tracers streamed upward at buzzing Black Hawk helicopters and, in the streets below, conventional mechanized infantry forces brought maximum pressure to bear on the PDF. In this deadly concert, the overloaded chopper, unlike a *Valkyrie* of lore, did not bear the men off to *Valhalla*, but was hit by ground fire and landed with an unceremonial thud on the street below. The iron–nerved aviator maneuvered it down the street like a taxi and pulled into a parking lot. Using several tall apartment buildings as a shield, the pilot again tried to make his getaway but the Little Bird was knocked down again, this time for good, and the men formed a defensive perimeter nearby. Seconds after one DELTA trooper held up an infrared strobe light, they were spotted by a Black Hawk, and the cavalry came to the rescue in the form of three 6th Infantry Regiment M-113 armored personnel carriers. Four DELTA troopers were hurt, one seriously, but unlike the events some nine years earlier in Iran, this plan was carried out and with the intended results.

(**Top**) The MH-6J Little Bird that lifted Kurt Muse to freedom is moved out of the street by US mechanized forces after they secured the area around General Manuel Noriega's headquarters. Note the three–man troop seats along each side and the large crane–like appendage for fast–rope operations. It folds forward against the side of the bird when not in use and inadvertently prevents troopers from easily exiting the interior from the right side. (**Right**) The battered *Comandancia*, located just across the street from Muse's prison cell. *Soldier of Fortune*

Air Support

Rotary– and Fixed–Wing Assets

The Holloway Report on Operation *Eagle Claw* laid bare the grevious deficiencies in special operations aviation that contributed to the disaster at *Desert I*; chief among them was the lack of interoperability between the armed services. The conglomeration of hardware fielded by special operations aviation was the most visible manifestation of this shortcoming.

Throughout the early 1980s, special operations aviation soldiered on with an unwieldy mix of helicopters. Depending on the mission (and what was available), a DELTA trooper might easily find himself working with CH-3 Jolly Green Giants, CH-53C Sea Stallions, UH1–1N Twin Hueys, CH-47D Chinooks, some newer (and extensively modified) UH-60A Black Hawks, HH-53B and C Pave Low IIIs, and substantially upgraded versions of the OH-6A Cayuse called AH and MH-6 "Little Birds." One highly capable helicopter that DELTA could *not* count on using, except, perhaps, in the most extreme emergency, was the RH-53Ds of *Eagle Claw*. The Navy's entire fleet of this counter–mine version of the Sea Stallion amounted to only twenty–four aircraft before a half–dozen were lost in the Dasht–e Kavir, severely degrading the fleet's mine–sweeping capability. They had been tapped for the mission because the stretched HH-53s, specifically designed for special ops, were literally too long to fit in the elevators of most aircraft carriers without time–consuming removal of their rotor blades, a problem that persists today, even though many of the vessels with smaller elevators have been retired.

Members of all armed services found themselves in general agreement with the Holloway Report's findings, and some organizational, equipment, and training improvements were made. But the most basic problem remained: the lack of "jointness" be-

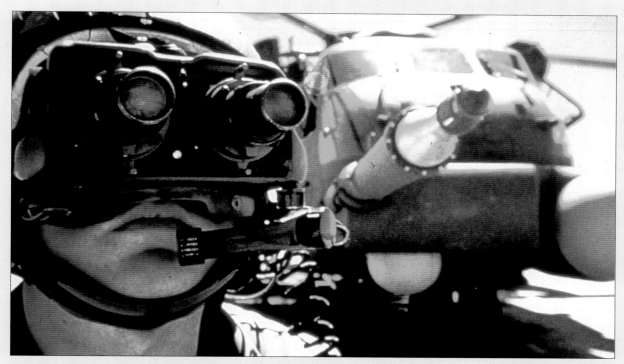

A Pave Low jockey wearing AN/PVS-5A night vision goggles. Even relatively lightweight goggles require that a counterweight be attached to the back of a pilot's helmet, and after a year of night flying an airman's collar size often increases a size or two from the increased exercise of his neck muscles.

tween the Army, Navy, Marines, and Air Force. Under pressure from congress, the Department of Defense attempted, unsuccessfully, to put an end to the interservice rivalries by advocating that the Army become the sole operator of rotary–wing special operations assets, while the Air Force continued to develop its long–range, fixed–wing capability.

Although this particular proposal went nowhere fast because of both congressional backpedaling and continued resistance within the Air Force to anything that would cut into its turf, the future security of the nation was immeasurably enhanced by passage of the 1987 Defense Authorization Act,

which established a unified command incorporating the special operations forces from all services. The new Special Operations Command (SOCOM) could train and deploy forces throughout the world and was given the authority to develop and acquire equipment, services, and supplies peculiar to special ops. Of particular interest to DELTA, was the funding and authorization to modify existing aircraft and develop new helicopter variants.

Under the act, the UH-60 Black Hawk would be reconfigured into three basic models to support all services. The Army's 160th Special Operations Aviation Regiment, Airborns (SOAR) would use the MH-60K Pave Hawk to replace its less–capable MH-60As* in the assault role; the HH-60H "Rescue

*The L variant Black Hawks, with their more–powerful engines, uprated transmissions, and HIRSS (Hover Infrared Supression Subsystem) would not enter service till the following year, 1988. All MH-60As and many UH-60As have since been retrofitted with the HIRSS.

(**Above**) The aftermath of an unscheduled Pave Low landing in Korea. No one was injured in the accident which occurred during a night training exercise. (**Opposite**) HC-130 Combat Shadow tankers and MH-53 Pave Low helicopters.

Hawk" would enhance the Navy's search and rescue as well as special warfare capability; and the Air Force MH-60G Pave Hawk would both replace its aging search and rescue aircraft as well as act as an armed escort for the new MH-53J Pave Low IIIs just entering service. All aircraft would be provided with tiedowns to allow shipboard operations.

The newest Pave Low III variant of the CH-53, called the MH-53J, was tasked to perform the heavy–lift, rotary–wing effort for the near future. A superb special ops aircraft, it is, unfortunately, rather short–legged, and even with the addition of a 600gal fuel bladder, it requires frequent air refuel-

ing during long missions. Congressional sponsors of the 1987 legislation—as well as the Air Force hierarchy—envisioned that it would be phased out of special operations and into search and rescue as MH-47Es came on line.

The special operations variant of the venerable, heavy–lift CH-47D Chinook would complement the MH-60K's mission. Unlike the Pave Low IIIs, MH-47Es can easily fit into the elevators of all aircraft carriers and, thus, offers planners more deployment options. The MH-47E would also have an interoperable avionics system with its smaller cousin and could engage in full and open competition with the CV-22A Osprey for the long–range strategic special ops mission. Unfortunately, the extremely versatile tilt–rotor Osprey, which incorporated the lift, range and speed of a fixed–wing transport with the vertical–lift capability of

a helicopter, was canceled by the Defense Department during the post–Cold War budget cuts.

Unlike other special ops helicopters, the AH and MH-6 Little Birds are not dealt with in the published versions of congressional defense appropriations. These descendants of the trusty old Cayuse were developd and fielded through the use of covert funds in much the same way as the F-117 stealth attack aircraft and, interestingly, started to edge out of the "black" at approximately the same time as the the F-117, primarily because of their high visibility during the 1987–1988 retaliatory attacks on Iranian targets in the Persian Gulf and the 1989 overthrow of Panamanian dictator Manuel Noriega.

The 160th SOAR, which carried out these operations, is known as the Night Stalkers, because of their effective use of darkness during missions, and many of its pilots have logged 2,000 or more flight hours wearing night vision goggles. The regiment, headquartered at Fort Campbell, Kentucky, is composed of four battalions: the 1st with eighteen AH-6s, eighteen MH-6s and thirty MH-60 (incorporating the forward–deployed 617th Special Operations Aviation Detachment (Airborne) in Panama); the 2d with twenty–four MH-47s; the 3d with ten MH-60s and eight MH-47s, based at Hunter Army Airfield, Savannah, Georgia, to support the 1st Ranger Battalion, as it did during the Grenada operation; and an Oklahoma National Guard battalion, the 1/245, based at Tulsa, Oklahoma, with more than three dozen aircraft including fifteen UH-60Ls which will eventually be replaced by MH-60s.

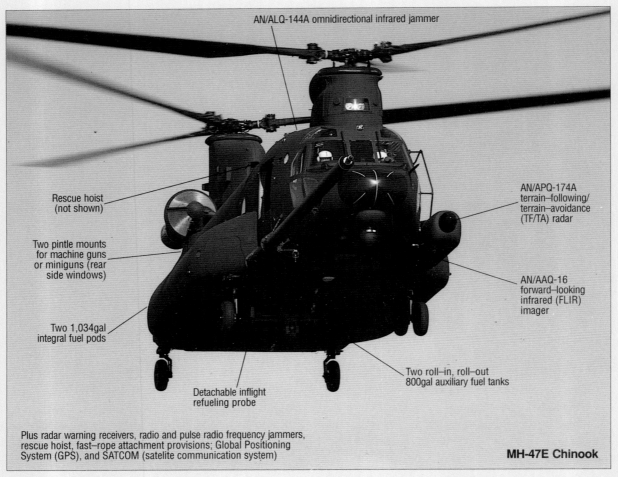

AN/ALQ-144A omnidirectional infrared jammer

Rescue hoist
(not shown)

Two pintle mounts
for machine guns
or miniguns (rear
side windows)

Two 1,034gal
integral fuel pods

Detachable inflight
refueling probe

AN/APQ-174A
terrain–following/
terrain–avoidance
(TF/TA) radar

AN/AAQ-16
forward–looking
infrared (FLIR)
imager

Two roll–in, roll–out
800gal auxiliary fuel tanks

Plus radar warning receivers, radio and pulse radio frequency jammers,
rescue hoist, fast–rope attachment provisions; Global Positioning
System (GPS), and SATCOM (satelite communication system)

MH-47E Chinook

MH-47E Chinook and MH-60 Black Hawk Variants

(**Above**) The MH-47E's highly advanced, integrated avionics system and extended range allow it to complete clandestine, deep–penetration missions. The aircraft can easily use nap–of–the–earth tactics at night and in any weather conditions while placing a minimum workload on the pilot. Special operations enhanced UH-60 Black Hawks have performed spectacularly in long–range combat operations from Grenada to Iraq. (**Opposite top**) An MH-60 Enhanced Black Hawk (sometimes referred to as a Pave Hawk) of the Army's 160th SOAR named *Executioner*, upgraded from either an UH-60A or L. (**Opposite center**) A newly built MH-60G Pave Hawk undergoing flight testing. (**Opposite bottom**) An Air Force MH-60K Pave Hawk upgraded from a UH-60A. All of these helicopters wear infrared–suppressing paint.

MH-60 Enhanced Black Hawk

Two pintle mounts for machine guns or miniguns (forward side windows)

AN/ALQ-144 omnidirectional infrared jammer

Hover infrared suppression subsystem (HIRSS)

AN/AAQ-16 FLIR imager

Two 7.62mm miniguns

Two nineteen–round 70mm rockets launchers

M–130 flare/chaff dispenser tied to missile detector

Plus radar warning receiver, rescue hoist, fast–rope attachment provisions, GPS, and SATCOM

MH-60G Pave Hawk

Wire strike protection

AN/AAQ-16 FLIR imager

Two pintle mounts for machine guns or miniguns (forward side windows)

Inflight refueling probe

AN/APN-239 weather radar (with ground mapping modes)

M-130 flare/chaff dispenser tied to missile detector (will be replaced by ALE-40 dispensers)

Plus radar warning receiver, radio and pulse radio frequency jammers, rescue hoist, fast–rope rappelling system, GPS and SATCOM

MH-60K Pave Hawk

AN/ALQ-144A omnidirectional infrared jammer

Wire strike protection

HIRSS

M–130 flare/chaff dispensertied to missile detector

Two crash–worthy 230gal external auxiliary fuel tanks

AN/APQ-174A TF/TA radar

Inflight refueling probe

Mounts for air–to–air or air–to–ground rockets

AN/AAQ-16 FLIR imager

Two pintle mounts for machine guns or miniguns

Plus radar warning receivers, radio and pulse radio frequency jammers, rescue hoist, fast rope rappelling system, GPS, SATCOM, and laser detector

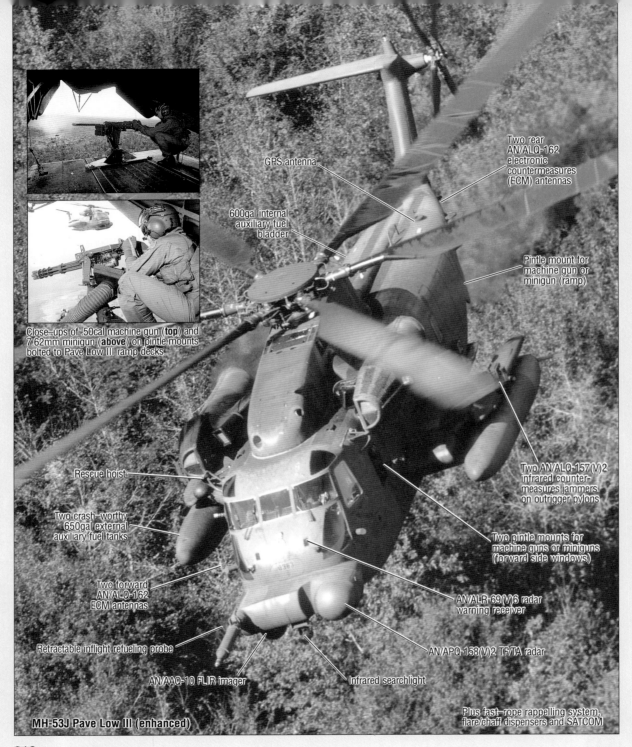

Close-ups of .50cal machine gun (**top**) and
7.62mm minigun (**above**) on pintle mounts
bolted to Pave Low III ramp decks.

GPS antenna

Two rear
AN/ALQ-162
electronic
countermeasures
(ECM) antennas

600gal internal
auxiliary fuel
bladder

Pintle mount for
machine gun or
minigun (ramp)

Rescue hoist

Two AN/ALQ-157(V)2
infrared counter-
measures jammers
on outrigger pylons

Two crash-worthy
650gal external
auxiliary fuel tanks

Two pintle mounts for
machine guns or
miniguns
(forward side windows)

Two forward
AN/ALQ-162
ECM antennas

AN/ALR-69(V)6 radar
warning receiver

Retractable inflight refueling probe

AN/APQ-158(V)2 TF/TA radar

AN/AAQ-10 FLIR imager

Infrared searchlight

MH-53J Pave Low III (enhanced)

Plus fast-rope rappelling system,
flare/chaff dispensers and SATCOM

MH-53
Pave Low III

The MH-53H and J Pave Low IIIs are descended from a long line of Sikorsky helicopters that have performed rescue and special operations from the Korean War through Vietnam and the aborted 1980 raid to free American hostages in Iran. Of a family that is second only to the Soviet–built Mi-26 Halo in size and heavy–lift capability, the Pave Low III is capable of operating with pin–point accuracy in all weather conditions and at night. It also shares many components with other Air Force assets, such as the FLIR on the AC-130 Specter gunships and MC-130 Combat Talons transports. (**Top**) Special operations forces exit the rear of a Pave Low III via a flexable ladder and (**above**) by fast–rope. (**Opposite**) An MH-53J skimming the trees. One recent night training exercise included seven Pave Lows receiving four inflight refuelings each during a nearly eight–hour flight. The exercise concluded with the helicopters arriving within two seconds of their target time and unloading thirty men each in five seconds.

MD 530MG

Little Bird Variants

Based on an extremely popular airframe that can be found in extensive use by both civilian and government entities in every corner of the globe, the Little Bird offers great agility, adaptability, and its own version of visual stealth if such is warranted by a mission. The aircraft is manufactured by McDonnell Douglas and carries a basic civilian designation of either MD 500 or MD 530. The 500, 500C, and 500D aircraft were produced with a round, bubble–like nose through 1982 when all subsequent helicopters of these types were manufactured with the more pointed nose of the MD 500E, 500F, and 500MG, as well as the slightly larger and more powerful MD 520 and 530 series aircraft. The US Army's orders for these helicopters after 1982, however, have generally called for the retention of the bubble nose to maintain the option of installing a TOW antitank missile aiming sight and keep visual commonality with the large number of pre–1982, nonmilitary aircraft of this type.

The high civilian and foreign–military demand for a small, reliable, inexpensive helicopter was coupled with the manufacturer's effort to fill that demand by incorporating a large variety of powerplant, transmission, rotor, and other changes on what is essentially the same airframe. This proliferation of different aircraft types found its way into the 160th SOAR's inventory since there was never a specific production line opened for the US Army, all purchases being made in bits and pieces over a decade of off–the–shelf buying to supplement its original OH-6A Cayuse helicopters. This proliferation has led to a mind–boggling alphabet soup of aircraft types in the 160th's 1st Battalion, the unit that most directly supports DELTA. Jane's *All the World's Aircraft* states that the MH-6B and AH-6C are derived from the OH-6A; the AH-6F and MH-6E from MD 500MG; and the AH-6G, MH-6F and MH-6J from the MD 530MG. "A" designations are given to the heavily armed attack versions of the Little Bird, which can be armed with a variety of miniguns, machine guns, rockets, and missiles. Nearly all Little Birds are equipped with a swinging, crane–like arm for fast–rope rappeling and Stabo operations, and the AH-6G, MH-6E, MH-6F, and possibly the AH-6F, have multifunction displays and forward–looking infrared (FLIR) imagers to be used in association with night vision goggles.

(**Opposite**) MD 530MG unleashing a salvo of 70mm rockets during weapons testing at the US Army's Yuma Proving Grounds, Arizona and closeups of seven–tube 70mm rocket launcher and TOW antitank missile pod. (**Top to bottom**) 160th SOAR AH-6G Little Bird bereft of any identifying markings or "sterile"; an MD 530N equipped with NOTAR (no tail rotor) system, including close–up of steering louvres on underside of tail; and MD 530N configured for transportation with louver cone and tail fins folded upward and main rotor blades stowed along tail boom. Note that the MD 530 models in the lower photos have both the pointed nose, for streamlining, and the pre–1982 bubble nose of the MD 500 series aircraft still used on most military variants.

Of great benefit to DELTA in urban counterterrorist situations is the 160th SOAR's conversion to the NOTAR system on its Little Birds. The NOTAR uses a variable–pitch fan and direct jet thruster to push cool air through longitudinal steering louvres on a circulation control tailboom. Although early tests by the 160th showed "higher than desired pilot workload" due to a tendency for the nose to wander at low speeds, yaw–only stability augmentation corrected the problem. With the NOTAR system, AH/MH-6 aircraft display a greatly reduced acoustic signature, increased hover stability, and roughly double the lateral and rearward speeds of conventional helicopters. The absence of a tail rotor also eliminates the danger of tail strikes on ground crew and allows DELTA troopers more freedom of movement around the aircraft during operations.

AN/ALQ-144A omnidirectional infrared jammer

Two seven–tube 70mm rocket launchers

AN/AAQ-16 FLIR imager

AH-6G

MD 530N

MD 530N

AC-130 Specter Gunship

The AC-130 Specter gunship is a basic C-130 modified with side–mounted weapons and various sensors that make it highly adaptable to a variety of special missions. When fielded against targets with few antiaircraft defenses and a minimal air threat, the Specter is able to provide close air support much more efficiently than a large force of fighter aircraft and is a particularly effective platform for interdiction and armed reconnaissance missions. The Specter has the ability to aid in perimeter defense, escort, surveillance, search and rescue, infiltration/ exfiltration, illumination, and landing zone support operations, as well as to conduct limited airborne command and control functions for other strike aircraft.

The AC-130H is armed with two 20mm Gatling–type guns, a rapid–firing 40mm cannon and 105mm howitzer supported by a laser rangefinder (which can also be used for marking targets for laser–guided bombs), an infrared sensor to identify heat sources such as people and vehicles, a beacon–tracking radar, a fire control computer, two–kilowatt searchlight and a low–light–level television capable of amplifying even faint traces of starlight to monitor both targets and friendly forces. The newer AC-130U models have retained the 40 and 105mm weapons but use a single 25mm Gatling–type gun fed by a two–canister, automated loading system instead of the H models' 20mm guns which required their linked ammunition to be hand–loaded. Other new features have also been added such as the F-15's fire control radar, lightweight Kevlar armor, inflight refueling capability, and a highly efficient, soundproof battle management center.

Depending on the type of target, threat environment, weather, and desired level of destruction, weapons can be accurately employed at altitudes from 3,000 to 20,000 feet above ground level. The Specter fires from a constant angle of bank and, at a typical slant range of 10,000 feet, the remarkably stable gun platform can deliver ordnance within ten feet of its target even under conditions of low cloud ceilings or poor visibility. Unlike fighter aircraft, which must make separate runs on hostile forces, targets are continually visible throughout the gunship's entire orbit and can be fired on at will. But even though the run–in headings required by fighter aircraft are not needed, no–fire headings may be imposed from the ground or automatically computed by the aircrew if there is a risk of short rounds hitting friendly forces from a particular angle.

The Specter's two–kilowatt searchlight can be used to illuminate targets and landing zones, aid in search and rescue, and supply light for the television sensor if its illuminator is inoperative. In combat, the searchlight is normally used in a covert infrared mode, to provide illumination for night vision devices, since its overt white light mode would easily pinpoint the gunship's position for hostile forces. Its effectiveness is reduced with altitude and weather.

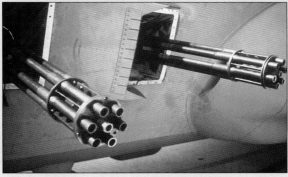

DELTA troopers in a tight spot can mark their ground position with a wide variety of items. First, Mk-6 and Mk-25 ground markers can be dropped by hand from the rear of the Specter, itself, and will burn for forty–five and thirty minutes, respectively. Next, transponders, including the handheld SST-101 miniponder, can be picked up by the aircraft's beacon tracking radar at up to ten nautical miles and the powerful AN/UPN-25 and SST-181x transponders can be received by the ship's navigation radar at up to sixty nautical miles. A standard survival vest strobe light with a removeable infrared filter can also be used either visually or with the filter installed. The infrared filter provides the same information to the aircrew as the unmasked strobe but prevents visible light from revealing the friendly ground position to the enemy forces. Positive identification is provided by turning one or more strobes off and on in response to radio instructions for the aircrew. The old standby, lightweight three–by–five–foot cloth reflective panels, can clearly mark ground reference points when illuminated by the Specter, either overtly or covertly. Other methods of marking positions include flashlights, vehicle lights, pen gun flares, tracer rounds, fires, fire arrows, signal mirrors, and simply running a vehicle engine with the ignition unshielded.

(**Opposite**) An AC-130H Specter fires its 105mm gun during a night exercise; (**top**) airmen loading a Specter's 40mm gun; (**left**) twin 20mm Gatling–type guns aft of the cockpit; and (**right**) 40mm and 105mm guns forward of the aircraft's loading ramp.

MC-130 Combat Talon and HC-130 Combat Shadow

The mission of the MC-130E and H Combat Talons is to conduct day and night infiltration, exfiltration, resupply, psychological operations, and aerial reconnaissance into hostile or enemy controlled territory using air landings, air drops or surface–to–air recoveries. The use of FLIR imagers enables aircrews to visually identify targets and checkpoints at night while terrain–following/terrain–avoidance(TF/TA) radar and an inertial navigation system allow extreme accuracy while navigating to unmarked drop zones. Missions are normally flown at night using a high–low–high altitude profile. The high portion is flown prior to penetrating and after exiting the target area at an altitude that minimizes fuel consumption and enemy detection. The aircraft then descends to the lowest possible altitude consistent with flying safety and uses its TF/TA radar to penetrate and operate in hostile territory.

The Talon's range depends on several factors, including configuration, payload, en route winds and weather, and the length of time spent at fuel–guzzling, low–level flight. For planning purposes, its range (without refueling and factoring in two hours at low level) is 2,800 nautical miles. With inflight refueling, the Talon's range is limited only by the availability of tanker support and the effect

that crew fatigue may have on the mission. The Talon is not a rapid response aircraft. Operating deep in heavily defended enemy territory requires extensive preflight planning, and units normally receive notification at least forty–eight hours out with a final briefing on threats and positions of friendly forces before takeoff.

Aircrews are capable of successfully operating at unmarked drop zones (DZs) but usually have something they can hang their headphones on. When ground and air component commanders agree to use a specific DZ, reception committee personnel coordinate with the aircrew on the type of markings to be used, configuration of the DZ, method of authentication and release point determination. The most frequent cause for mission aborts is a lack of coordination or confusion over marking procedures; it is important to note that terrain–following is made difficult during moderate showers and even further degraded during heavy thunderstorms.

Depending on mission, an aircrew makes either a static–line, low–altitude air drop; a high–altitude, low–opening (HALO) air drop; a surface–to–air recovery (STAR) using a Fulton extraction system; or may simply land the aircraft. For static–line drops during combat operations, a Talon is flown as low as 750 feet while a HALO drop, which requires a free fall before parachute opening, is never conducted from lower than 1,500 feet. For static–line drops combining both men and equipment (such as rubber rafts), troops exit immediately after ejection of equipment. A STAR can be used for the extractions dur-

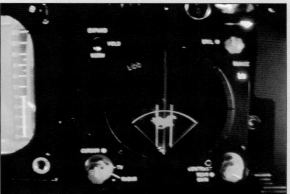

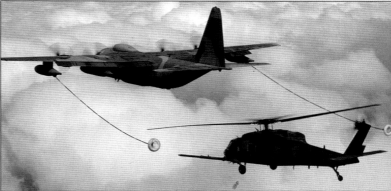

ing either day or night but requires fairly good weather to accomplish the mission safely. Either two people or 500 pounds of equipment can be picked up over land or water per pass. During air landings, the minimum length necessary is the takeoff/landing roll plus 500 feet for a total of approximately 3,000 feet. The Talon's minimum required runway width is sixty feet and, while the capability exists to set down at a landing zone that has no lights or is lit with infrared lights, use of the Special Forces seven–light panel marking system (which includes a 250–foot/ ten percent safety zone at each end out) is preferred.

The HC-130P Combat Shadow tankers have essentially the same extensive radar and navigational aids as the Combat Talon, as well as the ability to refuel two helicopters simultaneously in flight. After the tanker unreels its fuel line and slows to approximately 120mph, the Shadow's customer slowly edges its refuel probe closer to the drogue–tipped hose while making certain that it stays beneath or to the outside of the tankers turbulent slipstream. It generally takes an MH-53 less than ten minutes to top off and an MH-47, with its huge fuel blisters, can get its fill in about fifteen minutes.

(**Opposite**) The retracted nose prongs, which, when extended forward and out, snag the line of a target baloon during surface–to–air recoveries, can be clearly seen in this shot of a MC-130 receiving fuel from a KC-135 tanker. See page 120 for a complete recovery sequence. (**Top left**) A Vietnam–era MC-130 rigged for a pick–up with guard cables running from the top of its bulbous nose to its wingtips and (**top right**) a similarly configured MC-130E or H variant. Note the difference in radar bulge configuration on the newer aircraft, to accommodate its expanded TF/TA, FLIR, and other systems, as well as its lengthened prongs. (**Above left**) TF/TA radar screen, displaying an obstruction in the aircraft's path as a blob below the upwardly bowed line, and a portion of the FLIR display off to the left. These systems and all other internal controls can be made to glow in a subdued mode so that they do not interfere with the pilot's night vision goggles. (**Above right**) An MH-60 carefully maneuvering its refuel probe up to an HC-130's extended fuel line and drogue.

Chapter 5
Back to the Desert

The deep sleep of the early morning hours was interrupted by the familiar obnoxious sound of a pager going off. Reaching for his clothing, the young Sergeant kissed his wife's head and ambled down the hall to check on his son. Allowing the hall light to play over the boy's sandy hair, the trooper bent down to kiss him goodbye as he had so often in the past. Waiting until he had left the house, he sat on the front steps to pull on his well worn cowboy boots. He climbed into his pickup truck and drove to the post. In less than two hours, the young sergeant's troop was winging away from Pope Air Force Base near Fort Bragg. As the wheels of the lumbering C-141 Starlifter retracted into their wells, his troop commander was already scanning the initial intelligence reports from the agencies supporting the unit. Things were not so good in the land of oil and sand.

At 0400 on the morning of Thursday, August 2, 1990, mechanized elements of Saddam Hussein's elite Republican Guards stabbed across the desert frontier separating Iraq and Kuwait east of the disputed Rumalia oilfield. Iraqi forces had been massing steadily across the border for almost two weeks before the invasion, but both Western and Arabian governments believed this to be nothing more than a show of force to bolster Saddam's financial claims against the oil–rich kingdom. By midday, all meaningful resistance by Kuwait's tiny army had been crushed and its royal family had fled to a sumptuous exile in Saudi Arabia.

The Baathist government in Baghdad rejoiced over its quick victory and believed that it had been accomplished with such speed that the world was presented with a *fait accompli*. Saddam expected a toothless condemnation from the United Nations and perhaps even a half–hearted economic embargo that would soon fade away. But his analysis was fatally flawed. US and British leaders meeting in the United States immediately resolved that the rest of the Middle East's oil resources must be kept out of Saddam's bloodied hands, at all costs. Even before his generals gathered their forces for the next morning's move to the Saudi border, numerous elements of America's special operations forces were either already deployed or were going "wheels up" from bases in the United States and Europe.

From the first moment President George Bush was notified that Iraqi forces were plunging across

---

A thirsty trooper inhales bottled water in the shade of a C-141 StarLifter in Saudi Arabia.

Kuwait's border, one of the prime challenges to face him as the National Command Authority was the possibility—indeed probability—that large numbers of Americans would become prisoners in a dangerous diplomatic game. The specter of a second major Middle East hostage crisis loomed over the Pentagon and the White House. Although public speculation was kept to a minimum, no one needed to be reminded that the Carter administration fell because of the prolonged hostage crisis in Iran. The extreme vulnerability of the US Embassy staff and numerous Americans associated with Kuwait's petroleum industry was evident. When coupled with the Baathist regime's close ties with terrorist groups, history of wanton aggression against its neighbors, and deadly abuse of its own people, the president had no choice but to act. Although special operations forces assets already in the Gulf were capable of performing the hasty option response, the National Command Authority launched the first DELTA assets into the Middle East.

Crisis action teams were dispatched to Saudi Arabia and other friendly nations to establish C^3 (command, control, and communications) sites for future operations and to provide a terminal for information to and from Washington. Launch sites for missions were identified and staging areas hastily opened. Meanwhile, back at Fort Bragg, the Joint Special Operations Command (JSOC) worked hard to avoid being caught flatfooted and began building a massive workup of target folders for the "long war" that was sure to come.

Other important assets moving into the area were elements of the Intelligence Support Activity (ISA). Like so many other parts of the special operations force, ISA was an offshoot of the *Desert I* after-action review. A critical failing during the hostage crisis in Iran was the lack of information from human intelligence sources or HUMINT. In Iran, DELTA did not have an "eyeball" on its target. In Iraq and Kuwait, ISA would provide the needed eyes.

Various elements of the myriad special operations units in Europe and the United States continued to trickle in, and most of the burden of working with the resistance inside Kuwait was assumed by the Special Forces units that already had that mission in accordance with theater war plans. As predicted, US and other foreign nationals did indeed become "guests" at selected Iraqi strategic military and nuclear sites but were eventually allowed to leave as a "gesture of goodwill" when their continued captivity threatened to precipitate, not prevent, an assault on Iraq. DELTA remained.

Commencement of the coalition air campaign raised fears that hostages might be taken in retaliation at widely scattered locations around the globe, and additional target folders of possible hostage-holding centers began to take shape. While significant terrorist operations never emerged, the public display of Allied prisoners of war did cause concern at the highest levels, and plans were formulated to rescue those individuals. Small teams were also selected to carry out a number of sensitive, direct-action missions against targets in Iraq's command and control nets.

Initially, special operations units were faced with the same problem they have always had to deal with: How to get the conventional force commanders to use their capabilities properly or even at all. For example, the 75th Ranger Regiment's assessment team left the Gulf after finding out that there was very little they could do in the theater, and the elite light infantry of the 82d Airborne Division was severely handicapped on the billiard table–terrain without an immense amount of support.

Colonel Jessie Johnson, commander of Central Command's (CENTCOM's) Special Operations Command (SOC), drafted his campaign plans for the upcoming desert war from his headquarters at King Fahd International Airport near Dhahran. A

(**Right**) All–terrain Fast Attack Vehicles (FAVs) and motorcycles (**above**) saw extensive use by special operations forces, including DELTA, during operations in Iraq and Kuwait and operated from forward bases in Saudi Arabia or base camps established far behind Iraqi lines. Motorcycles with heavily muffled engines offered troopers individualized, high–speed movement coupled with the ability to approach a target from several axes simultaneously and, on some types of missions, would be used in combination with FAVs.

Capable of being armed with a wide assortment of goodies—machine guns, antitank weapons, grenade launchers and almost anything else one might think of—FAVs offered substantial hitting power and the ability to travel extended distances across the desert at speeds up to 80– plus mph. The vehicles pictured here both mount AT4 antitank missile launchers on the outsides of their frame roofs and M60E3 machine guns forward of the passenger seats. An additional gunner sits in the elevated, rear seat, which can swivel around for firing at targets behind the vehicle. In the top photo, this position mounts a .50cal machine gun while the vehicle above sports a 40mm grenade launcher. Note the dart board taped to the nose of the FAV at lower left, a not–so–subtle comment by its crew on their vulnerability. *Soldier of Fortune*.

veteran of *Desert I*, where he commanded the joint Ranger–DELTA road–watch teams, Johnson knew what difficulties awaited his forces. Luckily for him, his boss at CENTCOM, General H. Norman Schwarzkopf, had the utmost confidence in his special ops commander. Despite attempts by elements within the Joint Chiefs of Staff, to replace him with a two–star officer, Schwarzkopf kept his faith in Johnson, who in return, became the architect for several brilliantly executed operations.

Saddam's Vengence Weapon

As the war progressed, another in history's long line of terror weapons was unleashed in the Middle East: the Scud B medium–range ballistic missile, successor to Hitler's infamous V-1 and V-2 rockets

DELTA operated out of secure, remote bases dotting the desert wastes south of the Saudi–Iraqi border. (**Above**) A C-130, of unidentified type, sits baking under "big red" across from a special operations Black Hawk with external, add–on fuel tanks. (**Left**) Air base security armed for bear with a combination M16 assault rifle/M203 grenade launcher. His vest is packed with twenty 40mm grenades for the M203, and he is using night vision goggles, which turn even the blackest nights into a green day, to scan the perimeter.

of World War II. On those earlier weapons, The "V" designation was, itself, part of Hitler's psychological warfare campaign aimed at terrorizing the British people. Nazi English–language propaganda broadcasts gleefully warned Britons of the immense destruction that would be wreaked on their cities by the "vengeance" weapons. Since their target was an English–speaking public, the Nazis named their rockets the V-1 and V-2, instead of giving them an "R" designation for the equivalent German word, *rache*.

The Scud retained many of the V-2's basic characteristics, along with many deadly improvements. Highly mobile, it nevertheless required more than an hour to fuel and its involved targeting procedures took excruciatingly long to complete, even when performed by experienced crews at preplotted sites. To make matters even more interesting, homemade

(**Right**) A Scud B medium–range ballistic missile on its MAZ-543 transporter–erector–launcher and (**above**) a rare photograph of a Scud impact. Even before certain changes were made to the weapon that degraded its accuracy, it was not known for its ability to make pinpoint strikes. The weapon in the above photo was fired by Soviet forces at Afghan guerrillas who had surrounded Loyalist troops at an isolated garrison. It missed the guerrillas and instead landed within the government troops' defensive perimeter. Above: *Soldier of Fortune*.

versions of the missile, like the *al Hussein*, incorporated range enhancements that both reduced its warhead capacity and severely degraded its ability to strike near its target.

The Soviets designed the Scud to deliver small nuclear warheads, or as an area saturation system when fired in conventional battery salvos; the Iraqis instead used it as simply a fire–in–the–general–direction–of–your–adversary–and–then–wait–for–the–results weapon. Fixed launch sites containing both real and dummy missiles existed at airfields in western Iraq, targeting Israel, and in eastern Iraq, aimed at Iran and Saudi Arabia. These sites were well known to US and Israeli planners and could be easily removed from the picture. It was Saddam's surprisingly large number of wheeled

225

launchers for the Scud and shorter–range Frog missiles that proved to be exceedingly difficult targets for air reconnaissance assets to locate. This difficulty in targeting the mobile launchers in the wide expanses of Iraq set the stage for one role the troopers of DELTA never dreamed of or trained for: Scud hunting.

The scenario thrust upon DELTA was a far cry from the world of takedowns and hostage rescues each man became immersed in the moment he entered Wally World. Many, if not all, the troops deployed to the Gulf had extensive training in their initial Special Forces specialties and were already experts in carrying out such standard missions as unconventional warfare, special reconnaissance, foreign internal defense, plus search and rescue operations, to name just a few, but it was the introduction of Saddam's terror weapons that forced the counterterrorists to revert to these basic war-fighting specialties and become what the press dubbed "super commandos." Curiously enough, though, since Scud missiles served no real military purpose —when used as they were by the Iraqis— DELTA troopers could still be said to be involved in a new, unanticipated form of counterterrorism.

The war was going poorly for the Iraqi warlord, and he knew that his best bet to overcome the military setbacks around was to drive a wedge between the Arab and Western elements in the coalition arrayed against him. If attacks on Jewish population centers could push Israel into a knee–jerk military response, Saddam believed that indignant Arab masses would finally heed his call for a *jihad*, or holy war, and either overthrow unfriendly governments like President Hosni Mubarak's in Egypt or, at the very least, force their governments to withdraw from the coalition. Western elements isolated at the end of a very long logistics line would be forced into an ignominious withdrawal.

Saddam's strategy was not difficult to anticipate,

and the White House made it crystal clear through strong public statements (coupled with a rapid, showy deployment of a Patriot surface–to–air missile battery to Tel Aviv) that the drawing of Israel into the war would be prevented at all costs. CENTCOM had no choice but to commit its Air Force component to a resource–consuming search for mobile launchers with little to show for its efforts.* This same mission was also handed to the Army's Special Forces, who, if necessary, would actually target individual vehicles for air strikes— an extremely risky business for the troops involved but a mission that was, in light of the strategic situation, of immense importance. CENTCOM quickly discovered, however, that a critical shortage of trained special recon teams existed in the Kuwaiti Theater of Operations (KTO).

Every available Green Beret was committed to serving as liaison with the Saudi Army, training Kuwaiti resistance forces, or conducting intelligence–gathering missions for General Schwarzkopf's headquarters. When it became necessary to scrape together additional assets to help locate Scuds, the only force in the KTO was the counterterrorists of DELTA, as well as some British SAS personnel. Reports by the European and American news media later referred to this use of DELTA as if the unit were some sort of key reserve, when, in reality, it was all Schwarzkopf had at the moment.

Special operations assets made available by the coalition forces, primarily DELTA and the desert–wise SAS, were formed into teams and prepared for the upcoming operations.* At first, though, Colonel

---

*The continued success of the Iraqis at hitting Israeli and Saudi population centers necessitated that a full squadron of F-15Es be essentially pulled from the air campaign and assigned the task of eliminating mobile Scuds. Other air assets were soon added as the equivalent of three squadrons became tied up by the effort, and the number of sorties by Scud–hunting intelligence, refueling and strike aircraft sometimes climbed to more than 300 per twenty–four hour period. Although a severe drain on US resources, this heavy and prolonged commitment was instrumental in convincing the Israelis to call off two planned raids into western Iraq that could have had a disastrous effect on the war effort.

Johnson's professionals from Smoke Bomb Hill and the Ranch were understandably missing from the almost–continuous Gulf news coverage, while other forces from Fort Bragg, the XVIIIth Airborne Corps, 1st Corps Support Command, and the renowned 82d Airborne Division received their share of the limelight. But it wasn't long before reporters were hearing strange tales of parachutes gliding silently through the Arabian night to deposit their human cargo on the desert floor. The stories are many, but all have the same theme and similar scenarios. The following is just one of them. Maybe it's just a good piece of propaganda; then again, maybe it's true.

Prepping the Battlefield

An in-depth mission analysis was conducted on the upcoming Scud hunt by the intelligence agencies supporting the theater's special operations forces. The intel experts looked at such subjects as the terrain and infiltration/exfiltration routes

---

*The SAS not only retains a great deal of institutional knowledge on desert warfare but also makes frequent use of a training area in the Gulf state of Oman.

US special operations forces did not truly "own the night" as the often–repeated slogan claimed, but did operate extremely effectively in that environment, due to a combination of superb training and equipment. (**Above** and **above right**) Troopers viewed through a NVG move out under cover of darkness and rappel from a Black Hawk.

---

through Iraqi antiaircraft belts and known locations of enemy units were plotted on the situation maps. As this information was analyzed, a clear picture emerged indicating that the majority of the target areas could be easily reached by Army MH-60 Pave Hawks of the 160th Special Operations Aviation Regiment (Airborne) or Air Force MH-53 Pave Low IIIs of the 1st Special Operations Wing.

Unfortunately, the extremely heavy demand for the specialized helicopters in the KTO, as well as various other considerations, meant that they could not be used in every situation. For tactical reasons, it was decided that the target area around which this story centers necessitated that DELTA conduct a HAHO infiltration. HAHO (pronounced *hey–ho*)

is the acronym for high–altitude, high–opening and essentially means that the drop is conducted at about 30,000 feet or higher, with the jumper opening his parachute almost immediately after clearing the plane. The trooper then glides his maneuverable, double–canopy parachute through the sky and lands with pinpoint accuracy at a predetermined site. The distance from the point that the jumper pulls his rip cord and where he lands can be as much as fifty miles.

The team participating in this unique Scud–hunting mission is required to prepare a "briefback" on how each trooper will carry out his duties. The briefback is standard operating procedure within the special operations community and covers the friendly versus enemy situation, the mission, its execution, support requirements, command structures, and a short, concise, yet detailed narrative of how the trooper will help accomplish the mission. The briefback is normally given to the leadership of the unit and not only demonstrates to the commander that his men are ready, but also assures the team that everyone is playing off the same sheet of music.

After a few carefully considered questions, the team is given the go–ahead and conducts final rehearsals, equipment checks, and other preparations. On this mission, they are more concerned with the "sneak and peek" than direct–action aspects of the operation. If they can find the missile's elusive transporter–erector–launchers (TELs), they will call

An Air Force Special Operations combat control team member exits from the open ramp of a MC-130 Combat Talon. Control teams are often inserted before the arrival of special operations or conventional forces to mark landing or drop zones that must be used at night by pilots using NVGs and aircraft fitted with infrared imagers. For example, a control team member had already arrived at and marked the *Desert I* refuel site in Iran before the arrival of the aircraft bearing DELTA. The lack of weapon and rucksack indicates that this was taken during a practice exercise.

in an air strike and, if circumstances require it, use a portable laser to target the weapon for destruction by the fast–movers of the Air Force.

The basic plan is simple. The team will move undetected from their drop zone to a hidden observation point overlooking a likely area for Scud activity. When confirmed targets enter the area, SOC will be notified, and an E-2C Sentry's airborne warning and control system (AWACS) will vector strike aircraft into the target area. During their approach, the jets follow voice or signal beacon wavelengths to their prey. Air attacks will be conducted visually but any TELs obscured by darkness, camouflage, or poor weather will be lased, or "painted," by the recon team. Rolling in on their bomb runs, the fast–movers' sensors will lock on a laser guided bomb or rocket and release the "smart" munitions to glide along the laser's invisible path like a road map to the target. The jets will then maneuver away from the area, having only teased the outer perimeters of the lethal antiaircraft systems' kill zones, and the DELTA troopers, if necessary, will continue to lase targets for incoming aircraft from their concealed hideout. As many Iraqi units found out, the laser's invisible beam brought very visible destruction.

Reaching the austere departure airfield, the team is ushered into a secured hangar cordoned off from the rest of the facility. It is here that all of the specialized gear needed for the mission is stored. The departure airfield will also be the mission support site (MSS) for the operation, and a mobile communications van, mated to the main SOC communications bunker at King Khalid Military City,* has been moved into the hangar. The mobile van constitutes part of a duplex communications network

*Designed and constructed by the US Army Corps of Engineers during the Iran–Iraq War, King Khalid Military City is one of three huge base complexes around which the outer defenses of the kingdom are formed. The "Emerald City" (as it was called by many US soldiers, who were surprised at the sight of it rising out of the desert wastes) is located roughly 110 miles southwest of Kuwait's westernmost point almost halfway to the major Saudi Arabian city of Buraydah.

(**Above**) The control and reporting center outside King Khalid Military City which linked US and Saudi mobile and airborne communications. (**Left**) An internal view.

equipment. This union ends only when the mission is completed—or worse.

The six troopers wear sterile desert camouflage fatigues with the required face scarves and flop hats. Struggling mightily, they pull on cumbersome, insulated jumpsuits to help fight off the cold which sometimes exceeds –50 degrees at 35,000 feet, even in the Middle East. In addition to its insulation properties, the jumpsuits have radar–absorbing capabilities that will impede the enemy's ability to pick up the soldiers as they glide across the sky. Fortunately, the February night—cold even in the desert—engulfs the airfield, providing a small amount of relief as they don their main and reserve parachutes and oxygen masks. Before high–altitude drops like this one, both the jumpers and the crew of the unpressurized aircraft have to start breathing oxygen one hour before takeoff or "launch time." The team receives final jumpmaster inspections, and the troop commander arrives for that one last visit a leader makes. He is more of a fellow member than a

that ensured reception of the team's vital intelligence even if one part of the network went down from either systems failure or enemy action. Except for the team's communications specialist, who is coordinating preselected frequencies and transmission times, the troopers take little notice of the signals experts moving to and from the van and stay focused on checking and rechecking their weapons and field gear. All weapons had been test–fired before leaving the isolation site, and at the hangar, a ritual of sorts takes place, which will wed the jumper to his air items and other essential

230

A C-141 prepares for a night takeoff from an airstrip in the Saudi desert.

commander, and everyone in the hangar knows the way the boss feels. He'd trade in his major's oak leaves to be going with them into Iraq.

Following the safety NCO out into the desert darkness, each man finds his own release to the inevitable tension. A flick of a "bird" finger to the top sergeant with a muffled, "Up yours, Top," or "See ya at the NCO club," mark the beginning of another mission. Their transportation, a huge C-141B, rests majestically next to the hangar, its gaping clamshell doors exposing the broad tail. The team struggles up the StarLifter's ramp into the cavernous cargo bay, while the crew chief and loadmaster guide the men around the small patches of hydraulic fluid habitually dotting its deck. An oxygen console rests securely in the center of the compartment, and each jumper plugs into it after disconnecting the oxygen mask from his individual bailout bottle.

As the StarLifter slowly pivots and then begins to taxi, the crew chief switches the internal lighting to the red lights required for the team to gain their night vision. The pilot reaches the main runway, and as he revs up the four powerful Pratt & Whitney turbofans for takeoff, each team member is caught in the thoughts of the moment: the myriad details that must be covered so that the mission succeeds, his wife, family, or the girl back home— the same thoughts soldiers have had to deal with since the second–oldest profession began.

The Jump

The C-141B flies on an easterly heading to its rendezvous point with two B-52s flying in from the tiny island base of Diego Garcia deep in the Indian Ocean. Snuggling into the number three slot, the formation portrays just another inbound bomber formation for any Iraqi radar still operating.

As the unlikely trio nears Iraqi airspace, the jumpmaster receives updates from the navigator. At prescribed checkpoints, he notifies the team of their exact coordinates so that all know where they are in the event that they are forced to bail out early. Thirty minutes from jump time, the team prepares for the "infil." The men assist each other in making sure that their rucksacks ride snugly against the bottom of the main parachute. Checking their padded–leather jump helmets, goggles, and oxygen masks one last time, they prepare to change over from the oxygen consoles to the bailout bottle strapped to their left sides. On command from the jumpmaster, the jumpers switch to their bailout bottles and waddle toward the open troop doors on each side of the fuselage.

Staff Sergeant Len Rodgers and the rest of the recon team work their way to positions along the walls of the StarLifter as their communications man, serving as jumpmaster, completes his visual checks and gives the hand signal for "Stand by." The cabin's eerie red lights, green jump light, and the howling winds whipping in the open troop doors could easily meet the needs of a good nightmare, and Staff Sergeant Rodgers is nearly deafened by the roaring wind and mournful banshee whine of the engines. He marvels that some people actually think this is fun! Moving closer to the door, he receives the "Go!" signal, as the jumpmaster disappears out the open troop door.

Pivoting on the ball of his right foot, Rodgers swings out behind him and falls into the position commonly referred to as the "frog." He's immediately followed in quick succession by the rest of the team. Plummeting through the moonless night, arms and legs extended, Rodgers begins to feel the penetrating cold. Behind him, each man monitors the altimeter securely strapped to his left wrist and assumes the glide position as they prepare to deploy their parachutes. At 30,000 feet, the aerial ballet continues as the team members pull their silver ripcords.

To the casual observer, this particular maneuver looks like a giant hand shaking each jumper loose from his very life. In reality, the men feel very little, and each checks the double–layer canopy above to see if his is fully inflated. Fortunately for this team, all now resemble airfoil–shaped wings, and the jumpers line up in a rough, follow–the–leader formation, taking the planned westerly heading as Staff Sergeant Rodgers navigates through the frozen night air. Settling into the parachute harness, he scans the panorama unfolding before him. Far to the north, flashes appear from the bombing mission the team's C-141 had joined. Craning his neck around to the southeast, he can barely make out green* tracers darting skyward in a futile search for the destroyers of a known Scud site's command and control bunker and wonders if it was done in by one of the F-117 stealth attack aircraft. He turns back and looks toward the unseen drop zone and toys with the idea that the display is for their benefit. He knows,

*Munitions manufactured by former Warsaw Pact countries such as the Soviet Union and Czechoslovakia give off green tracers, but the spectrum of hues sometimes runs to a yellow–green. US and many Western munitions give off a red trace.

however, that the distant explosions mean that real, flesh–and–blood men are dying.

As the team continues on its noiseless flight, each jumper lines up on the dull luminescent strip on the helmet below. Altimeter checks show that the gradual warming they feel is due to the descent. At 12,000 feet, they remove their individual masks and inhale the night air. With each passing minute, the team gets closer to the drop zone. This is when the paratroopers are most vulnerable. All are sure that the entire Iraqi Army is waiting to pounce on them, but the only living things awaiting the DELTA troopers are some stray goats from a Bedouin camp that run bleating into the night when they strike the earth. The men are relieved

Special Forces trooper on a practice jump, taking up the "frog" position. Note that the soldier wears an altimeter on his left wrist. Rucksacks are always strapped below the main parachutes and, in the second photo, a rucksack can be seen dangling fifteen feet below the jumper so that it will be out of his way when he lands.

that no reception committee is on hand to greet them, but there will be plenty of time for surprises. One of the greatest shocks of this desert war for the special operations soldiers was the fact that whenever you thought you were in the middle of nowhere, someone was always showing up—usually at the most inopportune time.

Chapter 6

The Scud Busters

The Lord said to Moses, "Send men to spy out the land of Canaan, . . . from each tribe of their fathers shall you send a man, everyone a leader among them."

Numbers 13

The team quickly assembles after landing. The troopers move to a nearby depression, and while half take up defensive positions, the others strip off their heavy jump suits and then roll them up with their 'chutes and jump helmets to make compact, easily buried bundles. The gear is quickly buried and the now–unencumbered troopers silently take their turn guarding the perimeter. Preparing to move out, each man goes through his mental checklist to ensure that every piece of equipment is in place. Faint vehicle noise drifts through the black night and the telltale signs of light are seen to the south.

Staff Sergeant Christopher Gleason, the point man for this operation, silently moves to his right, where the team leader is making last–minute com-

Troopers in the desert viewed through an image–intensification device.

pass checks and using his handheld satellite navigation system to pinpoint the team's exact location. Chief Warrant Officer Gary Van Hee intently studies the tiny screen's luminous, digital readout, which arrived as coded signals from a Global Positioning System (GPS) satellite drifting in orbit above the desert. Only one–third of the complete twenty–four–satelite constellation needed to blanket the earth had yet been sent aloft, so the lack of full–time, three–dimensional coverage sometimes made reception problematic. Tonight, though, Van Hee is having no trouble and he smiles broadly as the staff sergeant moves within whisper distance.

Gleason points out the rather obvious activity to the southwest, "The whole place is crawling with ragheads, Chief!" Van Hee's camouflaged face breaks into a devious grin and he retorts with his typical, "No shit, Sherlock." The team leader's time–honored response reassures the edgy point man, who steps gingerly back to his position and prepares to move out.

Each man's personal equipment is designed for specific tasks. Black balaclavas have been replaced with desert flop hats and face paint of pale yellow and brown. "No sweat" bandanas and camouflage scarves are wrapped tightly around necks and tucked into the now–familiar "chocolate chip"–patterned camouflage jackets. The men carry ammunition in pouches hung from their vests, and distributed about their bodies are canteens, first–aid equipment, a powerful miniature flashlight, and a Beretta pistol. Two of the six–man team also carry silencers so that their Barettas can be used to noiselessly kill an enemy guard or nosey point man. The unique silencers are so efficient that, using subsonic rounds, only the sound of the hammer striking the firing pin and the gun's action cycling can be heard—a small sound in this noisy environment.

The threat of "getting slimed" by Iraqi poison gas is far more than rhetorical in this war, so each trooper also carries a gas mask, securely strapped within easy reach on his left leg, and a complete protective suit in his rucksack. Rucks for this mission are configured with extra ammunition and smoke grenades. Additional water, medical supplies, a small quantity of food, and limited decontamination gear, complete the major items. Personal weapons are based on the defensive requirements of the mission, and the team carries either Colt M16A2 assault rifles or Heckler & Koch MP5 submachine guns.

While these final checks are being made, the communications expert, Sergeant First Class Michael Cranson, sends the team's initial entry report, a codeword transmission advising the MSS that they have arrived safely at the drop zone. For this signal, Cranson uses his radio's burst–transmission capability, and with the touch of a finger, the pre-coded message is instantaneously sent. The split–second broadcast provides no time for hostile direction finders to get a fix on the team's position.

Armed with an integrally silenced MP5 SD3, Staff Sergeant Gleason slowly leads the way out of the depression and toward a large, rocky outcropping. The team members swing into their allotted positions behind him, forming a loose file. This and every action these soldiers will complete during the mission has been practiced over and over. Gleason and his fellow troopers use AN/PVS-7 night vision goggles to guide them through the rocky terrain. Popularly known as NODs, for night observation devices, the 1.5 pound goggles fit against a trooper's forehead and literally turn the desert darkness into a greenish, but very visible, day.

A Global Positioning System receiver.

By amplifying existing light, they enable man–sized targets to be recognized at almost 100 yards on all but the very darkest nights, with good moonlight extending their range by fifty percent or more. Operating under a last quarter moon, the men can see extremely well, but spotty cloud cover creates sudden, unexpected drops in visibility, in addition to the device's limited peripheral field of vision.

The point man's stubby, silenced MP5, his night vision goggles, and modified tactical vest give him an unearthly appearance. The bleak terrain, coupled with the patrol's appearance, could easily be mistaken for a Hollywood supernatural thriller. Walking behind the point man, the compass man, Staff Sergeant Rodgers, not only navigates for the patrol with his compass (for direction) and altimeter (for elevation), but also by watching his distance count (by how far he walks). The team leader occupies the number three position, and his communications, or "commo" man, Sergeant First Class Cranson, holds down number four. Positions five and six are rounded out by the team medic, Master Sergeant Frank Rodrigues, and the demolitions expert, another staff sergeant, who doubles as the patrol's tail gunner. His primary responsibility is to ensure that no one surprises the team from the rear and, like the point man, the tail gunner also resembles an alien stalking through a moonscape.

While approaching the low ridge where they will set up their observation post, it becomes painfully clear that they have, indeed, dropped into an area full of Iraqi units. Reaching their destination, the team immediately sets up security, sends out a two–man recon of the area, and digs in (one of the veterans later likened the experience to hacking into an asphalt parking lot). Flexible prefabricated covers are stretched over their holes to make the hide site complete, and the men will use disposable plastic bags to contain their bodily wastes so that no wild or stray animals will be attracted to their position—

a potentially disastrous occurrence that could attract curious Iraqi eyes and expose their position.

The troopers are prepared to lie low for days, watching for the elusive Scuds, but the arrival of dawn quickly reveals that part of Saddam's missile inventory is already operating in this area.

At first, only normal military, and civilian, traffic can be seen speeding along the east–west highway stretched out before them. It isn't long, though, before Van Hee recognizes some very familiar friends. Tailing along behind a westbound string of large civilian Mercedes tractor–trailers is a Ural-375 truck, mounting a mobile crane, and a pair of Type ZIL-157V tractors hauling elongated cargoes covered by tarps. The vehicles continue down the road for almost two miles and then pull off to the right about a hundred yards into the desert. Excitement is running high in the team and reaches a peak a half hour later when an eight–wheeled MAZ-543 transporter–erector–launcher (a TEL vehicle known to carry Scud missiles) and a ZIL-157V tanker towing a trailer appear to the east. They zoom by and continue on to the other waiting vehicles which, by now, include numerous supply trucks, C^3 vans, and a mix of towed quad 23mm and dual 30mm antiaircraft guns in the process of deploying on both sides of the highway. The top of the TEL is still well–covered by sand–colored tarps, but Van Hee is willing to bet his life and the lives of his men that it mounts a Scud missile.

The suspicious TEL remains with the other vehicles for only about ten minutes before all but the antiaircraft element suddenly begin to move off in column across the desert. After only a few hundred yards, the lead truck turns abruptly to the left into a deep wadi that arches back toward the road passing under it at a long, thin bridge a quarter mile past their original turnoff. As far as the team leader's concerned, this confirms it. There is no reason for an Iraqi unit this far afield of the main weight of coalition air attacks to go to this kind of trouble to hide itself unless it's a missile unit. At night, the TEL and select support vehicles will emerge back onto the flat, tabletop terrain to fire its terror weapon at Israel.

Sighting through his 7x40 Steiner binoculars, Van Hee begins to list what he sees as the vehicles disappear one by one down the now–apparent path bulldozed to the dry streambed. His time as an exchange member with one of West Germany's famed long–range reconnaissance companies is now paying off. As he reels off the NATO names, the team's radio operator writes them on his notepad. After one more sweep of the target area, Van Hee tells Cranson to inform headquarters that the "mother of all targets" is in front of them. He then slides back into the two–man foxhole, closes his eyes, and wearily tries to relax.

Opening his rucksack flap, Cranson closely examines the Satellite Communications System (SATCOM). From the ruck's outside pocket he pulls a miniature black satellite antenna folded in such a way that it looks like little more than a small, closed umbrella. Unfolding its legs and arms, Cranson places the device just beyond the lip of the hide hole and checks its frame to ensure that each prong is extended to its maximum position. With a diameter of only 17in, the antenna's profile will provide an observer with little clue as to what it is, even if the device could be seen from the highway. Cranson plugs the antenna's black, coaxial cable into the SATCOM and turns it on.

While the system hums and ticks through its self–checks and calibrations, the commo man listens through his headsets and consults the *Equatorial Satellite Antenna Pointing Guide* for the necessary elevation and azimuth angles required to orient the SATCOM's antenna for sending and receiving signals. Cranson moves the frame dish back and forth until he hears the unmistakable peep of the orbiting satel-

lite and then settles in to start his transmission. He speaks in slow, distinct tones into his microphone, sending the entire intelligence picture of what the recon team is viewing to a receiving station in the SOC communications bunker at King Khalid. Immediately, this vital information is passed through the US Air Force liaison officer to CENTCOM's air component tucked away in a basement corner of the Royal Saudi Air Force building in Riyadh.

Within minutes of the initial report being sent, coalition jets, pulled from the air campaign to hunt for Scuds, are vectored from their stations as others scramble from Saudi fields far to the southeast. Twenty–two minutes after the initial report, the first aircraft arrive over the highway. The jets briefly circle well out of range of the frustrated Iraqi anti-aircraft gunners while coordinating their attack, and then make straight for the well–camouflaged vehicles parked along the dry streambed.

Tipped off to the Iraqis' exact location, the ungainly looking A-10 Thunderbolt IIs (affectionately

A man–portable satelite communications system.

Mission accomplished. (**Left**) A missile and its mobile launching platform caught out in the open and destroyed. (**Above**) A missile rearm vehicle burned to the ground by Air Force jets.

called "Warthogs" or simply "Hogs") turn the wadi into a death trap. Resembling sharks during a feeding frenzy, the jets continuously roll in and pound the missile unit, and then begin to work on targets of opportunity up and down the highway. Their method of attack, however, seems strange to the hidden team members watching the show with intense interest. All had at one time or another seen live–fire exercises where the hog drivers swooped in and plastered targets from treetop heights, but now their hogs seemed to rarely venture below 8,000 or 10,000 feet because of the antiair assets.

Throughout the rest of the day, air strikes continue to hit what can only be described as "a target–rich environment." Periodic, huge explosions rend the wadi, and Cranson, who is monitoring the Warthogs' communications net, informs Van Hee that the hog drivers claim "two Scuds TANGO UNIFORM" (Tits Up—slang for "destroyed"). Later strikes are conducted almost exclusively by F-16s, with some help from Tornado attack aircraft of unknown origin. The team hadn't been briefed that

Tornadoes would be in on the show, and although Cranson picks up their cryptic transmissions, he can only state that they are *not* speaking *American* English. He can't make out if they are piloted by Brits, Saudis, or Italians (all of whom field the multirole jet), and is the butt of several rude jokes from his friends until they, too, fail just as badly at deciphering the jet jockeys' nationalities.

These aircraft, and all others working the many targets, fly no lower than the Warthogs and, consequently, there are a lot of misses. But even through the smoke and dust kicked up by the strikes, Van Hee can clearly see that the cumulative weight of the air attacks has destroyed nearly every vehicle in the area by using a combination of rockets, iron bombs, and cluster munitions. The medium–altitude attacks have, moreover, rendered the defenders' antiaircraft guns nearly useless by striking from beyond their *effective* range. No one in the team sees any coalition aircraft go down.

As evening draws near, the team leader fears that their position is becoming increasingly vulnerable.

(**Opposite**) A night–stalking F-15 taking on fuel during *Desert Storm*. (**Above**) A disabled fuel truck in Iraq, and (**left**) an actual Scud TEL targeted by an F-15E. Target identification was often extremely difficult at night, even with the most sophisticated ground and airborne systems.

Although well–hidden on a barely perceptible ridge, they are, nevertheless, located on the highest terrain feature in the area. It might only be a matter of time before the increasingly active Iraqi patrols unearth them. As soon as it begins to turn dark, the team picks up their gear, quickly sanitizes the area, and heads south across the previously active road, now silent except for the crackling of a few vehicle fires still burning brightly. Moving

carefully across undulating ground, the team settles into a steady, cautious march. Upon reaching a small depression dotted with low, thorny bushes, they form a perimeter and rest before continuing on to the exfiltration point that night.

But this is as far as they get. Gleason detects the hot thermal images of several trucks pulling off the highway barely 1,500 yards directly behind them. Both Gleason and Van Hee carry handheld AN/PAS-7 thermal viewers that pick up the heat of the vehicles several hundred yards beyond the system's stated range (the trucks can't be seen at all by the shorter–range NODs except for the occasional glint of reflected moonlight). Almost immediately, they are joined by a larger, semitrailer–sized vehicle.

Could it be another Scud TEL? Through their two thermal viewers, the team watches with nervous excitement—and no small amount of glee—as what appears to be more Scud launchers and support vehicles trickle in. Although the glowing, red, negative images provided by the viewers cannot produce an accurate picture at that distance, Van Hee and crew believe that their new neighbor is a full–blown battery preparing to launch a nasty surprise at the Jewish State.

Under normal circumstances, the lack of clear, sharp images would not prevent the team from determining if this is a Scud battery. With even the little elevation provided by a slight rise, they could look down on the spread of vehicles and make out the telltale signs unique to that type of unit's deployment pattern. Unfortunately, the recon team not only lacks altitude now, but is, in fact, slightly lower than the Iraqis. From their essentially eye–level view, all they can tell is that there are several dozen vehicles—some quite large—arrayed to the north.

Whoever they are, the darkness of night has given them a false sense of security and Van Hee can make out that they are neither properly dispersed nor making any effort at concealment. The team can easily call an air strike in on this unit, but even though the Iraqis are currently not well–dispersed, that could change in an instant. Moreover, if this is a Scud battery, even the fast–movers viewing the target area through their Maverick missiles' powerful infrared sensors will have great difficulty picking out the critical launch vehicles which, it turns out, are almost indistinguishable from fuel trucks and other lengthy vehicles at attack distances. Blanketing the area with cluster bombs will not guarantee the destruction of the mobile launchers either, although it would certainly "attrit" their crews and support personnel.

For obvious reasons, the Air Force was having a terrible time tracking down the nocturnal TELs and, true to the black humor that befriends men in war, the troopers nearly busted a gut a week earlier when they learned that a group of Jordanian tractor–trailer rigs had been rocketed and cluster–bombed when mistaken for one of Saddam's Scud units. It seems that their hapless drivers had pulled off the highway at one of its infrequent rest stops late at night and were inadvertently mistaken for a rearm and refuel site.* A Special Forces team on the ground soon confirmed that the blasted vehicles were civilian and, in any event, the Iraqis had immediately bussed foreign journalists to the scene to record "President Bush's most vile outrage." Word spread quickly from King Khalid "Emerald City" to the intelligence analysts, working out of prefab buildings on a Riyadh soccer field, and the shocked air unit that made the strike.

*If there was a plus side to the mistaken attack, it was the fact that fewer civilian drivers were now willing to brave the highway at night, thus making the job of target identification slightly less complicated.

Now, Van Hee finds the tables completely turned. Although the team leader is considerably closer than any fighter jockey releasing a Maverick missile and has all the time in the world to examine the glowing, shapes, there is no way he can confirm that they are what he believes them to be. Van Hee needs to know exactly what he is looking at before he calls in the fast–movers. Once committed to a strike here, on what is perhaps just some inconsequential heavy–lift unit, there might not be enough time or available air assets to immediately respond if a genuine Scud battery is detected.

Van Hee instructs Rodrigues and the tail gunner to move back toward the highway, to get a closer look, and hands over his thermal viewer. He wishes his team had gotten another of the precious thermal systems but is thankful that they

were able to get any at all. Many Special Forces long–range reconnaissance patrols didn't even have one of the scarce AN/PAS-7s, but the highly critical nature of DELTA's scud–hunting mission allowed Van Hee to get his mitts on two of the lightweight devices.

Gleason watches as their ghostly figures silently disappear into another depression, and settles into what is likely to be a long vigil on the perimeter. Everyone understands that the men may have to move in as close as 200 or 250 yards before their viewer will let them confirm the team's suspicions. If the approach to the Iraqi unit is difficult, the men might be gone for many hours. During their absence, the team checks and rehecks its equipment and notifies SOC of the situation.

The waiting is mercifully short. Helpful terrain features and a surprising lack of security have allowed the scouts to get their job done in barely three hours. Rodrigues reports that at least two of the mystery vehicles are "Spud" TELs, and Van Hee wastes no time setting back out with him to a spot where Rodrigues is confident that each of the confirmed launchers can be painted for incoming aircraft. When Gleason first spotted the gathering Iraqi vehicles at roughly 1,500 yards, they were beyond the effective range of Van Hee's AN/PAQ-3 MULE target designator, and the laser team has to travel almost one–third of the way back toward the road to ensure that their instrument can get a clear fix on the TELs. Newer, experimental handheld designators, that can accurately illuminate targets at roughly three times the distance had recently been sent to the Gulf, but Van Hee's team are not among the lucky few to receive one.

The route back is well known by this time, and the men are able to move with deliberate haste. The midnight hour Iraq often uses for launching its terror weapons is fast approaching, and through

A Scud missile erect on its launcher and ready to fire.

AN/AVS-6 Aviator's
night–vision imaging system

AN/PAQ-3 Modular universal laser
equipment (MULE) target designator

Comparative imagery from night vision equipment used by US forces in *Desert Storm*: (**top**) unaided, daylight photograph of an M606 Jeep and the same vehicle shot from a slightly different angle through (**center**) image intensification and (**bottom**) infrared devices.

AN/PVS-7A
Night vision goggles

AN/PAS-7 Thermal viewer

their thermal viewers, both the laser team and Gleason, at the hastily established patrol base, can see the unmistakable pillar of a missile raised on one of the erectors. A brief break in the clouds also allows a faint, grainy image to be seen from the NODs.

At the base, Rodgers peers intently at the shadowy image of assembled Iraqi vehicles and nervously fingers his M16. From his vantage point, he can see only one other trooper, the tail gunner, about twenty yards to his right, who has turned his way, as well, and gives Rodgers a thumbs up. Rodgers knows that he isn't the only man wondering if the fast–movers will make it before the Iraqis launch. He doesn't feel

himself to be particularly expendable and hopes that the Air Force will refrain from using cluster munitions against close–in, ground–lased targets as the team had been briefed before the mission.

Activity suddenly picks up near the road. Several of the smaller Iraqi vehicles start hauling off in all directions and a lone, dual 30mm antiaircraft gun, positioned slightly east of the launch site, begins to pop green tracers into the air. The team watches, mesmerized from their ringside seats as other antiaircraft artillery, or "triple–A," quickly comes to life, sending aloft crisscrossing streams of fire. Cranson, meanwhile, listens in on the approaching jets transmission: "Honey 1, sixty seconds, Maverick. . . . Honey 1, ten seconds. . . . Honey 1, laser on. . . . Spot. . . . Honey 1, lock–launch." *

The men have almost grown accustomed to the awe–inspiring spectacle of light and sound when a huge, double explosion bursts skyward. A Maverick air–to–ground missile has slammed into a TEL and ignited its fueled–up weapon.

Most of the triple–A falls silent for what seems like a long time, but one Iraqi gunner recovers from the shock of the explosion almost immediately and resumes shooting even before the fireball disappears into the air. Long strings of triple–A again arch into the sky as Rodgers and the others watch in fascination, knowing that Van Hee is already painting another Scud: "Honey 2, spot. . . . Lock–launch. . . . Honey 2, terminate." ** A second huge explosion lights the scene and more vehicles can be seen scurrying away from the carnage. As far as the Iraqi grunts are concerned, all Saddam's "little toys" do is attract death from above.

Secondary explosions begin to rock the target area as the laser team moves at a steady trot toward the patrol base. The Air Force is holding back from dropping its deadly packages of cluster bombs, to give them a jump at getting away from the target. Rodrigues and Van Hee's glowing green images can be seen quite clearly during their last 100–meter dash to the base, and some of the troopers can't refrain from greeting them with low–volume (*very* low–volume) whoops and hollers as they clear the perimeter. As if to join in the congratulations, the Air Force begins to hit the site again, and now the whole team moves out at a run. The troopers haven't covered a quarter mile when suddenly,

while cresting a wide ripple in the earth, they smack into an Iraqi squad barely thirty yards away. The Iraqis were apparently on patrol when the air strike erupted and are riding out the fireworks in this shallow depression.

The startled team comes under fire. Dropping to one knee, Gleason pumps two 9mm rounds into the nearest Iraqi's chest. Without pausing, he switches to the next target, who immediately crumples into a heap, his stomach perforated by two slugs from Gleason's H&K. Immediately sizing up the situation, Van Hee yells for the team to break contact. While moving through their leapfrog maneuver, a lucky round from an RPG-7 shoulder–fired rocket launcher lands between Rodgers and the tail gunner. Although most of the explosion is absorbed by the ground, shrapnel rips into Rodgers' right side and the tail gunner is killed instantly by a dime–sized piece of metal piercing his skull just above the right eye.

The four unhurt troopers immediately lay down an intense base of fire, which convinces the Iraqis to fall back to less dangerous surroundings. The firefight has lasted less than two minutes. One American is dead and another's life is leaking into the rocky earth. Hauling Rodgers and the fallen trooper along with them, the team hurriedly resumes their escape south while Air Force jets strike at Iraqi vehicles streaking pell–mell through the area. It is painfully obvious to all that they are in deep trouble, and, if action is not taken quickly, will either be killed or wind up being displayed on the evening news as prisoners of war.

Air–ground communications between the team and SOC is now being maintained by a "fast FAC," or forward air controller, who passes word to Cranson that immediate efforts are being initiated to get them out. They are instructed to keep moving south without delay, but each man knows that they are faced with a decision no soldier wants to make.

* "Sixty seconds to laser designator switch–on. . . . Ten seconds to switch–on. . . . Laser spot acquired. . . . Target locked–on and ordnance fired."
** "Laser spot acquired. . . . Target locked–on and ordnance fired. . . . Have visual contact; laser no longer needed."

The venerable A-10 Thunderbolt II "Warthog" and DELTA formed a deadly Scud hunter–killer team in Iraq. A-10s also proved themselves to be an effective search and rescue asset.

The young trooper's body hinders their movement to the extraction point, and they decide to bury him as quickly as possible. In a lonely defile, the team digs a grave for their comrade. It is not very much, as graves go, but it is made with love and respect, and the men dig as deeply as time will permit. Wrapping the staff sergeant up in his poncho liner, they gently lay his body into the desert soil. Van Hee carefully checks, then rechecks, the tight ten–digit grid coordinate he has plotted for the unmarked grave and silently swears to his fallen trooper that he'll be back for him. The team says a quick prayer over their friend, and then, carrying Rodgers, they strike out south again. Rodrigues, the team's medic, recognizes that the multiple shrapnel wounds are worse than previously thought. Rodgers is slipping in and out of consciousness and losing blood. Cranson radios the fast FAC that they have a man who will die if they don't get him out soon.

SOC knows that no special operations helicopters are currently available for a quick recovery, nor are there likely to be any until almost mid–morning. Virtually everything is already committed to the far–flung operations in progress throughout what the Israelis call "Scudinavia" in western Iraq. SOC decides to use a MC-130 Combat Talon equipped with a Fulton Recovery System to conduct a surface–to–air recovery (STAR) of Rodgers. This is not generally a preferred method of extraction because it takes so much time to set up the Fulton and is easily seen, but with helo assets unavailable, Rodgers' condition makes it necessary. Alerting the 1st Special Operations Wing, a hasty plan is worked out to recover the wounded DELTA trooper.

The Extractions

Arar Royal Military Airfield near Banadah is the launch site of some of *Desert Storm's* most inventive operations. It's not an unusual place to find one or two of the 1st Special Operations Wing's MC-130s, and when the call comes down, immediate preparations are made for the STAR. First, a modified delivery canister resembling an old napalm bomb is loaded with all the items needed by the team to set

(**Opposite**) Intense concentration marks the face of a trooper keeping watch on the surrounding terrain from a desert ruin. (**Right**) An E-3A Sentry at Dhahran, Saudi Arabia.

up the recovery. The canister is then affixed to a waiting A-10's weapons pylon, and the Warthog is immediately launched toward western Iraq. As the "Sandy"* Hog driver and his wingman speed north, the crew of the MC-130 receives their mission brief. Not uncharacteristically, the crew takes the briefing quite professionally; yet, underneath their calm exterior, there is a surge of adrenalin. They are going to execute a mission that they have trained hard for and has not been performed in combat for nearly twenty years. The airmen are confident that the improvements in technique and hardware introduced since the Vietnam War are sound.

Already deep in the desert, the recon team is now told to move beyond their original pickup point into an even more desolate area well away from any known military targets. After several hours, the exhausted team comes upon a group of ruined dwellings and sets up defensive positions as dawn begins to break. Rodrigues has just changed Rodgers' I-V and is connecting a new bag of saline solution when Cranson's radio crackles to life. The Sandy pilot is attempting to contact the team. Hopefully, it will appear to any nearby Iraqis that the hog driver and his wingman are out hunting for targets of opportunity and will avoid any curious overtures.

Van Hee is informed that he should mark their position for a "delivery." Using a mirror, Van Hee

*An A-10 pilot specially trained for rescue escort (RESCORT) missions. The rugged A-10's ability to loiter for extended periods of time makes it a perfect aircraft for conducting searches in a high-threat environment, and Sandy's are experts at locating survivors. By marking target locations and supressing enemy fire, they allow more vulnerable rescue aircraft to do their job. The term originated during the Vietnam war as a call sign used by A-1E Skyraider pilots providing gunfire suppression during rescue operations.

signals his location to the Sandys performing their lazy search pattern well away from the team. After receiving an acknowledgment from the pilot, Van Hee moves out about 175 yards from the perimeter, places a single orange panel in the gravel, and immediately moves back to the shelter of the ruins. The pair of Warthogs are continuing their indirect meander toward the ruins when they spot a group of Iraqi trucks moving parallel to the team approximately two miles out. Although they do not appear to be looking for the troopers, the Sandys take no chances and proceed to spoil the Iraqis' morning with fire from their 30mm Gatling nose cannons. As the hogs leave the burning vehicles, they approach the ruins indirectly by flying in a low, wide arc that, hopefully, will not draw attention to the hidden Americans. No extra passes are made over the site and the equipment canister is "pickled off" as the ugly jets roar overhead.

Thirty minutes behind the Sandys, the MC-130 Combat Talon penetrates into "Injun Country." While passing over the berm line, the special opera-

A surface–to–air recovery (STAR) of two troopers using a Fulton extraction system: (**Top row**) A canister containing the system is dropped by an Air Force fast–mover.' Helium bottles, balloon, line and attached suit in a recovered canister. The guard cables and whisker–like probes of an MC-130 yoke, opened to snare the Fulton's line. (**Center row**) Two volunteers with "Are we really going to do this?" looks on their faces. The line being snagged. Up, up, and away! (**Left**) The open rear ramp of the receiving aircraft as the soldiers are hauled aboard.

tions aircraft receives an ominous radio report from the E-3A Sentry orbiting in Saudi airspace behind them. Electronic warfare officers operating the AWACS's highly sophisticated sensors detect a number of hostile radar impulses. Despite the fact that the Air Force owns the sky, being painted over Iraqi territory always causes concern. Most of the Talon's crew had friends on the ill–fated AC-130 Specter gunship that failed to get out of Kuwaiti airspace when "locked on" by a surface–to–air missile. The result was charred debris floating in the Gulf and no survivors.

As the Talon closes on the team's location, Van Hee and Gleason open the canister. Extracting its contents, they find a balloon, nylon line, harness, and suit along with a bottle of helium. Rodrigues checks Rodgers' condition while Van Hee and Gleason prepare to inflate the balloon, and Cranson makes contact with the inbound Talon. Not only is the MC-130 approaching, but the pair of A-10s continue to ply the area in ostensibly random patterns, and a flight of F-16s has already assumed a guardian–angel role well to the east but within easy striking distance if trouble develops. The Warthogs again cruise past the ruins while Van Hee and Gleason affix the helium bottle to the balloon that will stretch Rodgers' lifeline in reach of the specially equipped rescue aircraft. As it inflates, the bulbous cream and silver balloon takes on the shape of a giant fish, its floppy fins growing firmer with each passing second.

While all this is going on, Rodrigues and Cranson gingerly ease Rodgers into the olive green recovery suit sewn firmly to the Fulton's harness. As its furlined hood is placed around Rodger's face, his glazed eyes open slightly to Rodrigues' familiar grin and thick, angular eyebrows. His medic friend has been in DELTA for a long time and has a well–earned reputation as a battlefield doctor. Patting Rodgers' thigh, he says with a chuckle, "You gonna go on a neat ride, my man. It's up, up, and away for you." Rodrigues does his best to put up a brave front for his buddy but fears that Rodgers may have lost too much blood. The furlined face is gray and expressionless, but it seems for a moment that he tries to acknowledge what the medic is saying.

Twenty minutes from the pickup, the balloon is allowed to creep slowly skyward. It reaches its full height and Rodgers sits securely attached to its tether while the team, minus the doc, stands guard in a circle resembling a herd of buffaloes shielding a wounded calf. Rodrigues continues his lively chatter to help keep his patient awake and gently pats and strokes his unhurt left arm. Although he doesn't know it, his determined "woofing" is paying off. Rodgers dimly comprehends that his buddies are doing everything they can for him and takes some comfort from the New Yorker's verbal blizzard.

At 525 feet in the air, the balloon attached to the tethered nylon rope is a beacon for all to see and is the reason that the team had to put so much distance between themselves and the highway. The incoming MC-130's unusual nose now resembles a snout with two large whiskers. These whiskers are actually probes swung outward to form the yoke. Their main function is to guide the line into place at the center of the nose as the plane makes the pickup.

Cautiously lining up on the balloon, the pilot throttles the fat, four–engine airplane down to 112, 105, then only 97 knots for the pickup and aims at the target area on the nylon rope marked by three orange streamers. Striking the target markers, the probes guide the line to the yoke and secure it as the plane flies over the DELTA team. With a minimum of fanfare, Rodgers is literally snatched from the gravity of earth and appears as a small dot hurtling behind the Talon. While the STAR is a nerve–wracking affair for the soldiers to watch, they know that Rodgers actually experiences less of a jolt during the pickup than he did when he opened his parachute.

In the gaping cargo bay, the loadmaster and crew chief now prepare to winch their human cargo on board. The nylon line is pressed firmly against the Talon's belly by the rush of air, and inside the bay, the crew chief and loadmaster move quickly to hook it, much as one snaps a fishing line. Reeling

A special operations helicopter streaking at low level across the night sky.

in the line and attaching it to the Talon's internal, hydraulic winch, the precious cargo is slowly drawn into the cargo bay. Soon, Rodgers is lying in the safety of the aircraft while Air Force Reserve trauma specialists work frantically to stabilize him. The only hitch during the pickup occurs when the balloon fails to release from the line. The Talon's navigator is forced to spear the playfully bouncing object with a harpoon–like device and cut it free with the help of the loadmaster.

As the MC-130 speeds toward friendly air-space, the remainder of the recon team moves out.

A well–timed air operation, centered mainly along the highway to the north, is initiated by the F-16s and a fresh pair of A-10s to mask their movement and the troopers head south by southwest toward a new pickup point several miles away. Although appropriate helo assets will be available in a few hours, SOC has decided to not make the extrac-tion until after dark since Rodgers has been rescued and the recon team is in no immediate danger.

The team had flung their prefabricated hide site covers into their foxholes and buried them when they sanitized their original position, but the rough terrain the men are now moving into offers many opportunities for natural concealment and there is no worry that they no longer have the prefabs. They soon come upon a wadi that offers a reasonable amount of security and decide that it is as good a place as any to go to ground till nightfall. After the midnight firefight, Saddam's forces know that American commandos are in the area, but ongoing airstrikes have given the Iraqis plenty of other things to worry about, and their movement has been heavily restricted for scores of miles in all directions.

The only enemy assaulting the men is a determined legion of sandfleas, which tirelessly press their attack as "big red" moved slowly across the sky. They do, however, also receive periodic visits from various Air Force jets. The pilots make it a point to fly close enough to the DELTA team to scout for hostile forces, yet their seemingly random passes are conducted at varied–enough intervals to give no clue to the whereabouts of the hidden soldiers.

Night comes quickly in this part of the world and the already–cool late January temperature drops like a stone even before the sun disappears from the horizon. As the four men make their final equipment checks before moving out, help is crossing the Saudi–Iraqi border 100 miles to the southeast. Boring through the gathering fog at sixty feet off the ground, a lone MH-60 Black Hawk is finally on its way to retrieve the soldiers.

Almost ten hours has passed since Rodgers was extracted, and Van Hee's team starts to move south again. The welcome night engulfs the dirty, unshaven troopers and their night vision goggles allow them to move with the assurance of prowling nocturnal beasts unencumbered by darkness.

In spite of the sophisticated vision devices and their apparent isolation, the desert holds one more surprise. As they near the pickup point, a young goat herder casually emerges from a depression forty yards to their right. Upon seeing the ghost–like apparitions, he runs screaming through the darkness, scattering livestock in all directions. Fearing a return of Iraqi soldiers, the team moves through the area quickly and sets up a defensive perimeter 600 yards from their encounter. Speaking in hushed tones with the inbound chopper, Van Hee guides the bird in until the troopers can be seen on its infrared imager.

As the Black Hawk's wheels touch the hard–packed dirt, the remaining four troopers scramble aboard and slide across the metal floor plates to hold each other in the embrace only those who have faced the ultimate challenge know. "We made it!" Gleason yells above the pitch of the engines as the helicopter begins to rise above the desert floor.

After looking out of the waist gunner's hatch for any signs of Iraqi forces, Van Hee wearily leans back and says "Christ, I hope so."

Epilogue

Fort Bragg, North Carolina

Along Ardennes Road, framed by a stand of regal North Carolina pines, the John F. Kennedy Special Warfare Center Chapel occupies a place of dignity and serenity. Against the hustle and organized chaos that characterizes this sprawling Airborne post, it provides a safe haven of sanity and peace whether the visitor is a regular church-goer or just passing through.

Framed against the buildup of an incoming spring rain, a memorial service is taking place. It is a closed service designed to avoid the prying eyes of nosy newspaper reporters still trying to write a story connected to *Desert Storm*. Although the service was unannounced, the chapel is crowded. Word has passed quickly around the special operations community that one of their own is being remembered today. Conspicuous in their off–the–rack suits, cowboy boots, and nonregulation mustaches

A soldier is laid to rest.

and haircuts, the members of a DELTA troop have gathered once more. Along with their wives, they are here to help the young widow weather one more storm. It is a unique scene—one that rarely occurred in the past few years but has often been repeated since the operations "over there."

The widow's five–year–old son, sandy blond hair neatly combed and out of character, sits on the edge of his front–row seat. Gently poking an imagined spot on the chapel's maroon carpet with the toe of his Sunday best, he absently wonders, not quite knowing or understanding why he is here. He is aware that his mom's world is in disarray, and her sadness is something he has never seen before. All he knows is that the man whose picture occupies the table in front of the chapel room is not coming home. His father left home late one night "on business." That was not an unusual occurrence in his young life, but now a new twist has occurred. Mom said that his best friend has gone to live with God forever.

His father's friends, gathered around the family in a supportive ring, knew the story all too well. The smiling young soldier, pictured with the coveted green beret had been their friend, and in this close-knit group of professionals, that one word, "friend," was all that required their loyalty.

The emotion of these men was not a complicated show. Each behaved simply but with a degree of maturity in combat that comes only to a veteran. They accepted what was thrown their way in a businesslike manner, hiding their hatred, fear, confusion, and pride behind the mantle of a well-trained special operations soldier. To this group and the many others like them, the specter of death was always an additional member of the team. In this particular case, their friend was no longer able to avoid death's embrace. Thousands of miles away, hidden in an unmarked grave deep in Iraq's rugged western province, their trusted friend and the young boy's father had rested until a subsequent team, under Gary Van Hee, recovered his lifeless form.

As the chaplain exhorts the group not to grieve but to pray for the Great Jumpmaster's protection of their comrade's soul, the thoughts of many of the group drift to other places, other actions, and other services. The veterans of *Desert Storm* looks back over the madness of the past weeks which characterized the operations in the desert.

Hanging back a little from the rest of the mourners, a grizzled old warrior remembers similar services after such operations—code-named *Desert I, Urgent Fury,* or *Just Cause*—and drifts further back in time to days before he left Smoke Bomb Hill to join DELTA at the old stockade. His thoughts go back to the Green Beret Parachute Club, its cold beer, warm friendships and the old jukebox nestled in the corner next to the pool tables. He smiles to himself as he remembers that one song, a song from an unpopular war that saw so many of the special operations community answer the requirements of the ultimate test. Though not all of the DELTA troopers were initially Special Forces-qualified, most ended with that qualification, and an old war song expressed best the thoughts and feelings of this moment: "Her Green Beret has met his fate."

It's not all glory and gunsmoke in the realm of special operations—especially in covert operations. It can be boring for months at a time and then spiked with moments of sheer gut-wrenching, piss-in-your-pants horror. But that is what they signed up for. No yellow ribbons, no victory parades, or grand celebrations would greet these secret warriors. Just a gentle hug, a kind word, or a pat on the back that seemed to say, "Well done." That, plus "Clean up your gear and get ready for the next one!"

And there will certainly be a next one—somewhere, sometime. The odds are that the professionals from DELTA will be used not as they were during Iraq's stinging defeat, but in their traditional counterterrorist role.

For over a quarter of a century, the former Soviet Union and its surrogates in Eastern Europe, Latin America, and the Middle East gave safe haven to the world's most dangerous international terrorists. The collapse of Soviet communism, coupled with the shutting off of the terrorist's revenue by oil-rich Persian Gulf states angered over their backing of Iraq, have left terrorist organizations in disarray. Increasingly isolated politically and cut off from training and supplies from Europe and money from the Gulf, they bicker among themselves over how best to satisfy their grudge against the West and any Middle Eastern government unappreciative of their past deeds. They are, to put it bluntly, out of work and out of cash.

But the breather this has given the West is likely to be short–lived. As the world speeds toward the twenty–first century, it finds itself with more wild cards in its deck of nations. The familiar bipolar dominance of the United States and the former Soviet Union is gone for good, as the "evil empire" disintegrates into numerous successor states of questionable stability. These new countries are, themselves, not homogeneous entities and are likely to be rent by factional fighting in the decade to come. They are also the inheritors of at least 27,000 nuclear weapons. Despite pronouncements of their good intentions, their desperate need for hard currency and sporadic control of their own territory may result in some leakage of nuclear weapons ("loose nukes") or, more likely, nuclear materials and production expertise into the hands of terrorists.

This threat to peace and a new, ghastly form of warfare—environmental terrorism—may also cause elite counterterrorist units like DELTA to retool their operational methods. The sight of massive oil slicks released on the Persian Gulf and black clouds boiling up from oil fires to shut off the noonday sun will not be lost on the next generation of would–be terrorists. Moreover, their twisted logic will lead some terrorists to use the results of *Desert Storm* to add fuel to whatever cause is fashionable at the moment.

Literally dozens of captured Palestinian and Shiite terrorists have been dumped into this cauldron of change, let loose by the Iraqis when they invaded Kuwait or released by the Israelis as part of the package deal that freed a handful of Western hostages. Like the wandering free–lance warriors of feudal Japan who traded their violent skills for gold and fame, these modern–day *ronin* are available to any would–be despot or group fanning the flames of ethnic or religious unrest across Europe, Asia, and the Middle East. Key terrorist networks remain intact, and a number of groups and individuals dropped from sight when the vigilance of America's intelligence assets were directed to combat in the Gulf. Now that the flex of security operations has fallen to its normal lull, the specter of terrorists finding new work in the developing chaos is very real and Americans abroad are, as always, notoriously easy targets for any group desiring big headlines.

The pros of DELTA are ready.

U.S. NAVY SEALS

HANS HALBERSTADT

Acknowledgments

Many thanks to the friendly folks at USSO-COM public affairs at MacDill Air Force Base, Florida, particularly Col. Jake Dye.

This book wouldn't have been attempted without the reassurance of RADM Brent Baker, now retired, former Navy Chief of Information, who responded very graciously to some criticism of mine with an invitation to try working with the Navy again. The result is this book. Sir, I salute you.

Another salute to LCDR John Brindley and JO1 Mike Hayden, as hard a pair of public affairs officers as you'll find anywhere, with one of the most difficult missions in the fleet—smack dab in the middle between the media maniacs and the Naval Special Warfare community (whose motto is *No pictures!!! No names!!! No kidding!!!*). To two fine people doing what is usually a thankless job, let me say: Thanks! Well done!

I'd like to personally thank the many folks at BUD/S and SEAL Teams Three and Five who helped so graciously, and against tradition, with this project. I'd like to, but I can't. National Security and all that. But the Desert Patrol Vehicle guys out at Niland, California, and the squad from Team Five went way out of their way to accommodate a bunch of media weenies and executed their op with a perfect blend of cooperation and consideration.

I *can* thank RADM Ray Smith—what a guy! He's largely responsible for a new, more open attitude toward public affairs within the Naval Special Warfare community, and it's about time. A salute to you, sir, as well.

CAPT Bob Gormly, USN (Ret.), and CDR Gary Stubblefield, USN (Ret.), both filled in the gaps in my Naval Special Warfare education, shared some wonderful war stories and lots of insights based on long careers in Naval Special Warfare. These are, despite the reputation of the SEALs, gentlemen—the kind of quiet professionals you seldom hear about in this community. It's too bad that more Americans can't know about the things these people and their teams have done for us all.

Chapter 1

Let Slip the Frogs of War

In the dark, damp hours before midnight, 19 December 1989, a small group of United States Navy SEALs put the finishing touches on their face paint, checked their weapons and equipment for the thousandth time, watched the clock, chatted nervously, and waited. There were twenty-one of them, all told, assembled and identified as Task Unit Whiskey.

As the time trickled away all of them knew that very soon blood would begin to flow. Whose and how much remained to be seen. At 0045 hours, according to the current plan, combined United States forces would initiate Operation Just Cause—combat operations against the Republic of Panama with the objective of seizing that nation's leader, Gen. Manuel Noriega. Tensions were high between the two nations, and there was no doubt that the operation would be costly.

The role of Task Unit Whiskey in all of this was small but potentially critical. Noriega had plenty of places to hide and lots of ways to escape. One of these was a Panama Defense Forces (PDF) patrol boat, the *Presidente Porras*, and the SEAL task force was detailed to immobilize it.

A scout/swimmer from Naval Special Warfare Group One. His fashionable attire is essentially the same as that worn by the dive pairs attacking the Panamanian patrol boat: wet suit with hood and a Draeger rebreathing system (not scuba).

The mission was launched from Rodman Naval Station in Balboa Harbor, one of many US Navy installations in the Canal Zone. At 2300 hours, not quite two hours before the scheduled kickoff, the men slid into their wet suits, donned their closed-circuit breathing apparatus, and clambered into their big, black rubber inflatable boats. When the Combat Rubber Raiding Craft (CRRC) were loaded, the engines were started and the boats pushed off from shore, moving into the soft, inky night at minimum speed to avoid notice.

In the first boat, CRRC number 1, rode two combat swimmers, LT Edward Coughlin and EN3 Tim Eppley (dive pair number 1); CDR Norm Carley (the on-scene mission commander); HMC George Riley (coxswain); and HT3 Chris Kinney (machine gunner). CRRC number 2 carried a second dive pair, ET1 Randy Beausoleil and PH2 Chris Dye; remaining in the boat would be IS3 Scott Neudecker (coxswain), OS2 Mark Dodd (communicator), and QM3 Pat Malone (automatic weapons man).

Ashore, within the Rodman facility but still within range of the objective, a fire-support team manned .50-caliber heavy machine guns, Mk 19 automatic grenade launchers, and 60mm mortars, all preregistered on likely targets and equipped with night sights. Afloat, in case of trouble, two PBRs (Patrol Boat, River) carried more SEALs ready to intervene if the vulnerable "rubber ducks" were engaged by the PDF.

As seems to so often be the case, there was tremendous tension in the boats. Special forces like the SEALs are in the business of high-risk, high-payoff operations. They are expensive, in every respect, and to be successful everything has to be planned, rehearsed, scheduled, and orchestrated in mind-numbing detail. Deviations from the plan traditionally mean mission failure and often death for the people out on the pointy end of the spear. So, at precisely one hour before midnight, an hour and forty-five minutes before the bullets will fly all over Panama, Task Unit Whiskey's operation was already turning into what SEALs call a "goatscrew."

All the planning and the schedules had been based on a 2330 hours insertion time to reach and attack the target at 0100 (H-hour), but then the COMJSOTF (Commander Joint Special Operations Task Force) changed the insertion time to 2300 hours, adding to the stress level. But late in the planning sequence,

just before the boats pushed off, Commander Carley was asked to push up his H-hour thirty minutes, to 0030. He refused; there wasn't enough time to get the swimmers to the target, arm the demolitions, and extract the swim teams with a thirty-minute advance in the schedule. The proposed change added another jolt of adrenaline to an already highly charged atmosphere.

Out in Balboa Harbor, the boats moved slowly and as silently as possible across the black water. There were bright lights ashore and boat traffic in the harbor, neither helping the SEALs with their stealthy approach to the point where the swimmers would slip over the gunwales and disappear on their mission. The outboards were not designed to run at such slow speeds; one began to run roughly and threatened to quit. But both boats made it to the shelter of a mangrove treeline on the north side of the harbor, across from Pier 18.

The SEALs waited and watched. Two

Hi ho, hi ho, it's off to work we go—with a Mk 138 satchel charge loaded with twenty pounds of water-resistant explosives, a dual priming system, and a pair of timers. The satchel charge is essentially iden- *tical to the old "mod zero" version of fifty years ago when the UDT swimmers cleared the beaches in Normandy and in the Pacific.*

boats moved across the harbor; was Noriega aboard? Were the Panamanians searching for US small boats or swimmers? The time for the boats to move out to the insertion point arrived. Boat number 1's engine fired up but boat number 2's refused to cooperate. Boat number 1 moved out alone while boat number 2, complete with frustrated boat crew and divers, stayed hidden in the mangroves.

In order to make up for the delays and still hit the required H-hour, the boat crew had to move a lot closer into the target than had been intended. At 2330 hours the first dive pair went over the side, into the water—on schedule. Commander Carley took boat number 1 back to the mangroves, took boat number 2 under tow, and got the second dive team out to the insertion point at 2335. Dive pair number 2 slipped over the side and disappeared.

After the swimmers departed, the SEALs were advised via radio that the H-hour for the whole show had been advanced fifteen minutes to 0045 local time, 20 December. This meant, of course, that the whole shooting match would kick off while the swimmers were at their objective and that their mission had suddenly become even more risky than anticipated. But there wasn't much to do except wait and watch and stay out of the way.

In the meantime, Commander Carley decided to take the boats back to Rodman and to change out the engine in CRRC number 2 with a spare. Boat number 2 was taken under tow again, and the little convoy slipped back across the water with practiced stealth. Two more Panamanian harbor craft transited Balboa Harbor; the SEALs evaded both and made it back to Rodman undetected and unscathed.

The dive pairs swam toward their objective about twenty feet below the surface. Instead of conventional scuba tanks, the swimmers wore Draeger rebreathing systems that recycle expelled air, clean it of carbon dioxide, then replenish it with oxygen. It is a closed system. No bubbles reached the surface to betray the swimmers' passage.

The swimmers had practiced for this mis-

A "rubber duck" is launched into the Pacific for some play time. The design is another bit of World War II surplus—a lifeboat that has been used for covert operations for half a century. It is simple, stable, reliable, cheap, stealthy, low-tech—just the ticket for special operators in US Special Operations Command.

sion for all their careers. For most it was their first-ever combat mission. Instead of employing some exotic, high-tech navigation system to find their way through the water, they used a system older than they were—determining their direction with a simple, luminous compass and measuring their distance by counting the number of kicks they made. It is a primitive system, decades old, that still works. After about half an hour underwater, dive pair number 2 (Beausoleil and Eppley) surfaced

263

Here's another simple, stealthy, low-tech piece of gear used in Panama: the compass board. Once trained and experienced in its use, a diver can navi- *gate with precision below the surface, using the compass to maintain course and measuring distance traveled by counting kicks.*

under Pier 18. It was a noisy place to be; a firefight began just as they arrived, visible to the fire-support teams ashore and to the boat teams. Who was firing at whom was unclear to the SEALs, and the mission proceeded as planned, despite underwater explosions in the area, probably from PDF personnel throwing hand grenades in the water to discourage just this kind of mission.

With the pier providing cover and concealment, Beausoleil and Eppley moved toward the target, still moored at its floating dock. They avoided swimming on the surface as they moved toward the patrol boat. At 0011 dive pair number 2 arrived at the *Presidente Porras,* positively identified it as the tar-

get, and executed the attack on the vessel. The two SEALs swam down under the stern, found the port propeller shaft, and began attaching and arming the explosive charge—just as they heard the engines of the ship start up.

The Mk 138 Mod 1 charge they'd carried through the dark water was a haversack loaded with twenty pounds of water-resistant explosive, complete with an MCS-1 clock, a Mk 39 safety and arming device, and a Mk 96 detonator, all designed to provide reliable delay and detonation of the main charge. In less than two minutes the charge was attached, armed, and ticking. Beausoleil and Eppley departed the target at 0013 hours, urged onward by explosions in the water nearby, and now made their way first to the shelter of nearby Pier 17, then to the extraction point where—they hoped—the boat would be waiting to pick them up.

A little late, dive pair number 1 arrived at 0014 and commenced their attack on the *Presidente Porras*. Despite the explosions and the firefight overhead, the SEALs moved along Pier 18 to the ship and installed their Mk 138 demolition system on the starboard propeller shaft. They tied a length of detonation cord from the haversack around the charge already in place on the port shaft, using a dual-priming technique to insure that both charges would detonate together for maximum effect.

At about 0017, after less than two minutes

at the target, Coughlin and Eppley removed the safeties and started the clock that would detonate the charges at 0100—if everything worked—and, as they say, got the hell out of Dodge. The PDF crews either knew or suspected what was going on and threw many grenades into the water, forcing the SEALs to the relative shelter of the pier pilings behind which they tried to avoid the effects of the nearby explosions. Finally they started to move away, but four more explosions sent shock waves through the water.

Because of the forty-five-minute delay on the charges and the enemy action in the vicinity of the target, both SEAL teams were trapped in the vicinity. They were still there

The first SEALs ashore are normally the scout/swimmer pair who precede the boat onto the beach, evaluate the threat level, then signal in the rubber duck with the rest of the crew. The wet suit is an important piece of gear, even for rough-tough SEALs—hypothermia is a problem for everybody.

at 0100 when the two Mk 138 demolition kits detonated as primed. While the swim pairs exited the target area, they noticed that all the PDF vessels in Balboa Harbor had started turning their propellers as an anti-swimmer defense.

The SEAL swimmers descended beneath the surface and swam out into the harbor on a course that brought them near the main shipping channel for vessels transiting the Panama Canal. In the grand tradition of military operations, yet another tactical problem presented itself now: a large, deep draft ship moving across the diver's intended course back to the extraction point. Although their Draegers were not designed for use at that depth, the swimmers descended to forty-five feet for ten minutes while the ship passed overhead, then ascended to the normal depth of twenty feet. At last they found the shelter of Pier 6 and from there proceeded to the pickup point at the end of the pier for extraction.

The two CRRCs were waiting. In fact, they'd been waiting for what had seemed an eternity, since about 0055. The dive pairs were extremely late for their planned extraction. The boat crews, the support teams, and the fire-support teams ashore had all seen the firefight in the vicinity of the target; they'd seen the charges go off on schedule. They'd endured a firefight of their own in the immediate vicinity of the extraction point, near Pier 6, where they'd held their fire while tracers zipped overhead, apparently at random. They'd monitored their radios, without word from the teams whose own waterproofed MX-300s had been unequal to the task of communicating with the support elements.

Commander Carley, worried that the dive pairs may have mistaken an adjacent pier for the extraction point, sent CRRC number 2 over to investigate, hoping that the swimmers were there; they weren't and the boat was recalled.

An hour later than planned, at 0200 hours, dive pair number 1 materialized from the gloom, much to the relief of the boat crews. About five minutes later the second group

A foundation for special operators from all services is the talent for popping up in the darndest places, unexpected and uninvited. This young lad looks a little waterlogged, as well he should because he and three teammates have been sitting on the bottom of San Diego Bay for an hour or so after navigating a few hundred meters below sailboats, water skiers, and the occasional recreational swimmer. He's been using a rebreather that recycles air, enriches it with oxygen, and emits no bubbles. The weapon is a Heckler & Koch MP4 9mm submachine gun, a favorite of special operators everywhere for urban and close combat.

showed up, too, intact. The four SEALs were hauled back aboard the rubber boats, and the teams executed a tactical withdrawal. Using infrared strobes as a preplanned recognition device, the boats returned to the relative safety of Rodman at 0220 hours. An hour and a half later, Task Unit Whiskey was declared ready for retasking.

Mission Overview

Task Unit Whiskey's little adventure in Balboa Harbor is a kind of classic in the SEAL bag of tricks, revealing the hazards and virtues of naval special operations. Naval Special Warfare (NSW), as it is called, has been a very important and much abused subject for the last fifty years. For the US Navy it goes back to the Underwater Demolition Teams of World War II, who cleared beach obstacles and surveyed gradients for amphibious landings in the Pacific and against European shores, many dying in the attempt. It is an extremely dangerous set of missions that cannot be practically executed with other, less demanding means.

The organization and the people of the Naval Special Warfare is actually two communities, one being the men in the water, the Sea/Air/Land "commandos" (or SEALs), and the other being the men on the water, the Special Boat Squadrons (SBS). Both have a long and distinguished combat record, and both

It can be a long, cold swim back to base, so when the bus stops to pick up the team there's always a scramble to get aboard. Here, a cargo net has been rigged off the bow to make recovery of the people in the water a bit more expeditious. The Naval Special Warfare community is well represented here, the guys in the water (SEALs) and the guys on the water (Special Boat Squadron members).

Membership in the SEALs is not for everyone. It requires tremendous toughness—some physical, most mental. While this healthy specimen looks as though he may have previously worked for a professional football team, most SEALs are of normal size and stature. These people are accepted into membership in a tiny community (about 1,200 men total) only after a long, rigorous process of testing, evaluation, and selection—more than actual training. Anyone can learn the technical skills required to do the things SEALs do, but few have the personal self-discipline to learn the internal, intangible skills needed to be a good operator.

to the same high standard of performance as the more notorious part of the team. This story is about both.

The men in Naval Special Warfare are just one part of a big, broad spectrum of American combat power—in fact, a tiny slice of the pie. There are only about 1,500 of them in the US Navy, far fewer than the US Army's 7,000 or so Green Berets (active and reserve). SEALs, along with the Army's Ranger regiment and Special Forces groups, comprise the United States most elite surface combat operations resources. All are masters of basic infantry tactics; each has its own area of expertise. All train together at some points of their qualification. All, despite their parentage as components of the Navy or Army, are really on-call assets for the highest levels of the National Command Authority (NCA)—the president, the secretary of defense, and the Joint Chiefs of Staff. When they go to war, their mission will probably start at MacDill Air Force Base, Florida, where the United States Special Operations Command (USSOCOM) is headquartered. It is that kind of organization: powerful, dangerous, expensive, and above all, *special*. There is also something traditionally a bit odd about these special forces soldiers and sailors. They are isolated and aloof from the rest of the military and especially from the public, partly by design and partly by tradition. So how and why do a book like this one?

This book is the result of a policy of the US Department of Defense and the Navy to release as much information as possible about military institutions and activities while maintaining operational security. That can be a tough compromise sometimes, particularly with communities in special operations. In this case, it means that this book is the product of a close collaboration with the Navy, with the SEAL community, and with individual SEALs. All the photography of active-duty SEALs in this book has been reviewed and approved by both US Naval Special Warfare Command (SPECWARCOM) and SEAL Teams Three and Five, who assisted with its production.

communities have been linked together as Naval Special Warfare for about thirty years. While the SEALs get most of the attention and notoriety, the SBS have been doing a lot of the shooting and bleeding over the years. While most of the SBS crews are not graduates of the Basic Underwater Demolition /SEALS (BUD/S) training program the boat officers are SEALs, and SBS personnel are held

The Big Picture: US Special Operations Command

Special Operations Command has become, in the years since the failed Iranian hostage rescue mission, one of the best funded, most secure, most competitive parts of the US force structure. All the services, including the Coast Guard, have been caught up to some extent in the reorientation away from what is called "high-intensity combat," with its need for nuclear weapons, long-range bombers, numerous tank divisions and aircraft carriers, to preparation for "low-intensity combat," the work of small teams of extremely adept people like SEALs and Green Berets.

USSOCOM is just one of eight "unified" commands within the US armed forces and has been a major player in the defenses of America since 1987. It integrates assets from all the services into one organization, with one commander, and with the same basic set of missions for everybody. That doesn't mean that everybody does the same thing; rather it means that the Navy, Army, and Air Force pool their talents and resources for planning, training, and executing missions.

Special operations forces have traditionally been the "bad boys" of all the services. Many senior officers have, over the years, been candid about their loathing of the "cowboys" within their large, conservative organizations. Special forces training and missions produce a kind of lunatic intensity that is accepted within these groups but that clashes badly with the larger Navy or Army community within which it is supposed to function. Special operators have a reputation (well earned by an earlier generation) of using their own, independent criteria for acceptable behavior. Green Berets used to say, when asked if they were in the Army, "No, I'm in Special Forces." Some still do.

Becoming a SEAL or a Green Beret has never, as a result, been considered the fast track to high rank. It was, and still is, a special place for special men (and, very rarely and not in the SEALs, a few incredible women) who consider these extremely demanding roles

Naval Special Warfare is an interesting blend of high technology and the most basic, simple warrior skills. This fire team, coming ashore in a practiced ritual, functions much as small units have for thousands of years—with the same kinds of missions, the same concerns, discomforts, stresses. Norsemen invading England must, with minor changes in equipment and uniform, have looked like this.

a kind of calling. They aren't in the business to get rich or famous but to be measured by the highest standard of military performance and found acceptable. That is the real lure and the real reward of the special forces.

While the special operators may not always be personally popular within their services, the additional stress and funding for such missions has made for a very competitive budgetary environment. Both the Army and the Marine Corps compete with the Navy for the missions done by the SEALs. In fact, you could stand on a beach being infiltrated by combat swimmers and be very hard pressed to

There is tremendous overlap of missions, training, aptitude, and command of all the organizations within US Special Operations Command. This Green Beret trains SEALs in the art and science of small arms like the German GPMG 7.62mm ma- *chine gun he's carrying. SEALs and Green Berets are essentially members of the same fraternity. They are likely to be on better terms with each other than with members of conventional units within their own branch of service.*

know who was about to kill you—American Army "Green Berets" or Rangers, Marine Corps Force Recon, or US Navy SEALs. All use precisely the same weapons, boats, dive gear, radios, and uniforms—and all train for what sometimes looks like the same exact mission. But it turns out that the missions are not quite exact, that there are distinctions, and that the overlap is not as great as it initially appears. Here, then, is a thumbnail description of how the confusing world of US Special Operations is split up and tied together.

JSOC

Joint Special Operations Command (JSOC) is a kind of planning and coordination cell, headquartered at Pope Air Force Base, North Carolina, (co-located with Fort Bragg). JSOC's primary mission is to study the techniques and requirements of all the Special Operation Forces (SOF) components, including Naval Special Warfare, to ensure that—as they say—everybody's playing off the same sheet of music.

USASOC

The Army contributes the "Green Berets" (properly but rarely called Special Forces), a

SEALs now have a hostage rescue/counterterrorist assignment to train for. These SEALs are training for it by being "proned-out" by some Marines during a training exercise aboard the USNS Joshua Humphries in the Red Sea. This kind of joint training is a standard feature of life in the teams.

regiment of Rangers, the Delta counterterrorist unit, a special operations aviation unit called Task Force 160 (TF-160), plus psychological, civil affairs, and signal units. Most of these units are headquartered at Fort Bragg, North Carolina, at the US Army Special Operations Command (USASOC).

AFSOC

The Air Force contribution to special warfare is the US Air Force Special Operations Command (AFSOC) with headquarters at Hurlburt Field, Florida. The Air Force provides special aircraft and crews to insert and extract Army and Navy combat elements and to support them from overhead. AFSOC owns and operates special versions of the C-130,

CH-53, and CH-60 within the 1st Special Operations Wing.

NAVSOC

The Navy's contribution to USSOCOM is called NAVSOC within the special operations community, but is in fact Naval Special Warfare Command—SEALs and Special Boat Squadrons.

SEAL Specialties

SEALs—by contrast with Air Force and Army special operators in the Ranger regiment and special forces groups—are generalists, although each will have a specialty (intelligence, submarine operations, weapons, engineering, communications), that he does in support of the organization in the planning process. But once the little squad of SEALs goes off to war, he has to be able to do the job of anybody else on the team. "If I'm the platoon commander on a mission and I take a hit," one SEAL officer says, "the assistant platoon commander can take over. It doesn't matter if he was the corpsman or the radioman—he can take over that operation and direct it to completion. I can pick up the radio, treat a wound, use any of the weapons. Green Berets say they can do that too, but I think we build *generalists* while they build *specialists*. That's probably because they operate in larger groups. We operate in groups anywhere from four to sixteen men, and any one of our guys can slip into the role of any other guy . . . within limitations."

SEAL Missions

Just about all the special operations forces have the same *basic* list of missions. Each of them adapts these missions to the unique talents of the force. For the NSW community the list looks like this:

1) Direct action (DA)—Short-term seize, destroy, damage, or capture operations. Attacks against facilities ashore or afloat; "prisoner snatch" operations; small offensive combat operations against hostile forces.

2) Special reconnaissance (SR)—Reconnaissance and surveillance operations. Covert beach surveys, listening posts, observation posts.

3) Unconventional warfare (UW)—training, leading, and equipping partisan and guer-

The Air Force contribution to Special Operations Command is two-fold: it offers a kind of bus service, like this SH-60 dropping a squad off in the Gulf, *complete with boat; and it provides a kind of bodyguard service overhead, with Spectre gunships.*

rilla forces, behind enemy lines.

4) Foreign internal defense (FID)—Training, advising, and teaching the military, paramilitary, and law enforcement personnel of allied nations. Professional development, normally in a noncombat environment.

5) Counterterrorist operations (CT)—Operations conducted against terrorist units and individuals. May be as direct responses to terrorist operations or as indirect, preventive, deterrence measures.

All these missions have implications for their missionaries. To accomplish missions like these and survive, the people and the organizations they belong to need to be agile (individually and organizationally), trained to a far higher standard than conventional military personnel, and provided with far more resources, man for man, than conventional units. This assignment makes for organizations that are expensive and exclusive.

The "Wiring Diagram"

SPECWARCOM is an interesting community and a tremendous challenge to command. Although the SEAL teams are its most famous component, they are only one part of the whole business of Naval Special Warfare—a fairly small part, in fact.

RADM Ray Smith commands two major combat resources, Special Warfare Group One and Two. Each of these groups include three SEAL teams, a Special Boat Squadron, and a Swimmer Delivery Vehicle team.

Group One operates out of Coronado, California, and generally deploys forces to the Pacific and the Persian Gulf; SEAL teams One, Three, and Five are assigned to Group One. Group Two is headquartered at Little Creek, Virginia, with teams Two, Four, and Eight assigned, and a responsibility for operations in and around the Atlantic, including Europe and Latin America. These two headquarters are the administrative foundations for special warfare and, despite the sneers from the operators in the field about the "puzzle palace" (as such headquarters are often called) they are essential for the efficient coordination of as-

The fundamental component of the SEALs is the dive pair. A cardinal rule of life in the teams is you never abandon your swim buddy. It is too dangerous a business for solo operators.

sets and activities.

Coronado is not only home to Naval Special Warfare and Group One, but also to the notorious Naval Special Warfare Center where SEALs are trained. Basic Underwater Demolition/SEAL training is conducted at Coronado, the entry point for all new SEALs and SEAL Delivery Team members. The center also conducts advanced training and professional development programs for members of the SPECWARCOM community.

Little Creek, besides hosting Group Two, is responsible for the Special Warfare Development Group. This is the SEAL think tank

273

where new weapons, tactics, communication systems, and dive equipment is tested, evaluated, and written into doctrine. Little Creek is also responsible for the development of special operations tactics for air, ground, and maritime forces, in and out of Naval Special Warfare. SPECWARCOM includes detachments in Alaska and Hawaii, plus five Special Warfare Units.

What you don't see advertised are the semi-covert programs called Development Group and Red Cell. Development Group provides support for a variety of classified programs that—sorry—we aren't going to tell you about. Red Cell is an offshoot from the Naval Security Coordination Team and has the interesting mission of assisting navy commands around the world with their security problems. This help is not always welcomed because it is done in a sneaky way when the Red Cell members sneak or break into what are supposed to be secure facilities. They are supposed to act like terrorists or subversives—and that's the way a lot of people outside Naval Special Warfare think of them, too. Some commanders seem to think Red Cell creates more security problems than it solves. This program was at one time extremely notorious and the subject of a book by one of its former commanders (written while in prison) that scandalized Naval Special Warfare generally. It appears at this writing that the program will be transferred out of NSW into the more conventional Naval Investigative Service.

SEAL and Special Boat Squadron Basics

Although we usually refer to this community as SEALs, it is a bigger, more complicated business than the SEALs alone. The other

This fire team represents half a squad, a quarter of a platoon. Units this size are perfectly suited to most SEAL ops—ideal for ambushes, for example, and many strike missions. The fire team is small enough to be fast and agile and almost invisible; it is big enough to provide mutual support and to have enough diversity and cargo capacity to go inland for a raid or a recon.

275

SEALs get considerable latitude in the kind of gear and weapons they carry and use. This officer's non-standard combat vest is based on a design concept developed by the Israelis and adopted by the British, along with some US Special Operations Forces personnel. Rifle magazines are stowed in pouches designed for easy access—and to provide some protection against enemy small arms fire and grenade fragments.

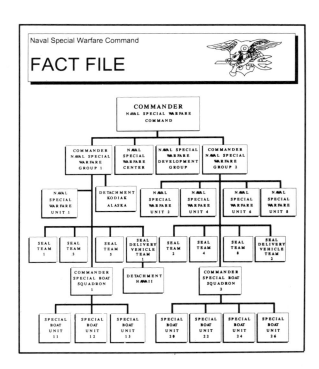
This is the "wiring diagram" for Naval Special Warfare—minus the "black" programs and units. Essentially it shows two major communities, Group One for the Pacific and Group Two for the Atlantic. The units are forward-deployment bases. Not shown are Red Cell and Development Group.

major part of SPECWARCOM is the guys on the surface who go through the same training at BUD/S, go off on the same missions, and bleed at least as much as the members of the SEAL teams—the Special Boat Squadrons and the members of the Special Warfare Units. They're all Naval Special Warfare members, although all the attention and glory seems to go to the SEALs alone. But, as the history of Naval Special Warfare in Vietnam and after shows, much of the combat and the killing has been done by the riverine warriors duking it out with the bad guys ashore with .50-caliber

machine guns and Mk 19 grenade launchers, all while roaring around in their PBRs in an unstealthy way.

The idea behind the boat squadrons is to provide the SEAL teams with dedicated, "organic" mobility, as well as some kinds of special patrol and surface strike missions. These squadrons are commanded by SEALs but manned largely by sailors from the surface warfare community, what SEALs often call the "black shoe" navy. Although part of the Naval Special Warfare community, they are not quite SEALs but SEAL support units.

The home base for SEAL/SBS operations seems somehow out of place on the luxurious, tropical paradise of Coronado, California, just

Far from the water but cold anyway, these two SEALs are participating in a training exercise in Norway. Special operators have to be extremely versatile and tolerant of extremes.

across the bay from San Diego. While tanned tourists frolic on the beach nearby, SEAL/SBS operations and training are planned and conducted at the Naval Special Warfare Command (SPECWARCOM), a component of US Special Warfare Command. The headquarters is just another rather modern concrete building, complete with the requisite lawn and landscaping, plus plenty of chain-link fence, guards, and razor wire.

The US Navy takes the prize for inventing and actually using the world's biggest and most awkward acronyms, one of which is SPECWARCOM. You might as well get used to words like this because everybody in the SEAL/SBS community uses them all the time; they are unavoidable. SPECWARCOM is the parent headquarters for all Navy special operations of which SEALs are only a part.

The commander of SPECWARCOM currently is a lean, bouncy, cheery, young-looking man with a star on his collar: he's Vice Admiral Ray Smith, fifty years old, who's been part of the community since 1970. Like all American commanders, he will have custody of

SPECWARCOM for two or three years, then hand it over to a new boss. During those years he will be responsible for the health and wealth of the community, its training, its tactics, its fitness for combat. He, like his predecessors and successors, will try to guide SPECWARCOM through the hazards of annual budgets and Department of Defense policy changes.

SEAL Teams

On paper at least, a full-up SEAL team includes ten platoons of SEALs plus a small support staff from the black-shoe navy. This support staff are the yeomen for administrative support, radiomen, ordnance specialists, a navy diver to help with the dive locker—about twenty non-SEAL personnel. There is an additional command element including the commanding officer, executive officer, and operations officer, all of whom are fully SEAL-qualified.

While in theory there are ten platoons in each team, it doesn't usually work out that neatly. Each team has an intense training program that cuts into the number of people actually available to participate in a platoon. But each of the platoons will have sixteen SEALs assigned: two officers and fourteen enlisted members. These are grouped further into two squads of eight, each getting an officer and seven enlisted. The squads themselves are split into fire teams of four men, the fire teams each having two "swim pairs."

The squad has traditionally been the organization of choice for SEAL operations and has turned out to be a very efficient group for many missions.

A lot of SEAL equipment is designed around these groups. The Mk V patrol boat is designed to accommodate sixteen SEALs. Fire teams of four fully combat-loaded SEALs fit very nicely into a Combat Rubber Raiding Craft. The Patrol Craft, Mk 1 is designed to carry a squad of eight SEALs.

SEAL Mobile Training Teams

SEALs (and Green Berets, too) are deployed all over the world, all the time, on quiet little assignments that you never read about in the papers—even when dramatic things happen, and the proverbial poop hits that fabled propeller. These deployments have a couple of functions: one is to put the special forces people out near the scene of a possible crime, before it is committed, ready to respond; the other is to train in environments a lot more realistic than are available in the United States.

One of these quiet deployments ("dets" in the trade jargon) nobody ever hears about is in support of the anti-drug war in Central and South America. Although US law prohibits SEAL/SBSs and other American military personnel from active combat, US policy is to use special operations forces personnel to train the "trigger pullers" to a high standard. And executing that mission is the team of Naval Special Warfare Unit Eight (NSWU-8) and Special Boat Squadron Twenty-Six (SBS-26), forward based out of Rodman in Panama but with people and boats busy in many Latin American nations.

These organizations, along with SEAL Team Four, are tasked with providing Mobile Training Teams (MTTs) to Bolivia, Argentina, Brazil, Colombia, Equador, and other nations where drugs are manufactured. All these countries have extensive river systems; there are more than 140,000 miles of navigable rivers in South America, with 20,000 in Bolivia alone. These become the highways for transportation of drugs. To control the drug flow requires efficient, effective patrol of the rivers, something the Special Boat Squadron folks do better than anybody.

The MTTs involve quite small numbers of US personnel and equipment to train rather large numbers of host-nation personnel. Sometimes the SBS/SEAL team doesn't even supply the boats. Once on scene the SBS team starts working with the boat operators from the host nation while the SEALs work with the police or military people who will do the patrolling ashore. In Bolivia this force is called the "Blue Devils"; it has been almost entirely trained by these MTTs. The SBS and SEAL dets have helped the Bolivians develop four bases for counterdrug operations deep in the jungle.

In Colombia the story is a little different. The US Marine Corps runs the show there,

Although the basic uniform matches that of Army and some Navy units, the CAR-15 version of the M16 is pretty much unique to the special operators. The CAR-15 has a shorter barrel and a collapsible buttstock.

Special operators place a high premium on surprise, stealth, and speed. A lot of all three come from the SBS crews and their exotic little boats, like this 30-foot rigid inflatable boat (RIB) seen here zipping around with a fire team of SEALs embarked.

Deep recon and strike missions are usually the province of the Army's Rangers or Green Berets, but SEALs train hard to do the same thing. Who will get the call for one of these assignments will have a lot to do with who is closest to the scene of the crime, *rather than any particular special talent. All are good, but if the op happens to be a coastal target it may be a platoon or squad of SEALs who "take it down."*

where they've had a long and chummy relationship with the Colombian marines. The Colombian det includes one officer and four enlisted SBS/SEAL personnel, all with a special interest in riverine operations and with Spanish language skills. MTTs in Colombia, as elsewhere in the program, last six months.

Special Warfare Units and Forward Basing

Since there are so few SEALs to go around, and since the "real world" has a way of blowing up in your face unexpectedly, Naval Special Warfare has developed forward bases closer to the potential hot spots of the world

than Coronado or Little Creek. These are the Naval Special Warfare Units (NSWUs), each with people, facilities, and equipment intended to speed up the process of planning and launching missions.

There are five NSWUs. When the "real world" starts acting up these are reorganized as Naval Special Warfare Task Groups and Units and start manning up with extra personnel from in and out of the NSW community. An emergency will probably find assets getting requisitioned from other NSWUs, particularly the exotic, complex Swimmer Delivery Vehicle (SDV), which may be flown in from the US.

Two SWUs serve the European Command area from bases in Spain and Scotland. The Naval Special Warfare Unit base in Spain (NSWU-6) uses Rigid Inflatable Boats (RIBs), Patrol Coastal boats (PCs), and Mk V patrol boats. The base in Scotland (NSWU-2) uses RIBs only. The Pacific Command is served by NSWU-1, recently repositioned from the Philippines to Guam; like NSWU-6, it uses RIBs, PCs, and Mk V patrol boats. NSWU-8 serves the extremely busy Southern Command out of Rodman Naval Station in Panama, supporting the busy counternarcotics operations with a mix of riverine and coastal patrol boats

This lieutenant commands a SEAL Team Three platoon conducting training in desert patrolling, small unit tactics, and live-fire exercises. Unlike many other units, particularly conventional ones, SEALs train their officers and enlisted people together at the same time. While it puts additional stresses on the officers, who must fulfill administrative duties as well as survive the program, it has the advantage of applying the same high standards to the commissioned officers, while their followers observe. The result is an extra measure of respect for a SEAL officer.

and the RIBs. Detachments in Hawaii and Alaska provide SEALs with a broad range of training options.

Besides these forward bases, two large Naval Special Warfare Groups on the east and west coasts of the US provide a continental United States (CONUS) foundation for operations "downrange."

For some Naval Special Warfare assets, forward basing is the only practical way to show up on time for the little "come as you are" wars that are the stock in trade of US Special Operations Forces. The PCs, for example, are far too big to go anywhere except under their own power. Although they are fast, it's a mighty big world. If they had to self-deploy from the US, it could take these ships almost three weeks to arrive at some possible operational areas.

Change of Mission

The "commander's intent" for American special operations has changed quite a bit since the idea was first used fifty years ago, at the outset of World War II. Back then the idea was to provide support for partisans and guerrillas in occupied France, Yugoslavia, China, and elsewhere. It involved very little—if any—direct combat. It was a training, leading, and supplying role for forces that tried their best to avoid direct contact with German or Japanese forces while collecting intelligence and sabotaging vehicles, railroads, and bridges and occasionally assassinating individual enemy.

Special Operations Forces today still train for that mission, and SEALs execute something like it every day, in nations all over the world. The trainees aren't guerrillas anymore, but soldiers, sailors, and law enforcement officers from nations such as Colombia, Bolivia, and Kuwait; and the "enemy" is now quite often the guerrilla-like forces who manufacture and distribute drugs or terrorists in Ireland, the Middle East, or Latin America.

The war against terrorist forces has, more than anything else, inspired much of the mission of today's SEALs and other SOF commu-

"Takedown" missions are complicated, dangerous raids that require tremendous skill to execute. When they go bad, they go real bad; the consequences aren't just death or embarrassment for the team, but possible dire international ramifications as well. Ever since the failed Iranian hostage rescue, this mission has been practiced over and over, in depth and detail.

Although SEALs try to avoid airborne insertions like this (as one team commander says, "If you have to jump—find another way!"), the technique is still used occasionally and is practiced as just one way of getting from here to there.

nities. The tasking for Naval Special Warfare is now, essentially, to be prepared to *conduct short-notice small-unit operations at night, over the horizon, to infiltrate from sea, air or land, in adverse weather.* Instead of training others to fight large, conventional battles, SOF units, including the SEALs, are much more like global SWAT teams that can be sent to fight almost anybody, almost anywhere. Like a good SWAT team, these forces are task-organized and are based on stealth, shock, surprise, and precision. While some SEALs still study foreign languages and are charismatic instructors for people of extremely alien cultures, the heavy emphasis now is on preparing SEALs to be able to slither deep into hostile territory, up to easy pistol range of

very specific bad guys, put 9mm bullets between their eyes—and then get out without being obvious about it. The battlefield can be a hotel, an airliner, a civilian cargo ship, an oil platform, a factory, or an embassy. And the enemy may be one hostile man—or woman—surrounded by innocents.

This is a tall order. In fact, it is sometimes too tall; SEALs aren't, despite what you hear, supermen. They get tapped to do impossible missions sometimes because they are so skilled, so sneaky, so confident . . . and they die in the attempt, sometimes, as in Panama and Grenada, when they're pushed beyond their limits. There are only about 1,200 of them for a global set of responsibilities. It is a small community with a huge mission.

This motley crew is a squad of warrior SEALs from long ago and far away. Standing are Pierre Birtz, Bill Garnett, Charlie Bump, and Bob Gormly; kneeling are Jess Tollison and Fred McCarty; the photo was made in 1967. With Gormly (then a lieutenant) as squad leader, these men operated around the town of Binh Thuy, helping establish the reputation of the SEALs as among the most elite American warriors. All made Naval Special Warfare a profession, and all are now retired except for Tollison, who was killed in an accident at the Niland, California, training facility in 1971. Gormly went on to command SEAL Teams Two and Six, UDT-12, and NSW Group Two before retiring in 1992 as a captain. Bob Gormly collection

Chapter 2

A Short History Lesson

The keel for today's SEALs and Special Boat Squadrons was laid in May of 1942 with the formation of the Naval Combat Demolition Unit at Fort Pierce, Florida. The men who were selected for the program came from the Naval Construction Battalions and the Navy/Marine Corps Scout and Raider Volunteers. All had extensive swim experience; some were commercial divers; all were in superb physical condition. The training was not too different, fifty years ago, from today—lots of physical training (PT), lots of swimming, lots of demolitions. The stress level was high, by design. Training continued day and night, in the swamps with the alligators, on the beaches, and offshore.

The motivation for the program had come toward the end of the previous year. After less than a year of war, the United States was beginning to strike back at the entrenched Japanese, first at Guadalcanal, then, in November, at Tarawa . . . "terrible Tarawa," as it will always be known to the United States Marine Corps.

The US was badly unprepared for war, and even more unprepared for large-scale, long-range amphibious operations. One of the things that makes wars interesting is the ways in which individuals and nations respond to the surprises and stresses imposed on them by events. In the case of the US Navy and Marine Corps in 1942, this meant a re-quirement for not merely the attack of Japanese installations in the Pacific, but the seizure of critical bases.

Guadalcanal came first—and the invasion phase of the operation, at least, was a cakewalk. The Marines were able to step ashore, essentially unopposed, often with dry feet. Getting the force ashore was just about the least of the problems at Guadalcanal—most of which came soon thereafter. The Navy had been lucky with that phase of the operation. Tarawa was different. D-day for Tarawa was 20 November 1942. Information about the island, its defenses, and its approaches was limited. Hydrographic data was sketchy, tidal data almost nonexistent. The assault force commander took a risk, knowing the stakes, and lost.

The Marines were sent in aboard conventional landing craft. Five hundred yards offshore, within the range of Japanese machine guns, the boats ground to a halt against coral reefs. The Marines, in the grand tradition, jumped off the boat ramps for the long wade into the beach . . . and died in droves. Many stepped into depressions in the coral reef; heavily loaded, they sank and drowned. The rest had to endure the heavy, interlocking fields of fire from the Japanese defenders. It was a disaster.

Hundreds of Marines died before the battle for Tarawa really even began. In a way,

Many of the basic "frogman" techniques in use today were invented half a century ago in the pressure cooker of war. That includes this technique for de- *ploying a line of swimmers off an enemy-held beach from a high-speed boat.*

their lives were wasted, but in another way, by dying this way, they taught the Navy a lesson. The lesson was, and still is, that amphibious assaults are high-risk operations that require careful preparation. And that need for battlefield preparation was the idea for the development of the Navy Combat Demolition Unit.

Their mission was to scout possible invasion beaches and to clear, with explosives, obstacles that might prevent the invasion force from reaching the beach as had happened at

Tarawa. It was recognized that there were essentially four hazards to the force: enemy action from fortifications ashore, enemy-built obstacles such as concrete blocks placed in the water, natural obstacles such as the coral reef that stopped the Marines, and the time and range of the tides.

That was the program for the sturdy volunteers at Fort Pierce. The survivors of the challenging training were organized as small units, structured with six enlisted men and one officer per Combat Demolition Unit and shipped off to England with the rest of the American contingent building up for the invasion of France.

When finally, on 6 June 1944, Allied forces were ready to take Europe back from the Nazis, the first men ashore were the Navy Combat Demolition Teams (NCDTs). The NCDT members were tasked with the nasty chore of surveying and destroying the beach obstacles emplaced by the Germans along the Normandy coast of France. These obstacles were an ingenious and extensive array of concrete blocks, steel spikes, mines, and barbed wire that cluttered most of the beaches suitable for amphibious landings. Left in place, they certainly would deter any large force from putting men ashore. And in 1943 the Germans knew the Allies were going to come, sooner or later, and were working as fast as possible to make a beach passage as costly as possible.

When the Allies finally struck, the NCDT men were out in front of the first wave. With the most primitive equipment, utterly lacking effective protection from the chilly water, they swam in to the beach in the small hours before the invasion. Working from one massive obstacle to the next, hanging satchel charges linked with detonation cord, they prepared to clear the beaches for the assault elements.

Dawn that day found an incredible armada off the Normandy coast, thousands of ships and boats finally bringing hundreds of thousands of soldiers back to Europe—and the beaches still hadn't been completely cleared. The NCDT men had been given a tall order, and not all the obstacles had been blown by the time the infantry started in to the beach. As the cloudy sky brightened, German gunners could see, and engage, the men setting charges on the beach whose mission was obvious. While the NCDT men struggled frantically to avoid the fire, emplace the explosives, and blow the lanes for the landing craft, the first wave closed on the beaches.

Even without clear access to some of the beaches, the craft disgorged their cargoes of infantry when and where they could, often under intense artillery and heavy machine gun fire. The NCDT men worked as fast as they could, but even so they found infantry sheltering behind obstacles rigged and primed for demolition, despite warning devices. Some charges blew with infantry nearby, killing them, while other obstacles weren't blown because of the proximity of men from the first wave.

Even so, four lanes were cleared and the assault elements generally made it ashore—if not in good order, at least in one piece, one infantry division after another. The cost for the NCDT force was far higher than for the infantry—about thirty percent at Utah Beach, about sixty-five percent at Omaha, about forty percent casualties overall. But, from the point

February, 1969. A SEAL ties a block of C4 into a line of det cord before placing the charge in aViet Cong (VC) tunnel complex. Vietnam honed the special warfare abilities of the little SEAL community to a sharp edge through an emphasis on small unit, independent operations that made individual platoons and squads responsible for "taking care of business."

of view of the planners, that was a small price to pay for getting a secure foothold on the heavily defended enemy shore.

Despite the losses and the problems the NCDT units encountered, their work was considered a success and adapted to the island-hopping campaign in the Pacific. They were rechristened Underwater Demolition Teams (UDT), each with 100 enlisted men and thirteen officers assigned, and retaining the seven-man unit foundation.

Out in the Pacific the UDT units developed a routine that became part of the standard operating procedure (SOP) for amphibious assaults, some of which survives to the present day. This routine started with a beach reconnaissance four days before the scheduled assault (D-minus-4) with the swimmers inserted just at first or last light. This recon would identify obstacles, natural and man-made, on the intended lanes for the landing craft and armored amphibious tractors (AAM-TRACs), recording each carefully and developing a chart of the offshore, nearshore, foreshore, backshore, and hinterland areas of the invasion beaches.

On D-minus-1 or on D-day itself the obstacles would be blown. The method developed fifty years ago is still taught today because it still works. Here's how they did it:

While naval gunfire and close air support aircraft light up the beach with guns, bombs, rockets, and cannon fire in this type of approach, a small, fast ship makes a high-speed run into the beach. During World War II, modified destroyer-escorts were used and designated APDs (Attack Personnel Destroyers). Several miles offshore the APD stopped and lowered four LCPR landing craft, each with a "rubber duck" lashed to the port side. These LCPRs then made a high-speed "splash run" parallel to the beach, about a thousand meters out, starboard side facing the shore. One after another the swimmers rolled out of the LCPR into the rubber duck and, on command, into the water, forming a line of swimmers. At a thousand meters the small portion of each man's head is essentially invisible, and while

the defenders might possibly have spotted one with powerful binoculars, the aerial bombardment and naval gunfire tended to make them worry about other issues.

The men swam ashore and executed their missions, either a reconnaissance or a beach clearance, then withdrew back to the thousand-meter line offshore for pickup, again forming a line of swimmers at intervals. The LCPR came zooming up the line again, with a rubber sling extended. By forming a crook with his right arm and kicking hard just before the boat came by, the swimmer could come up partially out of the water and snag the sling rigged from the inflatable boat, to then be smoothly plucked from the ocean slingshot fashion. One after another the line of swimmers could be quickly and (under the circumstances) safely recovered.

The actual demolition of the beach obstacles also became something of an art form, still practiced today. That technique sent swimmers in to assigned obstacles with satchel charges essentially identical to the ones used today. The flank swimmers at either end of the line carried long rolls of "det cord" instead of explosives; while the other swimmers were busy installing the satchel charges, the det cord was strung from one end of the beach to the other. The satchel charges were each tied into this det cord, and then most of the swimmers began to withdraw. Finally, the ends of the det cord were double-primed, once from each end, with a blasting cap and time fuse. Using waterproof fuse lighters, the fuse was lit, and the whole team formed up out at the thousand-meter line for pickup. When either of the fuses finally burned down to its blasting cap, the "powder train" was initiated; the det cord linked all the charges and caused all to go off within a small fraction of a second—hopefully while the swimmers were already well offshore and safe from the blast effect and chunks of concrete and steel that rained down after such a mission. After Normandy, UDT losses dropped to only about one percent from the approximately forty percent of the first large-scale operation, thanks large-

"Hey! You said the mud wasn't deep!" The op hasn't even started and this guy is already out of action—up to his knees in mud. The weapon is the infamous Stoner, a 5.56mm machine gun with a tendency to jam at embarrassing moments. When it worked, though, it could chew up whatever it was pointed at, and the idea behind it survives today in the lightweight version of the M60 still used by the squads.

ly to this technique. By the end of the war thirty-four teams, including about 3,500 officers and men, were in action in the Pacific.

Korea

In the grand American military tradition, much of the equipment and experience of the UDTs in World War II was discarded promptly after VJ-day—only to be reinvented a few years later. For UDT that came in September 1950 with the audacious amphibious landing at Inchon, Korea.

With United Nations (UN) forces trapped in a shrinking perimeter at the southern tip of Korea by a rampaging, nearly victorious North Korean army, Gen. Douglas MacArthur and his staff designed an "end run" operation on the enemy, with the port city of Inchon on the western coast of the peninsula, near the already fallen capital of Seoul, as the target.

The harbor at Inchon is a treacherous one, with an extreme range of tides that would make the timing and execution of any amphibious operation extremely critical. To minimize the danger, UDT was used to provide detailed information about channels, docks, tides, and defenses. They cleared channels of mines the hard way, by hand, swimming in line-abreast and attaching charges to the mines as they were encountered.

After the Inchon invasion totally changed the complexion of the war, with the North Koreans reeling back, the UDT units were used again, but not just for beach recons and clearance missions. Their skill and experience earned them assignments to blow bridges, railroads, tunnels, and similar targets well away from the beaches.

Korea was the first of a series of nasty little wars that didn't conform to the expectations of the strategic planners in Washington, but that didn't prevent soldiers, sailors, and Marines from having to fight them. Korea didn't really fit what the American public expected, either, and consequently support for the war and the men fighting it slowly ebbed a bit until the stalemate was formalized with a truce in 1953. But Korea expanded the mission of the organization that would soon be rechristened "SEALs" and included guerrilla operations behind the lines, parachute jumps, and other missions quite different from those envisioned ten years previously during the bigger conflict of World War II. And more was yet to come.

The Vietnam War

Although the ancestors of the units and the missions that would become the Navy's and Army's special operations forces existed during World War II, it was not until 1962 that they achieved real recognition and support. The support came from John F. Kennedy, a student of international conflict and unconventional warfare. Kennedy had read the works of Mao Tse Tung and Che Guevara, and he understood the changing nature of conflict away from nuclear confrontation to brush-fire wars. While the United States was reasonably well prepared for the former, he knew better than many of his generals and admirals how badly the US was prepared for unconventional warfare.

Kennedy was aware of the British success against guerrillas in Malaya in the late 1950s. The Brits learned to turn the guerrilla's tactics and strategies around on them, learned to live in the jungle—where they fought and won uncounted little battles. Kennedy perceived a warning and an opportunity. As a newly elected president, he was in a position to make things happen, and he did. He didn't invent the SEALs or the Green Berets—both organizations already existed but were allowed meager resources and roles.

The Army, in particular, loathed the fledgling special operations units that existed at the time. They refused to "play fair" in exercises and frequently disrupted the intended out-

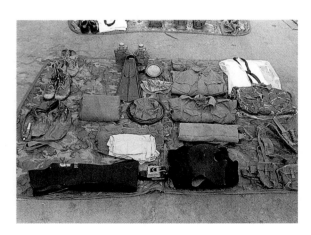

The basic issue of gear is laid out for inspection in this Vietnam-era photograph: coral shoes, canteens, flippers, weight belt, wet suit, web gear, uniforms, and unshined boots. Gary Stubblefield

come. As a result, wearing the green beret was a court-martial offense at Fort Bragg—until Kennedy showed up. The Navy wasn't as parochial, but the UDTs were still hardly a barnacle on the chain of command.

Kennedy put the whole Department of Defense on notice that there was about to be a change of mission. The change was from a focus on a northern European, NATO versus Warsaw Pact conflict, to the kinds of wars Kennedy thought the US was likely to actually have to fight. He said, "This is another type of warfare, new in its intensity, ancient in its art—war by guerrillas, subversives, insurgents, assassins—war by ambush, instead of by combat—war by infiltration instead of aggression; seeking victory by eroding and exhausting the enemy instead of engaging him. And these are the kinds of challenges that will be before us in the next decade, if freedom is to be saved—a whole new kind of strategy, a wholly different kind of force, and therefore a new and wholly different kind of military training."

Kennedy insisted not only on new training, new organization, and new strategies, but on new weapons and equipment as well. He was responsible for the development and introduction of the AR-15/M16 rifle and the jungle boot, with its steel insert to protect against punji stakes. But it was the development of what became known as a *special warfare* capability within the US Department of Defense that was one of Kennedy's most inspired and enduring legacies.

The Army's Special Forces (known popularly but unofficially as the Green Berets) and the Navy's SEALs and SBSs share many things, including missions, heritage, and a strong sense of mutual respect. Both were developed, at Kennedy's insistence, in the early 1960s. At the outset, both were envisioned as extensions of the World War II Office of Strategic Services (OSS) teams that parachuted behind enemy lines to train, equip, lead, and inspire the native population, a catalyst that used a few men to put hundreds of soldiers in the field. It was called *unconventional warfare* and it was a good idea. It worked—in some times and in some places.

Birth of the SEALs and SBSs

The SEALs were officially born on 1 January 1962, with President Kennedy doing the honors, commissioning Team One and Two, assigned to the Pacific and Atlantic theaters. The original mission was to conduct Naval Special Warfare—which then meant unconventional warfare, counterguerrilla and clandestine operations in maritime and riverine environments. This meant, theoretically, the capability to: 1) destroy enemy shipping and harbor facilities; 2) infiltrate and extract friendly force agents, guerrillas, and escapees; 3) conduct reconnaissance and surveillance; 4) conduct counterinsurgency civic action; 5) organize, train, and lead paramilitary forces.

The new organization got its first taste of real world operations shortly thereafter, conducting operations in support of the Cuban Missile Crisis in 1962, and again in 1965, in the Dominican Republic. Neither lasted long or received much attention, but both put the teams under the kind of pressure that only happens during genuine hostilities. It was a useful rehearsal for the big war that was about to begin. SEALs in small numbers shipped out to Vietnam in 1962, working out of Da Nang and functioning in an advisory role to the Vietnamese Navy, much as the Green Berets were doing for the Army of Vietnam at the same time.

SEAL Team One trained up and deployed two platoons to Vietnam in 1965, assigned to operate in the Rung Sat Special Zone near the capital city, Saigon. These platoons started operating in areas never previously visited by American or Vietnamese forces, deep in the mazes of rivers, creeks, and channels where the VC (Viet Cong, communist South Vietnamese rebels) had been safe. The platoons set up listening posts to collect information on VC activity and ambushes to turn the VC activity off.

The poor VC would come cruising back from a night on the town, shooting up the nearest government outpost, collecting "taxes" from farmers going to market, or assassinating mayors or other officials who might be friendly to Saigon, putting along a deserted stretch of canal in their sampans on the way back to base all fat, dumb, and happy. Then, suddenly, the canal bank would erupt as machine guns and rifles opened up from an artfully prepared ambush. The VC were either killed or captured, their operational routine disrupted, and their influence over the local population severely reduced. The American SEALs were turning a VC tactic around and using it effectively. It just wasn't fair, somehow! It was stealthy, sneaky, and utterly unexpected—just what Americans were not supposed to be able to do, setting the tone for the conduct of Naval Special Warfare to the present day.

The results from this preliminary experiment were quite successful, and four additional platoons were soon sent, two assigned to Nha Be, one to Binh Thuy, and another to My Tho. With a headquarters element, Detachment Alpha, set up at Subic Bay in the Philippines, the SEALs were ready to "lock and load." Detachment Bravo went aboard an APD as a component of a beach recon group, Detachment Charlie went aboard two fleet submarines (the USS *Perch* and USS *Tunney*), and Detachment Delta was sent to Da Nang, Republic of Vietnam. Detachments Echo and Foxtrot went aboard the Amphibious Ready Group standing off the coast, with assignments to assist with demolitions and beach surveys. But it was "Dets" Golf and Hotel, the riverine patrols, that most frequently closed with the enemy and where much of the legend of the SEALs in that war was built.

SEALs were again deployed to Vietnam in 1966, first to the area around Saigon and later to the rich, heavily populated Mekong Delta. The platoons did their workup together, deployed together, and returned together after six-month tours. This made for a kind of intimacy and unit cohesion far stronger than the main force Army units in the country at the time, where soldiers rotated in and out of units individually for one-year tours.

In some important ways, the lessons of the SEAL platoons and teams during the war in Vietnam have been ignored and overlooked. Within the limited areas in which they operated, these little units became highly effective in a generally ineffective war. Their efforts were independent of a larger strategy and so failed to have a lasting impact on the bigger campaign, but they did show what could—and still can—be done by extremely small, stealthy units operating in a maritime environment.

The platoons were given tremendous freedom to conduct their operations as they saw fit. They developed their own intelligence, plans, and procedures, and executed their missions pretty much without interference or support from the Army or Air Force or from the local Vietnamese military commanders.

Although they avoided working with the local Army of the Republic of Vietnam (ARVN) as much as possible, the SEAL teams often included Vietnamese SEALs. Some of these men were very good. They provided excellent translation services and often exhibited a high degree of combat discipline.

The most common and appropriate use of the SEAL teams were in ambushes, recon missions, and prisoner snatches. The small size of the units, even when supported with gunboats and ground-support aircraft, normally kept the platoons from engaging anything bigger than an enemy platoon or, if it couldn't be avoided, a company or even a battalion. Their

One of the most frustrating elements of combat operations in Vietnam was the way the VC and North Vietnamese Army (NVA) often used civilians for cover and concealment. Sorting out the good guys from the bad guys was always a problem, particularly within the heavily populated Mekong delta where SEALs did most of their operations. Gary Stubblefield

flexibility and experience, the effective and efficient support from the boat units, and the air and intelligence teams attached to the SEAL platoons all made for a successful fighting force and a style of operations that is extremely different than that used today.

In the Mekong Delta, particularly, SEAL operations ranged from simple ambushes to complex joint operations, staged from Navy ships located over the horizon, involving transit to the beach in small craft. SEALs used Army helicopter gunships, naval gunfire support, US Air Force "fast-movers," and Army helicopters again, this time the "slicks" for extraction from hot landing zones. SEALs also ran the Provincial Reconnaissance Units (PRUs) as part of the exotic Phoenix program.

Platoons at the time used fourteen men, but a typical mission usually called for no more than seven. Intelligence collection for an operation usually took several weeks and was developed concurrently with other operations. The platoon leader would design a mission around resources and objectives. Helicopters would be laid on for gunship fire support, the boats would be scheduled, an interpreter and a Vietnamese SEAL assigned. The helo crews were briefed, the squads received a warning order, and then, when the plan was fully refined, they got an operation order. Gary Stubblefield, a retired SEAL commander, says, "Briefings in those days took one hour, an hour and a half, max. We already knew our SOPs, we already knew our area. All we had to do was catch up with the changes required for the specific mission. The hard part was the 'actions at the objective' portion, where we got really detailed.

"Typically, we'd leave some time after dark, insert sometime before midnight, maintain an ambush until about daylight, break the ambush and get back in the boats to go back to the base."

A War Story

CAPT Bob Gormly has commanded SEAL Teams Two and Six, UDT-12, and NSW Group Two during a long career in Naval Special Warfare, just concluded. As a young lieu-

tenant he went to Vietnam with SEAL Team Two's first deployment to the combat zone in 1967. SEAL Team Two was sent to the Mekong Delta, a hotbed of enemy activity, in the first use of the SEALs in that part of the country—though Team One had been working for some time up to the north, around Saigon.

"Our operations at first were kind of 'touch and feel,'" he says. "We were always searching for a strategy that we fitted into—and we never found it—but we had a lot of fun. Us young lieutenants had tremendous freedom about how we wanted to run an operation. We couldn't be told by anybody to run an operation that we didn't want to do."

Back then the entire delta was considered "Indian" country—hostile territory. The only real US presence was the Navy's River Patrol Force (CTF-116), which used PBRs to patrol the major rivers for about a year, getting shot at regularly. The VC had pretty much free run of the rest of the area.

The problem for the newly established SEALs from Team Two was first to find out what was going on. That required an intelligence information program, something that began immediately with requests for overflights, interrogations of prisoners, radio intercepts, and similar information-gathering techniques.

Gormly developed his own little plan for how he wanted to operate. First, the SEALs wouldn't go where other friendly forces could operate—because there probably wouldn't be anything there, and to make coordination with friendly forces more efficient.

After considering the available intelligence information—the "intel" as it's called—Gormly would call for a Navy Seawolf helicopter and go for a ride. He flew over the area he was interested in to get a sense of the lay of the land, looking for signs of enemy activity. Although there were no US forces in the area, other than CTF-116, there were a few trustworthy American officers in the delta who could help keep the chaos and confusion to a minimum.

"Then I'd land at the subsector headquarters to meet with the senior US advisor, usually a US Army captain or major, who would be working with the local Vietnamese provincial and subsector commanders. I'd walk in and tell him, 'Hi, I'm Bob Gormly. I've got a SEAL team, and we want to operate in your subsector—and I don't want anybody else to know about it but *you*.' To a man, they all agreed to that condition. Then I'd tell them, 'I'm going to be out there sometime in the next three or four days. I'm not going to tell you when. Just, please, don't put H & I [harassment and interdiction artillery fire] in there.'

"Then I'd go back to base, get the platoon together, start running whatever intel we had on the place, setting up to go. We usually went the next night.

"Just before we launched, within six hours, I sent a UNODIR [unless otherwise directed] message . . . a *flash* message that went to all higher headquarters that began 'Unless Otherwise Directed,' and indicated where we were going. Never once was I told not to go. Then we'd hop in the boat and head down river.

"We traveled very light, only small arms, plus an M60 machine gun and an M79 grenade launcher. The briefing was simple: I made sure everybody had the equipment they were assigned, then I told them where we were going, when, and what we were going to do. 'Any questions? No? Let's go!'

"We jumped in the boat, a twenty-two foot trimaran and took off. The boat was a 75mph boat that we made into a 25mph boat by adding a lot of weight in the form of ceramic armor, weapons, and a lot of people."

The SOP for ambushes involved cruising down one of the main rivers or canals into the general area of the objective, inserting several kilometers ("klicks," in the trade), and walking in to the ambush site along another canal. A typical mission involved a boat trip of fifty kilometers or so up the lazy river, as fast as possible for most of the trip, then as quietly and innocently as possible for the last few klicks. Navigation in the confused maze of canals was a tremendous problem, generally one the skipper of the boat was responsible for. If he was good you arrived where you planned to go—if not, you could have a real problem.

The most dangerous and vulnerable concern was the problem of getting off the boat and into the local woodwork without being noticed. Nearly all insertions were done in the middle of the night. Rather than run the boat up into the weeds and debark the patrol in obvious fashion, the insertion was usually conducted in a more sneaky way. While the boat motored along in normal fashion, the team members merely stepped off the stern in patrol order, swam ashore, and slithered up on the bank. They all waited silently for ten minutes or so, listening for any movement that might indicate they'd been compromised and that enemy forces were moving in to investigate. If that happened, the boat could be recalled for an emergency extraction. Otherwise the mission proceeded according to SOP and to plan.

In the delta, the patrol would move out into the rice paddies, staying off the dikes and away from the treelines where enemy soldiers were most likely to be. Movement was extremely slow and careful, the SEALs moving quietly toward the intended ambush site, normally a canal bank, usually several klicks from the insertion point.

"Although we were in a free-fire zone where everything that moved at night was considered enemy," Gormly says, "we were more selective. Unless I actually saw weapons on the boats we would call the boat over to the bank and search it. If they were 'clean' I'd just take the sampan down the canal a ways and hold them there while we waited for somebody else to come along. One night we had to wait for four sampans before one came along that belonged to the bad guys."

SOP for that kind of contact was for the patrol leader to initiate the ambush, typically at quite short range where the M60, the M16s on full-auto, and the M79 grenade launcher's focused fire would shred the wooden vessel and its crew. The team would wait for the

From 1,000 feet overhead, the farms and rivers of the Mekong Delta look deceptively tranquil in this pre-op recon photo. Within the lush growth along the river are likely to be bunkers and fighting posi- *tions. Inland, among the fields and groves, may lurk more enemy facilities and stores—and the enemy himself. Gary Stubblefield*

leader to fire, sometimes with full-tracers, the signal to "hose down" the enemy vessel. "Seven guys carry a *lot* of firepower," Gormly recalls. "If it was a good hit and there were a lot of weapons aboard we might stick around to see what happened—maybe somebody would come over to investigate. Then we could ambush them too!"

After the patrol leader was satisfied with the evening's mayhem, the order to move would be given. The detained boats would be released, much to the relief of the fishermen aboard, and the SEALs would move off toward the extraction point. The pickup boat would already be somewhere in the vicinity for the scheduled recovery of the team, waiting for a radio call. The team would be recovered and would head back to base for debriefing and chow. In a couple of days it would be time for another briefing and another mission.

This pattern was used for the vast majority of SEAL missions of all types, including recons and prisoner snatches, with slight variations. Recons involved insertion around two or three in the morning, then patrolling into a predetermined overwatch location, setting up a "hide," and staying very still all day. Air or artillery fire could be called in on targets of opportunity. Finally, late at night, the SEALs would patrol back out to be extracted.

While this was a pretty efficient way of running operations, it was hardly without risk. Gormly was asked to send a team onto Cu Lao Tan Dinh, an island in the delta where enemy gunners routinely shot up passing patrol boats from fortified bunker complexes. With several patrol boats standing by for fire support, the team inserted at first light of 7 June 1967, loaded with hundreds of pounds of C4 explosive, blasting caps, detonation cord, and fuse.

Once ashore, Gormly's motley crew "sneaked and peeked" around for three or four hours, finding lots of bunkers in the process but not encountering any of the loyal opposing team. With the patrol boat supplying the demo materials, the team methodically blew up every bunker in sight. They did this for about four hours, moving steadily down the river from bunker site to bunker site. As they left what turned out to be the last bunker complex, Gormly noticed signs of human activity—bent grass where someone had stepped within the previous few minutes, leaving a trail away from the river. The patrol crawled thirty or forty meters forward, following the tracks, until Gormly (now on point) saw an enemy soldier, complete with helmet and weapon, in the weeds ahead. "I stood up and hosed him down. Then I got shot—and all hell broke loose! We had walked down the side of an L-shaped ambush—lucky us! We had a *big* firefight, then made our way back to the river where we directed fire on the VC until we could get a boat in to extract us. The helo gunships and the boats stayed there for about eight more hours, shooting it out with the VC. I got shot through the wrist. The guy that shot

me was no more than five feet behind me. We had a Vietnamese SEAL with us, and he hosed that guy down. I was *real* lucky—he shot me over my right shoulder. At first I didn't even know I was shot. I thought my rifle had jammed and blown up—then I noticed the gaping hole in my wrist and realized I'd been shot. That was kind of a stupid op but it was fun for a while!" It also turned out to be worth a Silver Star for Gormly after his SEALs wrote him up for the award.

Grenada

After Vietnam the armed forces of the United States suffered another postwar decline and was—as so often in the past—unprepared for the kinds of real world operations that always seem to materialize. But the failed Iranian hostage mission, among other factors, had begun to revitalize the conventional armed forces when, on 23 October 1983, the SEALs went off to war again, kicking off Operation Urgent Fury in Grenada.

Urgent Fury was, sad to say, pretty much a "goatscrew" for US Special Operations Forces generally, and for the SEALs in particular. The SOF community and the National Command Authority learned many lessons from the operation, but (as usual) it took the bloodshed of the former to educate the latter.

Point Salines Recon Air Insertion

On "point" for Operation Urgent Fury was one platoon of SEALs from Team Six tasked with a recon mission of Point Salines, a thin point of land at the extreme southwest end of the island on which the Grenadans had constructed a new airfield. The platoon's mission objective was a preinvasion recon of sites for amphibious and airborne landings. Their plan, which they developed themselves, involved an insertion by parachute of the sixteen men and their PBL (Patrol Boat, Light—a mil-spec Boston Whaler speed boat) near a Navy destroyer, the *Clifton Sprague*. Once in the water, the SEALs were to find the boat, assemble aboard it, rendezvous with the *Sprague*, take on more SEALs and three US Air Force combat controllers, and slip ashore for the recon. Planning such a complicated operation is one thing; making it happen in the real world is another.

Everything went wrong: instead of jumping at last light, as planned, the mission was late by six hours and the SEALs jumped into pitch black night, making link-up with the boats and the men extremely difficult. Then, overloaded with equipment, the SEALs were driven deep below the surface of the water on landing. Despite the use of flotation devices, three SEALs drowned at the very beginning of the insertion phase of the op. Others survived by jettisoning as much gear as possible from their 100-pound-plus loads. On the surface, one of the two PBLs couldn't be found. The five survivors simply floated on the surface, unable to execute the mission, awaiting rescue that would come at dawn with the arrival of the *Sprague*.

One of the SEALs in the other squad drowned on landing. That squad managed to recover its PBL, collect its survivors, and begin the execution phase of the mission. They found the *Sprague*, linked up with the other personnel, and headed in to the beach—only to encounter an enemy patrol boat and withdraw back to the destroyer.

They tried again the next night. This time another patrol boat came by; the crew killed the engine of their PBL and waited silently for the threat to pass. When the patrol boat was safely out of range, the SEALs tried to start the engine again—without success. They floated, dead in the water, for eleven hours before the *Sprague* came along. The airfield recon mission was, as they say, a "learning experience."

But elsewhere another SEAL recon mission was going off with more success. Using a more conventional (and less risky) fast boat insertion technique, elements from SEAL Team Four operated in direct support of the Marine Amphibious Unit preparing to conduct an assault on the Pearls airport, in the midsection of the little island. Bus service for SEAL Team Four was provided by Seafox crews from Special Boat Squadron Twenty. Late on the evening of 24 October the Seafox-es, heavily armed with machine guns and grenade launchers, got the SEALs ashore.

One element moved off to scout the airfield while the other conducted a beach recon. The result was good news and bad news. The bad news was that the beach wouldn't work for an amphibious assault; the reef and surf made it too hazardous. There was more bad news, too: the airfield was well defended. But the good news was that the SEALs provided the information before the assault was launched, enabling the task force commander to execute Plan B, a heli-borne troop lift. (The Marines executed their part of the show with precision and grace—then got back on their ships and went off to their original mission in Lebanon).

Beausejour Radio Station Takedown

The SEALs had two other assignments: the first was a takedown of the radio station at Beausejour; the second was a rescue, with US Army Delta teams, of the imprisoned British Governor General, Sir Paul Scoon. Scoon was being held under house arrest by Cuban and Grenadan forces involved in the coup at Governor's House, on a hillside above St. Georges. Both went badly.

After difficulties with helicopter insertion at the radio station, the SEALs from Team Six successfully captured the facility and defended themselves, first from an enemy vehicle that blundered into their perimeter, and then from a counterattack force that included a potent, Russian-built BTR armored car. Although the BTR was killed, a lot of the infantry with it were not, and the SEALs had to beat a hasty withdrawal to the sea. After a successful escape and evasion, they made it to the water, swam out from the shore, and illuminated their infrared rescue strobes. The strobes, invisible to the naked eye but brilliant on thermal imaging systems used by the helos and ships, attracted attention quickly, and the team was quickly picked up. More lessons learned for all hands.

SEALs to the Rescue at Governor's House

Meanwhile, over at Governor's House, another learning experience was in progress.

A Patrol Boat, River (PBR) noses into the shoreline to de-bus a squad of SEALs. Swift, stealthy, surprising ops in the Mekong delta essentially turned guerrilla warfare around on the VC and NVA, keeping them off balance and insecure. It was accomplished by a skillful combination of boat crews and SEAL teams, operating together in a way that still makes sense. US Navy

First, the helicopter pilots couldn't even *find* the landing sites on the maps and photographs. Finally, after a lot of thrashing around, the sites were identified, but—oh joy—although they look usable in the aerial photographs, they turned out to be utterly unsuitable in reality. The defenders, alerted by all the activity overhead, had plenty of time to collect their weapons, ammunition, and a spot to work from. Then, instead of rolling over and playing dead as expected, they sat up and took

notice—and aim at the helicopters, which they then shot up.

A force of about two platoons of SEALs fast-roped to the ground and made a dash for the compound, quickly seized it from a light force of police, and collected the governor and his family and staff. They then took up defensive positions—just in time. Another reaction force, again using a BTR, arrived on scene, complete with about a platoon of infantry. With the BTR beating up Governor's House

After calling for help, the squad runs off the mountain—right through this tiny pass. Overhead are the NVA, momentarily distracted by Cobra gunships firing up their positions. The squad, expecting a shower of enemy grenades at any moment, is on the run. Lieutenant Gormly leads the way, followed by Clay Grady and Ed Bowen, none of whom are too thrilled about the op. Bob Gormly collection

with its heavy machine gun and the infantry maneuvering on the place, the rescue operation was not going *quite* according to plan.

Among the many missing items from the SEALs bag of tricks was the radio they intended to use to call up support from the many gunships in the air. Instead, all that was available was a low-power, short-range squad radio designed essentially for coordination within the platoon. But at least it could talk to the Rangers and other units in the area and, by a series of relays, the SEALs were able to

get an Air Force AC-130 Spectre gunship overhead.

When a Spectre fires, it is essentially turning a firehose on the target, but with bullets instead of water pouring from its 20mm Vulcan rotary cannon. It is equipped with systems that permit incredible accuracy and precision target identification. And when the Spectre opened up on the reaction force, the party was over for most of them. According to one report, the crew of the aircraft reported to the SEALs after a firing run, "I see twenty 'flappers' and 'kickers' and seven 'runners.'"

Although the assault on Governor's House was held at bay, the enemy force was not driven off. The SEALs and the governor were to wait all night to be rescued by the Marines, over twenty-four hours after the operation began. It was, in the vernacular, a learning experience again.

While these operations were hardly textbook examples of the art, they were typical of the "first blood" encounters of inexperienced units throughout history. They revealed many inadequacies in doctrine, training, equipment, planning, and execution. Those lessons were studied and learned by all the armed forces, and major changes were then applied. The essence of these was to improve the integration of all the US Special Operations Forces into one force with different, mutually supporting talents: the US Special Operations Command assembled from Army, Navy, and Air Force units in 1986.

Panama

By the time Operation Just Cause kicked off in Panama in December of 1989, USSOCOM had come a long way in the process of integrating US special operators. In addition to better planning integration, all the forces had experienced better funding and received more attention as the NCA shifted the nation's military focus away from the Warsaw Pact threat toward the little brushfire wars and terrorist threats that now seemed more dangerous.

SEALs had two major assignments during Operation Just Cause: the *Presidente Porras* mission described earlier, and a mission with a similar objective, disabling Noriega's Neville Jet at Punta Paitilla airport. While the first mission went off pretty much according to the plan, the airport mission was a disaster.

The jet was identified as one of several likely ways Noriega might escape the noose prepared for him. While there were many options possible for taking it out of his game plan, the mission was assigned to the SEALs. The SEAL team, basing its plan on guidance from a higher headquarters, decided to send two platoons onto the airfield to seize the aircraft. When H-hour was pushed up fifteen minutes for the whole operation, the SEALs found themselves trying to play "beat the clock" and losing. The force of approximately forty men was discovered on the airfield and engaged in the open by some PDF who knew their stuff. The Panamanians fired low, skipping their bullets across the concrete. The SEALs took many hits—four dead, eight wounded. Although the Neville Jet was essentially destroyed, by accident, in the engagement, the mission was hardly a success. It even took an hour and a half to get the wounded out. Another learning experience, and a bitter lesson for all concerned.

But they did learn from it, directly and from the "after-action reviews" that followed, formally and informally. As the commander of the operation said to one critic, "You weren't there!" And he has a point—it is easy to be an armchair admiral (or lieutenant commander) and a different matter to do it under fire.

Persian Gulf, Round One

Special operations forces generally get tapped to fight the little wars and smaller skirmishes that tend to be forgotten rather quickly by the public and historians. One of these little operations, designated Ernest Will/Prime Chance, involved SEALs in the Persian Gulf long before that big "drive-by-shooting" called Desert Storm. These operations deployed US forces, in and out of USSO-COM, to the Persian Gulf during the war between Iran and Iraq. The purpose of the oper-

ations was to keep the sea lanes clear and secure for the passage of oil tankers, a rather tall order since the belligerents were indiscriminate about just who they were attacking and their use of mines, missiles, and the occasional small attack boat.

CDR Gary Stubblefield was one of the SEALs sent to the Gulf. His responsibility was to establish a kind of floating base to support a wide variety of "trigger pullers" from the Army, Marine Corps, and Navy—along with Air Force controllers—in a demonstration of what has come to be known as "jointness." The Army personnel operated AH-6 "Little Bird" attack helicopters and 20mm Vulcan cannons, the Marines provided defense for the platform, and all of them cooperated as a kind of guard force for the strategic waterway. For Stubblefield, the mission was twofold: support the guard force in the area with a secure, well-provisioned platform, and use the barge as a platform to stage offensive operations against hostile forces when required.

It was an interesting little operation. Several oil platforms were used by the Iranians as bases for offensive operations against shipping; the Marines took out some of these.

The SEALs *tried* to take down a couple of oil platforms, and probably would have done it well and perhaps with minimal loss of life. Instead, though, the "prep" cannon fire on the platforms that was intended to soften them up resulted in both platforms blowing up while the SEALs were about to land. As Stubblefield says, "We were *supposed* to capture the people on the platforms. But the wrong ammunition was used by the [navy gunners]; they were supposed to use armor piercing but used incendiary instead. While we were in the helicopters, on the way into the platforms, we got word that they blew up. There was no way we could land on them."

Persian Gulf, Round Two

Operation Desert Storm/Shield was the acid test for all the changes that had been incorporated in the US armed forces during the 1980s. SEALs and SBS crews played an active, early, and extremely successful role in

Urban combat skills have been a part of the SEALs' bag of tricks since the rise of terrorist groups and the necessity of hostage rescue operations began in the 1970s. This SEAL from Group Two is rehearsing his moves during a training op during Desert Storm. US Navy

the campaign.

One SEAL platoon, commanded by LT Tom Dietz, set up shop at a small naval base near the northern Saudi town of Ras al Mishab. After the air war kicked off in mid-January of 1991, the platoon started an aggressive reconnaissance program along the Kuwait coastline. Four special reconnaissance missions were executed, looking for any and all information about enemy defenses: Were there patrol boats operating in the area? Navigation aids still in place? Then, moving in closer to the beach, what kind of defenses were visible from offshore?

These recon missions had two or three phases. The first was supported by the SBS crews using their extremely fast, low, "cigarette" racing boats—designated HSBs (high-speed boats)—for a fast tour of the area. Although not really designed for the recon mission, the HSBs are normally tasked with training the bigger ships in the fleet against anti-ship attacks from such small, fast vessels, and they don't have an official tactical mission. But that speed made them excellent for these recons. With a Zodiac CRRC lashed to the deck, the boats made nighttime forays along the coastline. Dietz says, "We didn't know if there was going to be an amphibious invasion or not. We were told to look for a beach where one could be conducted—or where a deception operation could be conducted."

The first two missions identified two possible invasion beaches from well offshore. The next two missions sent the SEALs ashore to scout the defenses. The plan for the recon missions used two Zodiac inflatables for the run into the beach each night. There were sixteen guys in each platoon, who all wanted to go in, but only room for five in each Zodiac; Dietz had to decide who would go in the Zodiacs and who would stay in the HSBs. "It wasn't an easy decision," he says. "I integrated everybody into the missions, and everybody got to go, but there were some guys that went in every night and some that got rotated."

Three SEALs surface swam in to each beach, without scuba or closed circuit breathing apparatus, which seemed unnecessary. Despite the wet suits they all wore and the training and experience they'd developed, all were chilled. As Dietz says, "The difficult thing about these missions was the cold. We were wet the whole time, from dusk until around dawn. That's why we go through BUD/S and why we go through Hell Week—so we can be wet and tired and still think!"

The Zodiacs were put in the water from about ten miles out, then sent in to about a thousand meters offshore where the swimmers slid over the side into the chilly, low 50-degree water. The SEALs surface swam into the beaches, but not out of the surf. They lay on the sand, using the water for cover and concealment, watching and waiting for about an hour. Then, on schedule, they slipped back into deeper water and back out to the Zodiacs.

After reviewing the results of the intelligence collection missions, one particularly suitable beach was selected, just north of a point called Mina Sa'Ud. The fourth mission went in to the selected beach to confirm the assumptions of the earlier recons. Dietz, as platoon commander, went ashore to have "eyes on" the target, still not knowing if the platoon was supporting an actual invasion or a deception operation. Finally, the decision was made: execute the deception plan.

The plan for the deception operation called for three Zodiacs, and all the men in the platoon would be committed to the mission. Six would swim ashore, a swim pair from each boat; another three would stay behind to provide support. They were to install charges along the selected beach, primed with individual timers set for a two-hour delay. These charges were all supposed to detonate at about 0100 on the day the ground phase of Desert Storm kicked off, with coalition forces crossing their lines of departure at 0400. At about the same time the SBS crews and SEALs would close on the same beaches and fire them up with every suitable weapon they owned.

The charges and the gunfire didn't need to kill anybody or destroy anything to be effective. All they had to do was get the attention of the Iraqis and convince them that the Marines, who had been waiting offshore for just such an opportunity, were about to come across the beaches in a classic amphibious assault. If such an invasion actually happened and there was no one to meet it, the enemy commanders knew, the war would be over almost instantly.

But if there were no invasion and the enemy forces were still defending against one, that meant there were fewer enemy assets available to deal with the real assault, coming across the border to the west. So the SEAL platoon's sixteen men, plus the SBS crews in the HSBs, had the opportunity to take two whole divisions out of the war (about 20,000 enemy soldiers) with what amounted to a military version of a practical joke.

Execute The Deception Mission

"I've been asked how I picked the 'lucky' six who went in," Dietz says. "I basically chose the nine people who needed to stay back in the boats—my three best engine guys, three best machine gunners, three best radio operators—and the other six were left. But on the final operation I was able to take everybody. That's because we *needed* everybody."

Although the SEALs didn't see the need for Draeger scuba gear, they each took along a little "bail-out bottle" of air sufficient for about three minutes sub-surface swimming in case they made serious contact with any enemy defenders. The bottles were the kind of "field ex-

Desert Storm was a new test of Naval Special War-
fare people, tactics, and equipment. This RIB is
being prepared for a night operation in the Persian
Gulf.

pedient" solution to a problem that seems to materialize during war—they'd been acquired from a helicopter unit and adapted to an entirely different use (and a prohibited one) than that for which they were designed.

Of the six SEALs who swam in, three carried CAR-15s, the compact version of the M16A2 with a shorter barrel and a stock assembly that could be retracted. The CARs all had M203 grenade launchers attached for serious, long-range, indirect fire. The other three carried the German Heckler & Koch MP5 submachine gun with suppressers (not silencers) attached. "The idea was that if a couple of sentries showed up on the beach, and we thought we were compromised, we could take them out with the suppressed weapons without giving away our positions," Dietz says. "But if something heavy opened up on us—a machine gun, for example—at longer range, we could lay some grenades on it."

Each of the six swimmers carried a Mk 138 satchel charge. Two timers were attached to each, set for two hours. This kind of "double priming" is SOP. In the bags were ten two-pound blocks of C4 explosive, dual primed, the charges all carefully prepared ashore before everybody climbed into the water.

The swimmers went in to the beach on line, about twenty feet apart. Once they could touch bottom with their flippers, they spread out, about fifty meters from each other across the 250-meter-wide beach. "You could just see the guy on either side of you," Dietz says, "and we didn't have to wait for any signals. Once we spread out, we swam into the beach and placed our charges in about one foot of water—since the tide was now receding—pulled the pins on the timers and swam back out to regroup." The Zodiacs, which had been standing by about 500 meters off the beach, were signaled in for the pickup. Once the swimmers were hauled aboard, the "rubber ducks" headed out into the Gulf, about seven miles off the beach, to the rendezvous point with the supporting SBS crews in the speedy HSB cigarette boats.

Four of the HSBs participated in the operation. Two HSBs collected the Zodiacs and the SEALs, counted noses, and secured the inflatables. In the meantime, the other two zipped in to about two miles. Now, at about 0030 hours, the active part of the deception plan began as the two HSBs closed to 500 meters of the shoreline and opened up with every weapon aboard: mini-guns, heavy machine guns, grenade launchers. "They ripped the beach apart," according to the platoon leader. The firing continued for about ten noisy minutes. For any Iraqis ashore, this would obviously not be bombing or naval gunfire, but a large scale, close in attack of the type preceding an amphibious assault. On their final pass up the beach, the HSBs chucked several additional explosive charges overboard—more C4, wrapped in plastic, primed to go off in the water at irregular intervals. These detonated as the boats made a break for the exit. About five minutes later, almost exactly at the scheduled hour of 0100, the satchel charges ashore started exploding. All went off within about thirty seconds of each other, with a series of tremendous *booms* that were audible far out to sea, where the HSBs beat a hasty strategic withdrawal.

All four linked up out at the seven-mile mark, then headed back to base. At 0230 they debriefed. "It was a very low-key, matter-of-fact debrief," Dietz says. "The operation went according to plan. We were happy but not really excited about it. What we were really excited about was that the ground war was now kicking off! It wasn't until later, after we'd gotten cleaned up and had something to eat, that we got a message from CAPT (now RADM) Smith, the Task Group commander, reporting that elements of two Iraqi divisions remained on the coastline even as the ground forces were going up behind them. They remained in position to defend against the amphibious invasion. That's what really pleased us—that the Iraqis paid attention to us, reacted to us, and hopefully we saved some lives."

Chapter 3

Earning Your Flippers at BUD/S

So you think you wanna be a SEAL? No problem—piece of cake. Anybody can do it! It only takes twenty-six weeks, and the training is mostly done on the beautiful, sandy beach at Coronado, California, right on the Pacific Ocean near warm, wonderful San Diego, and the program is run by a large, kindly, attentive, cheerful, and well-trained staff of SEALs. There are always plenty of beautiful women strolling by to admire the handsome sailors; the famous and luxurious Hotel Del Coronado, with its superb restaurants and bars, is right down the road. There is plenty of sailing, surfing, scuba diving, and other recreation available in the immediate vicinity. The beach is always available for a nice jog. And, best of all, every instructor at the Basic Underwater Demolition/SEAL program is committed to making sure that every day of those twenty-six weeks are just *loaded* with activities and experiences you will *never* forget. Sound like fun? Sign right here!

Well, Navy recruiters don't actually sell

One of the first and most terrifying tests of BUD/S is called "drown-proofing." This involves spending a half an hour or so in the water—with your hands tied behind your back, floating at the surface, coming up for a breath, and then relaxing for a bit underwater. These students are practicing the maneuver before the test. They'll also have to retrieve the masks without using their hands, which are tied behind them.

prospective recruits that rosy view of the program. But despite many cautions, SEAL candidates often show up at BUD/S without a realistic understanding of what is actually involved in the training required to earn the "Budweiser" trident emblem of a SEAL. The truth is that it is one of the most difficult, challenging, and actually brutal learning experiences anybody can have, and one of the things most people learn is that they don't really want to be a SEAL quite badly enough to finish the program.

Like the Army's Green Beret Qualification Course (or Q Course), BUD/S is a *selection* and training program that weeds out people who don't belong. That usually means most of them. They are weeded out the only way that anybody has ever found for reliably selecting people who can hack the problem—by cranking up the stress so high that only the strongest survive and the quitters quit—or break. It is not nice and it isn't pretty. There isn't any other way. And sometimes it results in nearly everyone of an entering class of SEAL candidates being eliminated. In one class *not one* single man graduated. It is a calculatedly brutal experience that is not pretty to watch and pushes its victims to their limits of physical and emotional endurance, and beyond. Injuries are routine and deaths in training occasionally occur.

But, in a way, it is true that anybody can

When BUD/S students take a swim test it is not always a heap of fun. This class is about to be tested on drown-proofing skills.

survive it—if they have the appropriate state of mind. It takes plenty of strength, but most of it isn't muscular; it's mental. Little scrawny guys that you'd never pick for a badminton team sometimes turn out to have more of the kind of internal toughness and physical strength that it takes to survive BUD/S and become a SEAL than the big weight lifters who seem to be naturals. If you've got the mental strength to work through the discomfort, the fatigue, and the humiliation, you can probably develop the physical strength, SEALs tell you. The head is the hard part. And no other test has, so far, been able to figure out how to find the men who won't quit from those who will without pushing them

both far beyond the normal limits of civilized routine.

The BUD/S training takes twenty-six weeks, but it is only one part of the process of becoming a fully qualified SEAL. Before even applying for training a prospective candidate must: pass the very strict physical examination for Navy divers; have eyesight at least 20/40 in one eye and 20/70 in the other, correctable to 20/20, without color blindness; score high on military written tests; be male, twenty-eight years of age or less; and pass the physical fitness test (extremely high scores are expected) that includes swim test (500 yards, breast or side stroke, in less than 12:30), rest for ten minutes, then at least forty-two

Out on the "grinder," BUD/S students get an hour or two of formal physical training (PT) everyday. They get another ten hours or so of informal PT, too, paddling the rubber ducks, running up and down the beach, and frolicking around the obstacle course. During all this they are all expected to show a high degree of enthusiasm, no matter how miserable they may feel.

One of the kind and attentive staff of highly trained instructors helps a boat crew with their motivation. The technique is simple—a paddleful of sand, applied directly to the problem. Sand, it turns out, is a readily available, cheap, apparently effective material for helping people with their problems. It can be shoveled into boats and on hats, and the students can be rolled around in it, like a sugar cookie.

pushups in two minutes, at least fifty situps in two minutes, eight pullups, and run a mile and a half in boots and BDU pants in 11:30—all in less than an hour.

Applicants must come from certain Navy ratings, have the endorsement of their commanders, and have plenty of time remaining on their enlistment. If you fit all these require-

ments you can apply, and you might even be accepted and assigned a slot in a class. If that happens, don't wait to start your physical conditioning program. You don't go to BUD/S to get in shape; you *arrive* in shape, or you will fail almost instantly. "In order to even apply," RADM Ray Smith says, "you've got to be a top-notch sailor. We've got the pick of the guys coming out of the Naval Academy, more enlisted applicants than we can handle."

Although the published standards call for a cutoff age of twenty-eight, older men are sometimes accepted, and some are even recruited. Two thirty-six year olds have completed the program, and at least one man was thirty-two at the time. While the older bodies are a little less resilient sometimes, that can sometimes be offset by greater maturity and better self-discipline. One of these, a Polish refugee with extensive language skills, a former teacher and, at the time a competitive gymnast, was recruited for the program and made it through training on the first try.

New arrivals will indeed see the marvelous Hotel Del Coronado, the pretty sailboats, the girls sunbathing on the beach, and the glittering Pacific Ocean and will soon learn to loathe them all. They will soon learn that the Pacific is freezing, that the beach is for running on and rolling in, that the girls and the tourist attractions exist only as torture devices.

For seven long weeks the trainees endure a program of indoctrination and physical preconditioning, with long hours of classes, running, swimming, situps, pushups, calisthenics. They sweat and struggle . . . but they still haven't started BUD/S yet.

The Only Easy Day Was Yesterday

Phase One of BUD/S is the basic physical and mental conditioning portion of the program. It lasts nine weeks. It features a lot of running, swimming, and trips around the obstacle course. Every trainee is required to put his maximum effort into every test, every time. The minimum scores are raised each week. Each trainee is required to improve on his previous scores. Instructors watch and evaluate every hopeful trainee like hawks—or vultures—ready to pounce on any flaw or failure, real or imagined. It is an extremely abrasive, competitive process. The only way the instructors will leave you alone is if you've just beaten everybody else at an event; then you might be allowed a few minutes to gloat and relax while the rest of the class thrashes around in the surf zone.

This continues for five weeks. Each day the heat is turned up a little more. The instructors push harder and harder. The instructors never let up for a moment. As they say over and over, "The only easy day was *yesterday!*"

The students spend lots of time in the water, and the water is cold, even in summer. Hypothermia is a fact of life and occasional death. Wet suits are sometimes used, sometimes not; even with the suits, the cold Pacific Ocean seeps in, lowering body temperature. Students can be seen shivering violently sometimes after having come out of the cold ocean to stand in the cold wind. It is another stress, intentionally applied.

One by one people quit or are removed for injuries. Even quitting isn't easy, quick, or dignified; the trainee stands on the green painted frog footprints at one side of the "Grinder," the big blacktop space where calisthenics are performed, grasps the lanyard for the brass ship's bell attached to a column, rings the bell three times, and is gone. His green helmet liner remains in formation beside the bell with the others who've quit before him. While there is some disgrace to it, even these men get some credit (in private, away from the trainees) that it takes quite a man to get through any of BUD/S and that only a very select group even manage to get in the front door. While the quitters get credit for trying they are, just the same, an example to those who remain.

The O Course

One of the featured entertainments is the obstacle course—the "O course" in SEAL par-

"Get it up! Get that boat up! Get it up! Get it up! You guys are the worst—get it up!" the instructor screams. After their first jaunt out into the Pacific in the rubber ducks, a crew has a few moments of quiet reflection on what they've seen and done—their new-found skills in small-boat handling and teamwork, with the help of the staff providing a running commentary and critique. After a few minutes supporting the 250-pound boat aloft, the crew tends to have an improved understanding of the lessons of BUD/S.

lance. It looks like a big sandbox with lots of play equipment: telephone poles assembled into a wide variety of structures. The BUD/S trainees are assembled here about once a week for an hour or two of play time. One after another, on command, the students dash off for a circuit of the course.

310

You start by running to the first event, a set of pole stumps set in the ground, their tops about two feet above the deck. You must run across them, jumping from one to the next without falling off. Then, from the last stump, leap to the top of a low wall, swing a foot over, drop to the other side, and start running. You'll go about fifty feet before you dive under a grid of barbed wire—crawl under the wire, then emerge and dash to the next structure, the net climb. A tall tower suspends a rope net that you climb to the top, swing over, and descend; the flexible net offers unstable footing and it is slow going. Once safely back on the ground, dash off to the next position, a pair of simple structures about four feet apart; you climb up on one and jump to the other, catching the crossbar across your chest; this is a favorite way to break a rib. They call this one "The Ugly Name." There are about ten more obstacles to negotiate, and your progress will be closely monitored by one of the attentive, helpful staff who are always ready with words of encouragement and advice. If you have trouble with part of the course the instructors will probably let you try the event all over again, just to make sure you get it right. Finally you return to your starting point and your time is recorded.

If you haven't done well you may get to cool off with a quick dip in the ocean, on the other side of a tall sand berm. Then, to dry off, you'll be expected to roll in the sand, then hustle back to rejoin the play group. As the trainees quickly learn, the O course is highly competitive, and people who don't do well are subject to extra, undesired, attention from the instructors.

You're expected to go all out every time you run the course, and you're expected to do better every week. Minimum times for the course are published, and they get shorter every week. It is just one of the stresses that

Look like fun? The obstacle course tests strength, agility, and speed—and mental toughness, too. All are expected to improve over the weeks, and a trainee's times must get progressively better.

are applied to the trainees to test their motivation and physical conditioning. But, as one of the staff says, "It isn't supposed to break you but to build up your confidence. It reveals a lot about the character of an individual. By the time you've gone through about three-fourths of it, every fiber of your muscles is burning, and you still have another quarter to go—and it's all through soft sand."

Hell Week

After five weeks of this comes the real

The circuit begins with a dash across the tops of these poles, a leap to the wall, over the wall to crawl under some barbed wire, then off to the net climb. It takes about eleven minutes to do them all, if you're in shape. The instructors provide helpful comments and critiques at most stations.

311

challenge that all have heard about and dreaded: Hell Week. It starts just before midnight on the Saturday before the sixth week with a gentle wakeup call from the instructors . . . using blank M60 machine gun fire and artillery simulators as an improvised alarm clock. The noise in the compound is deafening. Besides the firing, instructors scream incessantly. Chaos reigns supreme.

The trainees begin five and a half days of virtually constant activity. They will receive an average of about twenty minutes sleep per day, if they are lucky. They will go from one event to another, constantly: running on the beach, boat drills, PT, swims. They will crawl in slime, roll in the surf, and for a little extra torture, do "log PT."

Log PT requires boat teams to lift and maneuver sections of log weighing from 400 to 600 pounds. If your boat team hasn't been doing well (or if the instructors think you need a little extra help with your motivation), you'll get the 600-pound model. Then you can do situps with it on your chest, or try holding it over your head for a while. Needless to say the whole team has to work together to do anything with it at all.

The sun comes up on the first morning, and the day proceeds much like any other at BUD/S. The sun goes down, and the trainees know that somewhere people are returning to homes and wives, to quiet evenings and friendly conversations. In the tall apartment buildings overlooking the BUD/S compound the lights will start going out around nine or ten. The PT continues. By 1:00 a.m. they are nearly all out, but the activity on the beach continues. "The only easy day was *yesterday!*" scream the instructors.

When the sun comes up the next morning, the trainees will be a bit tired but will try not to think about it. All of them know what the routine is, that the really tough part is still days away. The competitions continue with boat races in the ocean and on the bay. Gradually, individuals will fail. When they do, their teams are subjected to more stress from the instructors and from the other teams.

A recipient of the "sugar cookie" treatment—first get wet in the surf, then roll around in the sand. Then get back in line and try to do better. It's just one of the constant stresses and strains on trainees designed to separate those who will tolerate it from those who won't.

Although they don't get any real sleep, the trainees get plenty of food. They consume about 7,000 calories a day and still lose weight.

One day melts seamlessly into another without rest. There is no alternative but to tough it out, drive through the fatigue, and keep doing what they tell you to do. It is a test of mental toughness as much as the powers of physical endurance. After four days or so people start to hallucinate. And some people start

Log PT is another form of stress, this time applied to a whole boat crew all at the same time. US Navy

to quit. Hell Week is the most important part of the whole twenty-six week BUD/S experience, a physical and mental challenge that is intended to put the trainees under stress that is supposed to approach that of actual combat.

The hallucinations can be rather entertaining. While enduring a long night boat race out on the ocean, after a few days with no sleep and little rest, visions begin to appear. Sometimes it is mermaids, other times people picnicking on the beach, or a strange tunnel vision.

One of the rituals is the letter home. Toward the end of the week, when everybody is off in the ozone, they are all seated before tables and provided paper and pen. "Write me a letter explaining why you want to become a SEAL!" the instructor orders. This is not an easy thing to explain after going three or four days without sleep, wallowing in the mud, doing log PT, enduring endless boat drills, and slogging through competitive events like the "rubber duck" races on the ocean or the sixteen-mile runs on the beach. The students tend to stare at the paper for a while before attempting to write anything. The results tend to be gibberish. Later, after Hell Week is over, these essays are returned to their authors as an amusing reminder of the tremendous stress they were under and how it affected their performance of even this simple task.

As rough as Hell Week and the whole BUD/S program is, it has been toned down considerably from the past. Trainees no longer

Hell Week features rest breaks in the mud pit. Well, not really rest breaks but opportunities to work on your teamwork . . . and practice being miserable.

Not only do these guys get to stay awake for five and a half days straight, they get to do fun stuff like this day and night.

This is their first experience with a rubber duck in the ocean, dealing with the surf and having to function as a crew. Most will do rather badly and will overturn in the surf, lose paddles, and sometimes lose a man over the side. The instructors enjoy it all immensely—and pile on the punishment.

have to wallow in the mud of the Tijuana River, essentially an open sewer, after many came down with severe (and sometimes permanent) illnesses. That ended in 1983. A somewhat healthier goo is now available right in San Diego Bay. And after one trainee died on a five-mile winter swim around San Clemente Island, the staff started taking extra precautions to deal with extreme overexertion and hypothermia. An ambulance now trails along the beach behind the trainees on the long runs through the soft sand, trailing the "goon squad," as the slower runners are called; they can quit at any time, and many do.

BUD/S has been criticized, along with other extreme selection and training programs like the Army's Green Beret Q Course, for unnecessary extremes. The injuries, the high level of stress, the humiliation are all far more than anyone in civilian life or in normal military training ever must endure.

Why do it that way? As one SEAL officer explains, "One of the things I've noticed about many of the 'real world' combat operations I've been on is that you get a tremendous adrenaline rush—I call it *fear*. Once the operation begins that goes away, but on the way in you have a lot of time to sit and think. You *never* get that in a training situation! So one of the things I continually tell my troops while we are training is, 'Look, I can't give you the feeling of what it is really like to be in combat . . .

The famous bell is always waiting for anybody who's had enough. Then, you stand on the green frog footprints, grasp the lanyard, and strike the
bell three times—and you can go back to the regular Navy, to conventional hours and conventional missions.

because I can't shoot at you and make you hurt. It's illegal, and I wouldn't want to do that anyway. What I *can* do is to make the conditions so tough, and try to make you so tired, put you under such stress, that you will get something of a feeling of what it is like."

When the trainees recover from Hell Week they begin a period of study intended to prepare them for "hydrographic reconnaissance," as beach surveys are called. This involves even more time spent wallowing around in the surf, cold and miserable, while the ever-attentive staff offers suggestions and encouragement from the beach. Once through Hell Week students are treated with a bit more respect and affection by the instructors. Finally, Phase One is over.

Swim fins, mask, and booties are all pretty much standard commercial gear, used in unconventional diving.

Phase Two

Survivors of the first part of training go on to Phase Two, where they will learn about diving operations. Each will learn just about all there is to know about scuba, closed-circuit rebreathing systems, and dive physiology. They will learn more than they ever wanted to know about the nasty things that happen to people who make mistakes underwater. They learn to deal with equipment failures, lost regulators, the hazards of nitrogen narcosis. They make long swims beneath the surface and learn to navigate in the cold, murky, dark waters in which SEALs operate. After seven busy weeks the BUD/S class will be missing a few more faces. The survivors will have the knowledge necessary to be basic combat divers, and the program is about to get really interesting.

Phase Three

By now the BUD/S class is beginning to see light at the end of the proverbial tunnel, and are pretty sure it is not from an oncoming train. They are far stronger physically and mentally than four months earlier. They've acquired a great deal of knowledge and confidence. Now they get to start putting the skills and the stamina together in practical exercises that simulate SEAL missions.

Phase Three is the Demolitions/Recon/Land Warfare part of the program. The BUD/S students learn land navigation, explosives, small unit tactics, rappelling, and patrolling skills and become expert in the employment of all the small arms and weapons used by SEALs in combat. After four weeks of classroom instruction and practical exercises, the trainees deploy to San Clemente Island for five weeks, where they put it all together.

One of the evolutions involves clearing beach obstacles like those that faced the amphibious operations of World War II—concrete blocks and steel rails dropped in shallow water to block the passage of landing craft. The students first make a careful hydrographic survey of the landing zone, noting the location of all obstacles, then plan a mission to demolish them with explosives. The quantity of

A "stick" of jumpers exits a Navy CH-46 helicopter. All SEALs are jump-qualified after they complete

BUD/S at the US Army's Basic Airborne Course at Fort Benning, Georgia.

explosive has to be carefully calculated, fuse measured. The students use their "rubber ducks" to get into the area, then dive to emplace the explosives. All the charges are linked with "det" cord to insure simultaneous explosion, and the divers are recovered to the boats. The last dive pair pulls the safety pins on the fuse-lighters, retracts the striker, and pops the igniter. Now it is time to get back to the boat. The instructors will time the delay, and it had better be within a few seconds of what was calculated. With a satisfying *whump* the surface of the water will boil, and the obstacles will (usually) be shattered.

BUD/S is probably the roughest, most demanding training and selection program in the US armed forces, at least outside the covert organizations. It has been loudly criticized as excessively brutal. Although it might not be quite as dangerous as at times in the past, it is a guaranteed way to get miserable fast and stay miserable for most of six months—or more, if you get injured. And the

injuries are common, almost with the intent of the staff. No other program tolerates such a high level of injuries. A lot of people outside Naval Special Warfare think the BUD/S program is sadistic and ought to be reformed. CDR Gary Stubblefield has an opposing view:

"It is the toughest military training in the world, and it's done that way on purpose. The Army's Special Forces don't have anything to compare to it. It's been this way since the days of the Scout and Raiders in World War II, a *very* difficult selection process. Most of the people who make it through the program are not premier athletes—they are *normal* people who have the ability to stick with something.

"There are injuries, some severe, in every class. But the business we are in is inherently dangerous, combat or not. If you take away the risk that goes with the training, you take away the mental stress that you put people under to know how they'll respond in the real world, in actual combat. Landing on rocks, long cold swims, surf passages—training where we have people break arms and legs—has to be part of the program. You *have* to be sure that they will stick with you when the going gets tough, and they have to know that, if you don't do things safely, there are consequences that include injury . . . or worse. Death in training is very, very rare, and it happens, I think, when the student doesn't follow the rules. The deaths are an anomaly but the injuries are not—those happen when someone does something they aren't supposed to."

Jump School

But even after surviving BUD/S, a trainee is still not a fully qualified SEAL and does not wear the trident insignia of Naval Special Warfare. First comes three weeks at the US Army's Fort Benning in Georgia, undergoing the Basic Airborne Course. Here each will have to confront a different fear, that of jumping from an airplane, to become a fully qualified military parachutist.

The first week involves physical condition-

The Naval Special Warfare trident insignia (the "Budweiser" in the SEAL vernacular) is awarded only after completion of BUD/S, airborne training, and a probationary period on a SEAL team that lasts from six months to more than a year.

ing, and since the Army school's standards are comparatively low, the BUD/S graduates manage this part of the program more or less with one hand tied behind their backs. The Army instructors will try to make the experience a little bit challenging for any SEALs, Rangers, Marines, or others they can identify, usually requiring extra PT to keep their attention, but BUD/S graduates generally consider this part of the program a kind of vacation.

Week two teaches the basic skills of military parachuting: donning the parachute, actions inside the aircraft, door position, jumpmaster commands, proper exit techniques, emergency procedures, and the Parachute Landing Fall (PLF). The students endlessly practice door position, exits, and PLFs from training aids: the suspended harness, the thirty-four-foot tower, the C-130 mock-up.

Finally, they start week three, Jump Week. Five jumps are required, three "Hollywood" daylight jumps without combat equipment plus one night jump and one jump with loaded rucksack and weapons container. The night jump is usually a sunrise or sunset jump rather than one in full darkness.

Jump school is actually a lot of fun for many of the people who attend, and the BUD/S graduates hardly work up a sweat. The jumps are often exciting, the instructors fairly civilized, the drop zone a soft, fluffy plowed field. The last jump is generally done on Friday morning, and students often invite friends and relatives to watch from nearby bleachers. Then the Army instructors break out the silver wings of a qualified military parachutist and pin them to the shirts of the students.

The "Budweiser"

Completion of the Basic Airborne Course is the final academic portion of the program required to join a SEAL or Swimmer Delivery Vehicle (SDV) team but the students are still not bona fide SEALs. First, each man is assigned to a team where he must complete a six-month probationary period. It is still possible to fail, and individuals occasionally are filtered out, even now, if they don't fit into the team or fail to meet spec somehow. But at the end of the six months, a year or more after starting the process, a few young men will pin on the big, gold symbol of Naval Special Warfare and finally be able to call themselves SEALs.

They enter a tiny, select community with a big reputation that sometimes gets in the way of business. Within the military SEALs are sometimes known as "cowboys" or "glass-eaters" who glory in their superman image. Instead they find a different kind of man on the teams: extremely confident without bravado, a man with tremendous talents and abilities, a person who knows his own limits. "We like to think of ourselves as quiet professionals," one says.

RADM Ray Smith says: "We are essentially a *people* business. We use a lot of exotic equipment—scuba, parachutes, radios—but all those things are peripheral to the essence of what we are. Our focus at BUD/S is on the human being, the nature of the person we want to have come on a SEAL team and do the things we have to do—always has been, always will. The finest equipment in the world (which we have) is not sufficient to accomplish our missions. You'll see guys in BUD/S who don't look very impressive physically—little guys, young guys—who'll surprise you and make it through. You can *never* successfully predict who will make it through! You can't measure what is inside the individual without subjecting him to BUD/S. In fact, this is a course in the development of human potential; all we are trying to do is to make the young man understand that the limits of the human being are practically unlimited."

Of the fifty or sixty students who begin BUD/S, the staff will tell you there will be five or six who *know* that they are going to complete the program, no matter what, and that there is no stopping them. There is another five or six who don't really want to be here, are not really ready for the challenge, and who will never be SEALs. In the middle are the eighty percent the instructors focus their efforts on. They probe for the fears that every

BUD/S is a selection process more than a training program, challenging people to use far more of their personal resources than most will ever need to do. It is a rather brutal program, by design, intended to help people survive and function in the far more brutal and stressful environment of combat.

man has—a fear of heights, of water, of jumping from high platforms—and each is confronted daily with his perceived limitations and pushed past them. "You can't call 'time out' in combat," one of the instructors says, "and that's what we try to teach them here."

Officers and enlisted personnel go through training together, unlike some other programs where officers sometimes get an easier ride. Both suffer and perform equally at BUD/S. It is a team-building system, developing trust up and down the chain of command. About thirty-five new officers and 250 enlisted personnel graduate from BUD/S annually and join the world of SPECWARCOM on the SEAL, Special Boat, and Swimmer Delivery Vehicle teams.

Chapter 4

Movement to Contact

Despite the way it is shown in the movies, the business of going into combat is a lot more complicated than picking up your weapon and following some resolute-looking lieutenant or sergeant who growls, "Okay, men, follow me!" The movies always manage to leave out all the paperwork, meetings, and related homework that comes first. In fact, it is just about impossible for American combat units to go off to battle without a great deal of this stuff. It can take weeks to prepare an operation of any kind, conventional or covert, but at the end of this long process will finally come two quite interesting "management/staff" meetings. The first of these is called a Warning Order; the other is called the Patrol Leader's Order.

The Warning Order

Before SEALs and SBS crews go anywhere or do anything, the mission has to be authorized, approved, and planned. A long time ago the units did most of this internally, but for the last decade or so, the missions have been conceived and tasked from outside NAVSPECWARCOM. Somewhere during the process somebody decides it is okay to actually

A swim pair secure the beach. Depending on the mission, SEALs wear wet suits or standard uniforms (which will be wet suits, too, in a way). The man on the left is one of the more unusual members of the special ops community—a "long hair" SEAL.

let the teams know that they can cancel those weekend plans. The way this is done is that the selected team is herded into a compartment or room, the area is secured, the doors are closed, and somebody, normally the unit commander, will issue a Warning Order.

In various forms, warning orders have been around since the Mongol hordes, since Attila, since Alexander the Great. In its short form it sounds something like, "We're going to break camp in the morning before sunrise and attack the infidels, sack their town, rape their women, and put the place to the torch. Bring your sword, spear, and all your armor. Questions?"

The modern version is more complicated, but the idea is identical. It gives the people involved an idea, usually incomplete, of what they are going to be doing and what they should do to prepare. The formal version (used by the Army and Marines as well) includes a brief description of the situation; the mission; general instructions, including organization, uniform, weapons, chain of command, schedule, including time for the more detailed patrol order, and for inspections and rehearsals; and specific instructions for subordinate leaders and individuals.

Everybody then scurries around, collecting weapons, demolition material, MREs, fresh batteries for the radios, and night vision goggles. *Nobody* gets to call home and say, "Guess what, Honey, I'm not gonna be home on time tonight 'cause we're off to defend freedom and democracy . . . "

Instead, they just don't come home in the evening. Sooner or later the families might get some extremely vague information, but that's one of the costs of admission to the special op-

Although they wear the same uniforms and carry the same weapons as other US forces, SEALs are unique in their combination of talents and tasking. SEALs train and fight in extremely small units with missions in or around the water. These missions may be to support either a Navy boss or a joint theater boss who could be an Army, Air Force, or Marine officer. They may be extremely covert, or extremely unconventional. Regardless, the basic weapon of Naval Special Warfare isn't the rifle but the man behind it, and the tiny team of which he is a part.

322

erations and rapid-deployment military communities. And not only do these call-ups happen for real world events, they are called for training, too, with irregular frequency.

The idea behind the Warning Order is that, once the order comes down to the unit, a fixed amount of time will be specified before the operation is supposed to be executed—perhaps twelve hours. The platoon or squad leader is expected to take a third of that time to make his own preliminary plan, and allocate two-thirds of the time to the subordinates to do their preparation and rehearsals. While it often doesn't work out that neatly, the idea is a sound one and is applied as much as circumstances permit.

SOPs

Each platoon has its own set of Standard Operating Procedures, its own identity, its unique reputation and subculture, all based somewhat on the characters on the team.

SOPs make planning and executing operations far faster and more efficient than otherwise. When a Patrol Leader's Order is issued only the unique details of the mission need to be discussed—radio frequencies, rendezvous points, routes in and out of the objective, commander's intent. All the other essentials—patrol order of march, actions on contact, reaction to ambush, individual responsibilities—all these things have been long since memorized as a kind of "company policy" that doesn't need repeating. Most of the members of the teams, like Bob Gormly's SEAL Team Two, had known each other for four or five years and could just about execute an operation without a word ever being spoken.

Patrol Leader's Order

The five-paragraph format used to formally brief the mission has been in use since World War I, its format memorized by millions of servicemen over the years. It forces the unit to plan logically to deal with an extremely stressful and dangerous experience. The elements of the order are the situation, the mission, the details of the execution, how the mis-

When SEALs jump, the rubber duck goes out first, followed promptly by the SEALs. The hard part is hustling out of the aircraft with those darn fins on.

sion will be supported and supplied, and command and communications. Depending on the complexity of the mission, the Orders Brief can last a few minutes or six hours; an hour or so is typical. SEALs may get some of the most difficult and dangerous missions, but they also get some of the very best and most expensive intelligence support, often custom-made for the specific mission. This will almost always include "overhead" imagery, photographs from all altitudes, from low level all the way up to the secret satellites like the KA-11. There may be radio and telephone intercepts, and reports from agents in the operations area. And (in extreme and rare cases) a prisoner may be snatched out of the target area, brought back to chat with the team, and held until the mis-

sion concludes and the team is safely extracted.

SEALs like to rehearse their missions, and if it is practical to do so, some kind of run-through will be done. This might be no more than a detailed brainstorming conference somewhere in the bowels of a submarine, or it might involve the construction of a mock-up of a target and a complete rehearsal of the entire mission ashore. Regardless, once the Patrol Leader's Order has been given, none of the players will be going anywhere or doing anything except preparing to launch into the op area.

When it is time to go to work, SEALs commute in dramatic and dangerous ways. Although trained for insertion to an operating

Water parachute landings are potentially treacherous, particularly at night. The MC-1 canopy used by this jumper is steerable and has a moderate forward speed. Now, about a hundred feet above the water, the jumper should be facing into the wind, chest band and reserve unfastened, reserve parachute shoved to the side. Assume a good prepare-to-land position: head up, eyes on the horizon, knees bent. US Navy photo

services. When the orders trickle down the chain of command, the SEALs plan their mission and use the most stealthy technique of all to drop in on the enemy—submarine insertion.

US subs have a small chamber, the "escape trunk," installed forward of the sail. This little chamber has two functions, the first allowing for trapped submariners to escape a boat sunken in shallow water, and the second (a secondary use) allowing for the deployment and recovery of combat swimmers.

Locking out of a sub is not for the faint of heart. The swimmers don their wet suits and their combat equipment, collect weapons, explosives, and related equipment, and prepare to enter the chamber; scuba or Draeger rigs are, believe it or not, optional. Then, one after another, they climb into the chamber, a spherical space about six feet across. Up to five combat swimmers can crowd into the chamber, but all will be extremely cramped and uncomfortable. Even among trained and experienced SEALs panic sometimes occurs as the water is slowly allowed in. There are mouthpieces and air lines installed in the chamber, and it is possible to use the sub's own air supply for breathing until the chamber is unlocked and it is time to leave. But SEALs normally use their own rigs—if they have any. It is quite possible to ascend to the surface without scuba or rebreather, and SEALs train for this "free ascent" or "blow and go" technique—as well as the reverse technique required to come back aboard.

The sub will slither in as close to shore as the skipper and the SEALs can agree on. Subs are not normally content to be in shallow water close to a hostile coast; SEALs are normally not pleased to swim in from over the horizon. So the typical mission will bring the SSN attack sub into a mile or two off the coast on a dark and hopefully stormy night. The sub

area by parachute, that's really not the SEALs' forte. Except in rare instances, the mission will begin with an insertion over or under the surface of the water.

At any time there are SEALs deployed aboard US submarines operating around the world, waiting for world events to call for their

Here's another way to get to work—a Swimmer Delivery Vehicle being deployed by a submerged submarine. The SDV is kind of a submarine itself, although its passengers get cold and wet. US Navy photo

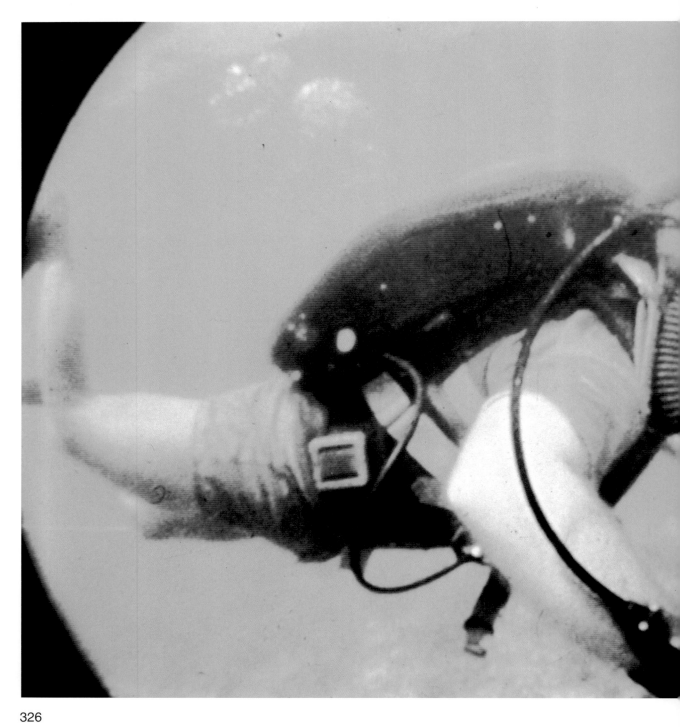

will come up to a depth of about forty feet, bring the periscope up for a quick peek at the neighborhood, then bring it back down. The 'scope makes a fair radar reflector, and if somebody is working a surface search radar tweaked for such targets, there could be a problem. So the sub crew gets extremely edgy about this kind of mission.

A typical insertion out of the chamber will have one man go out first, with scuba, and rig the Zodiac stored in the sail locker on deck. The boat will have to be taken to the surface while a tether is left attached to the submarine. This entire complex activity is done in darkness, almost entirely by touch, and takes about half an hour. When the diver has the boat properly infiltrated and on a tow, he signals the sub to send up the rest of the SEALs. Even this isn't quick or easy: he can flash a light signal at the periscope if the sub skipper is willing to raise it, he can swim down and rap on the hull, or he can even go back in the lockout chamber, repressurize and have a chat via microphone.

Usually, though, a simple rap on the hull will do it. Then the next batch of divers cram into the chamber, the water level rises, and finally somebody has to wriggle a hand over to the valves and latches that will open the hatch.

"You get into there, you've got all this weight on you, you close the bottom hatch, you stand there, doubled over—tanks on your back, equipment in your arms—three to five people jammed in there. Then somebody has to find a way to reach over to the valve so you can start to flood the chamber. There are some guys who are just more nervous about all this—everybody jammed in that small space, water coming up to your neck. I've seen guys panic in there."

It takes a long time, usually in cold, high seas, for the seven or eight men to rig the boats and exit the sub for a typical mission of

Locking out of a sub involves swimming out of a little chamber about the size of the hatch visible in this shot. US Navy photo

The M60 machine gun puts serious suppressive fire downrange. The M60 is an area weapon, used for delivering a heavy volume of fire at a distance.

this type. Hypothermia and seasickness will be a problem for those already in the boat up on the surface while the nervousness of the sub crew will be a problem for those still aboard. Even the rubber boats have a radar return signature, and if anybody is looking, the whole operation can suddenly become a target instead of a weapon. It is a very nervous time. But then, after perhaps a couple of hours, you're all set and its time to go ashore.

Dry Deck Shelter

There is an easier way, a bolt-on chamber that is called the Dry Deck Shelter (DDS). While it operates on the same principle as the lock-out chamber, it is far larger. The DDS is big enough to accommodate a whole platoon, with dive gear and rubber boats, radios and demolitions. It will also accommodate the Swimmer Deliver Vehicle, the SEAL-scooter

that is designed for zipping around underwater. Besides these handy features, it converts to a hyperbaric chamber for treating a diver who's been "bent" from staying under too long, too deep, and acquires the painful, potentially fatal condition called "decompression sickness."

While the general insertion technique for the DDS is the same as with the lock-out chamber, it is a lot faster and a lot less crowded. The whole evolution goes faster, much to the delight of the submarine crew.

To the Beach

Once everybody's safely in a Zodiak, it's time to break out the paddles or fire up the engine and head to the beach. Several hundred meters offshore, well outside the surf zone, a pair of divers—the scout swimmers—will slip over the gunwales of the Zodiac and, with weapons at the ready, move in to secure the section of beach where the landing is intended. After a quick check of the area, they signal the boats to come in. The "rubber ducks" run in through the surf, everybody alert for enemy contact, and the boats are promptly pulled up across the high water mark and either hidden or buried.

Once secure on the beach, the SEALs are ready to execute the mission. If it is a patrol or a "direct action" strike deep inland, the squad (or perhaps platoon if two boats have come ashore) assembles itself and prepares to move off into the hinterland without a word being spoken. Communication is done with hand and arm signals, visible and instantly recognizable even on dark, cloudy nights.

Out front, leading the patrol, is the point man who navigates the patrol to the objective. This is traditionally the most dangerous, difficult position in the patrol order, requiring superb land navigation skills and an extremely high level of alertness to the possibility of contact with enemy forces. A point man can walk you right into the kill zone of an ambush, or halt the patrol safely outside. Such choices can be (and often have been) the difference of life and death for an entire patrol. When contact with the enemy is made, the man on point is typically the first to fire or the first to die.

The point man's preferred weapon in wooded terrain is often not a rifle or machine gun but a military version of a standard twelve-gauge shotgun, loaded with five rounds of "double-ought" (size 00) buckshot. These are large, bullet-sized lead pellets that spread out in a lethal cone of destruction. One pellet will kill out to a range of about 100 meters, sometimes farther; at closer ranges, particularly within about ten meters, a well-placed load will punch a gaping hole through a torso, or rip off an arm or a head. It is the approximate equivalent of firing seven or so bullets at exactly the same instant in the same general direction.

An alternative load is the flachette round, with tiny steel darts in place of the buckshot. While these are not nearly as lethal or de-

structive individually, there are many more of them, and they produce a denser cloud of projectiles, a handy way of providing a group of enemy soldiers at close range with something to think about besides the SEAL patrol. They are lethal out to several hundred meters.

There's yet another handy twelve-gauge round for the point man's shotgun, a single, heavy slug useful for opening locked doors and disabling machinery or electronics in one quick, brutal way. It is accurate out to a range of about five feet, maybe six. If it hits some-

The M16 coupled with the M203 grenade launcher is a potent combination used to engage point targets out to about a quarter of a mile. The collapsible stock and short barrel make the weapon less awkward to get in and out of cramped places like lockout chambers.

This sentry doesn't know it but he's got a little problem. That's an invisible infrared aim-point dot on his personal center-of-mass. Since the aiming device is attached to a rifle, that means the bullets from the weapon will strike within that dot, probably creating some discomfort for the target.

thing, the target stays hit. This is no precision munition, but it will punch a hole in the cast-iron block of an automobile engine, or the concrete wall of a house or bunker—or, if they co-operate, a whole row of enemy soldiers.

Riflemen

If the point man bumps into a bad guy at close range and gets the first shot off effectively, the patrol has the choice of either "going to ground" and duking it out with the opposing team or making a run for the beach. In either case the point man's shotgun will soon have limited utility—it will be out of range, out of ammunition, or both. That's why there are several riflemen on a normal patrol, each with an M16 rifle and five or six thirty-round magazines stashed in their load-carrying web gear.

M16A2 and Car-15

The M16A2 rifle is almost the same weapon that the father's of some of today's SEALs carried and fought with in Vietnam a generation ago. It's no longer the most exotic weapon on the battlefield, or on the teams, but it is still a good, light, accurate, effective weapon that has proven itself in countless battles. The latest version is more reliable than the first, which had a failure-to-feed problem for a while. The A2 also lacks the "full-auto" feature of the original, a modification based on the discovery that in the heat of combat the weapon was being used as a "bullet hose," ineffectively spraying rounds downrange. Instead, the rifle has a BURST position on the selector switch on the left side of the receiver, above the trigger; this permits three-round bursts that economize on ammunition while encouraging the rifleman to aim rather than point the weapon.

While the basic rifle issued to SEALs is essentially the same as the M16A2 issued to Army and Marine Corps infantry privates (and just about everybody else, too), the SEALs version tends to be an upgraded, customized weapon with specialized sights and a collapsible stock or a compact version of the

The little MP5 "room broom" is a super-compact little squirt gun that's a favorite of SEALs and other operators who have to deal face to face with terrorists at short range.

M16 that has been popular with special operators for the last twenty years, the CAR-15. This little squirt gun uses essentially the same receiver components as the bigger M16, but with an ingenious collapsible stock assembly and shorter barrel. It trades bulk for a little fragility and a slightly greater inclination to jam. The decision to carry the CAR-15 or M16 is—as with similar decisions on a team— partly a matter of personal choice. SEALs, along with other special operators, are permitted to exercise a lot more latitude in the choice of accessories than are troopers in more conventional units.

Depending on the particular mission, the sights installed may be a night-vision scope or a laser aim-point system. The first of these, the night-vision scope, amplifies existing light and presents the shooter with a magnified, green and black picture of the target through a somewhat conventional rifle scope. The other device mounts a small laser pointer under the barrel; once activated it puts a bright red dot where the bullet will strike. You don't need to peep through a scope or iron sights—just put the red dot on your intended victim and squeeze. It is not a long-range, sniping system; but for night combat in confined spaces it is often the system of choice.

The M16 fires a small, 5.56mm (.223-caliber) bullet at high velocity. This makes for a very flat trajectory and a lot of retained energy at practical ranges. The Vietnam-era version of the M16 was supposed to be good out to about 300 meters; today's weapon/cartridge combination is rated to 460 meters—about a quarter of a mile. That means that a trained rifleman can hit a man-sized target at that range with about fifty percent of his carefully aimed shots. The bullet, of course, is lethal out to a couple of miles, but hitting things with it at extreme ranges has more to do with luck than gun control.

MP4 and MP5

The M16 and CAR-15 are not the only choices for a SEAL rifleman to take on a mission. His weapon can be almost anything that he and the patrol leader think is appropriate.

One favorite alternative is the Heckler & Koch (H&K) MP5 "room broom" submachine gun. It fires the diminutive 9mm Parabellum pistol round and is well matched to the laser aim-point sight system for urban combat situations. It is extremely compact—you can wear it under a jacket for those formal events. Like the shotgun, it is accurate and effective only out to fifty meters or so, and its projectiles aren't guaranteed to have the desired effect. But you can carry (and shoot) a lot of those little 9mm rounds; if you squirt a burst of them into a bunker the folks inside will probably wish you hadn't.

The bigger brother of the MP5 is a beefy submachine gun called the MP4 , brought to you by those fine folks at H&K, builders of fine military weapons used around the world. Both of these German weapons possess a qual-ity that, in many ways, is more important than accuracy, hitting power, weight or rate of fire: when you pull the trigger the gun goes *bang*. This reputation for reliability has sold a lot of H&K weapons to a lot of operators, and it is the reason you'll so often see them, drip-ping sea water and covered with sand, coming across a beach in the hands of SEALs.

Silencers

On the muzzles of all these rifles and sub-machine guns you'll sometimes see tubular de-vices about eight inches long and an inch and a half in diameter. These are sound sup-pressers, or silencers as they are sometimes called. For weapons such as the 9mm H&Ks, with subsonic ammunition, they can convert the loud report to a subtle pop by slowing the propellant gasses as they rush out the muzzle behind the bullet. This can be a very handy

The MP4 is very popular with the teams, and right-fully so. It is compact, reliable, and tolerant of salt-water immersion. Its little 9mm round isn't the *hardest hitting bullet on the block, but it works well enough at close range.*

feature in those sneaky, close-in fights that SEALs sometimes encounter.

Suppressers work on the M16, too, but not nearly as well. The standard ammunition for the weapon is designed to produce very high velocities, far faster than the speed of sound. Much of the noise from the firing of an M16 comes from the sonic boom produced by the bullet's flight through air. Even so, some of the noise can be reduced, and suppressers are often attached even to M16s, particularly in urban combat situations. As with the aimpoint and night sights and so many other tools of the trade, suppressers have their specialized role in the SEALs' bag of tricks.

M203 Grenade Launcher

One of the most interesting and useful weapons you'll find carried on a SEAL mission is the M203 grenade launcher, a fairly simple weapon with a complex variety of ammunition and uses. It isn't much more than a short length of aluminum tube with a breech block and trigger assembly. It bolts to an M16 rifle, under the barrel; the magazine provides the hand grip. The 203 fires a 40mm cartridge with one of several warheads. It is a bit like a mortar, although it is called a grenade launcher. Its lobbing trajectory allows you to toss projectiles over berms and other forms of cover that your opponent may use to hide from direct fire weapons. Within about two or three hundred meters you should, with training, be able to put one of the rounds through a doorway or bunker aperture (although it might take a few tries).

Projectiles come in several flavors. There is a high explosive model (HE) that is one of the most popular. It will reach out about 500

The M203 grenade launcher throws a 40mm projectile out several hundred yards with precision. It's not much more than a simple aluminum tube with a breech and trigger. The hand grip is the rifle's magazine. With it, you can pump a few anti-personnel rounds through the aperture of a bunker, or an illumination round up in the air, or an anti-armor round into the side of an armored personnel carrier, normally with the desired results.

In conventional units the automatic weapons man gets an assistant to feed the ammunition. SEALs manage this chore themselves. The orange bullet tip indicates a tracer round; the others are ball.

Another view of the M203. It's not much more than a simple aluminum tube with a breech and trigger. The hand grip is the rifle's magazine.

Combat Time

Although Naval Special Warfare represents some of the best trained, most experienced warriors in the US Department of Defense, there is still something just a little naive about the vast majority of the people in this community. While they train to the highest standards and with the most realistic training aids, there is still something missing from the resumes of nearly all the 1,200 SEALs and SBS crews today: combat time.

About twenty years have now passed since the end of America's last prolonged conflict. With those years have gradually gone the SEALs who planned and executed the missions in the Mekong during the long, difficult years the teams fought in Vietnam. The result of that is that, in some ways, the teams are becoming *less* qualified rather than more so as time goes by. The lessons learned from prolonged combat operations in what military folks call the "real world" cannot be duplicated in peacetime. Now, when SEALs go to war, it is typically the first real combat operation of a career, and perhaps the only combat experience a man will ever have. Of the 200-plus men on one of today's teams, there is probably not one left with Vietnam experience, and very, very few with actual trigger-pulling experience in any operation since.

Real combat makes people do things they don't do in training. The big, heroic guys sometimes go numb and ineffective on you while the wimpy little guys who always screw up during training execute the mission with calm and grace and not a trace of fear.

In training you shoot at a cardboard or plastic target that pops up for a few mechanically timed seconds, usually in a predictable place, then disappears. If you hit it, the target folds down, mechanically, and a computer records your hit. In combat your target will appear anywhere, often unpredictably, often for a fraction of a second. The target may be a woman or a child, may be trying to shoot you, or may not know you exist. You can see its eyes, sometimes; you can identify it as a person, somewhat like you. The target probably has a family, a mission of his own, and maybe a target of his own—you. It is a bit like hunting; you must expect the unexpected, be alert without fixation, all in a complicated, emotional, supremely frightening situation. When your target appears, it will probably be for a fleeting glimpse. If you are completely prepared, you may be able to get a shot off. If you do, you will certainly invite the same treatment on yourself.

Things they don't show you on television:

No matter how well you've maintained your weapon, no matter how full the magazine is or how carefully it has been loaded, there will be times when you pull the trigger on somebody and it will go *click* instead of *bang*. This can be quite embarrassing. It happens a lot more often than you can possibly imagine.

Gunfights on TV and in the movies are fought with weapons that have magical, bottomless magazines, that never run out of ammunition. Real world gunfights use weapons with magazines that are good for about three seconds full-auto, less if they jam (which they often will). And magazines that you can easily change in training, at night and with gloves on, you will find yourself utterly incapable of fitting into the well of the weapon. You will run out of ammunition far faster than you could imagine possible.

In a real world gunfight you can spot a target, align the sights, cut loose with a long burst from your trusty M60, and watch the tracers dance downrange at the man you intend to kill, when, just like in the movies, the dust kicks up around him, the bullets hammer his surroundings—and he runs off, untouched.

But if you somehow achieve that Zen-like state of mind that some men do, all things are possible. An enemy soldier can materialize out of the weeds, with your personal weapon jammed or broken, and now it is *his* turn to forget in nervous haste to move the safety on his AK-74 from "safe" to "fire." Then, perhaps, you will remember why you carry that Sig-Sauer 9mm handgun on your hip. If you get to the Sig quick enough, get it up, focus on the front sight, align with center-of-mass, and squeeze—if you are blessed this day—your bullet will strike your man in the lower sternum. He'll go down, and you can stay up; you'll live through another mission. If you're lucky and good, together.

None of these things will ever happen to you on an exercise or in training, but they will all happen to you if you go to war with a combat unit and stay there awhile. Trust me on this.

meters and will kill or injure anybody within about five meters of impact, a useful device when enemy infantry are closing in on your position. The 203 will also fire illumination rounds, like the mortar, that will light up the battlefield at night; and tear gas, white phosphorus, and flachette rounds for other times and places.

M60 Machine Gun

A SEAL squad with an inland patrol mission will carry plenty of "organic" firepower in the form of two stripped down M60 machine guns. The M60 is another old design that has been improved since the years when the dad of today's SEAL carried one back in the "big war." It fires the bigger 7.62mm (.308-caliber) NATO cartridge, delivering accurate, high-volume fire on area targets at ranges well beyond what the M16 can effectively engage.

It is a heavy weapon, with heavy ammunition, often cursed on those long walks in the woods and swamps—until, that is, the opposing team materializes out of the woodwork, spoiling for a fight. Then the M60 is worth its weight in gold or blood.

If this seems like a lot of choices, it is. A team commander explains his personal attitude toward weapons used by SEALs:

"I think we really do need a variety of weapons on the teams. Certain operations call for specific capabilities. I also don't think every guy should have a different weapon, just because he has his own personal preference. I should be able to switch magazines with the guy next to me if I run out and he hasn't. But, for the rifleman, the choice can be between the M14, the MP5, or the M16. The MP5 is for use in brush or urban combat situations. The M16 is a good, general, all-around weapon, and you can put the M203 under it. The M14 has extra power for penetration and range.

"Riflemen are for engaging *point* targets and they should be shooting single shots; personally, I don't even believe in three-round bursts. I don't even believe in 'double-tap' [firing two quick shots at a target instead of one], although the idea is currently quite popular. If you put the first shot where you're supposed

The M60 as used by the SEALs is a stripped-down, lightweight version that is a lot more tolerant of sand than the early versions were. After firing a hundred rounds or so the barrel will begin to glow.

to, you don't *need* another one! If you need another one, pull the trigger again. Why waste ammunition? You should be calm enough under fire to know what you are doing rather than just opening up 'full-auto' and spraying the riverbank.

"The automatic weapon man is not to take out point targets; he's supposed to keep the enemy's head down and to give you covering fire while the riflemen take care of the point targets."

RTO

The patrol can be far from a friendly face but still be in contact with the civilized world, thanks to the battery-powered high technology that the RTO (an old expression, short for radio telephone operator) carries. There are any number of systems he can carry, and with some of them you can chat with the big bosses

The RTO is the squad communicator. His duties include carrying the radio and batteries and managing the communications plan. The antenna will identify him as a prime target to any enemy snipers within rifle range.

in Washington and in the Pentagon—although that's not usually something the team will think is a good idea.

That's because you're on the ground, with eyes on the target, and the admirals and the assistant secretary of defense sitting next to him are both in a comfortable room in a safe place. When the sun goes down, they will go off for cocktails somewhere, have a nice dinner, and watch TV. You will crawl through the mud and perhaps have people shoot at you, all while attempting to do the bidding of these "experts" with the clean fingernails, thanks to that little "satcom" transceiver carried by the RTO.

Satellite radios are now extremely compact and can easily be taken along on operations with a very moderate weight penalty. They allow the team leader to communicate with almost anybody, almost anywhere (if he can get a channel on the satellite). That, believe it or not, can be a real problem. Although

you can call for help from almost anywhere on the globe with these little systems, if some politician in the "puzzle palace" comes up with a wild hair idea, they can call *you* and task you with this death-defying scheme, all from the comfort and safety of Washington, DC.

The RTO is, in some ways, a pack mule for the patrol leader; he carries the radio and operates it, but under the control of the patrol leader, whom the RTO shadows. The RTO is, along with the officer, a natural target for any sensible sniper on the opposing team who manages to identify ·and engage the patrol. The radio is the patrol's link to the close air support gunships overhead, the naval gunfire support offshore, and the "slicks" (unarmed helicopters) ready to swoop in to rescue the patrol in an emergency. By eliminating the RTO and his equipment, the enemy can isolate the squad and chop it to small pieces. That's why RTOs fold the aerials of their radios down and do their best to look as innocent as possible.

A funny thing about these radios, though, is that—despite their usually excellent reliability and reception—at moments like these they may suddenly stop working. As one officer explains:

"We have better communications now than we used to, but that works both ways. If I need to get ahold of somebody I probably can. It also means that guy can get ahold of me—and give me directions that I might not want. I can remember two times, during 1965 operations in Vietnam, when somebody tried to tell me what to do while I was on the ground. I didn't like it—and in one case I turned off the radio. Now, if the National Command Authority wants to talk to me while I'm on a hot operation, they very well may. This is not necessarily a good thing. To me, the guy on the scene calls the shots. He should receive *nothing* from those guys except support, when he calls up and asks for it. We make a plan and should stick to the plan, unless the guy on the ground wants to do differently. Now, if somebody has some information that can help you, if they see a platoon of enemy, for example, coming down the road toward you, they ought to be able to let you know. But don't tell me to go left or right in reaction to that platoon—let *me* make that decision!

"We have a tendency, because we have such good communications, to let responsibility slip upwards where sometimes it doesn't belong. Look what happened at Desert One [the failed Iranian hostage rescue mission]. Jimmy Carter was in the position where he could call up Colonel Beckwith [the on-scene commander] and tell him what to do. I don't like that! Most people in the SEALs don't like that. Some people submit to that. And some people automatically get their hackles up—don't submit to it; put the radio down and say 'Dang, something just went wrong with the radio!' The problem with letting decisions be made someplace, with letting somebody else be re-

PRC-112 squad radio is another example in the revolution in miniaturization that has transformed the command and control problem for managing SEALs during combat operations.

sponsible, is that I'm still responsible for the people who are with me. I want to make the decision for what happens once we launch the mission. Tell me what to do *before* I leave, and then if I buy off on it, fine. Just don't tell me what to do once I'm out there. While we have the advantage of better communications, we get with that the disadvantage of potential micro-management by people not on the scene."

Patrol Leader

The patrol leader on a SEAL operation is going to be one of the platoon's two commissioned officers, the platoon leader (normally a lieutenant) or executive officer (lieutenant junior grade or possibly ensign). The role of a combat leader is an odd kind of combination of duties that sometimes conflict. A combat leader has two heavy responsibilities: to complete the mission, and to preserve the force. That means that the leader takes himself and his followers to complete a mission that, in war, will probably involve great hazard. How much hazard is sometimes influenced by the officer; it may depend on how much risk he's willing to take in a given time and place. Just how important the mission is he has to judge. He has to judge how much it is worth, in time, effort, ammunition, and the blood of his men. So the patrol leader is stuck in the middle, with a responsibility upward, to his commanders who've tasked him with a mission, and downward, to his followers who trust his judgment.

The officer is part of the platoon, and he is aloof from it. He guards his men, is responsible for their welfare as a parent is for a child—and may send them knowingly to their deaths or dismemberment. He is trained, at Annapolis or OCS (Officer Candidate School), to be careful to avoid playing favorites and developing the natural kind of friendships that are common among civilians—fraternization, it is called.

The officer discovers, early in his career, that while the troops will automatically salute and call him *sir*, the respect may not be sincere. An officer learns that respect is earned in two phases: first through the commissioning process that awards gold bars and officer rank, then all over again in the units where real competence and leadership are demonstrated. For SEALs there is another part, BUD/S, where officers must perform alongside the enlisted sailors, suffer all the same insults and indignities, the same stresses and fatigue. It is an important part of the bonding between the leaders and the followers in the SEALs.

As officer candidates quickly learn at Annapolis, NROTC, or OCS, it's a complicated business to lead men in combat. It is a bit like leading an orchestra; you don't need to be the best player of every instrument, but you have to know perfectly what each can do—then to be able to make sure its resources are integrated into the big score. But the terrible,

This is one of the little compact SATCOM radios that have transformed the business of communicating in the field. This is the LST-5C transceiver; it weighs about ten pounds.

wonderful thing about military operations is that they are, always and invariably, partially improvisations. There is an old military saying: No plan survives contact with the enemy. That means that, no matter how well you think you've prepared, something is going to go wrong. And when it does, one person needs to be responsible for selecting an alternative course of action. That's what officers are for.

The platoon leader will normally have been personally given the mission and then designed the plan, with help from above and below. He takes the plan to the field and makes it happen with the help of his SEALs. When the shooting starts he is expected to direct, manage, and control the firing. When the ambush is triggered, he initiates it with a squeeze of the trigger or the "clacker" for the Claymore. His M16 magazines may be full of nothing but tracers, which he uses to indicate targets for the rest of the squad to fire on.

On the march, the patrol leader will typically be toward the front of the line of march. He may take the point sometimes, but usually will be the number two man, where he can provide direction for the man on point and still control the squad in case of contact. The RTO will be right behind the patrol leader, however, wherever he is.

Tail Gunner

The two most vulnerable areas for the patrol are its front and its back; it will either bump into trouble, or trouble will come sneaking up on it. That's why both the man on point and the last man in line, the tail gunner, have to be especially sharp. The tail gunner will probably have one of the squad's cut-down M60 machine guns—and eyes in the back of his head.

In actual combat, on deep penetration missions, he'll probably carry a variety of goodies to help break contact if the patrol finds itself compromised and on the run. Then he'll pull out the tear gas grenades, the devastating WP (white phosphorous) grenades, and perhaps a Claymore to rig as a booby trap against the pursuers.

Chapter 5

Actions at the Objective

As mentioned before, SEALs have five different general types of missions to perform: direct action, recon, foreign internal defense, unconventional warfare, and counterterrorist. This is a broad spectrum of responsibilities for a small organization, no matter how well trained or funded. Some of these are primary SEAL missions; others are secondary.

Counterterrorist operations, for example, are really the stock-in-trade for Delta, the Army's superb, extremely exclusive counterterrorist unit. The men (and—promise not to tell where you heard this—women) in Delta are going to get the call for such operations except under extreme circumstances. SEALs are trained and prepared to execute the operation, and there are a few "long hair" team members available for extremely covert ops, but it is hardly a prime talent for aquatic warriors.

Likewise, foreign internal defense (FID) and unconventional warfare (UW) are prime Army missions that are backed up by SEALs. Both require the language skills and charm of a diplomat, the charisma of an evangelist, and the patience of a saint. The FID mission turns

When you're a SEAL you don't have to worry too much about what the sign says, particularly when you've got a riot shotgun and an MP4. Close combat in confined spaces is a new skill required of SEALs. US Navy photo by PH2 Milton Savage

out to be one that a few SEALs excel at, about five guys of the 200 or so on a team, according to one team commander. This mission occupies a few SEALs in Latin America now, and it kept a lot busy during the workup to Desert Storm in training Saudi and other Arab naval personnel in the Gulf. As one of the team commanders says:

"I think we're quite good at the traditional Green Beret mission of foreign internal defense; we have a very high degree of success when we include foreign military personnel in our operations. For some reason we've thrown that back to the Army. We were very good in the Gulf when we took two or three SEALs and used them with ten or twelve host-nation personnel. We 'force-multiplied.' We had all the advantages of the host-nation expertise, plus our skills and experience in executing that type of operation. It was a Cracker Jack setup!"

But it is not one most SEALs find very appealing. It takes many months of study at DLI, the Defense Language Institute at Monterey, California, to acquire the skill to speak Arabic, for example, or Estonian, and that means time away from the teams. Unconventional warfare is the behind-the-lines version of FID, and hasn't really been used much since World War II—although it is still sitting there as a tasking for the Special Operations Forces.

So the principal missions, the ones that get the attention, the time, the rehearsals, are recon and strike. The first is stealthy and the second isn't.

Recons, Deep and Shallow

Despite all the wonderful, expensive technology that has gone into intelligence gathering, with billions of dollars spent on camera systems for aircraft and satellites, there is still no substitute for having someone go ashore for a "hands on, eyes on" study of a potential target. One of the lessons learned from Urgent

The SPIE (Special Purpose Insertion and Extraction) rig is one way to extract and insert SEALs in a hurry. It is a breezy and hazardous technique, but one that a lot of people actually enjoy. US Navy photo by PH2 Milton Savage

Fury was that overhead intel only begins to provide essential planning information and that things like landing zones can look completely different to a helicopter pilot than to a high-flying aircraft—with potentially catastrophic results.

Although not as glamorous as the strike missions, recon ops are just as important now as ever. As the recons in the Panama Just Cause op and the beach survey during Desert Storm both demonstrate, SEALs still get tasked with these jobs, and it is their particular art form.

The recon mission can be just about anything, anywhere. The classic one, of course, is the beach recon preceding an amphibious operation. While the Marines think their own recon guys can do this better than anybody, SEALs politely disagree. While it doesn't get much attention, it is still a tremendously important mission when you consider how much investment the US has in putting Marines across the beach anywhere in the world. The memory of Tarawa half a century ago haunts the Marines—and the Navy, too. Beach recons, consequently, are a big part of the course of instruction at BUD/S, where they're called "hydrographic surveys." They can be as simple or as detailed as you and your commanders want—and as circumstances permit.

There are many different types of hydrographic surveys and beach recons, from simple to complex. The amphibious task force commander who is planning an across-the-beach op will want to know gradient and composition of the beach, littoral current across the beach, surf size and type, beach exits, defenses, and obstacles underwater.

It takes a lot of people—or a lot of time—to develop this information. Without getting into the technical details, here's how they do it:

Swim pairs are dropped in the water off the beach at intervals of about twenty-five meters, on line, by a high-speed boat—just like they did fifty years ago out in the Pacific. Under command of the officer in charge (OIC), the swimmers move in toward the beach, mak-

342

A fire team (half a squad) fits neatly into a rubber duck for a semi-stealthy insertion. Although the little inflatable is rated for over-the-horizon ranges, you don't want to ride around like this for long out on the open ocean.

First ashore during a combat insertion are the scout swimmers, who secure the beach before the rest of the unit comes ashore. They operate in pairs, for mutual security.

ing soundings with a lead-line (a lead sinker on a line marked in one-foot increments). While one man measures the depth, the other records the data on a slate. Since all the swimmers make these soundings at the same time, a set of coordinated data is assembled across a wide frontage of possible landing zone.

The line of swimmers moves in to the beach together, with the OIC controlling the intervals between soundings. Both depth and composition are recorded on each swim-pair's slate. The Marine task force commander's staff will want to know what they have to contend with. Coral reef? Mud? Jagged rocks? Man-made obstacles with antitank mines attached? Is the foreshore (the surf zone) too shallow for LSTs, or is it steep and suitable for ramped vessels? Is the surf high and violent or short and mild? Is the current across the beach strong and likely to force the AAM-TRACs away from their intended beaches? Then, what's beyond the beach—will tanks and armored vehicles be "channeled" by sea walls, cliffs, embankments? Are there enemy-prepared fighting positions dominating the beach? Are they manned? Is there a beach patrol? Are there mines?

The survey party moves all the way into the beach and perhaps beyond, then withdraws back to the water. Under the direction of the OIC, they reform a line offshore for pickup. Then, perhaps aboard the flagship for the amphibious task force or wherever the SEAL unit has set up shop, the data from each swim pair is assembled as a detailed chart and presented to the plans-and-operations guys who are trying to figure out what to do. They (through their recommendation to the task force commander) make the call on the amphibious operation, not the SEALs, using the data provided.

There is another kind of recon for which the Army and Navy SOF communities compete, called *deep recon* or *strategic recon*, and this one might not involve even getting wet. Deep recon involves the study of a target or area of interest that typically requires covert travel overland or covert insertion inland. SOF teams did this during Desert Shield/Desert Storm in Kuwait and Iraq, watching for enemy SCUD launchers, for example, and reporting their location for attack by other "theater assets" like US Air Force F-15E Strike Eagle aircraft. A SEAL recon team was on the Saudi/Kuwait border when the Iraqis attacked the town of Kafji and participated in the coordinated engagement of the enemy armored column by air and coalition ground units.

HAHO and HALO Insertion

These recon teams can be delivered in some quite exotic ways. One of the sneakiest is by parachute, but SOF teams don't consider the standard 500- or 1,200-foot drop altitude used for mass tactical airborne operations to be very covert; having a C-130 fly low over the neighborhood is one sure way to get noticed. Instead, the drop aircraft goes way up to 30,000 feet or so—where the commercial airliners fly. The jumpers, rigged with special equipment to cope with the incredible cold and the lack of oxygen at that altitude, jump and free fall before deploying their canopies.

The HAHO technique (High-Altitude exit/High-altitude Opening) allows a jumper to glide for many miles under his canopy, through the dark, virtually without fear of detection, to a predetermined landing zone.

The HALO technique (High-Altitude exit/Low-altitude Opening) is a similar way to have the jumper move away from the ground track of the aircraft, making it difficult to find him. This time, though, the jumper uses free-fall parachuting techniques to "fly" through the air, opening his canopy only when very close to the ground.

Once down, the mission proceeds as planned. When it is over, one way or another, it is time to go home. While, again, there are many ways to do this, the quickest will again be by aircraft. Unfortunately, though, pickup aircraft are a lot less subtle.

STABO Extraction

An extremely unsubtle extraction technique, STABO (Stabilized Tactical Airborne Body Operations), involves having a helicopter arrive over the team on the ground with a special harness deployed, coming to a hover, and then plucking the SEALs out of harm's way. The SEALs all wear harnesses similar to those used for parachuting and attach the harnesses to the sling dangling from the helicopter. When all are secured, it's up, up, and away . . . for a very breezy ride.

Once the scouts determine the beach to be suitable for a visit, the rest of the squad comes ashore, but they are hardly complacent about it. This is a vulnerable moment for the SEALs, and they are extremely cautious at this phase of insertion.

Strike

The mission against the Panamanian patrol boat was a classic strike or direct action mission, a carefully planned, precision attack against a point target under difficult circumstances. Using any special ops unit for such an attack is a lot more expensive, in every respect, than using conventional resources to do the same kind of thing, so there is usually a good reason for sending SEALs to blow the propellers off a boat instead of (for example)

345

Airborne insertions are also typically done at night,
but that makes for dull photographs.

346

One way to make a quick getaway is to call the helo back for a pickup. The crew will toss a ladder over the ramp, and then it's up to the swimmer to climb back aboard.

having an F/A-18 drop a bomb or smart missile on the target. Collateral damage and loss of life has been one of the driving concerns lately; in Panama, certainly, and in Grenada, too, this caution has created risks of its own.

But ambushes and attacks on point targets are still a major talent of SEALs, another area where they compete with the Army's Rangers and Special Forces. These can be conducted in many imaginative ways, most of which are of the high-risk, high-payoff variety (although SEALs sometimes think some of these are high-risk, low-payoff missions).

Ambushes

The ambush is a kind of classic special op mission. SEALs conducted probably thousands of them in Vietnam—and were on the receiving end of quite a few, too. The "plain vanilla" version of the operation works like this: first, find a place where your enemy regularly travels—a road or trail—and find a nice sharp bend in the route. The "kill zone" will be determined by the patrol leader, normally the long axis of what is an L-shaped portion of the road. The leader will position himself at the corner and will control the whole thing, usually with his own fire and with the triggering of a Claymore mine or two.

Ambushes are marvelously effective when everything works properly—the carnage is *incredible*. But if you screw one up, the carnage can be on your end. And ambushes are easy to screw up; the key is fire discipline and timing.

The little $50,000 dune buggy called the Desert Patrol Vehicle is a fast, potent machine for rescuing downed pilots, scouting large sections of potential battlefield, or inserting snipers into an operational area. It will do at least 70mph, fly through space, and—with the machine guns and AT-4 rocket launchers—duke it out with carefully selected enemy forces.

SEALs practice executing raids on oil platforms and other semi-urban spaces. These guys have just landed on a ship and, like buccaneers of old, are swarming aboard to take control. US Navy photo by PH2 Milton Savage

The PAS-7 infrared viewing system. SEALs use a variety of sensor systems to inspect terrain at night; thermal imaging systems such as this make objects like people and vehicles instantly visible out of the gloom.

Ambushes don't take a lot of people or a lot of resources (depending on the target, of course), but they do take planning and teamwork.

If available, Claymores are installed along the kill zone with overlapping fields of fire and with careful attention to protecting the team from the substantial back-blast. If the ambush is along a road, detonation cord can be placed in the ditches that survivors will naturally use for cover after the Claymores fire, and they can be taken out with another squeeze on another "clacker," firing the electric blasting cap that will fire the det cord.

When all the preparations are made, the responsibilities and fields of fire assigned, you and the rest of the crew slither into the wood-work without a trace and wait . . . and wait . . . and wait some more. At last, in the distance, somebody is moving toward you; it can be chil-

dren on their way to school, innocent civilians going to market. You have to sit, silently, waiting for them to pass. What if one of the kids sees the Claymore? What if somebody notices your face peeping out of the brush? Anything that can go wrong, will go wrong to somebody, sooner or later—usually sooner—so it pays to set these things up with exquisite attention to detail.

The way these things are *supposed* to work, an enemy unit will come rolling down the road. With luck (for you, anyway) they will fit the ambush resources; don't pop a Claymore against a platoon of main battle tanks, for example. But if any enemy squad comes bopping down the bunny trail (laughing, playing radios the way they sometimes do), everybody in the ambush waits for the signal to fire. That signal is usually the patrol leader's detonation of the Claymores, hurling their pellets in wide, deadly arcs. If the timing is right and the patrol is within the kill zone, they will all go down—maybe. Some guys are just luckier than others, and fit into a hole in the pattern of the spray of ball bearings. Others may be outside the kill zone. Regardless, this is the time to use all those marksmanship skills they taught you at BUD/S and since. You engage the closest guy with a gun in your field of fire (got a round in the chamber? safety off?), and you keep engaging until there is no more resistance or the patrol leader calls, "Cease fire!" There will be a terrible mess where the patrol was, and this will be a good time to start moving toward the exits.

Ambushes go wrong in lots of ways. Often, the enemy doesn't cooperate. They either won't show up, or they send the wrong victims (like tanks), or they decide not to use the road today, but move along in the woods—where you're hiding. Or they notice you before they get to the kill zone, and then it's *turnabout is fair play.* Then it's your turn to be the vic-

Conflict resolution and power projection in the special operations community generally means something like this—either threatening or actually using deadly force against people to make them behave.

351

There is something extremely primitive about much of the work of a SEAL team; while drivers of stealth bombers and F-15 Strike Eagles operate multimillion dollar weapons systems in relative comfort, SEALs use skills as old as war. This swim pair crawls up out of the surf, just as their forefathers did in World War II, for a peek inland, hoping and praying that there won't be an enemy sentry on top of the sand dune.

USAF helos support US Navy SEALs in the new cooperative relationship called "joint operations." This kind of integration has had profound effects on things like radios, weapons, training, and doctrine, ensuring that different services can all "play off the same sheet of music," as the operators like to say.

tim—and practice those escape-and-evasion skills they taught you in BUD/S. Just remember what they told you at BUD/S: The only easy day was yesterday.

Raids

The diversion operation at Mina Sa'Ud that helped kick off Desert Storm was one kind of raid, as was the attack on the Noriega

Neville Jet, the rescue of Sir Paul Scoon, and hundreds of similar missions executed by SEALs since World War II. Raids are quick-in, quick-out strikes against high-value targets that can't be attacked efficiently or effectively otherwise. This is another area where SEALs compete with the Army, whose Rangers are masters of the art of the raid. Rangers, however, are specialists in the "blunt instrument"

This role-playing sentry might have a bit of a problem—and a headache not even Anacin could help. Much of the training, equipment, and doctrine used by SEALs today is oriented toward dealing with unconventional forces like terrorists.

353

style of raid, with lots of people (very large, muscular ones) and lots of firepower landing on top of an enemy target, typically by parachute, and ripping it to shreds.

The SEAL raid is more surgical and subtle. It still might arrive by parachute, but—unlike with our beloved Ranger Regiment—the enemy target of a SEAL op might never know what hit them. That's because a SEAL strike mission might only involve two men, a sniper and his spotter/security man. With their big .50-caliber sniper rifle and woodcraft skills, these two can move across terrain unseen and disappear into the woodwork.

(Rangers attempting this would leave a trail of scorched earth and destruction visible at a mile). Then the sniper team can sit and wait until the SCUDs come home—and then drill holes in their rocket motors from a mile and a half, without anybody knowing where the bullets came from or how it happened. That same sniper team can, if desired, kill a senior enemy staff officer or commander riding in his Mercedes, pick off a tank commander standing in his hatch, or disable an aircraft taxiing for take-off. In fact, people who weren't part of the Neville Jet take-down op during Operation Just Cause wonder why forty SEALs were

An electrical blasting cap, fresh from the box, ready to prime any military explosive. It contains three stages of material, each setting off the next. The last, *a material called PETN, will reliably set off just about anything.*

354

sent across the airfield to attack the jet when a sniper team ought to have been able to do it from the safety of the far side of the runways.

Among the most challenging kind of raid SEALs train for is the counterterrorist hostage rescue mission. This is the kind of op that you only get one shot at; it has to be done perfectly or the wrong folks get killed. Consequently SEALs practice all the ancient arts of rapid insertion, extraction, close-quarters target identification, and precision shooting. According to people who've been there, you've got seven seconds in a room with the bad guys to conduct business—sort out the good from the bad, kill the bad guys, protect the good guys—or the operation goes to hell. When you consider that this must often be done at night, in unfamiliar territory, with alert and fanatic enemies, this becomes a tall order. But it can be done, and has, successfully.

Killing People and Destroying Things

A sad but unavoidable consequence of all military missions involves taking perfectly good buildings, airplanes, vehicles, bridges, boats, and people, then taking them apart and converting them into smaller, less useful junk. This process is generally thought to help ac-

A mixed bag of things that go bump in the night— TNT, dynamite, and det cord, with a partial box of blasting caps (time fuse variety). These explosives are quite stable and difficult to detonate without a *blasting cap. For example, to prime the dynamite you have to poke a hole in it with a pointed tool, then insert the blasting cap-fuse assembly.*

Kids—don't try this at home! Somebody's used a lot of explosive to do a bit of body and fender work on this old car.

complish national policy objectives. While this behavior isn't always considered very nice, it usually works. This is conflict resolution, US Navy SEALs style.

There are many ways SEALs use to accomplish their mission, but basically there are only two fundamental techniques used by the teams. One of these uses individual weapons—rifles, machine guns, mortars—to engage other hostile forces. The other involves using explosives in one form or another to blow things up. "Hostile forces" is a military expression for the loyal soldiers or sailors opposing the SEAL mission, and "engage" is a military expression for the business of shooting up these folks in an organized way. If this seems like kindergarten, it is only because we generally talk around the seamier side of the business of war.

SEAL missions often involve the destruction of some enemy facility—a radio transmitter, a bridge, a bunker complex, a headquarters, or (as in the attack on the *Presidente Porras* in the beginning of this book) a naval vessel. This usually involves the use of high explosives in one of many forms, and one thing most SEALs quickly discover in BUD/S is that

explosives are *fun*. As one blaster says with a smirk, "There are very few of life's troubles that can't be cured with high explosives."

A Short Course in Demolitions and High Explosives

Despite what you hear, high explosives are quite safe to handle and are actually difficult to detonate. Most of the military varieties can be pounded with a hammer (old, runny dynamite excepted) without going off. One of the best materials for blasting passages through coral reefs is a simple mixture of fertilizer and diesel fuel. You can break off a chunk of TNT from a quarter-pound block and set fire to it; so it's not only a great explosive, it's also a great heat source for warming up your lunch. C4, the famous "plastic explosive," looks, feels, and acts like putty—a white material that you can easily form and shape with your fingers, in complete safety. The same is true of virtually all other military explosives, with the possible exception of dynamite, a combination of nitroglycerine and gun-cotton, that can become quite unstable if stored improperly. Most of these materials can sit on the shelf for decades without any significant decay, and it isn't unusual to be issued cratering charges, for example, that were made during World War II.

For these and other reasons, explosives are very interesting and useful materials, available in many forms. There is Primacord or "det cord," a material that looks like fuse, a flexible plastic-like quarter-inch cord that contains a very high explosive, PETN, and is used to connect main charges. The PETN cord is set off with a blasting cap or other charge—then it explodes at a linear rate of about four miles per second with enough force to detonate any US military explosive the cord is tied to. It is very handy stuff for making a lot of little charges all go off at the same time—and other, sneakier applications discussed later.

In every case, including that of dynamite, you must work hard and carefully to actually get the stuff to go off. And that's accomplished with a little device that is quite dangerous and that will go off if you fail to handle it with care, caution, and respect—the blasting cap. These come in two flavors: electric and fused. Both are tubes of aluminum or copper, a quarter of an inch in diameter, partially filled with a three-stage mixture of specialized explosives, an ignition charge, a priming charge, and a base charge. Although things happen quickly, these charges go off in sequence, and the last one, the base charge, is the one that *should* set off the main charge.

As an example, let's set off a one-pound block of TNT. The main charge comes in a cardboard tube with a threaded receptacle on the ends to hold the blasting cap. We'll use common fuse instead of an electrical cap for this charge; it's more traditional. Also less safe.

First we take the fuse, cut six inches off the end and discard it. This should remove any contaminated and unreliable material. Then we cut a section six feet long, light one end, and time the delay. After about four minutes, a little flash of fire will come from the end. Note the time, divide by six, and you know what the delay of the fuse is in seconds per foot; normally it is about forty seconds per foot. Now, using your combination tool designed for demolitions work, cut a good, healthy length of fuse sufficient for five minutes' delay. The ends should be clean, square cuts.

Remove a blasting cap from the storage box where they are kept for safety and inspect the fuse well for foreign matter. *Gently* slip the fuse into the open end—about an inch—and into contact with the ignition charge. Crimp the fuse to the cap with the crimper part of the tool, about a quarter inch from the end of the cap. Now gently insert the cap into the priming well of the TNT block, place it on the ground, and extend the fuse so that it doesn't coil over on itself. We could use a fuse-lighter to get things started, but you might as well learn the traditional way first: split the fuse end about half an inch, insert a match head in the core, and strike it. The match will ignite the black powder inside, a bit of flame will sputter, a little smoke will be emitted,

Emplacing an M18 Claymore. The device is not much more than a slab of C4 explosives and a lot of ball bearings, electrically primed. It sprays a cloud of steel pellets that will kill or maim anyone within about fifty meters to the front.

and it is time to vacate the premises. It is considered good manners to shout, "Fire in the hole!" at this point unless there are bad guys in the vicinity. You walk, not run, well away, take cover, note the time, and await developments.

When the fuse burns down inside a non-electric blasting cap, a little squirt of flame shoots out, into the cap. If everything works as planned, the ignition charge goes off, then the priming charge, which detonates the base charge of the cap, and that little blast will usually set off the TNT. There will be a loud *Boom!*, and dust and rocks will scatter for a hundred meters in all directions. But don't expect any gaping crater—even a pound of TNT won't do much unless it is artfully placed and prepared. Instead, we have a patch of ground that is lightly depressed and not much more.

Explosives are used to do very specific things and are used with mathematical precision. You can cut a twelve-inch diameter tree with a half-pound block and have it fall across

The M67 hand grenade is thrown like a baseball. With practice you can put it into a machine-gun pit, a bunker, or a room. Without practice it tends to bounce back, fall short, or otherwise embarrass its thrower.

a roadway, blocking traffic. You can make a ribbon out of C4 plastic explosive, stick it to a steel girder, and cut a bridge support. You can shape it into a flat diamond and wrap it around an eighteen-inch diameter ship's propeller shaft, prime both points with blasting caps, and cut off the shaft neatly when the charge goes off. Put two identical charges on both sides of a concrete wall or abutment and prime electrically so both go off at the same instant, and a small amount of explosive (a pound and a half per foot of thickness) will crumble the concrete.

The most common application of explosives for SEALs has been clearing beach obstacles prior to amphibious landings, a technique developed to a minor art form by the UDT swimmers during World War II and Korea. Besides that use, vast quantities of C4

went up in smoke in Vietnam and, more recently, in the Gulf, blowing up bunkers and creating diversions. You can make a foxhole in a hurry with it, crater a road, cut a railroad line or a thick telephone cable. In the form of a Bangalore torpedo (a long section of steel pipe filled with explosive) you can blast a gap through a barbed wire obstacle or a minefield. It is mighty handy stuff.

Det cord, all by itself, has an interesting application for those occasional ambushes where you have plenty of time to set up shop. It can be electrically primed and hidden in roadside ditches alongside the "kill zone." When the ambush is initiated, you can be reasonably certain that the survivors of the first blast of small arms fire will dive for the presumed protection of the handy ditch. If the SEAL with the "hell box" (as the blasting machine is called) remembers to twist the handle about now, the det cord will explode in the ditch, adding to the consternation and woe of the enemy force.

Claymore Mines

The Claymore mine was developed in Vietnam to deal with those nasty situations when a couple of hundred little fellers in black paja-mas were swarming across the barbed wire defenses of a compound with intentions of committing mayhem on the residents. The Claymore is a simple little package of C4 explosive and a few hundred steel ball bearings, fired with an electric blasting cap and a "clacker" (a one-handed electric generator that, when squeezed, will fire the cap). When the explosive detonates, the ball bearings

If this sniper team wasn't posing for the camera you wouldn't know they were there at all. The rifle is a bolt-action .50-caliber model designed specifically for special operations use. The bolt has to be removed to load each round. Its effective range is about two kilometers—more than a mile and a half.

Haskins .50-caliber sniper rifle. Despite the rumor, there is no prohibition against using the .50-caliber against individual enemy targets. This weapon is designed, among other things, to kill a man with the first shot at ranges over a half mile. The tremendous recoil is partly absorbed by twin hydraulic shock absorbers in the stock—and partially by the shoulder of the firer.

A sniper team in "ghillie" suits. These camouflage suits are handmade by the men as part of their training at the Special Operations Target Interdic- *tion Course. In them they blend into the terrain, virtually disappearing—although they do have a tendency to stand out a bit on the street.*

spray a wide area with deadly effect, usually helping to convince the enemy force that there may be other, better, things to do than to attack this particular place.

Claymores have since become favorites for temporary defensive fighting positions and for ambushes, where they excel. Like virtually all other weapons, they are not perfect or foolproof. One sneaky trick the VC learned was to find them and turn them around.

The guy with the "clacker" in an ambush setup has to be a very cool dude, sufficiently self-disciplined to wait until the enemy is properly within the kill zone before firing the weapon. Lots of perfectly good ambushes have been ruined by the premature detonation of the Claymore, removing the element of surprise quickly and completely.

SEALs carry a Claymore or two along on

some of their excursions, the whole kit of mine, clacker, wire, and blasting cap all stored neatly in a little bundle complete with carrying strap.

.50-Caliber Sniper Rifle

One fine, somewhat neglected military art is that of the sniper. SEALs and Green Berets study this skill at the Target Interdiction Course, part of the Special Operations Command Center and School at the Army's Fort Bragg, North Carolina. Here, out among the weeds and chiggers, apprentice SEAL snipers learn how to move invisibly across any terrain, to build a hide so natural that an enemy can stand on top of it and not know that two Navy SEALs are in residence below, and to shoot so well that enemy soldiers over a half mile away die with the first shot, tank commanders standing in the turrets of their tanks lose their heads (literally), and antennas and vision ports on armored vehicles become useless.

The key to all this is a relatively simple, relatively ancient weapon—the rifle. The one favored by special operators like the SEALs these days is the big .50-caliber single-shot, bolt-action model that weighs about twenty pounds with scope and bipod. For a variety of reasons the big half-inch bullet will fly very accurately, very far. It will reliably strike a man-sized target so far away that the noise from its firing is practically inaudible, out to ranges of two kilometers, more than a mile and a half. But to achieve such accuracy requires far more than just an accurate weapon and sights. A SEAL sniper team out in the bush must deal with wind, moving targets, slant angles, and heat distortion.

Snipers work as two-man teams: the shooter and the spotter. They are inserted near their objective by boat or parachute, or swim ashore from a submarine, or come by Volkswagen bus—whatever works for the tactical situation. They will travel the last kilometer or so to their hide by crawling. It can take a day or more. Their weapons and equipment are contained in a "drag bag," pulled along behind each. Under cover of darkness, they carefully, methodically carve a hole in the ground, then re-cover it so artfully that it seems perfectly undisturbed. In this hole the pair will live for a day or two, observing, recording, and possibly reporting by radio. Normally the sniper's mission will not include actually firing on an enemy force but calling in artillery or aviation to do the job.

Determining range to the target and wind effect are the two principal problems confronting the sniper team, and the pair will expend considerable effort preparing to fire the first shot. A big .50-caliber round is inserted into the breech, the bolt brought forward, locked, and the sights carefully aligned on a computed aim point.

The spotter uses a compact telescope to look downrange. Instead of watching the target, the spotter watches for the *bullet* as it streaks toward the victim. With proper training and the right weather conditions, you can actually see a bullet and the vapor trail produced as it flies through the atmosphere. The spotter reports the point of impact to the shooter for any corrections.

Another version of the .50-caliber sniper rifle, used in Desert Storm.

Chapter 6

Special Boat Squadrons—
The Brown Water Navy

As mentioned earlier, the Special Boat Squadrons have typically been somewhat neglected in favor of the higher profile SEAL teams in the development of Naval Special Warfare. That's too bad because the boats have as rich a combat history as the teams, and both have worked closely together for nearly three decades. In fact, one of the big selling points for Naval Special Warfare in the competitive business of special operations is the unique resource SPECWARCOM has in its fleet of boats designed to take the fight close to the beach and up all those lazy rivers.

The Special Boat Squadrons are teamed with the SEALs to provide a kind of mutual support. And, just as the SEALs have a variety of weapons to choose from for their missions, the SBS crews have a menu of boats as well. There are little IBS inflatables, RIBs, PBRs, and fast-attack patrol boats. Most are stunningly fast, with thirty-knot-plus speeds . . . although you only get speeds like that from an IBS (a little seven-man rubber duck) when all the BUD/S are screaming and the students are paddling like crazy.

Mission mobility for Naval Special Warfare provides an extremely diverse set of problems for the "Coronado Yacht Club." Here is a breakdown of the three basic areas of respon-

Thirty-foot rigid hull inflatable boat (RIB) with fire team of SEALs embarked. The crew are from the Special Boat Squadrons.

sibility for the SBS part of NSW. But don't think that there's a sharp line between any of these assignments—the real world has a way of mixing and matching them. The boat that is primarily intended for coastal patrol may find itself occasionally on a riverine mission, or executing some exotic special operations support assignment.

Coastal Patrol and Interdiction

The first of these, requiring the biggest vessels, is the coastal patrol mission. The offshore patrol and interdiction mission is very different than, say, the clandestine insertion of a couple of combat swimmers for a demolition raid. It takes a good-sized vessel to provide the kind of platform needed to stay offshore for very long, to provide reasonable comfort for the crew, and to have the speed and firepower to accomplish anything useful. These missions are currently assigned to the Patrol Boat Coastal (PBC), Mk III Swift Patrol Boat, and the Mk IV Patrol Boat.

Neither the PBR or PBL provide much speed or comfort out past the surf zone; they're flat water boats with a specific set of missions. For the offshore jobs, where the Sea State goes up to five or so and the waves swell up to twelve feet, even froggy SEALs want something sturdy and stable. That pretty well eliminates the light little flat-bottomed boats in favor of something longer and beamier,

The Naval Special Warfare community finally gets a real ship in the form of the new Patrol Boat, Coastal (PBC) vessel. While it isn't all that fast, light, or stealthy, it at least provides organic support for long missions offshore, with facilities for SEALs or other small teams of operators.

The Mk III patrol boat was intended to be a fast, inshore weapons platform that can mount mortars, heavy machine guns, and a big 40mm canon. With a length of 65 feet and three high-power, light-weight diesel engines and an extensive rack of radars and radios, the Mk III is a fast, potent little vessel. Its missions include coastal and river patrol, gunfire support, and insertion and extraction of a complete SEAL squad.

with a nice, sharp V-hull to slide through the waves instead of pound along on top of them.

Patrol Boat, Coastal (PBC)

The PBC is something of a major change for the Naval Special Warfare community—the introduction of an entirely new class of ship to support NAVSPECWARCOM missions. In the past such support has been improvised, based on whatever happens to be around. The PC-1 class formalizes the support.

Ships of this class, starting with the *Cyclone* (PC-1), are designed for serious patrol work, their primary mission. Naval Special Warfare support is secondary, but a dedicated assignment. With an overall length of 170 feet, the PBCs are big enough for serious offshore work, reasonably comfortable, and commodious enough for a rather large number of embarked SEALs and Naval Special Warfare players.

The ships are the biggest platform the Special Boat Squadrons have ever had. They're funded by Special Operations Command and are assigned to the NSW Groups at Coronado and Little River, but are likely to be forward based. There will be a total of thirteen of the PBCs when the program is complete.

Obviously, it is hard to be very covert with 170 feet of warship. Rather than sneaking and peeking like the little boats, the PCs will be used to "show the flag" while maintaining a US presence in regions where the National Command Authority wants a show of force. The ships will be tasked with monitoring and detection missions, escort operations, noncom-

The RIB is quite capable of getting airborne, and throwing its passengers overboard, too, if they aren't careful.

The coxswain's control console is pretty fancy for a rubber boat, but appropriate for such an expensive, high-performance craft.

batant evacuation, and foreign internal defense—all pretty much the plain-vanilla patrol mission assigned to any of the Navy's or Coast Guard's smaller ships.

The more interesting missions, and the ones the Naval Special Warfare community is involved in, are for long-range insertion and extraction of SEAL teams, tactical-swimmer operations, intelligence collection, operational deception, and coastal or riverine support.

The PBC's steel hull with aluminum superstructure has a beam of twenty-five feet and a draft of about eight feet; it displaces about 330 tons (full load). Propulsion comes from twin diesels that can drive the ship at thirty-five knots. A tank of fuel (about 13,000 gallons) will give a range of about 2,000 nautical miles at a moderate cruise speed of twelve knots. The ship will tolerate Sea State 5 conditions—rough seas with waves of 8–12 feet. There is a platform on the stern for launching and recovering combat swimmers, and the ships each have two CRRCs available for SEAL operations.

Normal complement is four officers and twenty-four enlisted personnel. Unlike previous SBS vessels, the commander of the PBC ships is not likely to be a SEAL but a surface warfare officer. While there is some apprehension about this, there is also the realization that this is an entirely new asset for the community, with a somewhat different mission—and how it all works out remains to be seen. There will probably be at least a few SEALs assigned. Besides the crew, there is berthing for a nine-man SOF or law-enforcement detachment aboard.

Appropriate to its size and missions, the

PCs will be the most heavily armed of Naval Special Warfare craft. A Mk 38 25mm rapid-fire gun is installed, along with a station for the Stinger antiaircraft missile system. Four mounts for heavy automatic weapons are available for the Mk 19 40mm grenade launcher, M2 .50-caliber machine gun, and the M60 7.62mm machine gun. For antiship missile defense, a Mk 52 chaff/decoy system is installed.

Mk III Swift Patrol Boat

The Mk III is a big, 65-foot boat designed back in the 1960s with a coastal mission in mind. These boats have been used extensively in combat over the years, particularly to patrol the waters off the coast of Vietnam and, more recently, the Latin American coastal waters used by drug traffickers and the Persian Gulf waters in support of Desert Storm. The basic mission is to serve as a high-speed weapons platform for Naval Special Warfare units. The deck is reinforced to tolerate recoil stresses from the many weapons that can be mounted on the Mk III—any mix of 20mm cannon, 81mm or 60mm mortar, Mk 19 40mm grenade launcher, .50-caliber machine gun, and the faithful old M60 7.62mm machine gun.

The boat is rated at thirty-plus knots, needs a crew of eleven, and can stay out up to five days. It is powered by three big diesel engines installed in an all-aluminum hull with a low-profile radar and acoustic signature (for this kind of boat, anyway) that makes it comparatively easy to accomplish some kinds of covert missions. The Navy will tell you officially that it is "reasonably" stable in "moderately" heavy seas, but most experienced offshore operators will tell you that a 65-foot hull fits neatly in the troughs of most any sea and will wallow like a pig in mud given half an opportunity.

But Naval Special Warfare boats aren't intended to be pleasure craft. The Mk III is tasked with patrol and interdiction missions, with fire-support missions against targets ashore or afloat, and the insertion of SEAL team elements. One of their users, an SBS unit commander, says of them, "They've lasted

SEALs support a US Marine Corps beach landing operation during Operation Desert Storm. US Navy photo

through everything we've sent them to, from Vietnam to the Persian Gulf—and in fact the Persian Gulf is where they've gotten their heaviest workout." The Mk III is an old boat now, nearing retirement. An improved model, the Mk IV, is in service, but a completely new version, to be called the Mk V, is in the long design and acquisition process.

Mk IV Patrol Boat

The Sea Spectre 68-foot patrol boat is an improved version of the Mk III, an evolution of a proven design with some substantial upgrades. The missions, specifications, and weapons remain about the same, but the boat is designed to be more easily adaptable to the wide variety of missions that such boats are tasked for. Like its older brother, it is not a heavy weather offshore boat (that doesn't mean you don't have to operate in those conditions, just that you'll be uncomfortable when you do).

Special Operations Support Mission

Support for special operations doesn't have the same kind of requirements for station time that patrol does, and the boats used for inserting and supporting SEALs and other

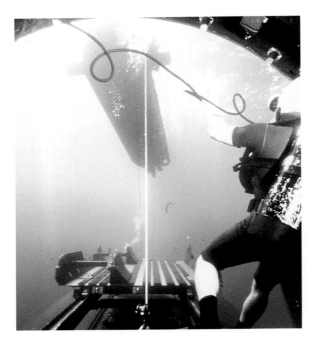

A Swimmer Delivery Vehicle (SDV) being deployed from a Dry Deck Shelter (DDS) of a submarine. US Navy photo

Locking out of a sub. Rigging the SDV is the business of the members of the SDV support unit, who are tasked with maintaining a complicated system plus maintaining their SEAL skills. US Navy photo

SOC operators are designed with things other than comfort in mind: speed, range, capacity, and a low radar signature are far more important than stability or fuel economy.

And the SBS crews and boats aren't always supporting strictly SEALs or Naval Special Warfare personnel; part of the idea of the Joint Special Operations Forces when it was established was to coordinate and integrate all the operators going downrange. So these SBS and NSW assets give rides to Green Berets and Rangers as well as to SEALs, and even to the occasional Force Recon Marine.

Rigid Inflatable Boats (RIB)

RIBs are the boat of the hour. Everybody's making and using them. Pretty soon you'll probably be able to take a Caribbean cruise on one. They're simple, cheap, fairly economical, and faster than a speeding bullet. They are used by the Navy, the Coast Guard, and many

foreign nations. They combine some of the best features of rigid hull and inflatable designs in one fast, stable, buoyant platform.

There are three variants of the big rubber duck used by the SEALs: 24-foot, 30-foot, and 10-meter RIBs. All use fiberglass hulls with a V-shaped cross section, offering stability, a rigid motor mount, and firm footing, along with an inflatable gunwale section. The inflatable part of the boat is fabricated from an extremely tough material, a combination of hypalon neoprene and nylon reinforced fabric. It won't shed bullets, but it will take a lot of lesser abuse, including the pounding you get from jamming around offshore, punching through the waves. The hammering a boat takes in normal service can be pretty severe, cracking fiberglass and aluminum hulls with the constant flexing. That is not a problem with an inflatable.

The RIBs are extremely tolerant, for a small boat, of heavy seas. With light loads the boats have operated offshore in extreme conditions—Sea State 6 and winds of forty-five knots. That means waves up to twenty feet high, when even SEALs would rather be ashore, even at BUD/S. While the boats can operate in such conditions, they normally don't go out when things get that bad; the SOP calls for a Sea State 5/thirty-four-knot wind limit on use. All the boats are normally crewed by three SBS sailors.

The 24-foot RIB weighs in at about 10,000 pounds fully loaded. It is powered by a single Volvo inboard engine/outboard drive powerplant and has a rated maximum speed of twenty-eight knots. Range is 175 nautical miles at twenty-five-knot speeds. Even this little boat mounts a radar—and an M60 7.62mm machine gun. Its principal mission is to deliver a single SEAL fire team (half a squad, four men) to an insertion point. It isn't the stealthiest way to insert a SEAL element on a covert mission, but not all missions require invisibility.

The 30-foot RIB is quite similar to the 24-foot version, but with two engines driving water jet drives and a higher rated maximum speed of thirty-two knots. The 30-footer is, as a result, half again heavier, weighing in at a combat weight of about 15,000 pounds. Range is slightly less, at 150 nautical miles, and the payload is a bit bigger.

The biggest of the breed is the 10-meter (33-foot) inflatable. This one will accommodate a whole squad. This means that an entire eight-man SEAL combat element can be cold, wet, and miserable while they huddle behind the dubious armor of two thin sheets of high-tech rubber and about two feet of compressed air on the run in to that hostile shore. The boat can be pumped up to forty knots, just in case the coxswain decides to race an aircraft carrier or perhaps outflank the fleet. And when he gets in range, this inflatable warship carries two weapons mounts accommodating either M60s or Mk 19 grenade launchers. There's enough fuel aboard for about an eight-hour mission, providing a range of around 250 nautical miles.

Combat Rubber Raiding Craft (CRRC)

One of the most used and useful boats in the inventory is a kind of war-surplus model left over from World War II, the CRRC—the legendary little rubber duck. Originally designed as a life raft, the boat has been adopted and adapted to all sorts of offensive missions. Marines use it, the Army Rangers and Green Berets use it, and of course the SEALs use it, for clandestine surface insertions and extractions. The CRRC weighs only 265 pounds. It gets tossed out of C-130 airplanes or from cargo helicopters, along with the SEALs, into the ocean. It is also launched from submarines, either from the surface or submerged, or gets chucked over the side of larger surface craft.

It's only about fifteen feet long, with a six-foot beam, but it will do about twenty knots. That, of course, requires an outboard engine, a single fifty-five horsepower powerplant with an eighteen-gallon fuel bladder providing a range of about sixty-five miles. That offers

The DDS is a temporary, hangar-like arrangement that bolts to the hull of the sub. It can accommodate a whole SEAL squad in relative comfort, or the squad and the SDV, in which case the squad is less comfortable. US Navy photo

over-the-horizon capability, but—trust me on this—you don't want to ride one in to the beach from over the horizon except on the *nicest* of days.

It is an extremely versatile piece of gear. While civilians spend hundreds or thousands of dollars on health clubs and Nordic Track exercise machines, the Navy uses the CRRC at BUD/S to build better bodies eight ways. In fact, the BUD/S instructors have discovered that you don't need fancy machines or chrome-plated weights, just a CRRC; if you have the students hold one overhead for a few minutes it *really* works those upper-body muscles. And, for a little extra help for those who need it, the CRRC can easily hold plenty of wet sand, bringing its weight up to something more challenging.

These inflatables have another virtue lacking in most other Navy property: they are, at times, considered disposable. Rather than go through the time and trouble to bring one back aboard a submerged sub, you may, during real world combat operations, stick your dive knife into one when you're done with your mission and let it sink to the bottom, engine and all. Just make sure that the submarine is standing by for you first!

SEALs are hauled back aboard a Patrol Boat, River (PBR)

Swimmer Delivery Vehicle (SDV) Mk VIII

Perhaps the most interesting, least publicized, most covert boat the Naval Special Warfare community operates is the wet submersible called the SDV Mk VIII. It's an odd little submarine SEALs use for fast, covert sub-surface insertions. The SDV is like a little speed boat, with rechargeable batteries and an electric motor for propulsion. Like other submarines, the SDV is visually blind and relies on sensors and instrumentation to navigate without bumping into things.

The embarked SEALs climb into a fully enclosed cabin. Although they wear scuba or closed-circuit breathing systems for backup and for work outside the vehicle, the SDV has its own supply of breathing air.

SDVs are launched from surface craft sometimes, but the dry deck shelter (DDS) attached to a submarine is a more typical point of departure. The DDS is like a small hanger, big enough for the SDV and with enough room for the swimmers to enter from the sub and climb into the SDV. The DDS is gradually flooded, the hatch opened, and out goes the SDV in search of adventure. The divers are now essentially in an expensive tin can full of water. It can be a cold ride. As one of its users says:

"It's a strange ride. You can't see out. You fly on instruments the entire time. You are a diver the entire time you're in it. The SDV provides more speed and range than swimming. Quite honestly, the boat will go farther than the man will. Exposure to the cold and to the ambient sea pressure put tremendous strains on the human body that become a limiting factor for missions with the SDV. I don't think it's used enough, perhaps because its reliability hasn't always been too great. It is a complicated thing to support and deliver. But if you plan its use properly, if you get it within its range, it is an extremely effective tool because it is almost nondetectable. The ability to deliver either SEALs or ordnance is just phenomenal!"

The vehicle has its own support unit, the SDV team, within SPECWARCOM. These teams maintain and operate the SDV, SEALs who actually man the boats on missions. An operator and a navigator are always assigned; both are fully qualified SEALs who have what amounts to a kind of bus driver job in addition to the usual combat assignments in the objective area.

The SDV is rated to carry six swimmers and their equipment, including the crew of two. A sonar sensor (for object avoidance) and an inertial navigation system allow the operator to cruise around underwater. A third sensor system is sometimes installed as part of a developmental program, but that remains "buggy," a side-scanning sonar for target identification of objects like mines as well as to record bottom contour. Not too surprisingly, a lot of specific performance information about these exotic little boats is classified. While the specifics are secret, we are authorized to hint a lot: The vehicle is about twice as fast as a submerged swimmer; vehicle endurance is probably a lot longer than crew endurance; and the SDV will tolerate up to 500 feet of water pressure without failing, and that's a lot farther than the crew will go before their subsystems start to fail! We could tell you more, but then we'd have to kill you.

Actually, though, the whole vehicle was extremely classified for a very long time. It couldn't be moved without being covered, and of course no photographs could be released showing it. But a few years ago, the then commander of SPECWARCOM decided the SDV would be a nice addition to the unit's annual float in the Coronado 4th of July parade and ordered it displayed on the flatbed trailer, along with the usual "cammied" Naval SPECWARCOM warriors. That's the way it is sometimes around Naval Special Warfare—things that are super-secret on one day and in one place are proudly displayed to the world the next.

Riverine Patrol and Interdiction

SEAL experience in Vietnam strongly demonstrated the need for good shallow-draft boats with plenty of speed, stealth, space for

Boat coxswain. Although the SBS coxswains don't go through BUD/S and aren't SEALs, they play an essential role in Naval Special Warfare.

combat-equipped SEALs, and provisions for both defending and attacking when in contact with enemy forces. That mission still exists today, in Latin America, where the US is involved in a quiet war in the backwaters of the Amazon basin and elsewhere. The boats from that previous war, along with some new ones, are helping to fight this one. Sometimes SEALs are embarked, sometimes not. In some cases the operators are foreign military or law enforcement people who are equipped and trained by the US, often by SEALs in the Foreign Internal Defense mission.

Patrol Boat, River (PBR)

The PBR has been around since quite

The SBS crews are the unsung heroes of Naval Special Warfare—or so they say, anyway. But at least they aren't shy when the media shows up.

early in the Vietnam war. It is still serving long after most of its crews have retired, a design with an interesting history.

When SEAL Team One packed its bags and shipped out to the combat zone in 1966 it was pretty much without a really good boat to support its new missions. Existing Navy LCPL (Landing Craft, Personnel, Launch) fleet craft had been modified for the purpose but just didn't seem suitable for the riverine mission of fast, long-range, shallow-draft patrol. That's why, in September 1965, the Navy's Bureau of Ships published a request for bids on a twenty-five to thirty-knot boat with a "dead-in-the-water" draft of eighteen inches and a draft at speed of only nine inches. A slightly modified commercial design from the Hattaras Yacht Company was selected, a 28-foot boat with "Jacuzzi" type propulsion.

The prototype was delivered only two weeks later. After testing, the design was modified, lengthened a bit to thirty-one feet,

and christened the PBR Mk I. The boats were being delivered to the Navy only a year after the program began. Not much later they were zooming around the Mekong Delta, trading shots with the VC and providing a kind of taxi service for SEALs off on nocturnal excursions.

The PBR was designed for high-speed patrol and insertion operations in rivers and bays. It is a heavily armed and armored boat, designed for combat at close quarters, with special ceramic armor similar to that used on tanks applied to the vessels' crew compartment. The hull is made of thick, reinforced fiberglass and is designed to accept the stresses of recoiling heavy machine guns and grenade launchers. The current PBR in service is 32-feet long, with a beam of about 12-feet. It weighs about 18,000 pounds—light enough to be transported on C-5 Galaxy aircraft.

While fairly ancient as military systems go, it is still an amazing boat. The two big

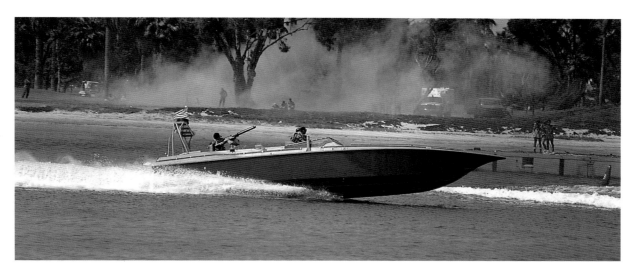

This High-Speed Boat (HSB) has just shot up a golf course with that big .50-caliber machine gun, terrorizing much of the tourist trade of Coronado, California, without so much as an apology. The HSB was originally intended to catch the small and medium-sized vessels that had been tormenting merchant and military shipping in odd corners of the world during the last decade or two. Very few of the costly, complex boats were purchased, and they've mainly been used as "adversaries" to train the Navy to deal with the fast, hit-and-run attacks of the sort mounted by Iraq and Iran. Even so, the HSBs were used during the deception campaign against Iraqi forces near Kuwait City, zooming along just off the beach, firing machine guns and tossing explosive charges over the side.

One of the 24-foot RIBs at speed. These extremely popular boats are used for many purposes by SEALs and other hard-charging units. They tolerate a lot of abuse (not including bullets), are fast, stable, and relatively easy to maintain and transport.

The Patrol Boat, Light (PBL) is a Boston Whaler with an attitude problem. The attitude comes from all those machine guns and the knowledge that, no matter how many holes the enemy puts in the hull, the fragments of the boat are unsinkable. US Navy photo

General Electric diesel engines will tootle along quietly or crank up 215hp each when required. Those engines each drive a 14-inch Jacuzzi pump; the water squirts out of 5.75-inch nozzles, making the boat go faster than thirty knots—in excess of thirty-five miles an hour to you landlubbers. Of course, that's with the water jets clean, and they do clog up. It has a range of 200 miles on 160 gallons of fuel. Normal crew complement is four.

A lot of bullets have dinged off the hulls and armor of PBRs, and a lot of crewmen have died aboard them. The boats have done a lot of shooting of their own. Standard equipment includes a tub-mounted twin M2 .50-caliber machine gun system in the bow; that's industrial-strength firepower guaranteed to "clean the clock" of almost any point target within two kilometers. There is also a pedestal mount for another M2 .50-caliber and a mount for the marvelous Mk 19 grenade launcher, a type of machine gun that fires 40mm, baseball-sized projectiles to better than two kilometers. As options you can sometimes get a 60mm mortar installed, with or without M60 machine-guns, and additional .50-caliber and 40mm machine

guns mounted amidship. Of the more than 500 PBRs built since 1966 only twenty-four or so remain in service. A new design is in the works.

Patrol Boat, Light (PBL)

The PBL is another modified off-the-shelf civilian design from that distant era; still in use is the 25-foot military version of the Boston Whaler, an unsinkable little boat powered by a pair of big engines and mounting two heavy weapons, the M2 .50-caliber machine gun and/or the Mk 19 grenade launcher. The PBL is a light, fast, air-portable, quiet, somewhat vulnerable boat that has evolved a bit over the years, but continues to support the riverine mission after almost three decades in the inventory.

Like the PBR, it uses water-jet propulsion to achieve better than thirty-knot speeds on flat water. It will turn on a proverbial dime—in fact, the boat will turn a lot faster than the coxswain and crew will probably find comfortable, a 180-degree about-face in less than 30-feet while doing thirty knots. While the G-load of such a maneuver could easily toss most everybody right out of the boat, it is a handy capability for those times you come blasting around a bend and find a horde of bad guys waiting for your arrival.

Two pedestal-mounted "Ma Duce" heavy machine guns are mounted just forward of the coxswain's position. This provides all-aspect firepower for breaking contact when the crew of three thinks it is necessary. There is also a third mount farther forward, and any combination of .50-caliber and 7.62mm machine guns can be installed.

Although the PBL draws about a foot and a half of water when stopped, at speed it will just about operate in a mud puddle, skimming along on the surface of the water rather than through it. The two engines will run at full throttle for eight hours on a tank of fuel, driving the boat across about 160 nautical miles of river or canal at more than twenty-five knots. It uses standard twin engines, with dual steerage, ignition, and controls for back-up redundancy.

It is an extremely mobile little boat, in and out of the water. The PBL can travel on a conventional trailer, be rigged as a sling load for a helicopter, or be loaded aboard a C-130. A lot of PBLs have traveled to Latin American military forces, where they are justifiably popular with the counter-narcotics forces patrolling the Amazon delta and other riverine battlefields.

Mini-Armored Troop Carrier (MATC)

The MATC is a kind of small landing craft similar to the ones Marines have been using to come ashore for decades, only smaller. It has a flat, ramp-type bow that drops forward to eject a whole platoon of sixteen combat-equipped SEALs onto a beach. It is a riverine craft with shallow draft and all the sea-keeping qualities of a cork. Like the PBR and most other riverine craft, the MATC has a water-jet propulsion system that "vacuums" the boat through the water, Jacuzzi fashion. A crew of three operates the boat.

Its hull is thirty-six feet long, made of aluminum, and is designed for high-speed patrol, interdiction, and combat assault missions on the relatively flat waters of bays, rivers, canals, and protected coastal areas. It is serious about all this—there are seven weapons stations for heavy machine guns or grenade launchers and a 60mm mortar can be installed. It comes with a high-resolution radar and a rack of radios for every taste and purpose. The boat weighs about 25,000 pounds, is good for about thirty knots and a range of 230 nautical miles from 430 gallons of fuel.

In the grand SEAL tradition, the boat is fast and sneaky. It has a low six-foot profile that's hard to see or pick up on radar (well, for a slab-sided metal-hulled boat). The engines are extremely quiet. What this all means is that you can pile a bunch of weapons and troops aboard, run up the river to a likely spot, slide into the weeds and woodwork along the bank, and wait, engine at idle. With good "comms" you can talk to surveillance aircraft overhead, other teams ashore and afloat in the area, and wait for your victim to come chugging down the creek. When the perpetrators of the crime arrive on scene, the MATC has the troops and the firepower to negotiate with just about anybody and win through intimidation.

Chapter 7

Leader's Recon

Before a combat operation, particularly ashore, a commander will, time permitting, travel to the objective area for "eyes on" the target, as LT Tom Dietz did before the diversionary raid on the Iraqi coastal defenses in Kuwait. This personal study by a combat commander of an area where conflict will occur is called "leader's recon." There is no good substitute for this kind of personal, direct contact by the combat leader with the battlefield. For people within military communities there are all kinds of battlefields besides the kind we usually think of. Some are institutional, within the unit, while others are the political, doctrinal, policy arenas. For the past fifty years, SEALS have had to adapt to changes in the world, in the US armed forces, in the Navy, and within Naval Special Warfare itself. These internal battles shape the nature of the institution that will fight the wars of the future. These institutional, peacetime conflicts are tremendously dangerous—not for the present, but for the time when push comes to shove, as it always seem to do.

Among the most dangerous things SEALs need to worry about is complacency on their own part, about bad tactical habits, about inexperience and overconfidence. Despite several combat operations over the last couple of decades, the SEAL community today is almost completely inexperienced in war—and this is a dangerous thing. War is different than training, no matter how tough that training may be.

Combat experience is slipping away from the Navy. The last Navy Medal of Honor winner retired in 1992, and nearly all the Vietnam combat veterans have left the formal military service. One of these men with a great deal of combat time is CDR Gary Stubblefield, recently retired but still actively working with Naval Special Warfare as a consultant and contractor. With retirement comes a greater freedom to discuss Naval Special Warfare issues. The following are a kind of "leader's recon" offered by Commander Stubblefield, a selection of opinions and insights about the life and times of SEALs today and in the future. His observations are a rare insight into the challenges of the present and future for Naval Special Warfare.

Deployment & Tasking

"Since the time I started in this business twenty-five years ago, I've seen a lot of changes. One is that now our people expect to receive their missions while sitting here in the States or in some forward-deployed base overseas—receipt of mission from higher authority, rather than developing our own missions from within the area where we will operate. In Vietnam we set up our own bases, designed our own missions, and, unless somebody thought we were doing something really stupid, we were left alone. Now we are directed by higher authority. When Ray Smith was operating in the Gulf, he was getting messages from the CINC saying, 'Conduct SEAL operations here, here, and here.'"

Planning and Accountability

"We've become very good at developing 'overhead' intelligence-collecting from aircraft and satellites. We've lost the ability to develop good 'human intelligence,' the ability to develop information from people, face-to-face. We were *great* at that, and it was so much better than what we even get now from the overhead systems. But you only get human intelligence by living there, by being part of the community, by building rapport with the host nation—it's the only way that will work. Now we do our planning in an insular way.

"Now I receive my intel, develop a concept or a series of options for an operation, and then I have to send it back to my boss and say, 'Here's what I intend to do; what do you think?' He may have to run the idea up the chain of command even further! Then he'll come back and say, 'This is the one I choose for you.' Then I have to develop that option—and send it up to my boss for approval again! It comes back with his changes . . . and only then can you brief your people. All this time the platoon is milling around, trying to get organized for something—but they aren't at all sure just what it will be.

"This kind of micro-management is the sort of thing we were getting into down in Panama. We were getting into operations where we required outside people, who weren't on the ground with us, telling us how we were going to do things, based on our written plan—asking for permission, which is asking for trouble.

"We tend to do more of our planning now for somebody else, rather than for the teams, to demonstrate that we know how to do something when we're evaluated by our higher authority, or in an exercise where we're demonstrating to an umpire that we're doing things according to doctrine. If you were to take that

same platoon and turn them out into an op area for six months where they eat, breathe, and live in the area, like we did on the barges in the Persian Gulf during the Iran-Iraq War, pretty soon you fall into the old habits. You know your operations area, you know your platoon—you go back to basics. You plan your operation on the basis of the lowest common denominator and use the KISS principle [keep it simple, stupid!]. That way you have fewer things go wrong, you have a simpler operation to run, you rely on your knowledge of your platoon to deal with contingencies. That's called *flexibility*."

SEAL Virtues & Vices

"We're quite good at maritime direct action missions—where we ourselves are out there, in the water, delivering the munitions, collecting reconnaissance. Second, we are capable of doing long-range, long-duration missions—but we haven't typically been very good at it. The reason is that when you do these long missions, with all their logistics support requirements, you lose the ability to be fast, light, mobile. The minute you start putting on hundred-pound packs you lose that ability to do what we've traditionally done best."

The Training Environment Vs. the Real World

"I see a lot of guys who just don't get serious about our business. People have a tendency in training, in noncombat exercises, to take shortcuts. We can't afford to do that in this business. The way that you train is the way that you fight. If you get used to taking shortcuts because it's not dangerous, you'll get killed by that shortcut out in the real world. The business that we do is inherently dangerous anyway—parachuting, diving with closed-circuit rigs, locking out of submarines, working with explosives, shooting close to each other—those things are dangerous, but there is a difference even between doing them in training and in combat.

"I cannot explain to somebody until they see it for themselves what it is like to have somebody fall down beside them with a bullet in them, blood coming out of them—to lose a friend—to explain to them that they are vulnerable. You feel like you are almost invincible until you see something like that—and you never get that same feeling in any exercise, no matter how tough we make it. It takes something like that to make you really get serious about this business.

"Because there aren't real bullets going by overhead, people today don't realize you don't go very far very fast in combat. We have a tendency today to say we can travel twelve nautical miles an hour—a figure that is only realistic in a noncombat environment. It was not unusual in Vietnam to take an hour to go 100 meters back then; you had noise control, mud to contend with, water up to your chest. A hundred meters in an hour was rather fast. But we typically expect much faster movement from our SEALs today.

"Another thing we need to learn is to stop carrying all this extra gear; lighter, faster, smaller is better! I see guys going out with 200 rounds—you don't need all that. You need to stay mobile, you need to stay light, you don't want to sink too deep in the mud. You need to go back to basics again . . . when you get in the real world.

"But when I left SEAL Team Three we had only five guys out of 205 people who ever had any combat time—and I'll bet that, out of those five guys, not all of them had ever seen anybody get hurt! So you've got five guys who are serious and about 200 who say, 'I like this job, it's neat, it's fun . . . ' Years ago, when we had teams come back with ten of the fourteen guys on a platoon having been wounded, we had a lot of guys who said ' . . . Uh, look, I don't want to do this anymore, I think I'll get out.' We don't have that now because we don't have all those casualties."

Technology—A Blessing and a Curse

"Our weapons system, operating gear, and radios are all better now than ever before. Technology has helped us in many ways—but now, we tend to load up on this stuff, because we have it. I've actually stopped people getting ready for an operation and had them weigh their packs—which turned out to weigh 110 pounds—for a three-day operation, and I say, 'What's wrong with this picture?' You don't need to do that! You need a couple of LRRPs [similar to MREs], enough water to get you by for that period, your weapon and ammunition—and *that's it*. Let's go! Batteries, maybe an extra radio, no more than that.

"We have a tendency today to do more 'whizbang' stuff—night vision sight systems, laser aim-point systems—it's smaller/lighter/faster today. If I had to go back over there today, I think we'd operate pretty much the same kind of ops. The radios are better now, the waterproofing is better.

"We don't have a tendency to move into an area and get to know it before an operation now, although the Persian Gulf was something of an exception. I think that's very important—you have to move into your area and become familiar with your territory. And we have a tendency to really overdo the briefings—I see briefings lasting five and six hours! It's ludicrous! A human being can't remember all that. When we're going out for a two-day operation, why do you need to brief for five or six hours? If you're working well together on the team, patrolling and training together, you're familiar with your op area and you know your guys, and you don't need to brief that long. Instead of briefing for the benefit of the senior commander present, I think we need to remember that you're briefing your *platoon*."

Joint Operations and the Multi-service Environment

"In Vietnam, our boat support units lived with us in the same hut. I could go over to the next bunk and say, 'We're going on an op tomorrow night—can you have this boat ready to go?' *Nowadays* assets like boats are coordinated by multi-services. If I need a boat now, even though it's internal, I have to make sure everybody knows about it because somebody else may be planning to use the same boat—so

I have to go to higher authority, tell them I need this boat, get my ticket punched, *then* I can go over to the guy on the next bunk and talk to him about it. If it's a helicopter that could belong to the Air Force or the Army, I might have to go all the way up the chain of command, find out if it's okay, involve them in my planning process, make them part of the mission planning. Since I'm not living in my op area, I have to rely on higher headquarters to 'de-conflict' my mission, to make sure that they aren't sending an Army Green Beret A team into the same area, where we might end up shooting at each other.

"We used to be well-segregated from other friendly units in Vietnam. We all had our assigned AO [Area of Operations], and you didn't cross over without checking with the other team. The same thing applied to the boat units—I could go to the riverine boat comman-der and say, 'You guys working in here? No? Well, we are, and I don't want you going in there with your boats now.' Nowadays you can't do it that simple."

Parachute Operations for Seals

"The rule for parachute operations is: If you *have* to jump, go find another way; if you still can't find another way, make sure you observe the restrictions on wind speed, weights, all that. We have a tendency to make things more complicated than they need to be—we should always go to the lowest common denominator. We have a tendency to send more people than we need when instead we ought to take the minimum. That makes for much better command and control. We get into trouble, as in Grenada and Panama, when we make things too complex."

One Foot in the Water

Special ops is a kind of military art form, a team sport that takes special talents and years to learn. Despite overlap of missions and training, each American special forces unit has a limited set of talents. For the SEALs, that means missions that are somehow linked to the sea. As one SEAL team commander explains, "The US military has Green Berets that dive, US Army Rangers that do across-the-beach operations with the same kind of Combat Rubber Raiding Craft that SEALs use—there are lots of similar examples in the Army and Marine Corps. We in the SEALs are the United States military's *small unit maritime special operations force*. We don't operate in larger than sixteen-man units. We don't belong in anything that involves multi-platoon operations—we've never been successful at it, we've never trained in it, and any time we've tried it we have failed. We keep our units small and separate from large force operations.

We have a niche there to be very good, in units most often less than eight men. That makes us harder to detect, easier to command and control, better at the small, unique operations that we train for. The Green Berets may conduct dive operations to get to their objective; we can conduct operations entirely underwater. US Army Rangers conduct large unit across-the-beach operations, and it isn't unusual to see them use twelve or more CRRCs. You probably will never see more than two in our business.

"We keep one foot in the water. That means that *if* we must do inland operations it is because they are attached to some maritime reason—that was the only available insertion technique, or it happens to be a coastal target. *Keeping one foot in the water* means that we don't get into areas that properly belong to other operators."

INDEX